Language and Languages

Chandler Publications in
ANTHROPOLOGY and *SOCIOLOGY*
LEONARD BROOM, *Editor*

LANGUAGE
and LANGUAGES

George L. Trager
Northern Illinois University, DeKalb

CHANDLER PUBLISHING
COMPANY

An Intext Publisher
SAN FRANCISCO • SCRANTON • LONDON • TORONTO

CONTENTS

An *Analytical Table of Contents* is presented on the
following pages.

v

ANALYTICAL
TABLE OF CONTENTS

PREFACE

Language and languages is directed at students of language—of many kinds. It is for the anthropologist who is not himself trained in linguistic analysis, but who needs to acquire an acquaintance with anthropological linguistic thinking and with the extent and kind of data available for "language and culture" studies, for exploration of the ethnography of speaking, and for the various kinds of sociolinguistic, psycholinguistic, and other metalinguistic studies that have been suggested or tried out. It is also for the educator in any field of learning who realizes that his own education is not complete without knowing more about language—the first prerequisite for human culture—than our educational institutions, from the lowest to the highest, teach about it. Specifically, social scientists of all kinds, and especially historians, should find much that is in some way valuable to their specialties, and perhaps even some things that will prove to be intensely pertinent.

Mathematicians, psychologists, and those technicians who call their recently developed specialties by such terms as "mathematical linguistics", "psycholinguistics", "mechanolinguistics", and other hybrids, may think there is little or nothing for them in this book. Their special approaches are absent here. But the DATA on which any treatment of language or any part of it must be based are to be found in or can be traced from this book. I recommend to all readers that they think about the uses of data.

Wherever possible, things have been phrased so that anyone who reads standard English will know what is being said; but the reader is not seduced into believing that he really understands everything without effort. He will have to work at understanding the technical materials and the theoretical bases for them. I hope that such work will be rewarding.

xiii

I have not directly worked with all the linguistic and cultural areas touched on in this book, but have had a wide array of contact and experience with many languages and cultures. In the instances of material that I have taken from the literature, I have attempted to interpret it in terms of the same analytical techniques that I use in my own work. The teacher who is himself expert in a particular area will add his own knowledge to the evaluation. Students can greatly profit from differences of opinion and critical comments.

In the References and Notes essential bibliography is presented, comments are made on the validity and availability of material, and references are given to material in the projected volumes to follow. No excuse is made for the lack of extensive or even completely up-to-date bibliographical material. The student who is sufficiently advanced to need it can start from the things that *are* listed; and he should know, or needs to learn, how to find the references himself. If some of the listings send him far afield, that is good; there is no better way to acquaint oneself with a discipline than to wander around in it at pleasure and repeatedly.

Language and languages was started as a textbook for my course "The Languages of the World", instituted in 1956–1957 at the University of Buffalo. The course was organized as a general introduction to linguistics as an anthropological discipline, and included not only theory and methodology in respect to description of languages, but also data on languages as such, on writing systems, and on language relationships. The book developed into a series of studies which have been organized into a projected major work in linguistics, in three parts, of which this book is the first. The intended future publications are: *English and its relatives* and *The Non-Western languages*. (In the References and Notes, reference is made from time to time to these future publications — abbreviated as *E&R* and *NWL* respectively — in the interest of the reader who wants to pursue certain specific topics further.)

It would be impossible to give sufficient credit to every individual who has furnished useful and usable ideas for this book, or to every publication from which data have been taken. In the References and Notes there are many bibliographical details, and some acknowledgments of communications from individual colleagues. A few persons whose general contributions have been outstanding may be listed here.

My friend and colleague of a lifetime, Henry Lee Smith, Jr., must be mentioned for his part in helping to establish the course "The Languages of the World" at the University of Buffalo in 1956 as part of the curriculum of the then new Department of Anthropology and Linguistics (since 1964, Department of Anthropology), with him as Chairman, and myself as Professor of Anthropology and Linguistics. For several years before coming to Buffalo, we had from time to time discussed such a course, and had developed the theory of where and how linguistics was to fit into the larger field of anthropology. There have been, over the years, many talks between us about all kinds of matters touching on the subjects treated in these books, and it would be difficult to find a section or subsection in which there was no topic that had been discussed by us at some time. In this instance, it is not so much a matter of thanks as an acknowledgment of a far-reaching community of thinking and the sharing of mutually thought-out ideas and conclusions.

Some two decades before 1956, I had the privilege of being a research fellow at Yale, which at that time included Edward Sapir and Edgar H. Sturtevant on its staff, as well as a number of other distinguished linguists. These two men had planned and established a course on the languages of the world; it was a graduate course, and was given by all the staff members who were linguists and who wished to participate, though Sapir and Sturtevant gave more lectures than anyone else. I had then recently started my work on the language of Taos Pueblo, and was greatly honored by being asked to give one of the course lectures, presenting some of my material; during a later year, when teaching at Yale, I participated more fully in the course. Not only did these two leaders give me the idea for the course, but many of their specific details of presentation—factual and methodological—have been retained to this day. To the memories of these two great linguists I wish to pay homage, emphasizing the intensely personal nature of the feeling involved.

To all my other teachers and associates since I entered the field of linguistics (and of anthropology as a whole), I owe some measure of thanks. Of those who are with us only in memory, I would like to mention Franz Boas and Leonard Bloomfield. It would be invidious to name some of the living and not others; but I had hoped to make an exception and thank Bernard Bloch for all the good ideas I have had from him; with sorrow, I must now list him also among the departed. The voluminous files of the correspondence between us were consulted many times in preparing this volume.

Acknowledgment of material prepared by, or with the assistance or collaboration of, certain individuals is made in the References and Notes. This is also the place to thank all those who contributed to the preparation of diagrams, tables of alphabets and special symbols, and other material which could not be set in type; their skill is evident in the results.

To my wife, Felicia, must go not only the usual thanks (which she has earned in full measure) for forbearance, understanding, and support during periods of discouragement or adversity, but also very specific acknowledgment of technical competence and substantive knowledge in many areas of the subject matter treated. She read the copy with a critical eye, helped in its preparation, and often suggested clarifications of analyses, not to mention improvements in style; in many places she deserves to be called coauthor. Where obscurities remain, the readers should blame them on my failure to accept suggested emendations.

All those named and unnamed contributed much to the merits of this work. I alone must be blamed for its defects; I am opinionated, reluctant to modify or excise a phrase once I have written it, and stubbornly insistent on writing about all I know or think I know, and on expressing my own views and conclusions, even when these are utterly at variance with the views of others (including my named and unnamed collaborators). For the acceptance of any new views of mine I shall be grateful, and I shall be equally—though possibly a little reluctantly—grateful for the demolition of any conclusions that prove to be untenable. If there are new editions following this first, they will be improved to the extent possible by eliminating error and incorporating criticisms and emendations.

—George L. Trager

Taos, New Mexico, August 1966, and
Dallas, Texas, March 1967

Difficulties in printing this work postponed its appearance until 1971. But the typescript, and the galleys and page proofs, were used in my teaching at Southern Methodist University from 1967 to 1970. In the academic year 1970–1971 xerox copies of page proofs were made and distributed to students, and to some colleagues elsewhere for experimental teaching.

The actual use of the book will begin in the fall of 1971. I shall then be teaching, on postretirement appointment, at Northern Illinois University, DeKalb.

—George L. Trager

Dallas, Texas, March 1971

Language and Languages

Part 1

LANGUAGE

Chapter 1

PEOPLE TALK

1.0. PEOPLE

1.00. Human behavior is so constantly and thoroughly accompanied by talking, that most people rarely stop to think about their speech activity, or to speculate about the nature and origin of the communication system which they use. But all people everywhere have always somehow recognized the very special advantage of being able to talk, and that it is precisely this ability that marks them off from the rest of the universe about them.

Many mythologies contain stories about how people learned to talk, and some of them account for the different languages that are known to exist. In all mythologies in which there are animals or objects which talk, their ability to do so is recognized as supernatural and out of the ordinary. In the rearing of children, it is usually taken for granted that a child shows evidence of being really a human being when he begins to learn to talk. Those—children or adults—who are pathologically prevented from learning to talk, by deafness, physical malformations, or mental deficiency, are everywhere regarded as unfortunates, and as specially afflicted.

Persons who do not speak one's own language are, at all times and in all places, looked on as different and strange, and possibly even as not quite human. They are often regarded as enemies, or as emissaries of evil forces. At the same time, the person who can speak not only his own language but also that of others is also everywhere singled out as different: whether his ability be highly prized or looked down upon, it is admittedly special and remarkable.

1.01. One of the purposes of this book is to examine basic attitudes and behavior patterns in respect to language, and to set them in a systematic frame of reference which will clarify them and make them understandable.

3

We shall consider in this chapter the origin and diversity of languages, and their situation in the whole of human behavior. This will lead to a definition of language, and to statements about its relation to the total communication situation, and about the general structure of all languages. From this will follow a discussion of the geographical, social, and other diversifications of languages, with exemplification from the varieties of English spoken in the world. Finally, some of the myths about written language, about correctness of style, and about the value or adequacy of different languages will be dispelled.

1.1. THE BEGINNING

1.10. The evolutionary history of the only existing species of man is not very well worked out. Fossil remains are scarce and scattered, and it is difficult to envisage the connections that may have existed between the different specimens that have been found. Linnaeus, the eighteenth-century naturalist who established the present system of biological nomenclature, named the species *Homo sapiens* 'man the knowing (or wise)', with obvious but perfectly proper human egoism; man is the one who knows, and though Linnaeus didn't say so, he knows because he can talk. With the development of the evolutionary hypothesis in the nineteenth century, the search began for the biological ancestors of this creature who was clearly superior to all other living beings in "wisdom" or "knowledge", and who must be the product of a special evolutionary development.

Remains of other manlike creatures have been found, and there has been much speculation about how near to or far from modern man they were. In the course of these speculations, there has come to be general agreement among anthropologists that in order to have become a maker and user of tools and other artifacts, man had to develop the ability to talk. There is evidence of the use of tools and possibly even of fire among the creatures whose fossil remains have been named *Homo habilis*, creatures quite far removed from modern man, but who walked erect and may very well be in the direct line of human evolution. The remains of these creatures must probably be dated as a million and a half years to two million years old. We can conclude that language was first used something over a million years ago, and it is reasonable to hold that it has been in use ever since.

1.11. How did language come about? An exact answer to this question can never be given, but informed speculation may be indulged in. All present-day language is used in a setting—the communication situation—in which it is accompanied by various other kinds of communicative activities (paralanguage, kinesics, and others—discussed in 1.2 below). The early ancestors of man certainly possessed the kind of ability to communicate that is found among many animals—communication by cries and gestures. Somewhere, at some time, among some group of *Homo habilis* prehumans, some small group of individuals, probably endowed with better than average mental ability, found themselves getting more and more precise and specific in the noises they uttered in specified situations. And one day, we may imagine, one or two of these individuals hit upon a specific series of sounds used always and regularly in a specific situation, and with systematic variation from other sounds in other situations. Such a happening may properly be described as an invention. Language was invented, and it was the first invention that man made. With this remarkably pliable device, all other inventions could follow, and the former pre-man could now be human, and could develop all the rest of what anthropologists call culture.

Whatever may be the exact way in which language was invented, we may be certain that it very quickly grew into the kind of extensive system that it now is (see 1.2). It was a matter of a few generations at most for the people associated with and descended from the first inventors to become fully fluent talkers. We shall henceforth define a human being as an animal that can talk, the only animal with this ability. Man is thus set apart from all the rest of living creatures on earth. Language made it possible to "think"—to talk to others and to oneself about anything, seen or unseen, real or unreal, present or past or future. It made possible the naming of persons and things, the giving of exact directions and instructions, the designation and recognition of members of one's own group (family, tribe) and the distinguishing of outsiders. Discourse about origins, values, and the nature of things became possible. Man could become *sapiens* by his own efforts.

1.12. It can be asked whether the invention of language took place once only, and spread from the original group to others, or whether the same kind of invention might have taken place several times. The question can never be answered with certainty.

If it happened once, the spread to other groups must have been extremely rapid. If it happened more than once, the several groups and occurrences must have been close to each other in time and space. Once the invention was made, once or several times, the spread and systematic development of language snowballed. To judge from observations of infants, the human mind is so made that its possessor constantly tries new activities, to see what will happen, so to speak. The inventors of language must have possessed this facility, and exercised it fully.

Within any one group, the snowballing system of words and sentences easily became known to every member, young and old. But separate groups were not in constant communication. So each developed its own innovations, many of which never got passed on to other groups. Thus from the very start, whether there was a single invention or several, language existed as languages. The extent of this diversification will be noted in 1.3 below.

1.13. Anthropologists use the word CULTURE to encompass the systematic behavior of human beings in its totality. Human beings react to time and space; they reproduce their kind by virtue of being of two sexes; they learn and they pass on what they have learned to others; they communicate by various kinds of symbols; they make artifacts of all kinds and extend their control over the physical universe by means of these artifacts; they attribute values to things and to behavior patterns; they divide up the work of the world and develop specializations and skills, and they learn how to enjoy the fruits of their labors; they extend their families into tribes and nations, and subdivide all these groups into hierarchies; they devise ways of protecting themselves as individuals and as groups from the natural and supernatural, and formulate guiding rules for an all-embracing way of life.

All the systematic behavior patterns of these kinds constitute human culture. Culture is a system of systematic behavior patterns; the system and its subsystems have to be learned; the system enables human beings to exist in social groups or societies, and to interact with each other in these groups. Culture is made possible and is carried on and implemented by the existence of language, which itself is one of the cultural systems. Without language, culture could not exist; but without the rest of culture, language would have no function. The phrase "language and culture" thus refers not to two things, but to an interrelated whole.

One of the ways of examining any cultural system is to establish its content—what it is made up of, then to see the setting in which the content operates, and then to study the functioning of the content in its setting. In these terms, the content of language is talking, the setting is the speaker-hearer situation, and the functioning is the conveying of the message. We shall see in the next sections how language is structured for the carrying out of its purposes.

1.2. TALKING

1.20. The word LANGUAGE is used by the ordinary person to designate the particular form of speech that he uses, in its various styles and applications. But the word is also used by extension in such phrases as "the language of love, ... of flowers", as well as more literally in talking about "the language of birds, ... of bees", etc. There is general agreement that in these kinds of uses, the word is extended in some way from its basic meaning. However, there is also the general use of such phrases as "the written language", "the language of Shakespeare", where reference is made to a recording of some form of language in writing, and various confusions and misconceptions often arise from this reference.

To indicate precisely that our primary concern is with talking, with language as spoken, we present a definition of language. In all that follows it is understood that language is both spoken and heard and that any normal human being is both speaker and hearer.

1.21. Language is defined as THE LEARNED SYSTEM OF ARBITRARY VOCAL SYMBOLS BY MEANS OF WHICH HUMAN BEINGS, AS MEMBERS OF A SOCIETY, INTERACT AND COMMUNICATE IN TERMS OF THEIR CULTURE.

The terms of this descriptive definition can be separately examined for further clarification. Language is LEARNED: no one is born with his language ready-made; he has to learn it from the people among whom he is brought up. Language is a SYSTEM: if we compare the initial babblings of an infant with his later production of sounds that are taken to be meaningful (the traditional "first word", for instance, something like *mama*), we can see what is meant by a system: the sound sequences in language are not haphazard, they are not random, but they are ordered and sequential in terms of some governing principles.

The system that is language is said to consist of symbols. A SYMBOL is something that stands for or represents something else: the word *sheep* is not the animal, the word *action* is not the activity, the word *from* is not the relationship of removal or apartness; the words are symbols of things or activities or relations. Symbolizing is the very essence of human behavior; human beings are able to make symbols for anything and everything, and they are able to interpret anything and everything as symbolic. In fact, human beings can deal with the universe about them ONLY by interpreting the reactions they get from the environmental stimuli as symbols.

The symbols of which language consists are VOCAL. This means that they are noises produced by human beings by means of the vocal apparatus, a set of muscles and other organs selected out of the whole because of their action in producing language.

The vocal symbols are ARBITRARY. This means that they bear no necessary relation to the thing symbolized. The word *house* could represent the number 10 just as well as a dwelling. This is borne out by the constant observation of similar-sounding items in different languages with different meanings. Thus *ten* in English is the number after 9; in Polish it means 'that [one]' with a so-called "masculine" noun; in Spanish it means 'hold' or 'have', the "imperative" of *tener*.

There exist in all languages words or phrases which are pointed out by native speakers as "sounding like" some noise occurring in nature, or as designating an animal because the word "sounds like" the cries the animal makes; such items are English *bang, buzz, crunch, slash, growl, meow, moo,* and many others. (The technical terms *onomatopoeia* and *onomatopoeic—*or *onomatopoetic—*are used to name and describe the phenomenon.) But these are always items composed of ordinary sounds of the language, they have to be learned and specifically identified as supposed "imitations", and a foreigner is likely not to recognize them as imitative. Thus *gang, hang* have none of the connotations of *bang; fuzz* is nothing like *buzz* (nor is *does*, pronounced as if spelled *duzz*!); the "imitative" nature of *crunch* can't be in the initial *cr-*, which certainly has no special connotation in *crow* or *cruise*, nor can it be in the *-unch*, which occurs in *lunch* and *munch* (an "imitative" word with quite different connotations); with *slash* compare *slow* and *cash; growl* is perhaps imitative because of the avowedly imitative *grrr* (which, however, also consists of ordinary English sounds except when made like an animal noise, and then it isn't language), but compare *grow* and *foul; meow* certainly does "sound like" a cat's cry, but *mew*, an older form for the same thing, hardly suggests it at all nowadays; *moo* "sounds like" a cow's noise, but *do* or *who* are not "imitative". That is, all supposedly "imitative words" (and not actually imitative cries) are arbitrarily assigned the meanings and connotations they have as a result of the history of the language and of the total culture of its speakers. The psychology of this process may well be worth studying but is not in the province of linguistics. Moreover, in other languages, the "imitations" of the same things often sound entirely different: compare English *purr* with French *ronronner.*

Language is used by HUMAN BEINGS. Only human beings talk, and we start from the admittedly circular statement that a human being is an animal that talks, and that language is the possession only of human beings.

The communication system that has recently been attributed to porpoises seems real enough, but has none of the special attributes of language that are being discussed here. It is a system of SIGNALS— like our warning lights, bells, some gestures—but not a system of symbols. The reported "dances" of bees are very interesting communicative devices, but they too lack the characteristics of language: they are iconic (that is, they picture or represent a situation) rather than symbolic; they are not arbitrary, but involve a specific connection with distance and direction; they are inherited rather than learned; they are closed systems, limited to specific information about location of food sources, and cannot be extended, while language is freely extended at will to any and all experiences. The talking of parrots and some other birds is mere sound imitation, and does not communicate as language does, though it may serve the same signaling purposes that the natural cries of these birds, and of other animals, serve.

All human beings are MEMBERS OF A SOCIETY. By SOCIETY we mean any functional and functioning group of human beings who carry on the bulk of their activities together. No human infant can exist except as a member of some such group, be it only a single family. Myths about persons brought up by animals—wolves or others—are just myths, and have no factual foundation. Individuals may grow up with minimal contacts with a society larger than the person or persons responsible for rearing them, and adults may live for long years in accidental or enforced isolation; but, once having grown at least to childhood, and having learned a language and the associated behavior patterns, a human being is a member of a society.

The activity of human beings is INTERACTION and COMMUNICATION with each other. By virtue of being members of a society, they must constantly engage in interaction with others. Even when seemingly interacting only with the physical environment, they are doing so in terms of their relation to other human beings.

The contact and interaction between human beings can only be IN TERMS OF THEIR CULTURE, because all human beings learn to behave in some cultural system, know no other basic form of behavior, and can not know—or even imagine—any other way to behave.

Language as just defined is manifested as particular languages. A language is the particular language system of a particular society. There are as many societies as there are languages; and as many languages as there are societies (see 1.3 for further elucidation of this).

1.22. Language is used in a total communication situation. When a person talks, his vocal activity may be called speaking, or speech. Speech consists of language in its environment of paralanguage. PARALANGUAGE may be described as consisting of voice set and voice quality, and the vocalizations accompanying the language material. Every individual when speaking has a voice set appropriate to his sex, age, state of health, social position, location in respect to his hearers and so on, and he varies it only under appropriate circumstances: one can whisper in a large room, or shout in a small one, one can use a high-pitched voice or a low-pitched one, one can sound infirm or vigorous, and all these differences have communicative significance. Voice quality is another factor that everyone possesses as a distinctive characteristic, and that can be varied when necessary: a grown woman can sound like a little girl, a grown man can whine, an orator can convince an audience by a cajoling wheedling or by a rasping irritation. Then there are the nontalking noises: one can laugh or cry, clear one's throat, use hesitating *uh*'s and *ah*'s; and there are the modifications of loudness, length, tempo, rhythm, pitch, and others, that one can add to one's talking.

Different languages are accompanied by differing paralanguage systems. Paralanguage is a cultural system like language—learned, arbitrarily symbolic, and systematically patterned. But, it appears from such studies as have so far been made, paralanguage is more simply structured than are languages (see 1.23). No one ever talks without paralanguage, if only the kind that may be characterized as neutral; special emotional effects are communicated by paralanguage, in different ways in different societies.

Because the things that we have described as constituting paralanguage may seem to resemble the noises made by animals, it might be conjectured that paralanguage existed before language. But the noises that were made by pre-human creatures before the invention of language were at best signals or icons, and not symbols. Paralanguage is by definition a cultural system, and accordingly it came into being with the invention of language. Paralanguage is then a communication system accompanying and subsidiary to language. The items included in paralanguage happen only along with or between linguistic events. And of those items that happen between, the special vocalizations (the nontalking noises referred to) are often converted into language; if one makes the noise "sh", that is paralanguage; if one says "hush", that is a conversion into an item of language.

In addition to paralanguage, language is always accompanied by body motion, facial expression, and gesture. These activities are also now known to constitute cultural systems, and the term KINESICS has been devised for them, though as yet little systematic study of kinesic systems has been made.

Besides paralanguage and kinesics, there may exist also tactile communication systems, involving touch and possibly other senses (odors, reactions to heat waves); and there are visual communication systems—one has to learn to see, and one sees what one has been taught to see.

1.23. In the definition of language given in 1.21, we spoke of vocal symbols and of the systematic arrangement of these, and indicated that the system functioned for communication. We can now restate this as follows, keeping in mind that the functioning of language is to convey a message (1.13):

Language in general is so structured that it has SOUND, SHAPE, and SENSE. All languages known are structured in this way, and it is assumed that all languages of human beings have always had this structure.

Language has sound: the "arbitrary vocal symbols" of the definition are the sounds of language. All languages are made up of sounds, and it is almost impossible for human beings to conceive of any other medium for language. Once language exists, it is possible to base secondary systems, in other media, on it; writing is such a system, and the various graphic arts, music, and other human activities are in certain ways based on language. But before any such developments are possible, language, as speech sounds, must exist.

Language has shape: the sounds are systematically arranged into sequences, the words of a language; and the words are systematically arranged, by various kinds of sounds accompanying them, into phrases and sentences. These arrangements are the shapes or forms of language.

Finally, language makes sense: the structured arrangements of sounds and shapes convey a message: this message stems from the arrangements themselves, and leads to an interpretation of the message as related to and symbolizing, in structured ways, the world around us.

Because all human beings are the same in general structure, it is possible for human beings to learn each other's languages, and to translate from one language to another. The details of structure differ, however, for each language. The differences in sound bring about different shapes. The different shapes result in different structures of arrangement. The different arrangements become more diverse as the messages conveyed are in terms of diverse cultural systems. With sufficient time and training, it is relatively easy to learn the sounds of another language; in English *mother* and French *mère* the first sound is practically the same, while everything else is different, but speakers of each can learn the other. And it is not difficult to learn even very complex systems of grammar, as far as the forms themselves are concerned; English verb phrases like *is doing, has been doing, had done, might do* as compared with French *fait, a été en train de faire, a eu fait, fasse* (none of these are exact equivalents, be it noted) are learnable as forms occurring in certain kinds of sequences. But when it comes to using the words and forms of a language to convey the right message, the problem becomes one of finding the equivalent in a strange culture for something in one's own, and often enough there is no exact equivalent. Though the words *mother* and *mère* generally mean the same thing, there are differences between English-speaking and French-speaking societies that bring about subtle differences in connotation. The verb forms cited, as every high-school student of French finds out, do not correspond at all closely in expressing time and duration of action. And when we get to so-called idioms, we enter completely into the realm of culturally different worlds; thus an American knows what *to strike out* means even if he is not a baseball fan; but this phrase cannot be translated literally into Russian at all because Russian speakers don't play baseball, and its connotation and general significance can be conveyed only by a paraphrase involving some Russian word meaning 'to fail'.

1.3. CROSS-PURPOSES

1.30. In 1.12 above it was suggested that after the use of language first began, a certain amount of difference developed between the language habits of different groups, and that this diversification came about very quickly.

Since that early beginning much time has elapsed, and the differences have grown. Thus an essential fact about the languages of the world is that they exhibit extreme diversity. That is, there are many of them, and they are very different in all the details of their structure—in sound, shape, and sense.

1.31. How many different languages are there, it may be asked. The question cannot be answered until we decide how to tell one language from another. It is clear that English and French are two different languages. But in Scandinavia, where Norwegians and Swedes and Danes talk to one another each in his own "language" and are mutually understood, is there one over-all language, or are there three? Is the English of the Mississippi fieldhand the same language as that of the Yorkshire farmer? Is Arabic as spoken in the Near East and Northern Africa one language or many? There are hundreds of such cases all over the world.

The answers to the questions can only be made in terms of the sound, shape, and sense structures of each language. The methods used for determining the nature of linguistic systems will be sketched in the next few chapters. But the science of linguistics has not yet reached a stage where it can do more than give approximate answers to the questions above. Very few of the forms of language in the world have been adequately surveyed and analyzed. As a result, the criteria for judging where one language stops and another begins are inadequate. It is necessary to rely on extralinguistic factors to get any kind of idea of language diversity.

The extralinguistic factors are, in part, group identification (different groups—tribes, nations—usually speak different languages); mutual intelligibility (different languages are usually not mutually intelligible); need for interpreters and translators; and other social and sociological matters. Linguistic factors are taken into account too, but the data are mostly superficial and inadequate. Different kinds of sounds usually distinguish different languages—but Americans who say *dance* with the vowel of *bad* and Englishmen who use the vowel of *father* are both speaking the same language; different grammatical forms count, but *you was* and *I seen him* are just as much part of English as *you were* and *I saw him*; different meanings are important, but consider the word *bonnet*: it means a kind of hat in both England and America, but only in England does it mean what Americans call the hood of a car.

But putting together all the factors listed, we can make some kind of estimate of the number of languages in the world. The estimate is highly elastic: there are perhaps as few as 2,500 languages, perhaps as many as 5,000.

Discussion in the next sections of how diversity came about, and of the notion of dialects, will help to make the extreme elasticity of the number more meaningful.

1.32. A homogeneous group of human beings living together and carrying on their activities together constitutes a society and forms a linguistic community—they speak the same language. This is true now and has always been so, though there are exceptional situations in which people who for most purposes are a single society have different languages, and there are in modern times examples of the same language being used by different groups. However, as soon as a society breaks up into two or more groups, geographically or socially separated, differences in the language begin to appear, and eventually there are several languages where originally there was only one.

The process of diversification begins the moment there is any kind of separation or difference in activities. This means that WITHIN a society diversification is actually going on all the time. Each individual tends to diversify his speech from that of others to the extent that his activities are unique. But in this case the necessity for continued communication irons out the incipient diversity constantly. When, however, groups of people become separated in space, or are kept apart by social barriers, the diversification proceeds without this check, and is in proportion to the lack of communication.

The first differences that arise are small. They result from the fact that the members of the separated groups now talk to others within their group, and rarely or not at all to persons in the other group. There are different persons to talk to, and different things to talk about. As time goes on, the sounds used may change, the words and grammatical forms may become different, the meanings may diverge. The new language forms, taken as a whole, constitute at first closely similar DIALECTS of the same language. With the passage of more time, the differences may become such that the two (or more) forms of speech come to constitute two different languages.

1.33. As has been said, no infallible criteria exist for deciding what are dialects of the same language, and what are different languages.

In a region such as the European area beginning at the North Sea and running across the Netherlands and northern Germany east to Poland, one can go from settlement to settlement finding only slight differences between the dialects in any two contiguous or adjacent areas. But by the time one has reached the Elbe, the dialects spoken there are very different from those in the Netherlands. It is difficult to say whether there is one language here, or more than one. Furthermore, the situation is complicated by virtue of there being two different literary languages, Dutch and German, set up as standards of usage. The diagram shows the kind of overlapping and gradual transition that is involved:

Dutch-German Dialects

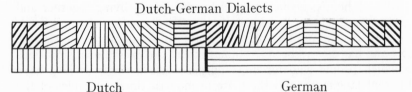

Dutch   German

In more recently settled countries, such as the United States, the settlers brought with them dialect differences. As population grew, the settled areas became contiguous or overlapped. The original dialect differences have remained, and are clear and distinct, but in border regions there may be places where people speak dialect A in an area completely surrounded by speakers of dialect B, and vice versa:

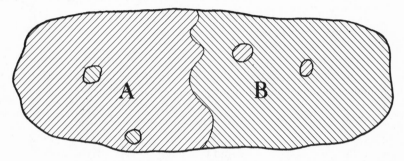

Where a colonial power has introduced its language as an official language, as in nineteenth-century India, the native population may acquire this language to such an extent as to make their use of it a new dialect of the language. Indian English and Philippine English are examples of this.

In areas where there are sharp social demarcations, based on class or caste and including educational differences, there develop social dialects in the same geographical area. In many parts of India even one small village may have several dialects, with persons of different social status speaking differently; the difference may be in any or all aspects of a language—sounds, grammatical forms, meanings may each be different in some ways.

Such social dialects, sometimes less clearly differentiated, are found in countries like the United States also: a word like *grass* is pronounced in the Central Atlantic area with a long, tense vowel starting somewhat like the vowel of *bed* and moving toward a central offglide like the last sound in *sofa*. Educated speakers do not over-prolong the sound, and manage to say it so that to those who use the vowel of *hat* in *grass* the described pronunciation is acceptable as an equivalent. Less educated speakers prolong the vowel and add a kind of twang to it, often with nasal resonance; this latter pronunciation, structurally the same (see 2.4), is socially different and less desirable. The person who says *I seen him* or *Between you and I* is speaking a socially different dialect from those who say *I saw him* or *Between you and me*. The person who has a dime left in his pocket and no immediate prospect of additional funds may describe himself as "broke", the rich man who forgot to cash a check and has only a dime left may also call himself "broke", but they are obviously connoting socially different images.

In summary, the kinds of dialects we have alluded to are:

GEOGRAPHICAL—forms of speech fairly homogeneous within an area and differing from those in other areas;

SOCIAL—forms of speech differentiated by virtue of the social standing (in a wide sense) of the speakers;

STANDARD—forms of speech used officially and differing more or less from local norms; often a standard dialect is based on one of the social or geographical dialects;

LITERARY—the form of speech codified as appropriate for use in writing, especially in writing what is called literature;

COLONIAL—a form of language imposed by an outside ruling group and often adopted as a second language by the natives.

In addition to the above, there are several other specialized kinds of dialects. A TECHNICAL JARGON (the word *jargon* here is a technical term, with no derogatory connotations) is a dialect used by the members of an occupational group; it is characterized chiefly by special vocabulary, but usually has the same sounds and grammar as the ordinary speech of members of the group. A PIDGIN or CREOLE is a form arising from more or less conscious simplification or adaptation of foreign vocabulary to native grammar to make communication possible between groups with widely differing languages. Pidgin English arose in the Pacific areas from the use of a restricted vocabulary and sentence structure by English speakers adapting to the supposed needs or limitations of speakers of Chinese or of Melanesian languages. Haitian Creole is a similarly derived form of French. Chinook Jargon was a grammatically modified form of a Northwest United States Indian language used by the Indians of that region to communicate between tribes having different native languages; it has now been replaced by English. Pidgins are often thought to be simpler in structure than "natural" languages, but this is not necessarily true.

1.34. To illustrate further the kinds of dialect differences there are, the different forms of English spoken in the United States will be briefly discussed.

The settling of speakers of English in what is now the United States took place over a period of time and on separate occasions, by groups of people rather than individuals; and at different times, the settlers came from different parts of the British Isles. They brought with them several varieties of English: that spoken around London; a West-of-England type; a northern variety which had spread to the north of Ireland (the so-called Scotch-Irish settlers came from there). Settling at various points on the east coast, they spread westward, crossed the mountains and began to expand in various directions, so that most of the central states show more than one dialect base in the English now spoken there. The greatest variety is naturally on the east coast, and the language is much more uniform in the most recently settled areas (except in urban concentrations).

The English spoken in the United States can be divided into eight areas:

A. Eastern New England (Maine, coastal New Hampshire, eastern Massachusetts, Rhode Island, Connecticut east of New Haven).

B. Western New England (interior New Hampshire, all of Vermont, western Massachusetts, central and western Connecticut north of the coast).

C. Central Atlantic Seaboard (southern and southwestern Connecticut; Long Island, New York City, the Hudson valley as far as Albany in New York state; New Jersey—except its northwestern quarter; southeastern Pennsylvania; Delaware; Maryland from Delaware to Baltimore and to Washington, D.C.).

D. Northern Middle West (central and western New York, northwestern New Jersey, the northern and western two-thirds of Pennsylvania, northern Ohio, Indiana, Illinois; Michigan, Wisconsin, Minnesota, Iowa, Nebraska, the Dakotas).

E. Midland (beginning west of Philadelphia, running generally south of the 40th parallel, and in a widening triangle to include the Ohio valley, Missouri, Kansas, Oklahoma, west Texas, northern New Mexico).

F. Coastal South (Tidewater Virginia, the coastal parts of North and South Carolina; southern and central Georgia, Alabama, Mississippi; Louisiana, east Texas).

G. Southern Hill (interior regions between Coastal South and Midland, to the Mississippi river).

H. Far West (west and north of areas D and E, to the Pacific).

In Canada the people in the eastern provinces speak what is essentially an extension of area A; Ontario and the prairie provinces are an extension of area D; British Columbia continues area H.

Alaska is a continuation of area H. Hawaii exhibits aspects of areas
A and C because of its special settlement history.

Within the several areas, New York City, Philadelphia, Chicago,
Saint Louis, San Francisco, and some of the southern cities have
special urban dialects differing in some ways from those of the general
area around them.

In 2.4, in the discussion of English sounds, examples will be given
to illustrate divergences in pronunciation between the above-men-
tioned areas. In 3.4 there will be some examples of dialect differences in grammar. In 4.2 divergences in vocabulary and meaning will
be given.

1.35. Most languages exhibit phonological variations in their dialects, even when the total linguistic community is small in numbers.
Examples analogous to those for American English could be cited
for numerous languages all over the world.

As stated, dialects also differ in grammar and in meanings, and
in the actual vocabulary items used. Within the scope of this book
we cannot illustrate such differences (see the References and Notes
for this section).

1.4. THE RECORD

1.40. The presentation of linguistic data that we have made so
far and the further discussion in the rest of this book depend on
there being a means of recording language. The principal record of
languages is contained in written material. In very recent years
there have come into being means of recording the actual sounds—
phonograph records, sound tracks on film, magnetic tape. The nature
and kind of written records, and of the newer sound recordings, need
to be considered before we go further.

1.41. It has been said (1.11) that language was probably invented
a million or more years ago. By its nature, as sound uttered by
interacting human beings, it was (and is) ephemeral: the sounds are
made and heard, and that is the end of it. Yet in another sense it is
not the end: the speaker and hearer both remember what they say
and hear, and much of what is said and heard is repeated many
times over. Language is thus recorded in human memory, has always
been so recorded, and gets passed on from generation to generation
in this way.

A long time ago man got the idea that visual representation of
events, people, animals, artifacts, and so on, could serve as an aid
to memory as well as a source of esthetic satisfaction. All the graphic
arts stem from this idea, and we have still existing wall paintings in

caves, pictographs on stone, images and statuettes, and other representations of things and events. But all these things, though describable in language, did not symbolize to the observer any specific linguistic content. In a cave painting anyone could point out the buffalo, the dogs, the men, the spears, and we can still look at the painting and do the same. But no two observers can possibly be sure of saying exactly the same things in their descriptive reports. The need for a direct and exact way of representing utterances, of recording language, may have existed for a long time. But there is no record of its having been acted upon until about 8,000 years ago. By that time agriculture had been invented and some animals had been domesticated. The consequent increase in availability of food served to free at least some individuals from ordinary daily chores. There was time for leisure, for thinking, for artistic creation. Somewhere in the Near East, apparently as far back as we have suggested, someone got the idea of symbolizing the elements of language—the words, or the syllables, or the separate sounds—by means of conventional marks on a smooth surface, such as a wall of rock, a large leaf, or a skin. This was how writing was invented. Languages are systems of symbols, and writing is a system for symbolizing symbols, i.e., it is a secondary symbol system.

In Mesopotamia and in Egypt, writing was already well developed about 6,000 years ago, probably by independent invention in each place. In China, writing began about 4,000 years ago, and among the Mayas of Yucatan there was writing over 2,000 years ago. The latter was almost certainly an independent invention, and each of the others may also have been. Our own writing system traces back to that of ancient Egypt. Writing is discussed fully in Part III (Chapters 7, 8) below.

The important point to note here is that writing systems have existed for, at most, 1/100 of the time that language has existed; and, more importantly, the majority of the world population is still illiterate (all young children everywhere, and most or many adults in many countries). Language comes first, and writing is at best a secondary symbol system of recent development.

The common belief among literate people in the societies that have a long-standing tradition of written literature is that the written language, as it is called (that is, the dialect that is written down by those who know how to write), is primary and superior, and that the language that is spoken is a kind of corruption of or degeneration from it. (The notion that written language is somehow superior may also derive from the fact that what is written is often edited, and thus is clearer than a spoken message). In view of what has been said about the relative ages of language and of writing, and the vast illiteracy of the world's peoples, the belief in the superiority of written material can obviously not be true. What then is the status of a written language?

In all societies in which writing has developed, it has been the possession of limited parts of the total population, and it has been limited in use and purpose. In ancient Egypt and Sumeria, writing was chiefly for recording sacred texts, but was also used for records of business dealings. When Egyptian writing spread to the peoples of the eastern Mediterranean, these uses persisted. In Greece, writing began to have use for recording general literature, and for making note of all kinds of activities. In China, writing was for literary and practical uses from the start. In Yucatan, writing was for astronomical and other priestly purposes, but the Aztecs secularized it. In the modern world there is widespread adult literacy, but writing is still used for special purposes: education, training and technical instruction, guidance and precept, warning, orders from superiors to inferiors, reports about technical matters, history, literary productions of all kinds, letter writing, business and technical activities. All of these uses, ancient and modern, necessarily call for special vocabulary and special style. What is written, then, is always a special form of language, aimed at producing a desired special effect. The written language is a special dialect, in any linguistic community. In fact, there are nearly always several written dialects. In our society, it is silly to deplore the fact that scientific reports do not read like novels; they shouldn't read like novels, but like scientific reports; and novels should read like novels. If the literary dialect has been established for some time, it may very well represent an older stage of usage. But the newer usages of the spoken dialects may not stem from the same dialect as the basis of the literary one, and in any case are not corruptions of it, or degenerations from it. They are simply examples of dialect differences.

1.42. Another notion about the development of languages in time is almost the direct opposite of the one just discussed, and is equally erroneous. It is believed by some that originally languages were "primitive"; this is supposed to mean that the sounds used were strange, few in number, not quite human; that the grammar was either extremely simple ("simple, primitive" minds couldn't remember) or extremely complex ("primitives" couldn't form abstractions); and the sense was limited to a few hundred notions at best, or else was highly unsystematic and too complex for anyone.

Since it can be assumed that all language began about the same time, every language must be just as old as any other language. If at the beginning (above, 1.1) language was "primitive", whatever that might be, then any language now existing is not primitive, but has evolved over an extremely long time.

But if there are no "primitive" languages, is there at least some worth in the notion of "civilized languages"? This notion can be supported only by definition of terms. We can say a language is a "civilized language" if the people speaking it are civilized; but here we will have to define in cultural terms what is meant by "civilized". True, the language of a people with technology, such as the people of the Western world, has a vast technological vocabulary. But the Navaho, with an elaborate ceremonial and religious structure, have developed a vast technical vocabulary for that activity.

We conclude that there are no primitive or civilized languages— just languages all equally old and equally complex. And we further decide that all languages are, by virtue of their age, prior to all forms of writing by many, many millenia.

1.43. The last conclusions raise the question of what attitude the scientific observer of language takes toward problems of "correctness" in speech and writing. An anthropological approach can easily answer this question.

It is quite true that literary language is only one of many dialects, for English as for other languages. It is also true, as stated, that any language is just as good as any other language—for its specific society and the culture of that society.

In the nations of the modern world, the official language or preferred literary style is the form of language that has been decided on—consciously or as the result of historical developments—to be the vehicle of the culture. Members of the society, to participate fully in its activities, need to control the national language fully. The schools can dedicate themselves to teaching the standards of usage of such a language; but they will have to do it with understanding of the anthropological and linguistic facts we have sketched previously, or their efforts will continue to produce the minimal results now seen. And it must always be recognized that the "correct" style or language for any particular purpose is the one that is best adapted for that purpose in anthropological terms, and that traditional notions of "purity", "correctness", "value", "beauty of sound", etc., have no pertinence. See the "Conclusion", Chapter 9, for fuller discussion of literary and official languages.

Chapter 2

HOW DOES IT SOUND?

2.0. THE STUDY OF LANGUAGE

2.00. Language is used in a total communication situation (1.22). This situation—talking or speech—occurs in a setting in which speaker and hearer are involved, and has the function of conveying messages (1.13). Language itself has sound, shape, and sense (1.23).

The field of knowledge that treats all of these phenomena together may be called MACROLINGUISTICS. This field deals with the totality of activity connected with and stemming from the use of language; it does not exist as a single unified science, and the term is used here only as an integrating label. The use of language occurs in a setting— the speaker-hearer situation (1.13). The examination of this situation, in terms of the physics of the activity and the physiology and psychology of the participants, may be called PRELINGUISTICS; it too does not exist as a unified science, but rather as a set of possible fields of investigation or in the form of writings whose basic goals are in the sciences of physics, biology, and psychology. The conveying of the message deals with the area of study that may be called METALINGUISTICS. The talking itself is examined in MICROLINGUISTICS, which exists in terms of a few studies of paralanguage and kinesics, and in the content of many thousands of books and articles on language and languages. The study and analysis of language as a whole, and of specific languages, is called LINGUISTICS.

The term ETHNOGRAPHY OF SPEAKING has been used for the study of actual speech occurrences in various social situations. In my terms, this study would be included in metalinguistics.

2.01. Linguistics must deal with the threefold description of language as having sound, shape, and sense. Linguistics is accordingly divided into PHONOLOGY, MORPHOLOGY, and SEMOLOGY.

23

The three terms just given are modern creations in imitation of Ancient Greek. *Phonology* means something like 'sound lore'; it is derived from Greek *phōnē* 'sound', *log-* 'talk', and from the noun ending *-ia* which gives English *-y*. Morphology is 'shape lore', from *morphē* 'form, shape'. *Semology* is 'meaning lore', from *sēma* 'sign, signal, symbol'. (See Chapters 7 and 8 for the Greek writing system and the Latin-letter transcription used here).

2.02. When language is looked at in the threefold way suggested, it can be seen that its central SUBSTANCE is in the shapes—the words, phrases, sentences. We ask, "what's the word for . . .?" or "What do you say for . . .?" This aspect will be considered in Chapter 3, where morphology is treated.

What are the words—the shapes—made of? For an answer to this question, see 3.12. If we ask, how are the shapes expressed, what describes or characterizes or identifies them, we can say that it is some aspect of the sounds. The sounds so considered may be called the DIACRITICS (Greek, 'describing', 'differentiating') of the substance; these are the units or components that describe, differentiate, compose the shapes. If the substance is described by the diacritics, then the functional RELATION of its parts is what constitutes or sets up or gives rise to the sense. This aspect will be considered in Chapter 4, dealing with semology.

2.03. The diacritics of the shapes of language, the sounds, are examined in the phonology. There is general phonology, the science of language sounds as a whole, and there are the specific phonologies of individual languages.

In treating phonology, it is possible to subdivide it into three areas. The substance of phonology consists of the actual sounds of speech, studied as PHONETICS, and their diacritics are the sound features or ARTICULATIONS; these two are examined in 2.2. The relations of the sounds are studied in PHONEMICS (2.3).

2.1. THE ORGANS OF SPEECH

2.10. The sounds of speech are produced by certain organs of the body. These organs have other functions also, and much of their study is outside the realm of macrolinguistics altogether, while their physical and physiological functioning in relation to speech production are in prelinguistics. In linguistics proper, when we treat the activity of these organs and its results, the organs can be called the ORGANS OF SPEECH.

The organs of speech are, for our purposes, the nose and nasal passages; the mouth and its parts—lips, teeth, gums, roof of the mouth, tongue, the throat passages; the passage to the lungs, the lungs themselves; and the diaphragm. We can examine their functioning in a general way, basing ourselves on the more detailed statements of various nonlinguistic sciences. These statements become, for the linguist, prelinguistic ones, and he bases his linguistic statements on them.

2.11. The accompanying diagram is as accurate and detailed as need be for linguistic purposes.

Diagram of the Organs of Speech

The NASAL CAVITY is a passive organ of speech. When the velum is lowered, as it is in normal breathing through the nose, air propelled from the lungs in the process of speaking can resonate in the nasal passages. Such resonance creates the sound features of NASALITY and NASALIZATION (see 2.2 and its subdivisions for discussion of these and the other sound features). In speaking, the velum is raised and the passage to the nose is closed except for sounds that are produced with NASAL RESONANCE. Sounds produced with resonance only in the mouth are ORAL sounds.

The oral chamber is divided for linguistic purposes into various areas, as shown. The UPPER TEETH, the ALVEOLES (pronounced /ǽlviyòwlz/—see 2.4 for the transcription of English), the hard PALATE (or, simply, the palate), and the soft palate or VELUM (/víyləm/) are surface regions against which the tongue can articulate. The UVULA (/yúwvyulə/) is a mobile organ which can be vibrated; uvulas differ in size and mobility, and some persons can hardly move them at all; snoring is in large part the involuntary movement of the uvula as one breathes during sleep.

The TONGUE, which is a muscle, has a movable tip or APEX, and its body can be raised, lowered, bunched up, or flattened. The upper surface of the movable forward part is the BLADE, the region back of that the FRONT, and the back of the tongue the DORSUM. The passage from the mouth to the throat is called the FAUCES (/fóhsìyz/). The tongue in its movements can be made to articulate against or close to the various parts of the roof of the mouth, and these points of articulation are labeled (see 2.2ff).

The throat is divided into the upper region called the PHARYNX (/fǽriŋks/), and the lower region called the LARYNX. The EPIGLOTTIS (/épi+glàtis/), controlled by muscles attached to the HYOID (/háyòyd/) BONE, closes the larynx during swallowing, so that saliva and food pass into the ESOPHAGUS (/iy+sáfəgəs/); if the epiglottis does not form a tight closure, coughing and choking result from swallowing. The upper portion of the throat below the epiglottis is the GLOTTIS; here are situated the muscle bands, one on each side, known as the VOCAL CHORDS (the spelling "cords" is also used, but is misleading; the term "vocal bands" is employed by some). The vocal chords can be brought together to close the passage, and can be made to vibrate rapidly. The ARYTENOID (/ərítinòyd/) CARTILAGE is used in producing some kinds of sounds when the vocal chords are kept immobile.

At the entrance of the mouth are the LIPS, which function to change the shape of the passage through which air is expelled in speaking, or to prevent the expulsion of air.

2.2. SPEECH SOUNDS

2.20. The organs of speech discussed in 2.1 produce the noises that we call speech sounds, the sounds of language. They also produce the often very similar sounds that occur in paralanguage (see 1.22). In the examination of the sounds of languages, the linguist has to learn to separate out the paralanguage noise from the language sounds. Such separation is facilitated by the examination of the articulations of sounds, in order to determine the various features composing them, and to arrive at descriptions of the sounds in terms of systematic arrangements of the articulatory features.

The study of sound features, called here articulations (2.03), is often carried out with the assistance of various kinds of instruments and apparatus. For this reason it may be referred to as "instrumental phonetics" or "experimental phonetics". The hearer's reaction to sounds is spoken of as "acoustic phonetics". The description of sound features in terms of the articulating organs is "physiological phonetics".

Our discussion of articulations includes results derived from all these specialized approaches. The phonetic system presented in 2.22 employs physiological labels, but embodies also the other descriptive techniques.

2.21. The articulations entering into speech sounds will now be set forth in terms of various sound features.

The sound features controlled by the action of the velum are NASAL RESONANCE (velum lowered and passage to the nasal cavity open) and ORAL RESONANCE (velum raised, nasal cavity shut off). Any of the sound features mentioned below may be accompanied by nasal resonance. When nasal resonance is the essential element in a sound, the sound is called NASAL, and the feature is described as NASALITY. When a sound has nasal resonance as a secondary feature, with other features more basic to its description, it is called NASAL-IZED, and we speak of NASALIZATION as the feature. Oral resonance is always described in terms of specialized features of articulation.

The vibration of the vocal chords produces the humming noise called VOICE. Sounds having the feature of voice are VOICED. Sounds without voice are called VOICELESS, and are considered to have the feature of VOICELESSNESS.

Sounds produced with free passage of the air stream without closure or constriction are called VOWELS (or "vocoids") and have the feature of VOWELNESS. Sounds produced so that there is noise resulting from closure or constriction at some point are CONSONANTS (or "contoids"), and have the feature of CONSONANTNESS.

Vowels are formed by differently shaped oral resonance chambers resulting from raising or lowering the tongue and pushing it forward or back, using the height and location of the front and dorsum in relation to the palate and velum. In addition, the conformation of the lips modifies the nature of the vowel. The features used in describing vowels are thus TONGUE HEIGHT, TONGUE POSITION, LIP FORM, and in addition RELATIVE MUSCULAR TENSION of the tongue; nasalization may be added also. The features named are each over-all labels for several detailed descriptions, and can be called DIMENSIONS.

Consonants are formed by various articulations of the lips, tongue, and other organs. The resulting conformations of the organs of speech can again be called dimensions. The consonant dimensions are MANNER OF ARTICULATION, POINT OF ARTICULATION, VOICING, RELATIVE MUSCULAR TENSION, and NASALITY. The last three of these occur also with vowels. Manner of articulation distinguishes closure and opening of the passage for the emission of an air stream. Point of articulation distinguishes the place at which the passage of air is stopped or most constricted. Voicing has to do with the vibration of the vocal chords.

Besides the dimensions by which vowels and consonants are described, there are dimensions of loudness, intensity, pitch, duration, and various other kinds of phenomena. The description of these kinds of features has been much facilitated by the various machines that have been developed in recent years. Many traditional views on these matters have been upset by the machine observations, and there is considerable disagreement on details between different students of the subject. See the next two sections for further discussion of these kinds of features.

2.22. The various dimensions listed above are each subdivided. Various combinations of the subdivisions produce the standard sounds discussed in this section. From these sounds, others are produced by described standard deviations.

In order to provide maximum comparability of observed speech events, certain sounds may be chosen as standards against which the actual sounds of languages may be measured. The standard or "cardinal" sounds are defined by combinations of the dimensions discussed above. The observer of language events, acting as phonetician, learns the kinesthetic and acoustic qualities of the standard sounds. Then he can describe the actually observed sounds by noting the deviations in any dimension from the standard. With practice, observers using the same standard system of phonetic notation usually arrive at descriptions and identifications of sounds that are substantially the same.

Learning to identify sounds in the manner suggested is always a matter of practice, and the phonetician can spend years refining his sensitivities, and can become expert in recognizing very small differences between sounds. Many different ways of teaching and learning phonetics have been set forth in books on the subject. Despite differences in technique, there is general agreement that the learner needs first to train his hearing, and then to learn how to make the sounds that he has heard. Many phoneticians believe that ear training is best achieved by listening to sequences of sounds outside of any real language context; they prepare dictation exercises, which in recent years have usually been recorded on tape. The learner is told what sounds (standard and with deviations) are to be illustrated, and he listens to the dictation—live or on tape. While listening he develops a feel for what muscle movements should be made to produce the sound. After listening, the learner is then subjected to a dictation during which he has to recognize the sounds being made. Later comes practice in reproducing the sounds. Other phoneticians prefer to teach hearing, recognition, and reproduction of sounds by actual language materials, concentrating on one part at a time. In any case, sounds being taught and learned must, in accord with the principle of going from the known to the unknown, be compared with or identified as "like" or "similar to" or "somewhat resembling" sounds of known real languages. In the light of this principle and the need for comparison, the use of actual language materials seems better than attempting to learn sounds outside of a systematic context.

The techniques just discussed are most effectively used, in various combinations, to study the vowel and consonant sounds—the SEGMENTAL sounds. The sounds involving features of intensity, loudness, duration, pitch, and the like—the SUPRASEGMENTAL sounds—are very difficult to study out of context, and to study them it is much preferable to listen to actual language occurrences. One reason for the difficulty is that the suprasegmental sounds often have scope extending over a considerable stretch of segmental sounds. This means that actual phrases and similar sequences of utterances have to be listened to in order to determine all the details of the phenomena.

The present book is not a work on phonetics, and therefore must present the necessary information about phonetics in comparative terms that can be written about in such a way that the reader can identify them from his own knowledge. In the next section systematic combinations of dimensions or sound features will be presented in the form of tables, and symbols for writing the sounds will be discussed.

In summary, phonetics deals with the recognition and reproduction of speech sounds. The sounds are ready-made groupings, so to speak, of articulatory features. In ordinary language, the word *phonetics* is often used for the symbols by which sounds are presented in writing. The important thing about a phonetic description, however, is the system of analysis of the sounds and the sound features.

2.23. The necessity of writing down phonetic details has led to the invention of phonetic alphabets. These are sets of symbols, based on ordinary alphabets, devised for the special purpose of denoting the sounds, basic or standard or cardinal as well as deviations, of a system of phonetic description. Alphabets are usually representations of part of the phonemic system of a language, adapted to morphophonic variation—see 2.3 ff, especially 2.32; 3.12, 3.40; and the chapters on writing (Part III, Chapters 7 and 8). When observers of languages began to note details of sound that were not represented in the usual writing system, they had to provide special symbols. In the eighteenth century, compilers of dictionaries invented such special symbols, but these were still essentially phonemic, that is, intended to make clear the significant sound differences within a specific language. By the nineteenth century, reports of unwritten languages were so numerous that it was clear that many sounds unknown to Europeans needed to be represented. This led to the beginnings of modern phonetics. Systems of description of sounds were elaborated, along the lines indicated in the previous section, and along with them came special alphabets. As the systems became more extensive, the alphabets began to be presented in systematic tables.

One of the best known phonetic alphabets is that of the International Phonetic Association (Association Phonétique Internationale)—usually referred to as the IPA. The IPA was founded in 1886, and its aims have always been directed at improvement of language teaching; many textbooks for teaching the most widespread languages of Europe and America use the IPA alphabet to show pronunciation. The general system of the IPA has, over the years, been extended to cover phonetics in general, and the alphabet has a large array of special symbols. The latest form of the IPA alphabet is reproduced below in 8.5.

Another widely known system was devised for the American Anthropological Association by Edward Sapir, was published in 1916, and has been very extensively used in American Indian (Americanist) studies.

The author of the present book collaborated with Bernard Bloch over a period of years in working out a system of phonetic description that would provide an improved and more systematic statement of phonetics, and an alphabet incorporating the best features of the two systems just mentioned. The basic tables of the present form of that system (see References, 2.1) are reproduced in this section.

In the vowel table, the high, higher mid, lower mid, and low vowels are defined as having the dimension of tenseness, while the lower high, mid, and higher low are lax by definition. This means that the first set of sounds are like actually occurring vowels in French, where the vowel sounds are generally tense; while the second

Table of Vowel Classification

	Front		Central		Back	
	Un-rounded	Rounded	Un-rounded	Rounded	Un-rounded	Rounded
High	i	ʉ = ü	ɨ	ʉ = u̇	ɯ = ï	u
Lower High	ɪ	ʏ = ü̇	ɪ	ʊ = u̇	ᵻ = ï̇	ʊ
Higher Mid	e	ø = ö	ɘ = ė	ɵ = ȯ	ɤ = ë	o
Mid	E	Œ = ü̇	ə	ʊ̈ = ȧ	Δ = Ë	ʌ̈
Lower Mid	ɛ	œ = ö̇	ɜ = ė̇	ɞ = ȯ̇	ʌ	ɔ
Higher Low	æ	ɶ = ö̈	ʋ = ä̇	ɷ = ö̈	ʌ = ä̈	ω
Low	Æ	ɒ = ö̤	a	ʋ	ɑ	ɒ
Semivowels	y	ɥ = ẅ	y = ẏ	w = ẇ	ɥ = ÿ	w

set are like English so-called "short vowels", these being generally lax. Thus the French vowels in *si, thé, nette, patte* can be represented by the unmodified symbols [i, e, ɛ, Æ] (it is customary to set off phonetic symbols by square brackets). On the other hand, the vowels in the English of the northern East Coast of the United States in the words *sit, set, sat* can be represented by [ɪ, ɛ, æ]; for many speakers the vowel in *sit* is retracted, and may be shown as [ɪ̞]; in parts of the Middle West, among others, the vowel in *sat* is raised and tensed, [æ̠ˆ] (this can still be distinguished from [ɛ]). In 2.4 below some additional details of English phonetics will be given.

Of the consonant sounds shown, the symbols [p, t̪, k] can well represent the initial sounds of French *pipe, tout, coup*; while the

Table of Consonant Classification

Point of articulation

Manner of articulation	Faucal			Dorsal			Frontal			Apical			Labial	
	Laryngal	Glottal	Pharyngal	Post-velar	Medio-velar	Prevelar	Post-palatal	Medio-palatal	Pre-palatal	Cacuminal	Alveolar	Dental	Labio-dental	Bilabial
Stop	ʔ	ʾ	⊖ ⊕	q ɢ (ḳ ġ)	k g	ḵ ɡ̇ (k̑ ɡ̑)	ȼ ɟ̇	ȼ ɟ	ȼ̑ ɟ̑	ʈ ɖ (ṭ ḍ)	t d	t̪ d̪ (t̟ d̟)	ȹ ȸ (p̣ ḅ)	p b
Spirant — slit	ḥ	h ʜ	ḥ ʜ̣	χ ʁ (χ̣ ʁ̣)	x ɣ	χ ʁ (x̑ ɣ̑)	x̀ ɣ̀	x̌ ɣ̌	x̑ ɣ̑		θ̇ ð̇	θ ð	f v	ɸ β
Spirant — groove							ż z̀	ʂ ʐ (ś ź)	z z (ś ź)	ṣ ẓ (ṣ ẓ)	s z	s z (ṣ ẓ)		
Nasal				ŋ̇	ŋ	ŋ̑	ṅ	ñ	ń	ɳ (ṇ)	n	ꞥ (n̦)	ɱ (m̦)	m
Lateral				ʟ̇	ʟ			ʎ		ɭ (ḷ)	l	ʎ (ḷ)		ʎ
Trill				ʀ ʀ						ʈ (ṛ)	ɾ ɹ	ɾ (ṛ)		ʀ
Affricate — groove							c̀ ʒ̀	c ʒ (ĉ)	c̑ ʒ̑ (ĉ)	c̣ ʒ̣ (c̣ ʒ̣)	c ʒ	c̑ ʒ̑ (c̑ ʒ̑)		
Affricate — lateral										ʎ̇	ʎ ʎ	ʎ̑		
Retroflex spirant										ɽ̇	ɽ	ɽ̑		

[j may be used for ǰ]

List of Diacritical Marks

advanced	ț, g̃	palatalized		t_y
affricated	t^s, t^>š, ɸ^š	pharyngalized		h̦o
alveolar (with θ, ð only)	θ̣, ð̣	pitch: falling		à
apicalized	p_T	level		ā
apicalized, strongly	ț or t_r	low, ... high	a¹ ...	a⁴
aspirated	t'	rising		á
aspirated, heavily	t^h	postpalatal		s̀
aspirated, voiced	d^H	prepalatal		ś
back unrounded	ë	quantity: extra-long		a··
backed	k>, a>	half-long		a^v
central	ė, ȯ	long		a·
click	t^Δ	overlong		a:
delabialized	w_M	short	ă or	a̯
flapped	n^l, r^l	raised		a^∧
fortis	d̲	released (general)		t^Γ
fricative	s^+	retracted		ṭ, ġ
frictionless	s^=	retroflexed		ṭ, t_r; ər, ɚ
front rounded	ü	rounded		a_w
fronted	k<, a<	stress: extra-strong		''a
glottalized	t'	medial		₁a
implosive	b''	strong		'a
inspirated	s^<<	strong medial		₁₁a
labialized	t_w	weak		ᵛa
laryngalized	h_ϲ	syllabic		n̥
lateral release	t^L	tense		I̯
lax	i̦	trill, heavy		r^2+
lenis	ț	unreleased		p^¬
lowered	a^v	underrounded		u_M
mediopalatal	š, ļ, ñ	velaric pressure		p^V
nasal release	t^N	velarized		l_x
nasalized	a̧	voiced		t̬
nasalized, strongly	a_n	voiced release		b^v
nonsyllabic	i̯	voiceless		b̥, ł
overrounded	o_w	voiceless release		b^∧

sounds in English *peep, too, coo* are aspirated and the *t* is alveolar, and can be shown as [pʻ, tʻ, kʻ]. The vowels in the French words are [i] and [u], while the English has gliding complex vowels, [ɪ^i̯] (a short glide) and [ʊ^u̯:] (a long glide).

The few examples of the use of the tables must suffice at this point. For additional examples of phonetic transcription used in describing the phonology of other languages see References and Notes.

2.3. PHONEMICS

2.30. When the sounds of a language are being studied phonetically, it is also necessary to determine the places where they occur, and the limitations, if any, on which sounds can occur in sequence with each other. These kinds of data give information as to which sounds are distinctive and contrastive, and which are automatically conditioned by their surroundings. After such determinations have been made, it becomes apparent that in all languages the comparatively large number of different sounds which occur can be grouped into a relatively small number of classes that are distinct from one another, but whose members are so conditioned that the native speaker is usually unaware of the differences within a class. An example is found in the sounds represented by the letter *p* in the English words *pin, spin, upper, up*. The first is released into the vowel with aspiration, [pʻ]; the one after *s* is lax and without aspiration, [p̬]; the single sound represented by *pp* is tense like the first *p*, but unaspirated like that after *s*, [p]; the last instance is unreleased in ordinary speech (the lips simply stay closed), [p˺]. To the native speaker of English these are all "the same sound" until his attention is called to the differences in a phonetic examination such as we are making here. In Danish the difference between the very lax voiceless unaspirated sound represented by *b* in *bar* 'bare', [b̬], and the strongly aspirated sound in *par* 'pair', [pʰ], is distinctive, and the two contrast, so that the native speaker is aware of the difference; in Danish the sound represented by *p* after *s*, as in *spansk* 'Spanish', is like the *b* in *bar*, [b̬], and goes with that sound into a class contrasting with the *p* of *par*.

The distinctive and contrasting classes or groups of sounds that are found by carrying out the techniques alluded to are called PHONEMES. A usable definition of the term is:

> A PHONEME is a class of sounds that contrasts with every other such class in the language; its members, called ALLO-PHONES, are phonetically similar, are in complementary (i.e., noncontrasting) distribution, and are congruently patterned with the members of some other phonemes.

The meanings of various terms in the definition need some further comment. *Class* is used in the mathematical sense—a grouping arrived at by noting some one or more features common to each member; a class may have only one member. *Phonetically similar* means having sound features in common; phonetic similarity of sounds always suggests that they may be allophones of the same phoneme, and the criteria of distribution have to be used to separate some phonetically similar sounds into different phonemes: thus English [pʻ] and [p] and [b] are all phonetically similar, but since [pʻ] and [b] are in contrast in such items as *pit* and *bit*, they are immediately seen to be members of different phonemes; on the other hand, the [p̣] of *spin* is perhaps equally similar to [pʻ] and to [b], and if we assign [p̣] to the same phoneme as [pʻ], it must be because of its distribution after [s] and other factors. *Complementary* or *noncontrasting distribution* means that the sounds so labeled do not occur in the same situations, and their occurrences may be predicted or delimited by their position: thus [pʻ] in English occurs initially, [p̣] occurs after *s*, [p] internally after a stressed vowel, [pᵓ] in final position; [p̣] is also in noncontrasting distribution with [b], but here the factors of what kind of sound precedes and of the congruence of patterning must be taken into account. Congruently patterned sounds are seen in the grouping [pʻ, p̣, pᵓ] and [tʻ, t̬, tᵓ] (in *tin, stand, it*); the fact that [t̬ᵓ] occurs in *list, missed*, and is similar to [t̬] in *stand*, but that [d̬] (voiceless release) occurs after [z] in *raised*, is a factor in deciding that [t̬] belongs in a phoneme with [tʻ] and [tᵓ], but not with [d]; and if [t̬] and [tʻ] belong together, then the congruently patterned [p̣] and [pʻ] also belong together, even though there is no contrasting final sequence [zb̬] in any English word.

The presentation of the phonemics of English in 2.4 below will illustrate the methodology to some extent. For further details, consult the References for the present section.

2.31. The phonological structure of a language has as its substance the phonetics, expressed in articulations as its diacritics, and functioning in the relations of the substance that constitute the phonemics (above, 2.03). For the purpose of examining the other aspects of language structure, the morphological and the semological, it is necessary to have a complete statement of the phonemics, the phonetics and articulations being subsumed under that statement.

The exemplification of phonemic techniques in 2.30 dealt with vowel and consonant phonemes. The analysis of languages, both ancient and modern, shows that all languages have vowel phonemes, which can be called NUCLEAR, and consonant phonemes, which are MARGINAL. The number of nuclear phonemes reported for different languages varies greatly: certain languages in the Caucasus are said to have only two vowel phonemes, while English as analyzed below

(2.4) has nine, and Norwegian seems to have ten, though each of these languages has additional vocalic nuclei, which are analyzed as units in other descriptions. Similarly, the number of marginal phonemes varies: Hawaiian seems to have eight, English has 24, some languages are said to have many more (possibly up to 50).

It was indicated above that among the characteristics of allophones that are looked for are the positional variations, especially initial, internal, and final. Such characteristics have been noted by all phonemic analysts, including the prescientific makers of alphabets. From this fact of the recognition of beginnings and ends of linguistic items, as well as of what happens inside, the modern linguist has drawn the conclusion that all languages have a third kind of phoneme —phonemes of TRANSITION. Let us consider the English word *nitrate* and compare it with the phrase *night rate*; native speakers hearing these said will recognize the difference easily. Observing what happens in pronouncing the two, we see that the main difference between them lies in the manner of transition from *t* to *r*. The sequence of phonemes in *nitrate* shows an uninterrupted smooth transition from one to the other; this we call normal transition, and it is not a phoneme but a characteristic of the other phonemes. In *night rate*, however, the *t* is unreleased [t⌐], and the *r* then starts as does an initial *r*. The manner in which transition from the *t* to what follows it takes place is described as open transition, in this case internal, and is considered as a phoneme. Transition phonemes occur at ends of utterances or parts of utterances, and they affect the preceding marginal and nuclear phonemes in various ways, principally by stretching the time during which they are produced, and by changing the pitch or stress in some way. In English there are three terminal transitions, as well as the internal one. The details will be found in 2.4.

The conclusion is drawn that all languages have transition phonemes because all of them have some way of marking ends of parts of utterances or of whole utterances. The study of transitions is the newest and most uncertain part of phonemics. But the fact that all writing systems have recognized word division in some way and have provided some kind of punctuation marks would seem to indicate a recognition of the existence of the phenomenon long before complete analysis was possible. Transition phonemes were first called JUNCTURES, and that term is widely used in discussion of this phenomenon.

For many generations it has been known that some languages had significant variations in stress and pitch and quantity, and partial analyses of these prosodic phenomena have been made. Recognition of accent differences, of tone or pitch differences, and of length differences is found in the phonological statements of many languages. In English it has long been known that one syllable of a word of two or more syllables was louder—had STRESS or ACCENT—and that there were some syllables intermediate in stress between the loudest ones and the weak or "unstressed" syllables. It has also been known that there are pitch differences at the ends of English sentences. Only recently, however, have these SUPRASEGMENTAL or ACCENTUAL phonemes been analyzed completely and by techniques analogous to those for the nuclear and marginal phonemes (together, the segmental phonemes).

The segmental, transition, and suprasegmental phonemes are three different kinds of phonemes, and all languages seem to have some of each; see 2.4 for English.

2.32. The grouping of the sounds of a language into phonemes makes it possible to devise a PHONEMIC TRANSCRIPTION in which only the phonemes are represented, and the phonetic details of the allophones are to be inferred from the phonetic description of each phoneme. If we recall that the native speaker of a language knows its phonological structure in terms of the phonemes—the distinctive and contrastive elements—and uses the appropriate allophones automatically and without being aware of them, then it can be seen that writing symbols representing the phonemes (as such, or as manifestations of morphophones—see 3.12) can be effective representation of a language. In fact, all alphabetic writing (see Chapter 7, and especially 7.02) aims at such representation.

A phonemic transcription is used in linguistic analysis to make up for the deficiencies and omissions of ordinary orthographies in the case of languages that are regularly written, and to supply a writing system in the case of languages not written by their speakers. A phonemic transcription as an orthography may represent only part of the total phonemic system: the early Semitic alphabets represented only the consonant phonemes (see 7.1 and 8.3); our own alphabet represents vowels and consonants as phonemes, but generally omits any indication of stress and pitch (see 2.4). A phonemic transcription of English would show all the phonemes, and would represent them consistently.

Phonemic transcriptions are devised by selecting for each phoneme a typographically simple and convenient symbol from the phonetic symbols which may represent the various allophones: thus the English phoneme including the allophones [p‛,p̣, p, p˺] is conveniently written by using the letter *p*; it has become customary to set off phonemic symbols by means of slant lines (solidi), /p/. In the case of a vowel like that of *sit*, the appropriate phonetic symbol is [ɪ]; we may use that symbol in the phonemic system, or we may decide to use /i/ instead, achieving greater typographical simplicity.

Transition phonemes are indicated by such devices as /+/ or /-/ internally, by spaces, and by various kinds of punctuation marks.

Suprasegmental phonemes are indicated by various accent marks (see the list of diacritical marks in 2.23).

The important point about any phonemic transcription is that all the phonemes be represented, that the symbols be typographically simple and available, and that there be no ambiguity or use of one symbol for more than one phoneme or representation of one phoneme by more than one symbol. In the working out of orthographies based on proper phonemic analysis, various kinds of adaptations can be made. Some phonemes may be left unmarked (as weak stress, for instance, where one or more strong stresses are marked); some phonemes may be represented by a sequence of letters (as *sh* for /š/, where *s* is used for /s/); some phonemes may be represented by cover symbols for a phoneme sequence (as a punctuation mark for a sequence of pitches and a terminal transition). The devices that may be used, and that have been used in traditional orthographies will be discussed in 7.2 and 8.5, as well as in the treatment of specific writing systems.

2.4. THE PHONOLOGY OF ENGLISH

2.40. The English language has been an object of phonological study for several centuries. One reason for this study is the irregular orthography, leading to a quest for answers as to how to pronounce words known to someone only in written form. The earlier studies were aimed at showing the "pronunciation of the letters"; newer ones discuss the phonetics of different forms of English, and the newest present the phonetic findings in phonemic form.

The consonant phonemes of English have been well recognized for a long time, and there is agreement on the analysis of most of them. The vowel nuclei have been recognized as distinct entities by all students of the subject; but the analysis into "short" basic vowels, "long" vowels, and "diphthongs" has given rise to many differences of opinion, and some entities have been overlooked. The transition phonemes were recognized first in 1939, and the first full analysis of them was presented in 1951; some disagreement on them still exists. The stresses and pitches have been fully analyzed for about the same length of time as the transitions, but there were previous analyses, and some scholars still hold to the older views, or have developed new views similar to some of the older ones.

2.41. The basic vowels of English are nine in number: three front, three central, three back rounded, with a high, mid, and low member in each position. Phonetically they differ in length in terms of the following consonants: short before voiceless stops, long before voiced stops (and nasals and liquids, i.e., /l/ and /r/), half-long before voiceless spirants, longest before voiced spirants. The length allophones may be illustrated for the phoneme /i/:

bit [ɪ]   *bid* [ɪ·]   *hiss* [ɪˇ]   *his* [ɪ:]

Before /m, n, ŋ/ the vowels are more or less nasalized: *bin* [ɪ̃·]. Before /y/ and /w/, and for many speakers before /h/, the vowels are raised and tenser than elsewhere.

The nine vowels are:

/i   ɨ   u
e   ə   o
æ   a   ɔ/

Names for the symbols, the general phonetic character of the allophones, and examples of them are:

/i/ is called by the name of the letter *i*—/áy/; it is [ɪ] in most forms of English, with some variation to a more central vowel, [ɪ>]; it occurs in *bit, bid, bin, bill, hiss, his* with primary stress, and in the second syllable of *habit, college* with weak stress.

/e/, "*e*"—/íy/; [E]; some dialects have raised tense [E^], and others, in some positions, have a lowered vowel, [Eᵛ] or [ɛ̱]; *bet, bed, Ben, bell, less, fez*; rare in weak syllables.

/æ/, "digraph"; [æ], in some dialects [æ^] or [æ̞^]; *hat, had, can* (auxiliary verb), *pal, has*; weak-stressed in *absolve* and the like; many speakers have a complex nucleus, /eh/ or /æh/ before voiced stops and nasals and all spirants; others have contrasts, as *can* (verb) with /æ/ but *can* (noun) with /eh/.

/ɨ/, "barred *i*"; [ɨ]; chiefly in weak syllables spelled with *i, e, u*, as in *limit, added, minute*; but also for many speakers with strong stress in *just* (adverb), and some other common words; some dialects have /ɨ/ in many or even most words that have /i/ elsewhere.

/ə/, "shwa"—/šwáh/; [ʌ<^] in most American English; lower in some British dialects, more central in some other regions, [ə] or [əᵛ]; *but, bud, bun, dull, fuss, fuzz.*

/a/, "*a*"—/éy/; [ɑ] in Eastern American (not New England), [a] or even [æ>] in most western American dialects; *hot, hod, on, doll, doff, Oz*; in New England, and in most British dialects, the words cited usually have /ɔ/ (see below) and these dialects often have /a/ where other dialects have /ə/.

/u/, "*u*"—/yúw/; [ʊ<], often relatively unrounded; *book, good, puss, room* in some dialects (others have /uw/ in *room*), *full*.

/o/, "*o*"—/ów/; [ɑ<], relatively unrounded; in New England in such words as *home, coat, road*, where others have /ow/; also for many speakers in *whole, gonna* (going to); also in weak syllables, as *obey, November*.

/ɔ/, "open *o*"; [ɒ] in some American English, in isolated items like *alcohol* (the last vowel), *gloss* (a translation), *doll, jolly*; regularly where most American English has /a/, in words spelled with *o—hot, hod*, etc.—New England has [ω], Great Britain, [ɒ^] or [ω] or [ω^].

The nine vowels occur in complex nuclei with following /y, w, h/. The allophones of these three semivowels, as they may be called (a subclass of consonants) vary in height with the vowel: /y/ is [i̯] after /i, i̯, u/, [ɪ̯] after /e, ə, o/, [e̞] after /æ, a, ɔ/; /w/ is similarly [u̯, ʋ, o̞]; /h/ is [i̯ᵛ, ə̯, ə̯ᵛ]. Before /y/ a vowel glides toward a high front position; before /w/ the glide is to a high, back, rounded position; before /h/ the glide is to a central, unrounded position, with terminal voicelessness in some dialects at the end of a word. The total number of possible complex nuclei is 27; no dialect regularly uses more than about 15, but each of the possibilities occurs somewhere. Examples are:

/iy/ in *beat, bead, be*.

/ey/ in *bait, bay*.

/æy/ in Southern U.S. where others have /æh/ or /eh/, as *half, pass*; also in London Cockney in *day*, etc., where others have /ey/.

/i̯y/ in some dialects (Philadelphia, London Cockney, Australian) for /iy/.

/əy/ in Canada, Scotland, and elsewhere where others have /ay/, as in *knife, light*; in older New York City ("Brooklynese") and in Southern U.S. Coastal, especially Charleston, S.C., and New Orleans, in words like *bird, first*.

/ay/ in *high, hide*; see also /ah/.

/uy/ in some dialects in *push*; also in *buoy, ruin*.

/oy/ in *boy, join*.

/ɔy/ in some dialects in *wash*; elsewhere instead of /oy/.

/iw/ in old-fashioned American pronunciation of such words as *few*; most standard speakers use /yuw/ in these words, or /uw/ after /t, d, n, l/ (*new, dew*); some dialects have /iw/ and /yɨw/ instead.

/ew/ in some Southern U.S. Coastal where others have /æw/ or /aw/, as in *house*; also in some Southern British where others have /əw/ or /ow/, as in *no*.

/æw/ in *out, loud, howl, how*, in most eastern and southern U.S. speech; northern U.S. and Southern British have /aw/ instead.

/ɨw/—see remarks under /iw/; also in many midland American dialects where others have /uw/, as in *do, soon*.

/əw/ in Canada and northern Middle Western U.S. in items like *out, house*, where others have /aw/ or /æw/; in Philadelphia and adjacent areas, and in some British usage, in words like *no, own*, etc., where others have /ow/.

/aw/ accepted standard in *out, loud, howl, how*, etc.; but see remarks for /ew, æw, əw/.

/uw/ in *boot, food, room, fool, do*; see also remarks under /iw/.

/ow/ in *note, load, own, coal, go*; see also remarks under /əw/ and /ew/.

/ɔw/ in Southern U.S. in words like *all, talk*, where others have /oh/ or /ɔh/.

/ih/ before *r*, as in *dear, fierce, beard*; see below, 2.42, for the pronunciation of *r* or its absence; also in *idea, theater, real* for some speakers.

/eh/ before *r*, as in *dare, scarce, cared*; also in *yeah*; many speakers in the eastern U.S., and also other speakers for some words, use /eh/ instead of /æ/ before voiced stops, nasals, and all spirants, as in *bad, slam, tan, laugh, path, pass, jazz*; but there is usually only /æ/ before /ŋ/, as in *sang*; in the Central Atlantic Coastal U.S. there are many speakers with minimal contrasts between /eh/ and /æ/: *bad* /eh/—*bade* /æ/, *cash* /eh/—*cache* /æ/, *adds* /eh/—*adze* /æ/; also *can*, noun and verb (see above under /æ/), and *pail* /eh/ (others have /ey/ here)—*pal* /æ/. See also /æh/. In U.S. Coastal Southern (e.g. Charleston, S.C.) many speakers use /eh/ in *bake, great*, etc.

/æh/ by many speakers where others have /eh/ (but not before *r*), or elsewhere instead of /æ/, as in some northern West Coast U.S.— *appetite* with /æh/, but *apple* with /æ/.

/ih/ by some speakers before *r* in such cases as *bird*, differing from *occurred* with /əh/; also by some instead of /uh/ in *sure, cure*. Some speakers use /ih/ in *milk*.

/əh/ before *r* in *hurt, heard, earn, purse, curve*.

/ah/ before *r* in *cart, card, barn, farce, carve*; also without *r* in *palm, father, drama*. Some speakers use /ah/ instead of /a/ in words like *cod, doll.* Some Southern U.S. dialects use /ah/ for /ay/ in many words; the items *I'll* and *I'm* are /áhl/ and /áhm/ in Southern U.S. and also widely elsewhere.

/uh/ before *r* in *poor, cure* (/yuh/).

/oh/ before *r* in *fort, lord, born, force, pours,* and without *r* in *law, broad, caught, cough, cause.* See /ɔh/.

/ɔh/ by many speakers instead of /oh/ in the words without *r*; some midland U.S. speakers have both /oh/ and /ɔh/ before *r*—*wore* /oh/, but *war* /ɔh/, *mourning* /oh/—*morning* /ɔh/.

A general comment on /Vh/ nuclei (V = any vowel) is: those listed as occurring principally before *r* are not found in this position in northern Middle Western U.S., nor in north of England and Scottish dialects, there being replaced by the simple vowel followed by a strongly retroflex *r* (see 2.42); other speakers show a similar absence of /h/ before *r* if there is a voiceless consonant following, as in *hurt, purse,* or in *here* and *there* when these are weak in a phrase. The /Vh/ nuclei exemplified for words without *r* are often without /h/ for many speakers, especially before voiceless consonants. On the other hand, every one of the possibilities occurs sporadically for some speakers in unpredictable items, as a lengthening of the simple vowel; the example of *appetite* under /æh/ above is an instance. In some dialects /Vy/ and /Vw/ are replaced by /Vh/ before *l*, and simple vowels become /Vh/ before *l*: /pehl/ for *pail*, /ahl/ for *I'll*, /puhl/ for *pool*, /dɔhl/ for *doll*.

2.42. The consonants of English are as follows (the symbols are called by the names of the letters, and the names of special symbols are given):

/p/: [pˤ] initial and before strong-stressed vowel, [p] before weak-stressed vowel, [pˀ] final, [p̪] after /s/: *pin, upon, upper, up, spin.*

/t/: [tˤ, tˀ, t̪] as for /p/: *tin, hit, stick.* Internally before weak-stressed vowels, some speakers have [t], but most American speakers and some elsewhere have a voiced fortis stop, [t̬] (with fortis muscular action, but lenis contact); many such speakers continue to distinguish this from [d], so that *latter* has /t/, *ladder* /d/, and similarly for *writing, riding*; but some speakers use [t̬] or [d] for both *t* and *d* between vocalics. In some dialects internal *t* is [ˀ], a glottal stop with or without accompanying *t*-closure; there are other special phonetic manifestations for /t/ (see References).

/k/: [kˤ, k, kˀ, k̪] as for /p/: *kin, lucky, luck, skin.* The allophones of /k/ also show fronting or backing depending on the following vowel: [k<] in *key*, [k>] in *cool.*

/b, d, g/ all show initial voiceless onset and final voiceless offglide, but are fully voiced internally: [b̥b-, d̥d-, g̥g-; -b-, -d-, -g-; -bb̥, -dd̥, -gg̥]. Examples: *bib, did, gig, rubber, fodder, logging.*

/č/ *"c-wedge"* or *"chay"* /čéy/, as in *church,* and /ǰ/ *"j-wedge",* as in *judge,* have been considered by some to be sequences of two phonemes—/tš/, /dž/, but the analysis as single phonemes seems preferable. The symbols /c/ and /j/ are also used. The phoneme /ǰ/ shows initial and final voicelessness, like the voiced stops /b, d, g/.

/f, θ, s, š/, the voiceless spirants, have essentially only one allophone apiece, [f, θ, s, š]. (/θ/ is called *theta* /θéytə/; /š/ is called *"s-wedge"* or *"esh").* Some speakers use a retroflex or retracted sound for /š/—[ʂ] or [s̱], and occasionally the prepalatal [ś] is heard. Examples: *fife, jiffy; thin, myth, mythical; sin, hiss, missing; shin, push, mission.*

/v, ð, z, ž/, the voiced spirants, show the same kind of initial and final voicelessness as do /b, d, g, ǰ/: [v̥v-, -v-, -vv̥], etc. The symbol /ð/ is called *"edh"* /éð/; /ž/ is called *"z-wedge".* Examples are: *verve, nervous; then, bathe, rather; zone, rose, rising; Zhukov, rouge, vision.* The phoneme /ž/ is initial only in recently introduced foreign proper names or other foreign words.

/m, n, ŋ/, the nasals, are long in final position, short elsewhere: [m-, -m-, -m·]. Examples: *mum, mummy; nun, funny; sing, singer.* /ŋ/ (called *"eng")* does not occur initially in English, except in New Zealand in names and words of Maori origin. Some speakers do not contrast *singer,* /ŋ/, and *finger,* /ŋg/, using either /ŋg/ or /ŋ/ in both; this is considered substandard or foreign.

/l/ has one allophone in most American speech, a slightly velarized [lˣ]. Other speakers use a nonvelarized [l] before /y/, as in *million, value.* In the south of the United States, and among British speakers, the velarized allophone occurs only final, or before a consonant, the nonvelarized one being used elsewhere: *lily* with [l], *hill* with [lˣ]. After /p/ and /k/ initial, /l/ has voiceless onset [l̥l].

/r/ before a vowel is usually the frictionless spirant [ɹ]. In the clusters /pr, kr/ it is partly voiceless [ɹ̥ɹ]. In the clusters /tr, dr/ it has friction noise: [ɹ̥ɹ⁺, ɹ⁺]. In Scotland many speakers use a slight trill, [r], initially and between vowels. In the south of England, some speakers use a flap, [r¹] between vowels. Some speakers use lip rounding with /r/, and the exaggerated form of this is often jokingly imitated as /w/. After vowels, before a consonant or final, /r/ shows great variation: in most of the United States, in Canada, and in the west and north of England, /r/ is a retroflex central vowel glide, [ə˞], in these occurrences, with the degree of retraction of the tip of the tongue varying widely (heavy in Middle Western America, slight on the East Coast of the U.S.). In Scotland, some speakers use retroflexion, others have a consonantal [ɹ]. In the south of England, in eastern New England, and the U.S. coastal South, as well as in the British colonial lands settled in the nineteenth century, postvocalic /r/ has in some instances completely disappeared, and elsewhere is usually a nonretroflex central glide, [ə], somewhat tenser than the /h/ that usually precedes it; these dialects are accordingly usually spoken of as "r-less". It is true that for some speakers of such dialects, and on some occasions, *lord* and *laud* may be exactly alike, /lóhd/; but most of the time the allophone of /r/ persists, so that *lord* has [ɒə̯ə], while *laud* has [ɒə̯]; in such cases, *lord* is phonemically /lohrd/, even though no retroflexion is heard.

/w, y, h/ in initial position show the same kinds of differences in height as they do postvocalically. In *wit, wet, watt* we have [u̯, ᴜ̯, ǫ̯]. In *ye, yet, yacht* we have [i̯, ɪ̯, e̯]. Initial /h/ starts voiceless and with some friction noise, but is otherwise an onglide from central position: *hit, head, hot* have [ɪ̯ᵛ⁺, ə̯⁺, ə̯ᵛ⁺]. The prevocalic and postvocalic allophones of these three phonemes are almost exact mirror images of one another: *woo, ye, hah* are phonemically /wúw, yíy, háh/; when they are recorded on tape and the tape is played backward, they sound almost the same as they do in normal sequence.

English consonant phonemes occur in clusters of two or three initially, and in greater number internally and finally. But the combinations are limited: some never occur, so that /sn/ is common but /fn/ doesn't exist; some are rare or foreign, as /vr/ and /šm̩/. The occurring two-consonant initials are: /pl, pr, py, pw, tr, ty, tw, kl, kr, ky, kw/ as in *play, pray, pure, pueblo, tray, tune* (in some dialects only), *twelve, clear, cry, cure, queer*; /bl, br, by, bw, dr, dy, dw, gl, gr, gy, gw/ as in *blend, break, beauty, bwana, dry, duke* (in some dialects only), *dwell, glad, grow, gewgaw, Gwen*/; /fl, fr, fy, vl, vr, vy/ in *flow, free, few, Vleet, Vreeland, view*; /θr, θy, θw/ in *threw, thews, thwack*; /sp, st, sk, sf, sv, sm, sn, sl, sy, sw/ in *spoon, stand, scan, sphere, svelte* (some speakers have /sf/ or /s+v/ here, and do not have /sv/), *smooth, snow, slide, sue* (in some dialects only), *swell*; /šm, šn, šl, šr, šw/—of this group, *shrimp, shrink*, etc. have the only originally English cluster, and some speakers use /sr/ instead of /šr/; the other instances of this last group of clusters occur in recent coinages and in foreign, names such as *shmoo, Schneider, Schleicher, Schwartz*;

/hy/ in *huge* (some speakers use /y/, but this is considered substandard), and /hw/ for the spelling *wh*, but most Southern British and East Coast American, as well as many urban speakers everywhere, use /w/ instead of /hw/.

The only three-consonant initials are: /spl, spr, spy, str, sty, skl, skr, sky, skw/, as in *splendid, spray, spew, street, student* (in some dialects only), *sclerosis, scream, skew, squeak*.

In final position there are many clusters ending in /t, d, s, z/ because these occur in freely added grammatical endings. The heaviest combinations of consonants are such as are found in *glimpsed* /mpst/, *chintzed* /ntst/, *sixths* /ksθs/, *jinxed* /ŋkst/; in *worlds* /hrldz/ the /h/ is a semivowel followed by four consonants.

2.43. English has four stresses: /´/ primary, /^/ secondary, /`/ tertiary, /˘/ weak. Every word or phrase in isolation has one primary and only one: *hót, hótter, hót-spòt, hôt fóod*, etc. In words of more than one syllable, one syllable has primary and the others may have weak or tertiary: *hóttĕr, hòtél, cóntènts, ópĕràte, òpĕrátiŏn*. In phrases, the primary syllable of one of the constituents remains, all the nonprimary syllables remain unchanged, and the original primary of the other constituent is reduced to secondary or tertiary or weak (secondary occurs only in phrases): *bláckbôard, bláckbìrd, òld máid, ôld hóuse, póstmăn, ăt hóme*. The process of stress reduction in phrases is important grammatically—see 3.3 and 3.4.

The internal transition phoneme, /+/ "plus", occurs within phrases and also within words: *black+board, black+bird, hot+house, old+maid, old+house, post+man* (but also /pówsmə̆n/ without /+/), *sly+ness* (but *highness*), *high+school* (but also /háyskù̆wl/), *a+bove, a way* and *away* both /ə+wéy/, etc.

The terminal transition phonemes are /|/ "single bar", /||/ "double bar", /#/ "double cross". Pitch is sustained before /||/, it rises before /|||/, it falls before /#/. These three phonemes have the effect of stretching the segmental material before them, from the nearest strong stress, by the following amounts, measured in terms of the average length of a phoneme: /|/ adds one average phoneme length, /||/ adds two, /#/ adds three or more. By contrast, /+/ adds only about half a phoneme length, and doesn't affect pitch contour. The average phoneme length has been reported as 7 centiseconds, but this estimate is perhaps 1 or 2 centiseconds too high.

There are four pitch phonemes: /¹/ low, /²/ middle, /³/ high, /⁴/ extra high. They occur in combinations of two, three, or four, with a terminal transition. In two-pitch sequences, the first one coincides with a primary stress: ³*Dó+it*¹#. In three-pitch sequences, the second is usually coincident with the primary: $^2Al^3l\acute{o}w{+}m\grave{e}^1\#$; but such items as $^2W\acute{o}n^3d\breve{e}rful^1\#$ occur. The four-pitch sequences are of two kinds: primary with the third pitch, or with the second: $^2Sh\grave{e}$'s $\breve{a}\ ^3n\^{i}ce\ ^3g\acute{i}rl^1\#$ or $^2Y\grave{o}u^4r\acute{e}ad\ \ddot{\imath}t^1first^1\#$. The pitch and transition sequences, called INTONATION PATTERNS, are important in syntax—see 3.3 and 3.4.

2.44. In the examples for 2.41 and 2.42 above there were references to dialect differences. In 1.34 the United States was divided into eight dialect areas: A, Eastern New England; B, Western New England; C, Central Atlantic Seaboard; D, Northern Middle West; E, Midland; F, Coastal South; G, Southern Hill; H, Far West. Now that we have a phonemic statement for English, we can exemplify the dialect differences by a list of words each of which represents a whole group of words and characterizes the different dialects. The words are *merry, marry, Mary; wash, water; on, off, dog, oft, lot, log, sorry; greasy, gone; about, house; father, park; first, bird, burred; any, penny; ash, ask; can,* verb, and *can,* noun; *food, moon.* (See References). Below is a discussion of each group of words and their areal differences; references are to the eight letters designating the areas.

merry, marry, Mary. In areas A, C, and F, these words all have different vowel nuclei: that of *bet*, /e/, in *merry*; that of *hat*, /æ/, in *marry*; that of *fair*, /eh/, in *Mary* (or that of *may*, /ey/, in older-generation area-F speakers); around Philadelphia, and in area E, *merry* has the vowel of *hurry*, /ə/. In all the rest of the United States these three words are usually pronounced alike, all with the vowel /e/ or else /eh/; in urban regions there are speakers who may distinguish *marry* from the other two by /æ/, or *Mary* by /eh/ contrasting with /e/ in the other two.

wash, water. In area A, the vowel of both these words is short, being low back rounded, /ɔ/. In area B, *wash* may have the unrounded vowel of most American pronunciations of *hot*, /a/, while *water* has /ɔh/, or a more rounded vowel, /oh/ (like the vowel in *more*); some speakers have an *r*-sound in *wash*, as in the comic-strip spelling "worsh". In area C, *wash* has /a/, *water* has /oh/. In areas F and G, *wash* often has a *y*-sound following the vowel, /ɔy/, while *water* has /ɔh/ or /oh/.

on, off, dog, oft, lot, log, sorry. These words show variations in the vowel from /a/ to /ɔ/ to /ɔh/ to /oh/. In area C north of Philadelphia, *off, dog, oft* have /oh/, and the others have /a/; but south of Philadelphia *on* has /ɔ/ or /ɔh/ or /oh/. In area F, *on* has an offglide *w*, /ɔw/. The words *dog, off, oft* have /ɔh/ or /oh/ in most other areas, as does *log* most often; *sorry* has /ɔ/ in areas B and D, and *on, lot* have /a/.

greasy, gone. South of 40° in C, E, F, and G, *greasy* has a /z/ for the spelled *s*, and *gone* is like *on*—with /ɔ/, /ɔh/, or /ɔw/. North of 40°, it's "greassy", and *gone* is like *on*—with /a/.

about, house. In A, C, E, F, and G, these words have the complex nucleus /æw/, often reflected in the dialect spellings "naow, abaout". In B, the western parts of D, and in H, the nucleus is /aw/. In the eastern parts of D, and in Canada, the sound begins like the *u* of *hut*, /əw/ (but it is /aw/ when a voiced sound follows).

father, park. In A and B, these words have a vowel that is phonetically [Æ], lower than the vowel of *hat*; in A, it is long, and there may be no *r* in *park*, /æh/; in B, it is long in *father*, /æh/, short and with *r* in *park*, /ær/. In the other regions the nucleus begins with /a/; *father* has /ah/ in C, E, F, and G, and often simple /a/ in D and H; *park* may have no *r* in F and in New York City (in C), and the vowel is /ah/; elsewhere in C the vowel may be /a/ or /ah/, with *r* pronounced.

first, bird, burred. In A, there is the "r-less" *r*, and the vowel is like that of *u* in *cut*, but long, /əh/, or it is higher, /ih/. In New York City many older speakers have /əy/ in *first, bird* (the so-called Brooklynese "foist", "boid"), and /əh/ with or without *r* in *burred*; other New York speakers have /ihr/ in *first, bird* and /əhr/ in *burred*. Area F has /əy/ and /əh/, as in New York City. In B, D, and H, the vowel is /ə/, with a strong *r*, in all three. In E and G, the vowel is /əhr/.

any, penny. In F and G, words of this type have /i/ instead of /e/, so that *pin* and *pen* sound alike.

ash, ask. In A and B, these words have the so-called New England "broad *a*", /æh/. In C, they have a vowel like that in *fair*, but without *r*, /eh/. In D and H, they have /æ/ or /æh/. In E, F, and G, *ash* has /æy/, and *ask* has /æ/ or /æh/ or /æy/.

can, verb, as in "Yes, I can"; *can*, noun (and verb, "to put in cans"). In area C, the auxiliary verb has the vowel of *cat*, /æ/, and the noun and its derived verb have the long tense vowel /eh/, found also in *man, bad*, and the like. In other areas the two items are usually alike, having either /æ/ or /æh/ or /eh/.

food, moon. In Philadelphia, and in area E, these words have a nucleus beginning like that in the adverb *just*, i.e., /ɨ/, and ending in *w*, /ɨw/. Elsewhere the vowel is /uw/.

Other characteristics of the regional dialects may be mentioned. Final *r* and *r* before a consonant are reduced to a very slight vowel-like prolongation of a preceding vowel, or are lost entirely in some cases, in areas A and F, and in New York City (in part) in C. In B and C outside of New York City, *r* is pronounced clearly, but less strongly in C than in B. In D, *r* is very strongly pronounced, while in E and G, it is about as in C; in H, *r* varies from the strong kind in the more northern areas to a weaker one in the south. The dialects of C, E, F, and G show the greatest incidence of the lengthened vowels transcribed /ah, eh, oh/, and they all have many more internal open transitions (/+/) between syllables than do the dialects of A, B, D, and H. The southern dialects in F and G have the greatest number of these open transitions, this being part of what is called the "Southern drawl".

Chapter 3

HOW DO YOU SAY IT?

3.0. WORDS AND SENTENCES

3.00. The words and sentences of a language—as behavior events or occurrences, and thus as objects of observation and analysis—are its substance (2.02), and the substance is treated in morphology. In treating morphology, we follow the same procedure as above for phonology (2.03), and divide the study into three parts or aspects. The central or substance aspect of morphology deals with the grammatically significant forms that make up words: this study is called MORPHEMICS, and is treated in 3.10 and 3.11. The diacritic part of morphology, which examines the items of which MORPHEMES are composed, may be called MORPHOPHONICS (more commonly the term is *morphophonemics*, but there are good theoretical reasons for omitting the *-em-*); this aspect is treated in 3.12, in terms of the forms of morphemes.

Morphemes enter into the formation of WORDS; words as linguistically definable are wholly composed of morphemes. The LEXICON of a language is the list of its words and their constituent morphemes. The different kinds of morphemes are discussed in 3.11. In 3.2, the formation of words is taken up; also treated there are the grammatical changes that are called INFLECTION, and such notions as "parts of speech" and "derivation".

The relations of morphemes are studied in terms of the sequences and arrangements of the morpheme complexes known as words, as these sequences and arrangements—called PHRASES and CLAUSES— are delimited by suprasegmental (accentual) and terminal (transition-contour) patterns. This part of morphology is here called SYNTAX and is treated in 3.3 (see 3.01 for other terminological usages).

Morphology as a whole covers what is usually meant by the term *grammar*. It deals with the grammatical structure of a language. A sketch of English grammar is presented in 3.4. It builds on and stems from the phonological statements about English made in 2.4.

3.01. In many treatments of grammar the term *morphology* is used for what is here called morphemics, or for morphemics and morphophonics, while syntax is considered a separate subdivision. In such cases, *syntax* is usually so used as to include a considerable part of what will here be called SEMOLOGY (Chapter 4). The use of these terms, and the question of where syntax stops and semology begins, are important theoretical differences in today's linguistic discussions. For the reader of this book, however, it is more important to know the kinds of problems and possible solutions that have been worked out than to follow the theoretical differences. The definitions and boundaries of the various aspects of linguistics that are used here are consistent, and are relatively easy to equate to other usages and practices.

3.1. MORPHEMES

3.10. In the grammatical examination of any language it is necessary to look for items that recur and for patterns of recurrence. The processes will first be illustrated here by means of English examples.

The body of material that the linguist examines is the CORPUS. Suppose our first corpus consists of the following material:

boy	*girl*	*man*
one boy	*one girl*	*one man*
boys	*girls*	*men*
two boys	*two girls*	*two men*

These words would have to be said as phrases, and in isolation as sentences, but we will at this point ignore those details and consider only the single words and the sequences of two words.

Examination of the corpus shows certain recurring items, which we shall call RECURRENT PARTIALS: *boy, girl, one, two, m-n, -s*. It is clear enough that *boy* and *boys*, *girl* and *girls*, *man* and *men* occur alone, but when we use *one*, only *boy, girl, man* appear, while when we use *two*, the accompanying terms are *boys, girls, men*. Both *boys* and *girls* have the final *-s*, which is clearly added to *boy* and *girl*, and which occurs in the presence of *two*. The relation of *man* and *men*, in which at least *m-n* recurs, seems to parallel that of *boy, girl* and *boys, girls*. We can postulate that *boy, girl*, and also *man*, represent basic or unchanged forms, and that *boys, girls, men* represent forms that have been added to or changed. We then conclude that we have been dealing with some base words—*boy, girl, man* (as well as *one, two*), and that these can be INFLECTED by the addition of -*s*, or, in the case of *man*, by a change of vowel.

Our small corpus is not yet fully exhausted. By comparing the possibility of varying the phrases, such as óne+bóy or óne+bóy, etc., we can also establish that each of the words in the phrase has a stress even if it has only one syllable. As soon as we consider longer items such as wómǎn, ánǐmǎl, or ácǒlyte, we see that the stresses on words occur in patterns where there is always one primary stress and there may be others—weak or tertiary, if the word is said by itself.

At this point we rewrite the words phonemically, getting /bóy, gǝ́hrl, méhn/ (or /mǽn/ or /mǽhn/), and /bóyz, gǝ́hrlz, mén/. The recurrent partials that are analyzed out are morphemes, and may be written thus: √boy-, √gǝhrl-, √mæn-, √-z, √(æ⟩e)-ᴓ. These are to be read by interpreting the symbols as follows: √ means "the morpheme" or "Don't name the symbol [the root sign], but interpret it as showing that what follows is a morpheme"; the hyphen at the end of an item means that it is a base morpheme, so we read "The base *boy*" (or "The base *b, o, y*, hyphen"), etc. The hyphen before an item means "the suffix"; the symbolization √(æ⟩e)-ᴓ is read "digraph is replaced by *e* in the presence of suffix zero". In this last instance, zero, ᴓ, is a positive entity; it is NOT nothing; it is postulated because in the other items there is a suffix, √-z; it is further established that the latter is the usual pattern and that ᴓ is the exception. Stating this item in this way provides the basis, or "cause" (conditioning factor), for the change of /æ/ to /e/. The suffixes √-z and √(æ⟩e)-ᴓ are variants of what can be called the "plural morpheme". There is also in all these items the recurrent partial √ᶻ, "the superfix of primary stress".

The base morphemes listed above are taken to be invariable. Morphemes being classes (analogous to phonemes), they contain members which are called allomorphs. Invariable morphemes are said to contain one allomorph only. The suffixes listed are characterized as variants of a "plural morpheme"; we can reword this and say that there is a suffix morpheme √-Pl which contains the allomorphs √-z and √(æ⟩e)-ᴓ. The relationship of /æ/ to /e/ in the last item is called a MORPHOPHONIC alternation, and alternations of this kind will be examined further in 3.12; the use of æ to include the suggested pronunciation variants /æ, æh, eh/ (and others) will also be discussed in that section.

3.11. In the previous section there were illustrated three kinds of morphemes: bases, suffixes, and superfixes. There are numerous other kinds; some can be illustrated from English, some occur only in languages other than English. For every language the kinds of morphemes that exist have to be determined from its own material, and there are few, if any, statements applicable to all languages. It is true, however, that something like a base exists everywhere, and that suffixes are very commonly used in many languages; not much has been reported on superfixes, but it may be conjectured that some equivalent of them exists in all languages.

It should be remembered that although the terms used in the present book are largely traditional, often their explicit use may depart widely (or even wholly) from tradition. Moreover, in innovating, it has at times been necessary to use established terms in new ways, and to devise new terms or modifications of old terms in some instances.

In addition to bases, suffixes, and superfixes, English also has morpheme types that can be called PREBASES and POSTBASES: *ab-*, *ad-*, *be-*, *con-*, *de-*, *ex-*, *in-*, *un-* are examples of prebases; *-an*, *-er*, *-ish*, *-ic*, *-y* are examples of postbases; in traditional terminology the prebases are called "prefixes", and the postbases are called "derivational suffixes". Further discussion of the functioning of these kinds of morphemes in English will be made in 3.40. English also has special morphemes limited to small groups of words, such as the *n-* in *never*, *no*, *not*; the *wh-* in *where*, *when*, *what*; etc.: these may be termed PREFIXES. Similarly, the *-t* of *it*, *that*, *what*, the *-ce* of *hence*, *thence*, *whence*, and a few other such items may be called POSTFIXES. English prefixes and postfixes as described here are derivational, like prebases and postbases, but are limited in their uses to small groups of words, with no new formations taking place.

In many languages inflectional suffixes are complex, and have to be treated in sets. In French, a form like (*nous*) *donnerons* 'we'll give' may be analyzed as having a base $\sqrt{}$don-, a 'future-tense' suffix $\sqrt{}$-ər-, a 'multiple-subject' suffix $\sqrt{}$-on-, and a final suffix of the first person $\sqrt{}$-ᶻ (manifested as phonemic /z/ in some cases where a vowel follows).

Many languages have prefixes which are inflectional rather than derivational. In Taos, a noun like *kána* 'mother' may have prefixes of possession, 'my', 'thy', 'his', etc.; for instance, *'ąnkána* means 'my mother'; the prefix *'ąn-* consists of the initial glottal stop, which is an allomorph of the morpheme of '1st person possessor', $\sqrt{}$'-, and of the second-position allomorph $\sqrt{}$-ąn(ą)- 'singular possessor' (the part in parentheses is automatically lost under conditions not pertinent here). The form *'ąnąmp'inemą* means 'my head'; here the prefix complex is *'qnąm-*, consisting of $\sqrt{}^{a}$- and $\sqrt{}^{a}$-ąn(ą)-, which are the same as before, and the third position $\sqrt{}^{a}$-m(ą)- 'possessed noun of class B'. The noun *kána* is put in class A because of its suffix *-na* (whereas 'head' has the suffix *-nemą*), but the possessive prefix with a class A noun shows nothing following the second prefix position; this is considered to be a real absence of a prefix, and not a zero allomorph.

The Taos nouns of class B can also provide an example of the kind of morpheme that is usually called an INFIX: the prefix complex *mąpęn-* before a verb stem means 'you 2' as subject, and noun of class B as object of the verb; it consists of $\sqrt{}^{a}$m-, 1st position allomorph, '2nd person subject', followed by the dual morpheme (elsewhere $\sqrt{}^{a}$-ąn(ą)-), in the form $\sqrt{}^{a}$-ą..n(ą)-, into which has been infixed the form $\sqrt{}^{a}$..pę.., which is an allomorph of the morpheme for class B as topic (object, etc.).

In the Semitic languages the most usual form of a base morpheme consists of three consonants. Thus in Classical Arabic, the base $\sqrt{}$ktb means 'write, writing'. Verb and noun forms are derived from the base by insertion of discontinuous morphemes that are called VOWEL PATTERNS, after which suffixes (as well as prefixes and prebases) may also be added: *kataba* is 'he wrote', with vowel pattern $\sqrt{}$-a-a-Ø, where the hyphens show the position of the three consonants—the final $\sqrt{}$-a is a suffix; the pattern $\sqrt{}$-a-a-Ø appears also in *katabta* 'you (sg., masc.) wrote', where $\sqrt{}$-ta is a suffix; the pattern $\sqrt{}$a--u-u appears in *yaktubu* 'he writes, will write', where $\sqrt{}$y- is a prefix. The Semitic vowel patterns are in some ways like infixes.

Another kind of morpheme is that found in so-called REDUPLICATIONS, as in Greek *léloipa*, perfect of *leípō* 'I let, leave'; Latin *cecinī*, perfect of *canō* 'I sing'. If the Greek base is set up as $\sqrt{}$l(e $\sim$ o)yp- (where the sign $\sim$ means 'alternating with'), the "reduplication" can be stated as a prefix (or prebase?) of the form $\sqrt{}$R:C_1V_1-, to be read "reduplicate as a prefix having the form first consonant of the base followed by first vowel". The Latin base is $\sqrt{}$kan-; the change from /a/ to /i/ in the perfect is taken care of by a morphophonic statement; the "reduplication" is of the form $\sqrt{}$R:C_1e-. Instances of complete repetition of a base such as English *choo-choo* must be analyzed as phrases (see 3.3), and similar formations elsewhere are probably best treated in this way too.

The example in 3.10 of English *man* : *men* was analyzed as having a plural formation of the form $\sqrt{}$(æ > e)-Ø. Here the suffix is taken as an allomorph of the form "zero", but with the power, so to speak, to induce a change in the base. In English the many instances of base

change (*mouse* : *mice*, *take* : *took*, *sing* : *sang* : *sung*, etc.) are probably best treated as zero-suffix allomorphs with base-changing
power. This treatment is possible because the zero can be considered
an allomorph of some suffix that has other allomorphs with phonemic
expression. If all plurals were to be made by internal change, with
no phonemically expressed suffix, we could call the plural a PROCESS
MORPHEME. An example of a process morpheme may be found in the
French subject pronoun *je* 'I'; the form *me* 'me' is postulated as the
basic form, base √mə-; the subject is formed by a process morpheme
which can be treated as an addition, a suffix of 'subject': √-S; this
has the allomorph $\overset{a}{\sqrt{}}$/m > ž/ (the symbol > is read as "replaced by,
becomes") with 1st person, √mə-; with 2nd person, √tə-, the allo-
morph is $\overset{a}{\sqrt{}}$/ə > ʉ/, resulting in *tu*; with 3rd person (masculine),
√L(ə)-, the allomorph is $\overset{a}{\sqrt{}}$/i/→, that is, "prefix /i/ to the base",
giving *il*. Some linguists prefer to treat such forms as *je*, *tu*, *il* as
irregularities, which are said to be in SUPPLETION with the regular
bases.

The following kinds of morphemes have been presented: base,
B-; prebase, *p*B-; postbase, -*p*B; suffix, -*s* and -*s*-; prefix, *pf*→; postfix, ←*pf*-; superfix, $\overset{s}{ }$; infix, ..*if*..; vowel pattern, $^cv^cv^cv$-, etc.;
process, -*Pro*(*x* > *y*)-. Several varieties of these morphemes have
been shown. There are probably other kinds of morphemes in languages that have not yet been adequately described. Superfixes will
be further discussed in 3.2.

In cases like those of the English words *slide*, *slip*, *slick*, or *crash*,
crunch, *crack*, and others, the question has been raised whether the
sl- and *cr*- and similar consonant clusters might not be some special
kind of morpheme that carries with it the similar meanings that
such groups of words connote. A recent treatment has called them
"psychomorphs", and has rejected the notion that they are morphemes. The present author thinks that in the morphemic aspect
of analysis, these kinds of elements can be considered prefixes in
English: √sl→, √kr→, √fl→, etc. This would mean that the remaining parts of the items would have to be called bases. If we
write √æš-, √ənč-, etc., however, there is not only the risk of confusion with other bases, such as that in the word *ash*, but we also
conceal the fact that these elements never occur as the only segmental
morpheme with a superfix to form a word (see 3.20). A tentative
solution would be to write √.ayd-, √.ip-, √.ik-, √.æš-, √.ənč-,
√.æk-, and so on, with the dot indicating that a prefix is obligatory.

Further examination of English reveals that there are other instances of parts of words and phrases that occur in the places where

bases are expected, but, like $\sqrt{}$.æš-, etc., never form words with the addition of only a superfix. Examples are *-ceive* in *deceive, receive*; *cran-* in *cranberry*; *-lim-* in *sublime, sublimity*, and many others. All these can be called BOUND bases, and can be further described as PREFIXATE (/príyfiksit/) 'always having a prefix' ($\sqrt{}$.æš-); PREBASATE (/príy+bèysit/) 'always having a prebase' (*-ceive*); PHRASAL 'only in phrases' (*cran-*). Further, it appears that bases like that in *liberty, liberate* should also be called bound, in this case POSTBASATE (/pówst+bèysit/). In detailed treatments, we could symbolize these as follows: $\sqrt{}\rightarrow$.B-, prefixate bound base; $\sqrt{}$-.B-, prebasate bound base; $\sqrt{}$B.-:, postbasate bound base; $\sqrt{}$B.-+, phrasal bound base; the symbol $\sqrt{}$B.- could mean 'bound base' in general.

There are many languages in which many, perhaps even most, bases are bound. Wherever most words have to be analyzed as having other elements besides a base and a superfix, bound bases would occur. Languages like Greek, Latin, Sanskrit, have many bound bases. In the Iroquoian languages of North America the base of a word is often a small element (consonant alone, or consonant followed by vowel), preceded and followed by several other kinds of elements. In Semitic, the three-consonant base alluded to above is bound, never appearing without a vowel pattern.

It is interesting to look at the kind of pattern that appears in recently spread English phrases like *cancer : shmancer, rain : shmain*. Should these be analyzed as having bound bases, with prefixes? Such a solution would not be the most economical, for any initial consonant or consonant cluster (in the first word of such a pair) would then have to be considered as a prefix. It seems better to set up a prefix that is also a process: $\sqrt{}$šm → $(C_1 > \emptyset)\cup$, to be read as "prefix /šm/ causes the first consonant or cluster of the base to disappear, and is itself joined in normal transition to the rest of the base". In the syntax and semology there would have to be further explanation of the kind of phrases in which forms with this prefix occur. This formation seems to have been consciously introduced into American English from Yiddish; in Yiddish it seems to be imitating a usage found in Ukrainian; somewhat similar formations have been reported from other, wholly unrelated languages.

3.12. It has already been shown that morphemes may exhibit more than one phonemic shape, or may require—in certain combinations—changes in the phonemic shapes of other morphemes. The relation of a phoneme in one form of a morpheme to another phoneme in another allomorph is called, as indicated in 3.00, a morphophonic relation, and may be abstracted as a morphophone.

If this is true, we may then go on to say that morphemes with more than one allomorph are made up of or composed of morphophones, and it follows that morphemes with only one allomorph are also composed of morphophones. That is, the phonemes in which morphemes are expressed are manifestations of the constituent morphophones of the morphemes. The morphophonic alternations that occur can then be considered as relations between (simple) morphophones, or they can be held to be themselves morphophones of a higher or more complex nature embodying the alternations. When we write the base of *man* as √m(æ > e)n-, this can be understood as meaning that this base appears with the morphophone √æ/ in its primary form, and with the morphophone √e/ in other situations (which have to be stated); or we can understand it as meaning that the base has a higher-order alternating morphophone written by the sequence of symbols √(æ > e)/. The older term "morphophoneme" usually referred to the latter notion of an alternation or complex of what were thought to be phonemes. Further discussion below will seek to clarify the theory applicable to these matters.

It will be recalled that the relations subdivision of phonology deals with phonemes (2.03). Under morphology, however, it is the substance that deals with morphemes (3.00). The term phonemes was defined as a "class of sounds" (2.30), where the important word in the present connection is *class*; phonemes are CLASSES of the kinds of entities that are found in phonetics; those entities, the sounds, are themselves DISTRIBUTIONS (or arrangements in patterned ways) of the articulatory features; and the articulatory features are OCCURRENCES—that is, behavior events. This way of looking at the aspects of a language gives us another threefold descriptive device, alongside of the description as diacritics—substance—relations. But, as has been pointed out, morphemes, which are classes of allomorphs, are the substance of morphology, while phonemes are the relations of phonology. From this the suggestion follows that while the sequence "diacritics—substance—relations" holds at any level of subdivision, the "sequence occurrence—distribution—class" does not fit with the previous one in one-to-one correspondence. It is suggested that the diacritic subdivision of an aspect of language will involve occurrences if the higher-level aspect is itself occurrences, but will involve distributions or classes if the higher level fits those descriptions.

More simply, phonology as a whole deals with occurrences, and its diacritics—the articulations—are occurrences. If morphemics deals with classes, then morphophonics deals with distributions, and morphology as a whole deals with distributions (of the occurrences which are in phonology). Schematically we have:

phonology
(diacritics)
(occurrences)

articulations (diacritics) (occurrences)	phonetics (substance) (distributions)	phonemics (relations) (classes)

and:

morphology
(substance)
(distributions)

morphophonics (diacritics) (distributions)	morphemics (substance) (classes)	syntax (relations) (occurrences)

The fact that the diacritics of morphology are not classes is responsible for the preference in the present text for the term *morphophonics*, since we prefer to use terms with *-eme* and *-emics* only for the subdivisions which are classes.

The morphophones are then distributions of the occurrences that constitute the phonology (taken as a whole). As the diacritics of morphology, they are what morphemes are made of.

Suppose we look at the morpheme that occurs in the verb (*to*) *knife* and its form (*he*) *knifes*. The base seems always to be /nayf-; it may be said to be composed of the morphophones /n/, /ay/ (/ay/ is a unit on this level), and /f/. In the noun *knife* and its plural *knives* something else seems to be true: there are the morphophones /n/ and /ay/, but the last one differs in the two forms; the difference involves the relationship of phonemic /f/ with phonemic /v/ (in the presence of the plural morpheme). Such a relationship is a morphophonic alternation; we can speak of the "morphophone *f* alternating with *v*", and symbolize the alternation as /(f ~ v)/. The morpheme in the verb and noun is perhaps best represented then as /nay(f ~ v)-, and is stated to be subject to certain rules in terms of which /(f ~ v)/ appears as /f/ or /v/. In *life* : *lives* we seem to have the same kind of thing, but the verb (*to*) *live* shows that here there is a further alternation, and we construct the base as $\sqrt{l}$(ay $\sim$ i)(f $\sim$ v)-. This last example shows why we consider /ay/ and the other complex nuclei to be morphophonic units, $\sqrt{}$ay/ etc.

Automatic morphophonic alternations are those that result from the limitations on the phonemic arrangements of a language. In English the plural of *lid* has a final /z/; the plural of *cat* has a final /s/; the plural of *kiss* has a final /iz/. This distribution is automatic, in that /z/ occurs after all voiced finals except those that cannot enter into a cluster with it, /s/ occurs after all voiceless finals except those that cannot enter into a cluster with it, and /iz/ occurs when neither /z/ nor /s/ can occur. (The statement of this distribution will be found in 3.41.) The relationship of *man* and *men*, however, involves a nonautomatic morphophonic relation.

It was said above (3.10) that /æ/ could be used as a cover symbol for the pronunciations /mǽn, mǽhn, méhn/ (and others) of *man*. This is an example of the morphophonic relations between varieties of a language. We can say that the morphophone symbolized as $\sqrt{}$æ/ represents phonemic /æ/ or /æh/ or /eh/, etc., according to inter-dialect rules.

In English the vowel alternations in such items as *sing : sang : sung, sane : sanity*, the consonant alternations in *narrate : narration*, the stress alternations in *define : definite*, are all examples of mor-phophonic alternations.

The best way to state morphophonics, and a fully worked out morphophonic system, have not been agreed on. In brief, any phonemic difference between allomorphs of a morpheme may con-stitute a morphophonic alternation, and an examination of all of the latter makes possible a listing of the morphophones that a lan-guage has, and the relations they enter into. English has morpho-phonic alternations like $\sqrt{}$f $\sim$ v/ and the parallel $\sqrt{}$θ $\sim$ ð/ (*bath, bathes*), $\sqrt{}$s $\sim$ z/ (*advice, advise*)—but no *$\sqrt{}$š $\sim$ ž/ (* here means 'nonexistent'); $\sqrt{}$ay $\sim$ i/ (*life, live*), $\sqrt{}$iy $\sim$ e/ (*keep, kept*), $\sqrt{}$ey $\sim$ æ/ (*sane, sanity*), etc. In French we find $\sqrt{}$v $\sim$ f in *vive, vif*, which is like English $\sqrt{}$f $\sim$ v/, but others are quite different ($\sqrt{}$nd $\sim$ n^t/ in *grande, grand*, $\sqrt{}$e $\sim$ ə/ in *mène, mener*, etc.). Every language has its own set of morphophonic relations, based on its phonological system as used in the grammatical system.

3.2. WORDS

3.20.   It can be said that in the ordinary meaning of the term, all languages have WORDS. The problem arises, however, of how to define a word. Traditional definitions are often based on meaning,

and, much worse, on how things are written. If there is a white space
before and after an item, it's a word! If *car* and *automobile* mean the
same, then traditionally both are "words". If English has *highway*,
and French *route*, then both are "words". But if English says /wáynčə/
for "Why don't you", and French says /imlapa+di/ for *Il (ne) me l'a
pas dit* "He didn't tell me", how many words are there in each
example? (Our answer in this book is that English has four and
French six—or perhaps seven).

The definition of a word has to be arrived at for each language in
terms of its own structure. And the level of analysis at which the
term *word* is being used must also be kept in mind. The present
discussion is of words in terms of morphemes. Statements about the
structure of words in English and other well-known languages will
lead to some general principles or definitions.

The study of morphemes above (3.10–3.11) showed that in English,
items like *man, boy, milk, thought, big, nice, clear, you, it, do, go, walk,
how, when, by, in, and, but, no, yes, oh* have to be analyzed as having
a base morpheme and a superfix morpheme. Suppose we consider
this as a first definition of a word in English: a word is a structure
consisting of a base and a superfix. The words cited may be written
morphemically as follows: √mæn-´, √boy-´, √milk-´, √θoht-´,
√big-´, √nays-´, √klihr-´, √yuw-´, √it-´, √duw-´, √gow-´, √wohk-´,
√haw-´, √hwen-´, √bay-´, √in-´, √ænd-´, √bət-´, √now-´, √yes-´,
√ow-´. This is the simplest type of word possible in English, since
everything said in isolation must have a stress; words of less than
two morphemes are impossible.

A look at longer items shows other superfixes, and begins to present the various kinds of affixes, though there are items of more than
one syllable which may still be unitary bases. Some two-syllable
words may be listed: *manner* √mænər-´ˇ, *boyish* √boy--iš-´ˇ, *nicer*
√nays--ər-´ˇ, *going* √gow--iŋ-´; here there is a base, followed in
boyish and *nicer* by one postbase each, and by a suffix in *going*, and
ending with a superfix.

Still other items, of the same length or longer, show prebases
(√...⁻), and/or several postbases following each other: *alone* √ə⁻
lown-ˇ(+)´, *defeat* √di⁻fiyt-ˇ(+)´, *incantation* √in⁻kænt-⁻ey-⁻t-⁻Y-⁻ən-
ˋ+ˇ´ˇ, *collision* √k(a ∼ ə)[n]⁻l(ay ∼ i)d-⁻Y-⁻ənˇ(+)´ˇ, *animateness*
√ænim-⁻(ey ∼ i)-⁻t-⁻nis-´ˇˇ+ˇ, etc. The symbol (+) means that the
superfix may or may not include /+/ for different speakers; Y means
a morpheme that palatalizes preceding /t/ to /š/, /d/ to /ž/, and so
on; (a ∼ ə), (ay ∼ i), etc., indicate morphophonic alternation; [n]
means loss before the following base.

From the words exhibited, and from those that were used in 3.11 to establish prefixes and postfixes, we can conclude that a full definition of a word in English can be the following:

> In English a WORD must have one (and only one) base morpheme, and one superfix morpheme; may in addition have one or more prebases, and one or more postbases; may in some cases have a prefix or a postfix (or both); and may be concluded by a suffix.

By this definition such items as *phonology, automobile, locomotive, photography*, and many others, cannot be words because they seem to have two bases: *phonology* has the bases of *phone* and *logic, automobile* those in *auto* and *mobile, locomotive* those in *local* and *motive, photography* those in *photo* and *graphic*. Such items must then, by definition, not be called words, and will have to be examined below in the discussion of syntax (3.31).

When we look at a language like French, there is no stress superfix to help us define a word. But it has been shown that the nonphonemic "final stress", as it is called, locates the end of a French word, and we can accordingly say that the definition of a word in French is like that of English, except that there may be more than one suffix at the end. A French word superfix consists only of the indication of where an item ends for purposes of phrase transition and placing of intonation (pitch patterns).

If we examined more languages, we would find that everywhere there are morphemes comparable to bases, and that always there seems to be some way to state a word-closing superfix. Accordingly, we may venture a general definition of a word:

> A WORD is a phonologically separable item, in a language, that is morphemically analyzable into at least a base and a superfix of some kind, and may in addition have or require such other morphemes as the language possesses.

The determination of the nature of bases and other morphemes as to their morphophonic makeup has to be made for each language.

With this kind of definition of a word, some very general structural appraisals of different languages may be made. In older works on linguistics, and in popular discussions, there is often found a classification of languages into "isolating", "agglutinative", and "inflectional" (sometimes the last is further divided into "fusional" and "polysynthetic"). The typical "isolating" language is usually given as Chinese; we can give meaning to the term "isolating" by pointing out that Chinese (i.e., the Mandarin or Northern Chinese, the standard literary language) has no segmental affixes, and its words consist of bases and superfixes only; and, to anticipate syntax, its grammar consists chiefly of the arrangement of words under phrase superfixes. A typical "agglutinative" language is Turkish: here words consist of a base followed by (potentially) numerous postbases and/or suffixes, and closed by a superfix; apparently there are few, if any, prebases; and the morphophonic structure of the affixes shows little alternation, and they seem to be clearly identifiable and separable. Typical "inflectional" languages are Latin, Greek, Russian; here there are words containing a base and a superfix, with prebases and postbases possible, occasional prefixes and postfixes, and terminal inflectional suffixes; moreover, the suffixes and often also the other affixes show considerable morphophonic variation, and often call for morphophonic change in the base. This last is the characteristic often called "fusional", and in many instances a separation of an affix into separate morphemes has to be done by postulating processes with special morphophonic effects (the English $\sqrt{}$-Y- illustrated above is an example). The term *polysynthetic* (or *incorporating*) has been applied to some American Indian languages, where a word like Taos *timį́* 'I saw it [object of class A]' can have inserted into it, as it were, the base of another word, say *kána* 'mother', to give *tikà+mį́* 'I saw the mother'; this last item has to be described as a "phraseword" (or the like), and the conditions under which more than one base may appear in a wordlike item have to be examined and stated.

Given the definition of a word, and the morphophonic description of different kinds of morphemes, it is possible to compile the lexicon of a language. The words may be listed, though obviously no list can ever be exhaustive, since new words are constantly being formed. The bases may be listed by showing what part of a word is the base, or for some languages (e.g., Arabic), the bases may be the principal entries in the list, with the words containing them listed under the base; here too the list can never be exhaustive, since new bases can be formed. The various affixes may also be listed in the lexicon, or, depending on their number and kind, it may be more convenient to gather them up in one or several collections, and to indicate them in the lexical list only as parts of words.

A dictionary is usually a word list, and thus a partial lexicon. Further discussion of dictionaries will be found in 4.4.

3.21. In discussing morphemes and words above, the terms *inflection, inflectional* have been used. In English the forms *boy's, boys,*

boys', and *man's, men, men's* are described as inflectional forms of *boy* and *man*, respectively; they illustrate the inflection of the words *boy* and *man*. Similarly, *goes, went, gone, going* show the inflection of *go*.

A set of inflectional forms going with a "name form" of a word (i.e., the form by which a word is cited or named) constitutes a PARADIGM (/pǽrədim/ or /pǽrə+dàym/) of inflection.

The existence of paradigms enables us to divide the words of a language into various morphemic classes or PARTS OF SPEECH, according to the different paradigmatic (/pǽrə+digmǽtik/) sets that exist. Thus in English there are the paradigms of nouns like *boy* or *man* and of verbs like *go* or *walk* (*walks, walked, walking*). The only other paradigms of inflection in English are those of the personal pronouns (*I, me, my, mine*; etc.). In a language like English, then, we can divide the words into inflected and noninflected, and subdivide the inflected by their paradigms into NOUNS, VERBS, and PRONOUNS. By this process, the terms *noun, verb, pronoun* become technical terms with precise meanings, and it is no longer necessary to deal with the traditional vague and philosophical definitions ("A noun is the name of a person, place, or thing"; etc.). The specific definitions of *noun, verb, pronoun* in English will be given in 3.4.

Having defined and sorted out the inflected words, the rest of the words of a language have to be classified by other means. Part of this, and also the subclassification of the inflected words, can be done by examining their derivational structure (see 3.22). The bulk of the classification, however, of noninflected words has to come out of syntactic analysis (see 3.3). The traditional list of "parts of speech" includes those identifiable by inflection—nouns, verbs, (personal) pronouns; and the rest identifiable by syntactic function—adjectives, nonpersonal "pronouns", prepositions, adverbs, conjunctions, interjections. In a language without inflection (e.g., Chinese) all parts of speech can only be defined syntactically.

Many languages have inflected parts of speech more or less similar to English nouns, verbs, and pronouns. In many of the languages of Europe adjectives also may be sorted out on the basis of inflection. In some languages all or most bases can be inflected, in one or more ways, so that inflectional paradigms are classed as nominal or verbal or the like; an example is the Nootka language (an American Indian language originally spoken on Vancouver Island). In Japanese only verbs are inflected (and adjectives are a subclass of verbs—'to be good', etc.). In Taos, nouns and verbs are inflected (verbs include items translatable by English adjectives); there are a few inflected demonstratives; and all the other words are noninflected.

3.22.   The mention of postbases and prebases, as well as of prefixes and postfixes, has already brought attention to the matter of DERI-VATION. It is necessary to give the term a precise definition.

In most, if not all, languages, there are words which, regardless of whether they have inflectional affixes, show partial resemblances in form such that, if one of the words can be established as having an unmodified base, the others can be said to be DERIVED from it by means of the affixes that are present. In English, if *starve* exhibits a base ∤stahrv-, then *starvation* is DERIVED from it by the addition of the postbase complex -*ation*. In English most derivation takes place by means of one or more postbases, but there is also derivation by means of prebases, and there are forms derived by prefixes and post-fixes. A derived form to which inflection is added may be called a STEM; a stem is an extended base.

There are many traditional studies of derivation in many lan-guages, but there are few in which the morphophonic and affix structures are thoroughly examined and systematically described. A few examples will have to suffice here.

The English complex of affixes spelled -*ation*, -*ition*, -*ution*, -*tion*, -*sion*, -*ion* has been studied (see References, 3.20). There is the terminal postbase of the form ∤-ən-, preceded by the postbase ∤-Y-; the latter is added to stem-final /t, d, s, z/ with great regularity of morphophonic change; in many cases the /t/ and /s/ are them-selves postbases, but elsewhere they are base-final consonants, as are /d/ and /z/ usually; there are also instances of some other base-finals, and in many cases the alveolar finals /t, d, s, z/ are preceded by /m, n, l, r/ and other consonants. Some examples are:

> *narrate* : *narration*
> *expedite* : *expedition*
> *absolute* : *absolution*
> *act* : *action*
> *emit* : *emission*
> *evade* : *evasion*
> *pretense* : *pretension*
> *confuse* : *confusion*
> *reg(al)* : *region*

The consonant relations shown here are the following (→ 'results in') :

> ...t-ːY-→/š/
> ...d-ːY-→/ž/
> ...s-ːY-→/š/
> ...z-ːY-→/ž/
> ...g-ːY-→/ǰ/

In *equate* : *equation* most American speakers have ...t-ᴛY-→/ž/;
...nd-ᴛY- regularly produces /nš/, as in *intend* : *intention*; ...rs-ᴛY-
and ...rt-ᴛY- result in /rž/, as in *disperse* : *dispersion, divert* : *diver-
sion*.

The words ending in *-tion* etc. also show regular stress-pattern relations, with the related bases and stems: *óperàte* : *òperátion*; the
rule is that the primary stress must be on the syllable preceding /ən/.
There are also regular morphophonic vowel relations: *expedite* with
/ay/ and *expedition* with /i/.

Derivation by prebase is shown in *base* : *debase; cognition* :
recognition; -ceive : *deceive, conceive, receive*, etc.; *like* : *unlike; board* :
aboard.

Derivation by stress shift, that is, by change of superfix, is exhibited in: *permít* : *pérmit; transfér* : *tránsfer*. Stress shift is also
combined with affixation in the *-tion* words, and elsewhere (*áble* :
abílity).

There are other kinds of relations too: *advise* /z/ : *advice* /s/;
intend : *intent; authentic* /k/ : *authenticity* /s/; etc.

The derivational processes illustrated for English occur widely in
other languages; and there are also others, involving relationships of
tone (pitch), of initial consonants, and in fact of any part of the
morphophonic structure of a morpheme.

3.3. SYNTAX

3.30. The subdivision of morphology that deals with the relations
of morphemes is here called syntax. Syntax treats the occurrences
of the classes that are the morphemes. It is concerned with the sequences of morphemes, as words (since morphemes are found only
in words), and with the phenomena that mark the ends of word
sequences and indicate the manner in which succeeding sequences
are connected. In common parlance, syntax is understood to be
concerned with words as put together in phrases, and with phrases
as put together into clauses and sentences.

In this kind of linguistic analysis, the definitions of any of these
entities—the boundary phenomena, phrases, clauses, and sentences—
must be based on objective linguistic criteria, and may not be arrived
at by invoking meaning. Indeed, if any objective analysis of meaning
is ever to be achieved, it must be done by basing the meaning on
the syntax, as stated without the aid of meaning. The linguistic
meaning of utterances is studied in semology, and this meaning
must proceed from—not be a requisite for—the syntax. Semology
will be examined in Chapter 4 (especially 4.1ff).

The theory of syntactic analysis which will be briefly presented here developed from the study of English. A small amount of similar analysis of other languages has also been made, and corroborates the advantages of this approach over some others. For one thing, it is based on objectively apprehensible phonological phenomena as boundary markers, and on morphemically defined entities (the words) as constituents. For another, it validates many of the traditional syntactic statements, differing from them chiefly in its avoidance of the use of meaning, and in clarifying those points on which grammatical tradition is uncertain by explaining them in terms of objective criteria or by removing them to the higher realm of semology.

The basic approach is that the primary units of syntactic analysis, the PHRASES, are always binary in structure, and are marked by a transition phenomenon between the two parts, and some kind of suprasegmental phenomena that indicate the end of the phrase. Simple phrases are then composed of two words in one of the possible transitions, and have a suprasegmental pattern of stress or something analogous. Two simple phrases may be combined into a complex phrase, but always binarily, and this process may continue through several layers. A simple phrase or a complex series of phrases may be further held together by an INTONATION pattern, consisting of pitches or some analog of them, and a terminal contour; this higher unit is a CLAUSE. Some clauses, alone, or following others, may constitute or close a SENTENCE. Syntax stops with the sentence.

The relations of words to each other in phrases, of simple phrases to each other to form complex phrases, of phrases under intonations to form clauses, and of clauses to form sentences—all these are determined in the first instance by phonological criteria, and by actual occurrence. There need be no philosophical discussion of whether some sentences are real, or "grammatical", or the like; of supposed ambiguities found in written forms but not present when the items are spoken; or of which constituents belong with which. Any utterance that occurs in a language as used by its speakers is real and/or grammatical, and must be analyzed. Any such utterance may be ambiguous in meaning outside of its context—that is, its semology may be unknown at the time its syntax is being examined; but the syntactic structure itself, based on the morphemic identification of words within sequences that are phonologically marked, has no ambiguities. The constituents are delimited by their phonological markers, and syntactic analysis ends with these phonologically marked arrangements. Generally, there will be agreement with "common sense" and with known semology; where there is seeming disagreement, one must develop further analytical procedures, beyond syntax, and handle the items semologically.

So much for the theory. Some examples from English syntax follow, with an indication of analogous phenomena elsewhere.

3.31. There are many two-word sequences in English that are regularly used as lexical items, and which are usually called "compounds" or "compound words". By the definition of a word given above (3.20), these sequences cannot be called words, since they have more than one base. But they certainly fit the definition of a phrase, given in 3.30. They are binary in structure, there is a transition (plus or normal) between the two parts, and there is a single stress pattern over the whole—a primary stress on one part, some other stress (secondary, tertiary, weak) on the other. Examples, marked for stress and transition, are: *stréet+câr, ráil+ròad, pláce+ nâme, bláck+bìrd, ìce+créam* or *íce+crèam, mílk+trùck, óffice+mânager, rént+pâyment, òld+máid, dòwn+tówn, sét+ùp, sèt+úp.* The phrase superfixes illustrated here can be written separately, using the "long s", ʃ, as an identifying symbol for a SYNTACTIC OPERATOR (an analog in syntax of the morpheme in morphemics; other names will be mentioned later): ʃ'+^, ʃ'+`, ʃ'+'. Other English phrase superfixes will be discussed in 3.45. It should be remembered that word superfixes are stated in terms of all of their actual stress phonemes, and are morphemes. Phrase superfixes are shown not as actual stresses, but as indicators of the strongest stress of each of the two parts; it is for this reason that we call them operators rather than a special order or variety of morphemes.

The kinds of phrases above enter into more complex phrases. The phrase *gréen+hòuse* is binary and simple; *bìg+gréen+hòuse* is complex: *bíg+(gréen+hòuse).* How is this arrived at? First, we look at the sequence of three words *bíg+gréen+hòuse*: if we start with *big*, we may discover that *bíg+gréen* is possible, but only in such an instance as *they have a big green*, with a terminal after *green*; if there is in addition the item *house*, then we may put *green* and *house* together first, under the phrase superfix ʃ'+'. This now is a unit, and may be put into a phrase under either the primary or the nonprimary stress: ʃ^+' will give us *bíg+'(gréen+hòuse)*, while ʃ'+^ gives *bíg+^(gréen+ hòuse).* In simple phrases the primary stress of one of the words is reduced. In complex phrases, the primary stress of one of the constituent simple phrases is reduced. This principle works up through as many stages as necessary:

ʃ'+ˋ: gréen+hòuse
ʃˆ+':   bíg+'(gréen+hòuse) = bíg+gréen+hòuse
ʃˆ+':   nîce+'[bíg+(gréen+hòuse)] = nîce+bíg+gréen+hòuse
ʃˇ+':   the ˇ+'(nîce+'[bíg+(gréen+hòuse)] = thĕ+nîce+bíg+gréen+hòuse

Above in 3.20 it was pointed out that by the given definition of *word*, certain items like *photography*, *phonology*, *automobile* must be considered as phrases. Let us analyze a few of them.

In *photography* we have the word *photo* /fówtow/, and a "bound word" *-graphy*, which, we may suppose, would be pronounced */grǽfiy/ if it occurred—but it doesn't. *Photo* has the base found in *photon*, and a postbase *-o*: √fowt-, √ᷱow-, √ᶻˇ; *-graphy* has the base found in *graph*, and a postbase *-y*: √grǽf-, √ᷱiy-, *√ᶻˇ (postulated as such because of *graphic*). Now what happens in *photography*? The words composing the phrase are *photo* and **graphy*. The phrase superfix is ʃ'ᴗˇ, because **graphy* appears as /ᴗgrəfiy/ in the phrase. How do we account, however, for the shift of stress in *photo-* from /'ˇ/ to /ˇ'/, with accompanying morphophonic vowel changes? We must say that the affix *-o-* has the special properties of "drawing" stress to itself and exhibiting vowel changes when it occurs in a normal-transition phrase between two bases the first of which takes /'/, that is, under ʃ'ᴗˇ. Rather than calling this affix a postbase, we prefer to call it an INTERBASE. This interbase could be symbolized thus: √ᷱ(ow ∼ á)ᷱ.

Let us now look at *phonology*: here we have the first base the same as in *phone*, and the second as in *logic*; the words are *phono* /fównow/, which actually gets said, and *-logy* */lájiy/; the morphemic structures are: √fown-, √ᷱ(ow∼ á)ᷱ, √ᶻˇ; √laǰ-, √ᷱiy-, *√ᶻˇ. The phrase superfix is again ʃ'ᴗˇ. But there also exists the word *ology* ("there are many ologies"), pronounced /áləǰiy/; here the interbase seems to function as a prebase, √aᷱ, coming under the primary stress of the word superfix √ᶻˇˇ. This peculiar affix is perhaps best called an AMBIBASE, and described as able to appear as a postbase or as a prebase or as an interbase: √[ᷱ](ow ∼ á)[ᷱ].

In *automobile*, *locomotive*, the ambibase √ᷱ(ow ∼ á)ᷱ appears between the two bases, but the phrase superfix is ʃˋ+', so the ambifix has the automatic weak form /ᴗə/.

It may be noted in passing that the accent-shifting character of this affix *-o-* was found in its language of origin, ancient Greek, and was brought into English ready-made, so to speak, in the words in which it was first introduced; for instance, Greek *philosophía* 'love of wisdom, philosophy' (*phílos* 'loved, liked, dear'; *sophía* 'wisdom'), but *philósophos* 'loving wisdom, philosophical'. The details of Greek phrase superfixes have not been worked out.

The examples that have been given show that in a language with a stress system like that of English it is not difficult to establish phrase superfixes. But what happens in French, where there are no stress phonemes? The answer is that since the establishing of words as entities is based on morphemic criteria, and the markers of phrases are taken from the phonology as a whole, there need not be stress phonemes but only some phonological phenomenon that can be correlated with word ends. This is precisely what occurs in French. The words are defined morphemically much the same as in English (above, 3.20). Phonetically French words are known to show a greater loudness or prolongation on the syllable containing the last vowel (the so-called "mute *e*" is not a vowel phoneme for this purpose). This establishes the point of termination of the word phonetically and is one of the features on which transition phonemes are based in French. When words are put into binary phrases, the second one retains the loudness and prolongation, but in the first one various things can happen: loudness and prolongation may both be retained, though to a lesser extent than in final position; or loudness is lost, with some prolongation retained; or the syllable becomes completely like an internal syllable elsewhere. These phenomena are analyzed as, respectively, /+/ "plus", the open internal transition; /·/ "dot", the less open internal transition; and normal transition in the third instance. French has only one word superfix, the indicator of the place where the word ends phonetically; it may be written /-⌐ ('root sign', 'hyphen', 'raised upper right corner'; or, 'the morpheme word-closer'). The phrase superfixes, with the possible variation of the internal transition, are: ʃ-+-, ʃ-··-, ʃ-.-. Examples for these are: *beau retour* /bo+rətur/, *au retour* /o·rətur/, *aurevoir* /o·rəvwar/ or /orəvwar/.

In Japanese there are words with an accent and others without: *hana* 'nose', *anáta* 'you'; and there are phonologically dependent items which only appear as the second part of a phrase, after /+/; these are the particles. Phrase superfixes are of the types ʃ˘+˘, ʃ′+˘, ʃ˘+′, and ʃ˘˘˘, etc. Examples: /hana+wa/ 'nose (as tópic of discourse)', /haná+ga/ 'flower (as topic)'—but 'flower' in isolation is /hana/ because the accent never occurs on a final syllable; /anáta+wa/ 'you (as topic)'. In complex phrases the phenomena are of the same order: *watakushi wa hon o yomu* 'I'm reading a book' is structured thus: /yómw·/ 'reading takes place' enters into a complex phrase with /hóŋ·+˘o/ 'book (as goal)', itself a phrase—/(hóŋ·+˘o)′+yómw·/;

/watakw·sy·ˇ+ˇwa/ 'I (as topic)' is a phrase, entering into the higher complex ([watakw·sy·ˇ+ˇwa]ˇ+'[(hóŋ·+ˇo)'+yómw·]). This last example anticipates the treatment of complex phrases as clauses, although the clause-closing terminal is not shown.

3.32. Clauses are bounded by intonation patterns. In English these patterns consist of sequences of pitches, with a terminal contour. Many languages have similar kinds of intonation patterns (French, German, Russian). In others, intonations consist of terminals alone, with effect on preceding pitch or other accentual phenomena; such a case is Japanese. Still others have stress or intensity patterns with terminals; Siamese (Thai) has pitch differences within its words, and stress differences in intonations.

In analyzing clauses, which are often composed of a complex of phrases, it is necessary to know where to begin. The answer must be in heuristic terms, and is arrived at by experimentation. In English it has been found necessary to enter at the finite verb, then proceed to the right to the end of the clause, and then take up the material preceding the verb. If there is no verb in a clause, one starts with a noun. Details will be given in 3.47. Here one example must suffice: *The tall man was entering the house.* This can be said in the following way:

$$/ðə+^3\text{tóhl}+\text{mǽhn}^2 \mid {}^2\text{wəz}+\text{êntəriŋ}+ðə+{}^2\text{hǽws}^1\#/$$

First we identify the words morphemically: article, noninflected, noun, finite verb, participle, article, noun. Then, leaving the intonations aside for the moment, entering at the finite verb, we establish the phrases:

wəz+éntəriŋ
ðə+háws
(wəz+éntəriŋ)^+'(ðə+háws)

tóhl+mǽhn
ðə+'(tóhl+mǽhn)

At this point it is necessary to begin the syntactic description and identification of the phrases and their relation to each other in the clause. After that, the intonation is put back on, as it were, the two clauses are brought into relation, and the syntactic analysis is finished.

The present book is not a complete presentation of linguistic analysis, so the remainder of this exemplification will have to be taken on faith, so to speak.

The phrase *was entering* is described as a VERBAL phrase, consisting of auxiliary and participle; *the house* is a NOMINAL phrase, definite, and is postverbal. The clause is a VERBOID (a term designating a higher level within syntax than *verbal*), containing a finite verbal phrase with a nominal complement, and constituting a predicate. The first clause is a NOMINOID, containing a definite nominal, the nominal consisting of an adjunct uninflected word and a noun; this clause is said to be arranged to the verboid, and being a nominoid and preverbal, is the SUBJECT. The whole sentence is a complete predication.

The Japanese example in 3.31 above can be analyzed thus: *yomu*, the inflected verb, enters into a verboid phrase with the goal-nominal phrase *hon o*; the nominal, being preverbal and with the goal particle, is the complement; the phrase *watakushi wa* is a topic nominal, and enters into a complex phrase with the verboid, as a subject. The clause is bounded by a falling terminal, /#/, and is a complete verboid sentence.

3.33. The establishing of the phrases and clauses in terms of their boundaries and morphemically identified constituents makes possible the necessary description and identification of their relations with each other in objective terms.

Proceeding from the morphemically identified inflected or other word classes, we note their relation to each other and to noninflected words in simple phrases. Using terms like NOUN, VERB (in English) for the inflected forms, we label their syntactic functions NOMINAL, VERBAL. Then we extend these terms to complex phrases of similar functions; arranging word classes in a hierarchy, heuristically, we take verbs and verbals as primary, nouns and nominals next, and so on. The relations of those lower in the hierarchy to those higher are then noted, by such terms as PREVERBAL, POSTVERBAL, ADNOMINAL, ADJUNCTIVAL, and so on. Finally clause functions are described by such terms as NOMINOID, VERBOID, and the relations as SUBJECT, PREDICATOR, PREDICATE, COMPLEMENT, and the like. For each language, the terms and relations are based on its own material; see 3.47 for English.

In Japanese the terms *noun*, *verb* seem to be usable on the first syntactic level, since there is only one kind of inflection (verblike). Then come the more complex structures, nominal, verbal; and finally the -*oid* terms or special terms of the same hierarchical value are introduced.

In the languages so far examined by the techniques of phonologically based syntax, there seem to be several hierarchies of syntactic behavior. In English, phrases with tertiary or weak stress on one part seem to behave differently from those with secondary; the ones with weaker stresses may be called CONSTRUCTS, the others CONSTRUCTIONS—or by some analogous difference of terms. In much the same way, a part of a sentence may be made into a separate clause and the relation of such a clause, said to be ARRANGED or ATTACHED, to the rest of the sentence, is of a different order than if it were simply an included phrase.

In syntax, then, the hierarchy of relationships depends on the kinds of morphemic classes there are, and on the kinds of phonological markers of the classes—in the form of phrase superfixes, intonation patterns, and the like—that exist.

The pitch sequences of the intonation patterns, or their analogs or absence in some languages, seem to lead into semological analysis, and out of syntax as such.

3.4. THE MORPHOLOGY OF ENGLISH

3.40. In 2.4 above the phonology of English was set forth briefly. The present section focuses on the morphophonic organization of the phonological material, and its use in morphemes and in syntactic structures; in short, this section presents the grammar of English.

For the present purpose, all of English as spoken and written everywhere in the world by educated people is taken as "the English language". There are some 250,000,000 native speakers of this language, and an equal number of persons use it as a second language or have some knowledge of it for educational or administrative purposes. Despite differences of pronunciation (see 2.44), and extensive local variation in vocabulary, this language is remarkably uniform over all the areas where it is in use. This uniformity is probably in part the result of a long literary tradition, maintaining the written form largely unchanged for many generations (see 5.1).

Since the uniformity of English is manifested to a great extent in the morphemes which enter into the formation of its words, largely conventional spelling will be used in the present discussion. But it is useful to establish an over-all morphophonic pattern for the language as a whole.

The vowel morphophones are seven in number: $\sqrt{i}$/, $\sqrt{e}$/, $\sqrt{æ}$/, $\sqrt{u}$, $\sqrt{o}$/, $\sqrt{ɔ}$/, $\sqrt{ə}$/. These morphophones (excluding $\sqrt{o}$/) occur in *pit, pet, pat, put, pot, cut*; the morphophone $\sqrt{ɔ}$/ is phonemically /a/ in most items in most American dialects. The phoneme /i/ appears in some words and for some speakers where others have /ə/ or /i/, and is most probably not to be regarded as a separate morphophone; we shall write it as such, however, in places where there is always a weak vowel which cannot be identified as one of the seven other morphophones. The phoneme /a/ is an American manifestation of the mor-phophone √ɔ/, or a British (for some speakers) manifestation of the morphophone √ə/. The morphophone √o/ is manifested as /ɔ/ or /ɔh/ or /oh/, and is different from √ɔ/.

The complex nuclei are unit morphophones as constituents of morphemes (except in some pronominal forms, see below); there are nine: √iy/, √ey/, √ay/, √oy/; √aw/, √ow/, √uw/; √ah/, √əh/. The phonemic complex nuclei other than the nine written with the same symbols as these nine morphophones are manifestations in various dialects of these nine, or, for those ending in /h/, may be manifestations of simple vowel morphophones before √r/. The morphophone in *man* and many other words is written here as √æ/, and is manifested phonemically as /æ/ or /æh/ or /eh/ (and in some other ways) in different dialects; similarly, that of *fog* is written √ɔ/, and is manifested as /a/ or /ɔ/ or /ɔh/ or /oh/. The details of such variation would constitute a full morphophonic study of English dialect variations (see References—Smith).

The consonant morphophones and morphophone clusters used here are the same as the phonemes and clusters; √hw/ is manifested as /hw/ or /w/ according to dialect.

Alternations of morphophones in allomorphs of morphemes are symbolized thus: √(ey ∼ æ)/, as in *sane, sanity*.

The morphemes of English are of the following kinds; base, √B-(also √→.B-, √-.B-, √B.-, √B.₸, see 3.11); prebase, √pB₸; postbase, √₸pB-; prefix, √pf→; postfix, √←pf-; suffix, √-s; superfix, √ˢ.

3.41. English has paradigms of this kind:

man	*men*
man's	*men's*

These establish the inflected category of nouns. The four forms may be called "name form", *man*, "plural", *men*; "possessive", *man's*, "plural possessive", *men's*. A noun is morphemically defined as an inflectible word having a possessive or a plural or both; if it has both, it will also have a plural possessive.

The allomorphs of the inflectional suffixes are:

√ᵃ-Pl: √ᵃ-s after base final /p, t, k, f, θ/

√ᵃ-iz (phonemically /iz/ or /iz/ or /əz/, depending on dialect) after base final /s, z, š, ž, č, ǰ/

√ᵃ-z elsewhere; except that there are so-called "irregular" plurals which have to be listed. Some of these are:

√ᵃ-ən in *oxen*

√ᵃ-Ø in *sheep*

$\sqrt{}$-(Bay > i)rən in *children* (such a formula may be read "suffix -rən with change in the base from /ay/ to /i/")

$\sqrt{}$-(Baw > ay)ፀ in *mice*

$\sqrt{}$-(Bu > iy)ፀ in *feet*; etc.

$\sqrt{}$-Po: $\sqrt{}$-s ~ ['alternating with'] $\sqrt{}$-iz ~ $\sqrt{}$-z, as for plural, and $\sqrt{}$-ፀ after a plural allomorph in /s/ or /z/ (and also for many speakers in proper names ending in /s/ or /z/)

The last remark refers to such forms as *Charles'*, *James'* instead of *Charles's*, *James's*. The zero allomorphs are written with an apostrophe—*Charles'*, *boys'*—and are the only instances of zeroes indicated in the conventional spelling of English.

Instead of such summarizing symbols as $\sqrt{}$-Pl and $\sqrt{}$-Po, we could use $\sqrt{}$-Z_1 and $\sqrt{}$-Z_2. Morphemic formulas for some noun paradigms may be illustrated; in these examples, the part of the formula after the word *or* spells out the detail of the allomorphs:

man: $\sqrt{}$mæn-ʻ; $\sqrt{}$mæn--Z_1ʻ or $\sqrt{}$mæn--(Bæ > e)ፀʻ; $\sqrt{}$mæn--Z_2ʻ or $\sqrt{}$mæn--zʻ, $\sqrt{}$mæn--Z_1-Z_2ʻ or $\sqrt{}$mæn--(Bæ > e)ፀ-zʻ

boy: $\sqrt{}$boy-ʻ; $\sqrt{}$boy--Z_1ʻ or $\sqrt{}$boy--zʻ; $\sqrt{}$boy--Z_2ʻ or $\sqrt{}$boy--zʻ; $\sqrt{}$boy--Z_1-Z_2ʻ or $\sqrt{}$boy--z-ፀʻ

child: $\sqrt{}$čayld-ʻ; $\sqrt{}$čayld--Z_1ʻ or $\sqrt{}$čayld--(Bay > i)rənʻˇ; $\sqrt{}$čayld--Z_2ʻ or $\sqrt{}$čayld--zʻ; $\sqrt{}$čayld--Z_1-Z_2-'ˇ or $\sqrt{}$čayld--(Bay > i)rən-zʻˇ

Charles: $\sqrt{}$čahrlz--ʻ; $\sqrt{}$čahrls--Z_2ʻ(ˇ) or $\sqrt{}$čahrlz--ፀʻ and $\sqrt{}$čahrlz--izʻˇ

fungus: $\sqrt{}$fəŋgəs-ʻˇ; $\sqrt{}$fəŋgəs--Z_1ʻˇ or $\sqrt{}$fəŋgəs--(Bəŋgəs > ənǰay)ፀʻˇ

Another way of doing this is as follows:

$\sqrt{}$mæn- & ('combined with') $\sqrt{}$-Z_1 & $\sqrt{}$ʻ→ ('results in') /mén/

$\sqrt{}$fəŋgəs-& $\sqrt{}$-Z_1 & $\sqrt{}$ʻˇ→/fónjày/

3.42. A second kind of English paradigm is found in words like *do* and *walk*. The forms are:

do	does	did	done	doing
walk	walks	walked	walked	walking

This paradigm establishes the inflection of VERBS.

The forms of verbs are: the NAME FORM—*do*; the GENDER-MARKED SUBJECT FORM—*does*; the PAST—*did*; the PAST PARTICIPLE—*done*; the -ING FORM (often called the "present participle")—*doing*. The forms *do* and *does* together constitute what is usually called the "present", which may perhaps better be designated as the NONPAST. Examination of the corpus of the language shows that there are many verbs—including all new formations—that are like *walk*, with four different forms and perfectly regular and predictable inflection; these are traditionally called WEAK or REGULAR verbs. Then there are the verbs with five different forms or with changes in the base in the past and the past participle; these are the STRONG or IRREGULAR verbs. Beside these there are a few DEFECTIVE verbs, with no past participle or -*ing* form. And there is one verb with a few extra forms: *be, am, is, are, was, were, been, being*. In addition, there exist some special forms for the special subject pronoun *thou* (see 3.43), but these forms are not in the ordinary spoken language: *dost* or *doest, didst, walkest, walkedst, art, wast* or *wert*. There are also alternate forms for the *does, walks* forms: *doth* or *doeth, walketh*; these too exist only in special archaic usage.

From these inflections, we may conclude that a verb is a word inflected for PAST, and also in most cases for four other forms—two of which may turn out to be alike. We shall designate the five usual forms as V, Vz, VD, VN, VG; the forms of *be* are B, BM, Bz, BR, BDz, BDR, BN, BG. The forms in -(*e*)*st* may be designated as VT, VDT, BRT, BDzT, BDRT.

The regular (predictable) allomorphs of the inflectional suffixes of verbs are:

Vz: $\sqrt[a]{}$-s after /p, t, k, f, θ/
$\sqrt[a]{}$-iz after /s, š, z, ž, č, ǰ/
$\sqrt[a]{}$-z elsewhere

Irregular allomorphs are some instances of $\sqrt[a]{}$-z with base change (*does*), and the $\sqrt[a]{}$-θ in the verbs we shall call auxiliaries (below). All these are the morpheme $\sqrt{}$-Z₃.

VD: $\sqrt[a]{}$-t after /p, č, k, f, θ, s, š/
$\sqrt[a]{}$-id after /t, d/
$\sqrt[a]{}$-d elsewhere

Irregular allomorphs are instances of $\sqrt[a]{}$-t with base change (*went*), $\sqrt[a]{}$-t where $\sqrt[a]{}$-d would be expected (*burnt*), $\sqrt[a]{}$-d with base change (*sold*), and various kinds of $\sqrt[a]{}$-θ with base change; the latter are the typical strong verbs, of which some sixty are still left in the language (*sing, sang, sung; come, came, come; take, took, taken*; etc. This morpheme is $\sqrt{}$-D.

VN: same as VD for the regular forms $\sqrt[a]{}$-t, $\sqrt[a]{}$-id, $\sqrt[a]{}$-d; often same as VD also for the irregular forms, but there are also $\sqrt[a]{}$-n, $\sqrt[a]{}$-ən (both of these with and without base change), and $\sqrt[a]{}$-θ with base changes different from those in VD. This morpheme is $\sqrt{}$-N.

Vɢ: $\sqrt{}$-iŋ, always regular, and found with all verbs except the auxiliaries. This morpheme may be written $\sqrt{}$-G.

The modal auxiliaries may be defined as verbs that have $\overset{a}{\sqrt{}}$-θ for $\sqrt{}$-Z₃, have a past, and do not have any other forms (no Vɴ or Vɢ): *shall, should; will, would; can, could; may, might.* They may be symbolized as M, Mᴅ.

The forms of the verb *be* are morphemically as follows:

B: $\sqrt{}$-biy-²;
Bᴍ: $\sqrt{}$æ--m² (phonemically /ǽm/ or /ǽhm/ or /éhm/; weakened to /ˬm, ˬim/);
Bz: $\sqrt{}$i--z² (weakened to /iz, ˬz, ˬs, z, s/);
Bʀ: $\sqrt{}$æ--r² (phonemically /áhr/ or /ár/; weakened to /ər, ˬhr, ˬr/);
Bᴅz: $\sqrt{}$wə--z² (/wə́z, wəz, wiz/);
Bᴅʀ: $\sqrt{}$wə--r² (/wə́hr, wər/);
Bɴ: $\sqrt{}$biy--n² (American /bín/, British /bíyn/);
Bɢ: $\sqrt{}$biy--iŋ²ˇ.

In the syntax it will be found that verbs occur as the nonpast (V, Vz) and past (Vᴅ), these being the FINITE forms; and that the NONFINITE forms (Vɴ, Vɢ) occur in phrases with auxiliaries and in various adjunctival and nominal uses. For clarity of reference, the various verbal phrases may be listed here (for the superfixes with which they occur see 3.45):

Bᴍ, Bz, Bʀ, Bᴅz, Bᴅʀ with Vɢ: *am going, is doing, are talking, was seeing, were looking,* etc. These are the "progressive" or "durative aspect" phrases.
have, has, had with Vɴ: *have gone, has done, had come;* etc. These are the "perfect phase" phrases.
M, Mᴅ with V: *shall* and *should go; will, would do; can, could talk; may, might see.* Also used in this way are *do, does, did,* and (rarely) *dare* and *need.* These are the "modes", which can be named simply by their auxiliary. The traditional "future" consists of the *shall* and the *will* modes.

The forms of *be* occur with Vɴ to give what may be called the "resultative-passive voice" phrases: *is gone, is done, was seen,* etc.

Combinations of perfect with durative, the modals with perfect and perfect-durative, and others are discussed in 3.45.

3.43. A small group of words—*I, he, she, we, you, they, who*—exhibit special inflectional forms, and constitute a small relic class, the (personal) PRONOUNS. The special word *thou*, and also *it*, may be included here, and there are a few other words that have some relation to these (see below).

The pronouns show a name form, which may be called the SUBJECT form, an OBJECT form, a POSSESSIVE, and a SECOND POSSESSIVE; these are usually called the CASES (after the usage in Latin and other languages where nouns and possibly other parts of speech have several inflected forms of this kind). It is customary to call *we* the "plural" of *I*; *they* the "plural" of *he, she, it*; and *thou* the special singular of *you*. For our present purposes, it is best to treat each of these as a separate word—FIRST, SECOND, (third) MASCULINE, (third) FEMININE, (third) NEUTER, FOURTH, FIFTH, SIXTH PERSONS; *who* is the RELATIVE pronoun.

The forms found are:

	1	2	(3) M	(3) F	(3) Nt	4	5	6	R
Subject	*I*	*thou*	*he*	*she*	*it*	*we*	*ye*	*they*	*who*
Object	*me*	*thee*	*him*	*her*	*it*	*us*	*you*	*them*	*whom*
Possessive	*my*	*thy*	*his*	*her*	*its*	*our*	*your*	*their*	*whose*
2nd possessive	*mine*	*thine*	*his*	*hers*	*its*	*ours*	*yours*	*theirs*	*whose*

The forms of *it* are really just like those of a noun, name form *it*, and possessive *its* (but spelled without an apostrophe), with no plural. The form *ye* is archaic and special, like the whole paradigm of *thou*. The form *whom* is literary, and is going out of use even in written language; without it, *who* is like *it*—name form and possessive (special spelling) only.

For pedagogical purposes it is only necessary to present the forms as given above. There is some interest, however, from a structural point of view, in analyzing these forms into a base and affixes, as a relic inflectional class no longer productive in the language. Most of the forms have an initial consonant, and all have a vowel and a final consonant or a semivowel. The most consistent structural analysis is to set up the vowel as a bound base ($/.B-$), the general pronominal base, with several different vowels as its allomorphs. The initial consonant, or its allomorph zero, is the person prefix; *it* is taken to have no prefix, but has a postfix; the final consonant, or the semivowel /y/, is analyzed as a suffix of case. (The separation of /y/ from the preceding vowel is the only instance in English where a VS nucleus is treated as two morphophones rather than a single one.) The analyzed forms are:

	1	2	(3)M	(3)F	(3)Nt
Sb	Ɵ→.a--y˒	(ð₂→.aw--Ɵ˒	h→.i--y˒	š→.i--y˒	□.i-‹t˒
Ob	m→.i--y˒	ð₂→.i--y˒	h→.i--m˒	h→.ə--r˒	□.i-‹t˒
Po	m→.a--y˒	ð₂→.a--y˒	h→.i--z˒	h→.ə--r˒	□.i-‹t-z˒
2Po	m→.a--y-n˒	ð₂-.a--y-n˒)	h→.i--z-z˒	h→.ə--r-z˒	□.i-‹t-z-z˒

	4	5	6	R
Sb	w→.i--y˒	(y→.i--y˒)	ð→.e--y˒	hw→.uw--Ɵ˒
Ob	Ɵ→.ə--s˒	y→.uw--Ɵ˒	ð→.e--m˒	hw→.uw--m˒
Po	Ɵ→.aw--r˒	y→.uw--r˒	ð→.e--r˒	hw→.uw--z˒
2Po	Ɵ→.aw--r-z˒	y→.uw--r-z˒	ð→.e--r-z˒	hw→.uw--z-z˒

In 1 and 4 the person prefixes have zero allomorphs in one and three instances respectively; in 5 the subject form, and in 2 the whole paradigm, are archaic and special; the object form is generally used as subject in 5, and 5 is generally used instead of 2. In the 2nd possessive the final suffix in (3)M, (3)Nt, and R could be interpreted as a zero allomorph, $\sqrt{}$-Ɵ, in which case it would be like the possessive of nouns. The technique used here is that of presenting the morpheme in its basic morphophonic form, the allomorphs here being automatically conditioned: /s/ in the Nt, and nothing phonemically in (3)M and R. The first possessive is perhaps best regarded as a separate morpheme, though it could be argued that the two possessives are syntactically conditioned variants of each other; the second possessive is more like the possessive of nouns, in that it can appear after the first possessive as the noun inflection can appear after other inflections (the plural) and after whole phrases. The first possessive appears after the postfix of Nt, while the subject and object suffixes do not appear in this position. The relative prefix is set up as $\sqrt{}$hw→ because of the presence of /hw/ in syntactically related forms like *what*, *when*, etc.; the morphophonic rule is that $\sqrt{}$hw/ appears as /h/ when the following nucleus is /Vw/ (compare *how*, $\sqrt{}$hw→.aw-). The first possessive allomorph $\sqrt{}$-r results in automatic preceding /h/ (in many dialects) in F and 6, preceding /ə/ and an extra weak syllable in 4, change of /w/ to /h/ in 5. In Nt, where there is a postfix, there are no Sb or Ob suffixes. Many of the forms have special allologs in syntax.

A summary of the morphemes is:

$\sqrt{}$.Pr-: $\sqrt{}$.a- ∼ $\sqrt{}$.i- ∼ $\sqrt{}$.aw- ∼ $\sqrt{}$.ə- ∼ $\sqrt{}$.uw- ∼ $\sqrt{}$.e-

$\sqrt{}$1→: $\sqrt{}$Ɵ→ ∼ $\sqrt{}$m→

$\sqrt{}$2→: $\sqrt{}$ð₂→

$\sqrt{}$M→: $\sqrt{}$h→

$\sqrt{}$F→: $\sqrt{}$š→ ∼ $\sqrt{}$h→

√←Nt: √←t
√4→: $\overset{a}{√}$w→ ~ $\overset{a}{√}$θ→
√5→:   √y→
√6→:   √ð→
√R→:   √hw→
√-Sb: $\overset{a}{√}$-y ~ $\overset{a}{√}$-θ (does not occur after √←t)
√-Ob: $\overset{a}{√}$-y ~ $\overset{a}{√}$-m ~ $\overset{a}{√}$-r ~ $\overset{a}{√}$-s ~ √-θ (does not occur after √←t)
√-Po₁: $\overset{a}{√}$-y ~ $\overset{a}{√}$-z ~ $\overset{a}{√}$-r ~ $\overset{a}{√}$-s
√-Po₂: $\overset{a}{√}$-n ~ $\overset{a}{√}$-z

This analysis of pronouns makes possible the recognition of several groups of words that have syntactic (and, at a later stage, semological) functions that resemble those of pronouns. They are substitutes for large groups of other words, or even for whole phrases and clauses. The analysis here presented resulted from the recognition of the possibility of occurrence of prefixes and postfixes in English, and led to the identification of these affixes and their limited and non-productive functioning.

The word *what* is analyzable as consisting of the morphemes √R→.Pr-←Nt, in the shapes √hw→.a-←t; the pronominal base here is $\overset{a}{√}$.ə- for many speakers. The word is uninflected for case, but can be called an uninflected pronoun by virtue of having the postfix √←t; it is the relative neuter pronoun.

The word *that* can be analyzed in similar fashion: √6→.Pr-←Nt; the pronominal base exhibits a new allomorph, $\overset{a}{√}$.æ-. Shall we call this the "6th person neuter pronoun"? This denotation would certainly be correct enough as to the analysis; however, the "6th person" is perhaps better seen as a general DEMONSTRATIVE prefix, which happens to have plural concord syntactically in the paradigm of the personal pronoun. Another way would be to call the /ð/ of the demonstrative a separate morpheme, √ð₃→; we prefer the identification of √6 and demonstrative for later use in semology. The word *that* is a pronoun, and is inflected, but only for √-Pl: *those*, √6→.Pr--Z₁ = √ð→.ow--z; again the pronominal base has a different allomorph; the plural allomorph is regular; note that the postfix of the name form is not present when there is a suffix.

In similar manner the word *this* can be analyzed as containing √6→.Pr- and a postfix √←s indicating, in semology, proximity or the like; this may be called the "demonstrative nearer pronoun". If we do this, we have to analyze *these* as containing not only √6→.Pr- and √-Pl, but also something representing the "nearer" postfix; one way is to say that before √-Pl, the √←s- is replaced by an allomorph

√⁺y-; this would mean, however, that we have here an instance of both a postfix and a suffix. A simpler treatment for both *those* and *these* is to say that once *that* and *this* are formed, they are treated as nonanalyzable nouns, with irregular plural inflection.

The words beginning with /ð/ are all (except *thou*) seen to be so used, and to have enough parallels with other initials, to enable us to say that they are all "demonstratives" with a prefix √ð→: *than*, *then*, *thence*, *there*, *thither*, *though*, *thus*; the portions following the initial /ð/ are to be treated as various forms of the pronominal base with postfixes, or as special bases, some with postfixes also. The full treatment would take too much space here; the reader might enjoy making trial analyses, in conjunction with the other words about to be listed. The DEFINITE ARTICLE *the* (/ðíy, ðĭy, ðə/) also belongs with the demonstratives.

The various "relatives" are *when*, *whence*, *where*, *whither*, *how* (√hw→ with loss of /w/ before /Vw/), *which*, *why*.

The words *here*, *hence*, *hither* show a prefix √h→ of "nearer demonstrative" meaning.

Analyses with prefixes and postfixes can also be made of such words as *any* : *many* (and then *much*, *more*, *most*—the /r/ and /st/ here are the "comparative"- and "superlative"-deriving postbases), *ever* : *never* (and then *no*, *none*, *not*); *no* : *so* (and then *some*, *such*). The words *once*, *twice*, *thrice* show a postfix √⁺s, probably different from the ones in *this*, *hence*.

See the next section for other morphemic subclasses of words.

3.44. The word classes or parts of speech that are distinguished by inflection are, as we have seen, nouns, verbs, and pronouns. And as was seen in the last section, the analysis of English pronouns suggests ways in which subclasses of words may be determined morphemically among the uninflected words. Moreover, the examination of words of any class that contain prebases and postbases indicates how further subdivisions may be made, into simple words, bound words, prebasate words, postbasate words, and others. The items with prebases and postbases are the words traditionally called "derived".

In the study of inflection it was seen that some bases undergo change in form in the presence of certain suffixes. This kind of change is traditionally called by the German term *Umlaut*, which may be pronounced with English phonemes as if spelled "oom-lout", i.e., /úm+làwt/. The term *metaphony* (/metǽfəniy/) has also been used; the basic meaning is something like "change of sound". However, the historical basis of umlaut in the older Germanic languages was one of change of sound under the influence of a following sound. In cases like those of the strong verbs, the alternations in the base were thought to be inherent in the base by virtue of a kind of derivation from an original (often by means of accent change), and this is called *Ablaut* (as if spelled "op-lout", i.e., /áp+làwt/), or *apophony* (/əpáfə-niy/), '[change of] sound from [something else]'. The way English works suggests that a single term be used for all these phenomena, and the term chosen here is ABLAUT. Ablaut variations are found especially in the words with prebases and postbases, and among these, most markedly in the ones that are technical terms and are known to be of Latin and Greek origin; often they are combined with extensive but systematic changes in the word superfix also.

Among the uninflected words that are traditionally called adjectives are found sets of three words that are related in form, one being base, and the other two having *-er* and *-est* (the so-called "comparative" and "superlative"). Syntactically these are all adjuncts, with much the same syntax (see 3.47). Morphemically such sets may be set apart from other uninflected words by virtue of the presence of the postbases in two of the three, and there is no reason why the term ADJECTIVE should not be used. However, in this use, the term must be restricted to those words that show the *-er* and *-est* postbases, and must include all such words, even those traditionally called "adverbs" or something else. Some adjectives, as here defined, exhibit various kinds of ablaut.

Sets like *nice, nicer, nicest; tall, taller, tallest,* etc., show the postbases in their most usual forms, √-ər-, √-ist; they are the "regular adjectives". However, no one can say with certainty that some particular word is or is not such an adjective, for usage varies: some say *pleasanter, pleasantest,* others use phrases (*more, most pleasant*). There are some sets with suppletion: *good, better* (√bet--ər-), *best* (√be(t)--st-); *bad, worse* (√wər--s-, where -s- is an allomorph of √-ər-), *worst* (√wər--st-). Then there are the so-called adverbs, prepositions, and other words that show one or the other of the two postbases; examples are:

much, more, most: √məč-, √-(Bəč > ow)r- (here /ow/ automatically becomes /oh/ before /r/), √-(Bəč > ow)st-;

less, least: √le--s-, √liy--st-, with different base vowels (is the original base that of *little?*), and the ᵃ√-s of √-ər;

far, farther or *further, farthest* or *furthest:* √far(ð)-, with regular √-ər, √-ist, or the same forms of the postbases but with change of vowel (Ba > ə).

nigh, near, next: √nay-, √-(Bay > i)r-, √-(Bay > ek)st-;

fore, first: √for-, √-(Bo > ə)st-; or possibly *fore* is a form with √-ər, and the base is perhaps to be found in *fro* (as in *to and fro*), in which case the analysis would be √frow-, √-(Br > θ)r (with /ow/ > /oh/ before /r/), √-(Brow > ər)st-.

A postbase (or is it a postfix?) that shows ablaut in the base is -*th*: *long* : *length*, *wide* : *width*, *strong* : *strength*, *broad* : *breadth*. Here there are some special forms: *high* : *height* (but "highth", substandard); *dry* : *drought* (and *drouht*), *foul* : *filth* (which are not always recognized as connected), *hale* : *health*, *weal* : *wealth*, *steal* (a verb) : *stealth*. But *warm* : *warmth* and the substandard *cool* : *coolth* show no ablaut. This affix √-θ results in nouns.

The postbase complex -*ation*, -*ition*, -*ution*, -*tion*, -*sion*, -*ion* has already been referred to above (3.22). When the sequence of -*t*-, -*d*-, -*s*-, -*z*- (and some others) preceding √-Y--ən- is found, then the primary stress always falls on the vocalic nucleus preceding the -*t*-, etc. But in the related forms that end in -*t*-, etc., (i.e., without the -*ion*) there may be various stress patterns: *ănĭmátiŏn*, but *ánĭmăte* (verb), and *ánĭmăte* ("adjective"); *sólve, sólŭte, sŏlútiŏn*; *ădjóin, ádjŭnct, júnctiŏn*; *fínĭte, dèfĭnítiŏn*; and so on.

The postbase -*ty* or -*ity* always has a primary stress two syllables before the -*ty*: *líbĕrty, ĭnfínĭty*. The postbase -*ize* has a similar pattern: *cívĭlìze, órgănìze*.

The stress rules just exemplified, and others like them, are tied up with the greatest number of ablaut relations; and the ablaut affects both the bases and the postbases. On the addition of prebases, still more ablaut relations are found. We cannot in this book enter into the details of these relations, which would furnish data for many specialized monographs. Therefore, a few examples will have to suffice:

> *sŭblíme* : *sŭblímĭty* : *sŭblĭmăte* : *sŭblĭmátiŏn*
> ə́ áy ə̆ í ə́ ĭ ə̀ ĭ
> *ĭnfínĭte* : *ĭnfínĭty* : *fínĭte* : *fínĭsh* : *dèfĭnítiŏn*
> í ĭ ĭ ĭ í ĭ́ áy ày í ĭ ĭ́ í
> *sóciăl* : *sŏcíĕty* : *ăssóciăte* : *ăssòciátiŏn*
> ów š° əsáy ówsĭy òwsiy
> (° means on vowel and accordingly no stress)

Instances of consonant relations are found in some of the above examples, and in various prebases:

accede, adapt, attrition, assent: k ~ d ~ θ
offer, obtain: θ ~ b
concede, combine, collect, correct: n ~ m ~ θ, etc.

The spelling changes in the prebase reflect an original assimilation to the first consonant of the base, but in English in most cases this assimilation is not represented phonemically, since English does not have phonemic doubling of consonants.

From the systematic examination of the prebases and postbases there can emerge several classifications of words: all words, whether inflectible or not, can be classified as containing a simple base, or a stem consisting of a base with one or more postbases, or a base with one or more prebases, or a stem with one or more prebases; certain postbases can be seen to form nouns or verbs from nouns or verbs or noninflected words; certain other postbases form groups of noninflected words, which have consistent syntactic functions ("adjectives" in -ate, in -ish, in -ose, in -ous, etc.); the various prebases form words with consistent semological functions (de-, ex-, re-, in- ['negative' and 'local'] un-, etc.).

The subclasses arrived at by full examination and systematization of the morphemic structure of English words can serve as very useful guides to the syntax and the semology. But it must be clearly seen what the direction of development and guidance is; morphemic structure leads to the higher levels, but one cannot take them for granted and try to classify words by the traditional meaning groups.

3.45. In the discussion of syntactic theory and methodology above (3.31), some of the English phrase superfixes were exemplified. Here will be given a list of all of them, but obviously a full discussion of English syntax is not possible in the short space available.

The phrase superfixes of English are defined as syntactic operators consisting of a primary stress, another stress (or the absence of stress) which may precede or follow the primary, and a transition between the two—open or normal. All the phrase superfixes are binary, and all phrase structures are binary. In terms of the definition, there can only be sixteen phrase superfixes in English. They are:

$$\int {}^{\prime}\!+^{\wedge} \qquad \int {}^{\prime}{}_{\smile}{}^{\wedge} \qquad \int {}^{\wedge}\!+^{\prime} \qquad \int {}^{\wedge}{}_{\smile}{}^{\prime}$$
$$\int {}^{\prime}\!+^{\backprime} \qquad \int {}^{\prime}{}_{\smile}{}^{\backprime} \qquad \int {}^{\backprime}\!+^{\prime} \qquad \int {}^{\backprime}{}_{\smile}{}^{\prime}$$
$$\int {}^{\prime}\!+^{\vee} \qquad \int {}^{\prime}{}_{\smile}{}^{\vee} \qquad \int {}^{\vee}\!+^{\prime} \qquad \int {}^{\vee}{}_{\smile}{}^{\prime}$$
$$\int {}^{\prime}\!+^{\circ} \qquad \int {}^{\prime}{}_{\smile}{}^{\circ} \qquad \int {}^{\circ}\!+^{\prime} \qquad \int {}^{\circ}{}_{\smile}{}^{\prime}$$

It should be remembered that these symbols have the following meaning: ʃ is "syntactic operator", the analog in syntax of the morpheme in morphemics; ' (acute) means 'the primary stress of the word or phrase that constitutes this part of the binary structure remains unchanged'; ^ (circumflex), ` (grave), ˇ (breve), mean 'the primary stress of the word or phrase that constitutes this part of the binary structure is replaced by secondary, tertiary, or weak respectively'; ° (zero superscript) means 'the primary stress ... is replaced by no stress due to the morphophonic disappearance of the vowel that bore the primary stress originally'; + (plus) means 'the transition between the two parts of the phrase is open'; ⌣ (tie line) means 'the transition between the two parts of the phrase is closed up'. In most instances of ˅ and ⌣, and in all instances of °, there are automatic morphophonic changes of several kinds.

Illustrations of the phrase superfixes are:

ʃ ′+^: *bíg+trúck* (contrasting with a small one)
ʃ ′+ˋ: *íce+crèam*
ʃ ′+˅: *postman* pronounced /pówst+mə̆n/
ʃ ′+°: *John's going* pronounced /ján+z+gôwiŋ/, from *John* and *is góing*
ʃ ′⌣^: in some dialects items like *blackguard* may be pronounced /blǽgârd/
ʃ ′⌣ˋ: items like *grapefruit* are pronounced /gréyfrùwt/ by many speakers
ʃ ′⌣˅: *postman* pronounced /pówsmə̆n/
ʃ ′⌣°: *He's going* /híyz+gôwiŋ/, from *he* and *is góing*
ʃ ^+′: *bîg+hóuse*
ʃ ˋ+′: *òld+máid*
ʃ ˅+′: *thĕ+mán*
ʃ °+′: *If I* pronounced /f+áy/
ʃ ^⌣′: in some dialects items like *canned fruit* may be pronounced /kǽhn⌣frúwt/
ʃ ˋ⌣′: *old maid* pronounced /òwlméyd/
ʃ ˅⌣′: *and then* pronounced /ə̆nðə́n/, where /nð/ is phonetically [nd̦], that is, stop nasal gliding into spirant nasal
ʃ °⌣′: *'Tis*

The application of the binary-phrase technique to clauses containing several phrases may be illustrated by a number of sentences (intonations are omitted—see 3.46):

John arrived: /ján+əráyvd/, ʃ ^+′
John arrived early: /ján+ərâyvd+ə́hrliy/, ʃ ^+′(^+′)
John's wife arrived: /jánz+wâyf+əráyvd/, ʃ (^+′)^+′
John's wife arrived early: /jânz+wâyf+ərâyvd+ə́hrliy/, ʃ (^+′)^+′(^+′)
The man smiled: /ðə̆+mǽhn+smáyld/, ʃ (˅+′)^+′
I told him: /ày+tówldĭm/, ʃ ˋ+′(⌣ ˅)
You said it: /yúw+sêdĭt/, ʃ ′+^(⌣ ˅)
I told him the truth: /ày+tôwldim+ðə̆+trúwθ/, ʃ ˋ+′([⌣ ˅]^+′[˅+′])

It is probable that there are no instances of more than three phrases combining into a clause; and there are not many instances of more than three words combining into a complex phrase. The handling of larger combinations and the procedures for the full analysis of clauses and sentences by what is here called "phonologically based syntax" involve operations with the intonation patterns, which are considered next (3.46); they will be summarized and exemplified in 3.47.

3.46. The phrases of English, when said as part of normal speech, or, for that matter, whenever said, alone or in sequence, are accompanied by pitches, and terminate (simple phrases said alone, or complex phrases alone) in one of the terminal contours. We can now examine the nature of the pitch sequences and contours. As stated (3.32), phrases with such pitch (or analogous) sequences and a terminal are taken, in any language, as clauses. The pitch (etc.) sequences together with the terminal constitute an intonation pattern (3.30).

English intonation patterns are of several kinds. They always have a pitch (the nuclear pitch) coinciding with the primary stress of the phrase, and also have a terminal pitch, and a terminal contour. This first instance may be illustrated thus:

No.   /³nów¹#/
Never. /³névə̆r¹#/
Never? /³névə̆r³||/ or /⁴névə̆r⁴||/

If there are syllables preceding the primary one, then the intonation pattern has an initial pitch, a nuclear pitch, a terminal pitch, a contour. Such intonations are the most common in the language. Examples are:

Again.   /²ə̆³gén¹#/
The idea!   /²ðĭy+à y⁴díh²#/
John went home.   /²jân+wênt+³hówm¹#/
It's quite impossible.   /²ĭts+kwâyt+im³pásibəl¹#/
He got up, and went out.   /²hìy+gàt+²ə̆p²| ²in+wênt+³áwt¹#/

It soon becomes apparent in examining the corpus of the language, that the above two types of intonation patterns are not enough to take care of all the occurring phenomena. Moreover, the two kinds are clearly the same thing, since in the first examples there simply aren't any syllables preceding the nuclear one.

Many clauses have a fourth pitch. In some instances it precedes the primary or pitch nucleus, in others it follows the nucleus. Examples are:

That's a nice house.   /²ð\u00e6ts+ŏ+³nâys+²háws¹#/
Read Chapter 1.   /²rîyd+²č\u00e6ptŏr+³wŏn¹#/
I want it done now.   /²ày+wântᴗit+³dŏn+¹nâw¹#/

From the examples so far given, it seems warranted to draw the conclusion that intonation patterns in English may be defined and described thus:

> An INTONATION PATTERN in English is a sequence of not more than four pitches, with a terminal contour, such that the penultimate or antepenultimate pitch coincides with the primary stress of the phrase (being thus the nuclear pitch), the ultimate pitch is phonetically affected by the terminal contour (hence is the terminal pitch), and there is an initial pitch. If the penultimate pitch coincides with the primary, then an antepenultimate pitch may coincide with a secondary (or tertiary or weak) preceding the primary, being itself preceded by an initial pitch. If the antepenultimate pitch coincides with the primary, then the penultimate usually but not always coincides with a secondary. If no syllables precede the primary, the pitch on it coincides with the initial.

This descriptive definition may be summarized thus: an intonation pattern has the form

$$[a(b)]\acute{c}(d)eT$$

Here a is the initial pitch, $\acute{c}$ is the nuclear pitch, and e the terminal pitch; T is the terminal contour. If b is present, d is excluded; if d is present, b is excluded. If $\acute{c}$ comes first, then $a(b)$ simply do not occur.

The most common pitch in initial position (a) is /²/; the most common nuclear pitch ($\acute{c}$) is /³/; the most common terminals (eT) are /¹#/. Prenuclear (b) is most usually /²/ or /³/. Postnuclear (d) is often /¹/. In reading the examples below, the reader should remember that there are in many instances several different ways of saying a sentence. The sentences are of varying length and complexity, and exhibit a good number of the most frequent intonation patterns. The syntactic function of intonation patterns is to delimit clauses, and to indicate hierarchical dependence of clauses. The actual pitches, however, do not affect syntax, but the location of $\acute{c}$ in relation to the contour is an important factor in the developmental procedure from syntax to semology. The nature of T does affect syntax: if T is /||/—a minor terminal—the clause is in some way dependent in respect to a following clause; if T is /||/ or /#/—a major terminal—the clause is independent syntactically. The intonation patterns as syntactic operators may be symbolized thus: ʃ₁aće|, ʃ₁abće|, ʃ₁aćde|; ʃ₁aće||, ʃ₁abće||, ʃ₁aćde||; ʃ₁aće#, ʃ₁abće#, ʃ₁aćde#. In each one a or ab may be absent, this being marked if desired by parentheses: ʃ₁(a)će#, ʃ₁(ab)će#, etc. To repeat, at the syntax level there are only these nine intonation patterns, and they are basically only two—with minor or major terminals; subdivisions are determined by whether three or four pitches occur, by the presence of either b or d if there are four pitches, and by the kind of major terminal.

Examples of intonation patterns in conversational speech are:

Hello, James. How've you been?
²hɨ³lów² | ²ǰéymz²# ²hâw+v+yùw+²bín¹#

Oh, hello there. Just fine. And yourself?
¹ów¹# ²hɨ³lów+²ðêhr¹# ²ǰɨs+³fáyn¹# ²ɨn+yùr+³sélf³||

Not bad. I got back from Chicago yesterday.
²nât+²béhd¹# ²ày+gàt+²bǽk² | ²frðm+ši+³káhgŏw² | ²yéstɨdɨy¹#

Chicago? What were you doing in Chicago?
²šɨ+³káhgŏw³|| ²wât+wðr+yð+²dûwɨn+ɨn+šɨ⁴káhgŏw¹#

One of those business trips. Not very exciting.
²wðn+ðv+ðôwz+³bíz+nɨs+trîps¹# ³nát³ | ²vêrɨy+ɨk+²sáytɨŋ¹#

That's the way ... Excuse me, there's my bus. See you.
²ðǽts+ðð+wêy[*break*] ²ɨk+³skyúwz+mìy² | ²ðêrz+mày+³bðs¹# ³síyyð¹#

Yeah. Good-by. Say hello to everybody.
¹yéh¹# ²gŭ+³báy² || ²sêy+hɨ+³lów² | ²tð+²évrɨbàdɨy¹#

In literary language the variety of intonations is less than in speech, and the sentences are usually longer. The example below is given in the form it might have in silent reading to oneself:

²Cŏm²pútĕr+dĕ+sîgnĕrs² | ²hàve+bèen+²knówn² | ²tŏ+cŏnstrûct+mă+ ³chínes² | ²clêvĕrĕr+thăn+³théy²# ²ăs+whên+ă+³chéss-plâyĭng+mă+ ²chîne² | ²cŏn+²sístĕntlŷ² | ²bêats+thĕ+³búildĕr¹# ¹Bút¹ | ²thĕre+ìs+ă+ pràg+mâtic+³límɨt² | ²tŏ+thĕ+²clévĕr+nĕss² | ²thăt+căn+bè+²pút² | ²ɨnto+a+cŏm+³pútĕr¹# ²Àftĕr+ă+³whíle² | ²ɨt+bĕ+cômes+³nécĕssàrȳ² | ²to+²lînk+ă+mă+²chíne² | ²cóm+pĕtĕnt² | ²ɨn+³séveral+rĕspêcts² | ²tŏ+sŏme+³óthĕr+mă+chînes² | ²cóm+pĕtĕnt² | ²ɨn+⁴óther+wâys² || ²ănd+lêt+³áll+ŏf+thêse² | ²ôpĕràte+ăs+ă+³sîngle+cŏm+²púter¹# ²Prĕ+ ³súmably² | ²sûch+ă+²gádget² | ²wòuld+³nôt+bê+²pórtăblĕ¹#

3.47. When the phonological markers of phrases and clauses have been established, as in 3.45 and 3.46, we can then proceed to identify the relations of the parts to one another, and to make the syntactic statements. Since the syntax of English by the methods described here has not been completely worked out, and there is no publication detailing the procedures, we shall simply consider a few examples of analysis and the kinds of relationships that exist.

Traditional syntax lets us know in advance that we are concerned both with complete sentences, containing verbs, and with various kinds of fragments or incomplete sentences. It was indicated above (3.33) that in English there is a hierarchy of structure that has verbs and verbal sequences superior to other word classes. So we begin with what are usually called simple declarative sentences.

The first example is:

> *People talk.*
> ^{2}pîypɨl+^{3}tóhk^1#

There is a single clause consisting of a single phrase of two words. We take off the intonation pattern, $\int_1{}^{2\text{-}3\text{-}1}$#, and see that the phrase that is left consists of a noun (we check this by the paradigm *people, people's, peoples, peoples'*), and a verb (paradigm *talk, talks, talked, talking*). The conclusions are noted thus:

> (pîpɨl+tóhk)${}^{2\text{-}3\text{-}1}$#
>   n   v

The phrase superfix is then noted:

> (^+')

Beginning with the verb, we establish that as a FINITE VERBAL, V_F; then, since there is nothing following the verb, we go immediately to the noun, which we call a NOMINAL, N. The nominal is PREVERBAL (symbolized by □), and we have here a construction. We write:

> N □ V

and add a closing symbol to remind us of the presence of the intonation:

> N □ V ◊

The nominal is then identified as a NOMINOID, N, the verbal as a VERBOID, V, and the preverbal position of the nominoid is named the SUBJECT, s; the terminal verboid is the PREDICATOR, p_r. Noting now the intonation as a major one, $\int_1$aće#, the clause, standing alone, is a sentence, a PREDICATION, p_n. The full analysis can be symbolized thus:

A	^{2}pîypɨl+^{3}tóhk^1#		D	(^+'), aće#
B	(pîypɨl+tóhk)${}^{2\text{-}3\text{-}1}$#		E	N □ V_F ◊
C	n v		F	(N s V p_r) p_n

We can give the several lines just above the following descriptive labels: A, the sentence as given us is the DATUM, here presented phonemically (but when first cited given orthographically); then we have the first presyntax line, B, CLAUSE-MARKED (with intonation separated); the second presyntax line, C, is WORD-CLASSED; the next line, D, is the first in syntax, the PHRASAL and CLAUSAL constituent line; line E is the second in syntax, the PHRASAL STRUCTURE line; line F, the third and last in syntax, is that of SENTENCE STRUCTURE. Summarizing, we have:

The datum is presented orthographically and phonemically;
it is clause-marked;
it is word-classed;
phrasal and clausal constituents are identified;
phrasal structure is identified;
clause and sentence structures are identified.

The sentence analyzed is the simplest possible, but represents the most common sentence type in English. Each part of the sentence structure can be expanded; as expansion takes place, the single clause is replaced by at least two clauses, one containing the subject, s, and the other, including the predicator, being now the PREDICATE, p$_t$. Each clause can be further expanded; the subject can contain PRENOMINAL or ADNOMINAL elements, which can become separate clauses, said to be ARRANGED with the nominoid clause; the predicate can contain postverbal elements, COMPLEMENTS of one kind or another, and these can become separate clauses arranged with the verboid; the subject clause is ATTACHED to the predicate.

The following examples show various kinds of constituents and clauses:

a. *The audience paid attention.*
²ðiy+²óhdiyəns² | ²pêyd+ə+³ténšən¹#
(ðiy+óhdiyəns)²⁻²⁻² | (pêyd+ə+ténšən)²⁻³⁻¹#
 d   n   v   n

The word *the* is uninflected, but is identified as the DEFINITE ARTICLE (d) by its structure with /ð→. Continuing, we have:

(˘+'), aće | (^+'), aće#
Dò- N ◇- □Vᴅ △ N ◇

The new symbols mean: D 'definite'; ò- 'prenominal in construct' (the dot indicates construct; a construction would be shown without the dot); ◇- minor terminal; VD 'verb in past'; △ 'postverbal follows'. Next we have:

$$[N(=A.N)s(Vpr \cdot Nc) p_t] p_n$$

The sentence is a predication consisting of a nominoid subject, which itself consists of an ADJUNCT prenominal to a nominoid, and a predicate consisting of a verboid predicator and a nominoid complement.

    b. *The audience paid close attention to the speaker.*

²ðiy+²óhdiyəns² | ²pêyd+klôws+ə+³ténšən² | ²tu+ðə+²spíykər¹#
(ðiy+óhdiyəns)²⁻²⁻² | (pêyd+klôws+ə+ténšən)²⁻³⁻² |
   d   n   v   xᵃ   n

(tu+ðə+spíykər)²⁻²⁻¹#
 x d   n

The symbol x^a means 'uninflected word' identifiable morphemically as an 'adjective'; x means simply 'uninflected' (and morphemically unidentifiable). We continue:

(˘+'), aće | (^+'[^+']), aće | (˘+'[˘+']), aće#
DÒ- N◇-▢} VD△ Ao- N◇-◄{ P ⊻ DÒ- N◇
$[N(= A \cdot N)s(Vp_rN[= A \cdot N]cA[= P \cdot N(= A \cdot N)] c_2) p_t] p_n$

In the next-to-the-last line the middle clause is the main one, with a finite verb in the past (VD), a postverbal adjunctival (A), which is adnominal (o-) to a nominal (N); the last clause is arranged (◄{) to the middle one and consists of a prepositional (P) preposed (⊻) to a definite (D) adnominal (in construct, ò-) to a nominal (N); the first clause consists of a definite (adnominal, in construct, ò-) to a nominal (N). The first clause is preverbal (▢) and is attached (}) to the middle one.

In the last line the first clause is seen as nominoid (N), and consisting of an adjunct (A) and a nominoid, the whole being subject (s). The second clause is a verboid predicator (Vp_r) followed by a nominoid complement (Nc) which itself consists of an adjunct and a nominoid. The third clause is an adjunct (A) serving as second complement (c₂); it consists of a preposition (P) and a nominoid, the latter consisting of an adjunct and a nominoid; the (Vp_rNcA) sequence of these two clauses is the predicate (p_t). The sentence as a whole is a predication (p_n).

Chapter 4

WHAT DOES IT MEAN?

4.0. UTTERANCES AND MEANING

4.00. In the analytical scheme for language that is being followed in this book, there is a rubric, SEMOLOGY (2.01), that covers many of the relations that are said to be treated in traditional "syntax" (3.01). Semology is the aspect of language analysis that deals with the relations of the parts of the substance of language. The substance, which is treated in morphology, consists of distributions of occurrences. The occurrences are the behavior events treated in phonology. The relations, then, embody the classes of the distributions of the occurrences. Semology thus deals with classes, and these classes are units called SEMES. The subdivisions of semology are: SEMEMICS—dealing with the classes of semes, the SEMEMES; OCCURRENCES of sememes; and DISCOURSE, the distribution of the occurrences.

The occurrences are examined by recording the various collocations of items (words, phrases, clauses) that occur in speech. These are then described in terms of their diacritics, the sememes, which are classes. The collocations are further described by their distribution in discourse.

The theory and practice of semological analysis are very new, and there have been few studies in terms of the present frame. (See References and Notes.)

4.01. The reader, confronting the term *semology* for the first time, may wonder why it is needed, when there exist such terms as *semasiology* and *semantics*, the latter being almost a word of everyday usage.

As usually employed, *semantics* refers to meaning in general, and is only a little more technical than the word *meaning* itself. In the special sequence "general semantics" there is reference to an area of communication studies which undertook, some decades ago, to popularize certain useful notions about language and thinking; much good has come out of some of the philosophical and psychological speculations of the "general semanticists", but there has also been some treatment of the area as a kind of cult, good for "what ails you", and it has not become a part of the mainstream of linguistics as an anthropological study.

The term *semasiology* is occasionally found in linguistic works, but has not come to be a regular part of the terminology of the science.

In the traditional use of terms like *semasiology* and *semantics*, the areas covered begin with syntactic structures, and go on to involve the whole relation of language to all the rest of human activity, that is, to what was designated as *metalinguistics* in 2.0. It is necessary then to delimit our term *semology* in respect to such other uses. In semology we are concerned with the LINGUISTIC MEANING of the language. Connotations, exact messages in relation to other activities than talking, emotional reactions and stimuli—all these are outside of the language itself; they are in metalinguistics. But the linguistic structure itself imposes meaningful relations, and it is these we want to look at now.

4.02.   The well-known poem "Jabberwocky" from Lewis Carroll's *Through the looking-glass* will serve to illustrate some of the points made in the preceding section:

> 'Twas brillig, and the slithy toves
> Did gyre and gimble in the wabe:
> All mimsy were the borogoves,
> And the mome raths outgrabe.

It has been pointed out many times that this makes sense. Alice herself says, at the end of the poem, "Somehow it seems to fill my head with ideas—only I don't know exactly what they are!" What Alice meant, in our solemn terms, was that she understood semologically, but that metalinguistically there were not many references she was able to recognize. Let us see why this is so.

The title, *Jabberwocky*, is clearly a phrase, composed of *jabber* and *wocky*. *Jabber* is clear enough, and *wocky*, at least to Americans, suggests *wacky* or *whacky*. As we read further, we learn that there is some kind of dangerous creature around called a *Jabberwock*; this tells us, BECAUSE OF WHAT WE KNOW OF THE STRUCTURE OF THE LANGUAGE, that *Jabberwocky* means "referring to the Jabberwock". The word *brillig* is unusual in its ending, but syntactically it follows a form of *be*, and is a descriptive word of some kind, a postverbal noninflected item; we conjecture that one could say either *brilliger* or *more brillig*, and we decide it is a so-called "predicate adjective"; it may be connected with *brilliant*, and we conclude it refers to the weather or the sunshine, or the like. The *slithy toves* are obviously unpleasant creatures; what a *tove* is we don't know, but there are several of them (because of the plural ending); they are described in a phrase that must be read with the superfix ʃ ^+', regular for the "adjective-noun" sequence. The "adjective" itself has the prefix *sl-*, the bound base ✓.ayð-, and the postbase *-y*; we think of *slide* or *slime* and *writhe*, and decide that toves must move something like snakes, only more unpleasantly! (Lewis Carroll himself tells us, in the Preface to *The Hunting of the Snark*, that *slithy* is pronounced with /ay/, as in *writhe*; also, that *toves* rimes with *groves*, and that *borogoves* begins like *borrow*.) In the next line, we have *gyre* and *gimble*; the first is perhaps /ǰáy(ə)r/, but is the second /ǰímbil/ or /gímbil/? We could decide that it is /ǰímbil/ because the language "likes" alliterative sequences; but Lewis Carroll, speaking through Humpty-Dumpty, says it's /gímbil/, as in *gimlet*; so *gyre* must be /gáyər/. These are obviously verbs, after *did*; *to gyre* must be something like a *tove*-ish version of the twist; while *gimble* may be something like *gambol* (so it is /g-/ and not /ǰ-/!). A *wabe* must be some sort of place, where *toves* have their habitat. The *borogoves* (stress must be ✓́ ˇˇ) are again some type of strange animal, and their description as *mimsy* (cf. *flimsy*?) does not endear them to us. As for *raths*, they are still another animal, they are *mome*, an unpleasant quality, we may be sure, and they do something called *outgribbing*, if we may form *outgrib* from *outgrabe* on the analogy of *give* and *gave*. (Or should we use the analogy of *speak* and *spake* for its archaic flavor, and get *outgreab*? Or perhaps *outgrub*—cf. *come, came*—is even better.)

   In the second stanza of *Jabberwocky* we are told about the *Jubjub* bird and the *frumious Bandersnatch*. This latter must be a dangerous creature; *-snatch* 'one who or that which snatches'; *bander-* tells us either what the snatch snatches, or the kind of snatch he is; moreover, he is *frumious*, which might mean 'possessed of or exercising *frumy*', if we compare with *fury, furious*; but Lewis Carroll tells us, again in the Preface to *The Hunting of the Snark*, that *frumious* is from *fuming* and *furious*: "Make up your mind that you will say both words ... If your thoughts incline ever so little towards 'fuming', you will say 'fuming-furious'; if they turn ... towards 'furious', you will say 'furious-fuming'; but if you have that rarest of gifts, a perfectly balanced mind, you will say 'frumious'".

In the third stanza the protagonist takes his *vorpal* sword (cf. *voracious, lethal,* possibly *supple*), and seeks the *manxome* foe (*handsome* but *manic?*). We also have a *Tumtum* tree; this, like the *Jubjub* bird, must be exotic somehow.

The next stanza may be cited in full:

> And, as in uffish thought he stood,
> The Jabberwock, with eyes of flame,
> Came whiffling through the tulgey wood,
> And burbled as it came!

Our hero can't feel complimented by such a term as *uffish*; we think of *oaf* and *foolish*, there being few other models. But the *Jabberwock* can't be too terrible, either, for it came *whiffling*, and it *burbled*. (The present author's family dialect has *burble* as a term for noises made by babies—a portmanteau of *burp* and *gurgle*.) The wood wasn't too pleasant, however, being *tulgey*.

In the next stanza the *vorpal* blade goes *snicker-snack*, and the hero goes *galumphing* back. These terms are almost normal usage, and they are definitely not suggestive of heroic actions. After this, the hero is welcomed as "my *beamish* boy", and the day is called *frabjous*. We conclude that the boy beams with pride, or maybe it's his welcomer who beams. The day is perhaps fabulous, or joyous, or similarly notable.

The serious dissection we have performed on a delightful piece of nonsense is a mixture of several kinds of analysis. There is recognition of morphemic structure, of syntactic relations, of semological grouping, and of metalinguistic reference. The reader or hearer of such a passage regularly performs ALL these activities, because as a speaker of the language and a member of the culture he knows all the things involved, and carries on his cultural interaction on all necessary levels at the same time. The linguistic analyst who wishes to get at the structure of linguistic meaning— the semology—must untangle the different things that are happening. This we shall now do.

4.03. The analysis of the title of the poem, *Jabberwocky*, started with recognition of the first part as a known word of the language, and a guess, by phonemic resemblance, at the rest of it. The way in which English spelling regularly functions is what made us read the item as a phrase, /jǽbər+wàkiy/, and analyze it as we did. As soon as we discovered that there was something called a *Jabberwock* we discarded the first attempt at analyzing *-wocky* as somehow like *w(h)acky*, and replaced it by the decision that *-y* is probably the postbase found in *crazy, sunny, woody, sunshiny*, so that the analysis is *jabberwock-y*. Already at this point we can note that the poem is stylistically special, titles like this being unusual. What a *wock* is, or, for that matter, a *jabberwock*, remains unknown, but there is now no question that *wock* is a noun; semologically, nouns may indicate agents, receivers of action, abstract behavior patterns, and other referents, and this one seems to deal with a unit agent or receiver of action, which is animate.

As we went on, we noted various nouns, some possible adjectival words, some verbs, and additional phrases of various kinds. Some of the items, as *slithy*, suggested the presence of prefixes. By the time we came to the end of the poem, the semological classes of the unknown words and of the phrases consisting wholly or partly of unknown items were so well established that all kinds of metalinguistic conclusions were inevitable. Connecting *brillig* with *brilliant* starts from morphemics and syntax; it then suggests a semological class of items connected with the base *brill-*; and then we come to the metalinguistic guess that the state of the weather is involved. When we decided to see the prefix *sl-* in *slithy*, we also decided on the semology that includes *slide, slip, slimy*, and other items; the decision about the obvious unpleasantness of *slithy* is a metalinguistic one, however.

The reader should, at this point, review the comments made above on the various words and phrases involved, and see for himself the phonological, morphemic, and syntactic features that lead to semological conclusions, and delineate the latter from the further metalinguistic responses. The exercise will prepare him for the more technical consideration of how syntax and semology are separated.

4.1. SYNTAX AND SEMOLOGY

4.10 In the discussion of syntax (3.3–3.33; 3.45–3.47) certain categories were arrived at. First of all we established phrases on a phonological basis, and then intonation patterns, tying phrases into clauses and sentences. It was indicated that many phrases constitute what are usually called "compound words" or "compounds". Here we can point out a first difference between syntax and semology. In English, a word like *kitchen* and a phrase like *bedroom* have identical syntactic functions as nominals, but they have different syntactic structures; they also can be shown to have similar semological structure, going with other terms dealing with the description of parts of a house; metalinguistically, they are quite different in their relation to the rest of the culture and in the activities carried on in them.

The phrases that are the so-called compounds are not only interesting in themselves in terms of being semologically like words, but can also be examined for the semological relations of the parts: in *bedroom* the relation is something like 'object contained' to 'place'; in *headroom* it is 'object for which' there is 'space'; in *living room* it is 'activity carried on' in a 'place'; syntactically these three are all alike, phrases with the superfix ʃ '+` (though *headroom* may be said with ʃ '+^), and they are all nominals. Semologically they are all concerned with allocation of space, two of them deal with the parts of a house, but the internal relations within the phrases are quite different. The interest of this discussion stems from the fact that all three phrases contain as their second part (what is often traditionally called the "head") the word *room*.

The kinds of structures just discussed for English are very common in the world's languages. But there are some languages which do not have "compounds", or which only form a few special kinds. In modern French, for instance, there are many compounds of Latin origin, with special morphophonic and morphemic characteristics, but only a very few are newly formed from existing native material: *abat-jour* 'lampshade' (*abat* 'decreases', *jour* 'day, light'); *passetemps* 'pastime' (the English is a translation loan from the French) (*passe* 'passes', *temps* 'time'); *porteplume* 'fountain pen' (*porte-* 'carry', *plume* 'pen'; here the semology is different from the previous examples). Very interesting contrasts in semological structures can be seen to result from study of such differences. The metalinguistic worlds of French and English are much alike; but their semologies show some striking differences.

The discussion of syntax also established such terms as *verbal, nominal,* and *verboid, nominoid; subject, predication; preverbal, postverbal, adnominal, adjunctival; predicator, predicate, complement.* These terms are for English, and analogous ones are established for other languages. Such distinctions as *construct* and *construction* may well be of importance in many languages, as may also be the difference between *arranged* and *attached* clauses.

As was stated at the end of 3.33, the intonation patterns (and their analogs) are beyond syntax, in the semology. But within the syntactic structures themselves semological differences are found, as has already been exemplified above for English compounds; and there are also instances where syntactic and semological structures simply do not correspond directly.

4.11. Semology, as defined here, has been indicated to be a new and as yet relatively unexplored area of linguistics. A few examples of semological structures will have to suffice, therefore.

It is a well-established notion in traditional English syntax that there are direct objects and indirect objects. In the sentences

John gave Bill money.
John told Bill a story.
He gave me it.

and the like, everyone "knows" that *Bill* and *me* are "indirect objects" and *money, story, it* are "direct objects". Syntactically, we can see only that there are some verbs that can be followed by two nominal or pronominal complements. What is the objection, it may be asked, to calling the first of these the "indirect object" and the second the "direct object" on the syntax level? There would be none if these were the only kinds of instances of the sort. But consider these sentences:

He gave it me.
John made Bill captain.
John called Bill a name.

In the first example "direct" and "indirect" objects are reversed; it is true that this structure is now uncommon (indeed, it is absent from American usage), but no one has any difficulty knowing what it "means". The next two examples show syntactic structures exactly parallel to the examples cited above for two complements, but the first complement is certainly the "direct" object, and the second is just as certainly not an "indirect" object. These two sentences are examples of the so-called "object complement"—a sort of second "direct object". It is clear that the differences between the three examples first given and these last three do not stem from anything in the phonologically marked phrases or in the morphemics of the words; that is, the differences are not syntactic. The differences arise from the specific verbs or nouns or pronouns used and the order in which they appear. In other words, the differences are semological. Such notions as "direct object", "indirect object", and "object complement" are semological categories.

Another firmly established notion in traditional English grammar (though this one is a much newer tradition than the previous one) is that of "mass" and "count" nouns. Such words as *milk, water, wine* are "mass" nouns; such others as *boy, man, house* are "count" nouns. "Mass" nouns are said not to occur with the indefinite article *a, an,* or the numerals. "Count" nouns, on the other hand, don't occur without the indefinite article or a numeral. Let us look at the actual evidence.

Examples of "mass" nouns are:

> *Milk is good for you.*
> *Water is necessary for life.*
> *Wine is a favorite drink in France.*

Examples of "count" nouns are:

> *A boy soon grows into a man.*
> *A house on a hill is a good thing to have.*

So far, so good. But now consider these sentences:

> *A milk apiece was all they had.*
> *A water without minerals is to be preferred.*
> *A wine I like is Liebfraumilch.*
> *There's a lot of boy in every man.*
> *That's quite a hunk of man.*
> *That's too much house for them.*

In these last examples, *milk, water, wine* are now "count" nouns, while *boy, man, house* are "mass" nouns.

It thus becomes clear that the categories of "mass" and "count" nouns in English are not syntactic, but are semological. In fact, they are not categories of nouns at all, but categories based on phrases with or without the indefinite article and certain other words. The semological categories stem from the presence of the article or its absence, and the particular collocations of nouns used.

As was indicated at the end of 3.33, the intonation patterns of English are grammatically significant in the semology, and not in syntax. It is probable that analogous clause- and sentence-closing phenomena in other languages have analogous functions.

The following sentences differ in intonation patterns:

> ²Thât's ă nîce nêw ³hóuse¹#
> ²Thât's ă nîce nêw ³hóuse²|
> ²Thât's ă nîce nêw ³hóuse²||
> ²Thât's ă nîce nêw ³hóuse³||

The first one is an ordinary statement. The second is an assertion that implies that there is more to come, that the comment is not complete. The third is like the second, but also involves contrast, and definite disapproval. The fourth is a question (an echo question). Syntactically all four sentences are alike—all the syntactic categories to be extracted from the phrasing being completely the same. The different meanings come from the intonation, and these meanings are semological. Categories like "statement", "assertion implying further comment", "assertion implying contrast", "question" are semological categories. The last is especially interesting in this connection.

Traditional grammar speaks of questions, interrogative pronouns, and so on. Words like *who, what,* etc. are indeed question words, but only in the appropriate semological setting, including intonation. In some languages questions are indicated by special morphemes, but in English a question is neither morphemic nor syntactic (inverted order occurs in nonquestions too), but semological.

A phenomenon like the shift of stress for emphasis is even beyond semology in English. Syntactically the sentences

    Ì wênt hóme.
    Ì wént hôme.
    Í wênt hôme.

are of the same over-all structure, though the phrases are differently arrived at:

    Ì+′(wênt+hóme).
    Ì+′(wént+hôme).
    Í+^(wênt+hóme).

In the first two, the phrase superfixes in the verb-complement sequence differ, though the final phrase is the same. In the third, the final phrase is different. The selection of these superfixes is something done in the mind of the speaker, we may say. The resulting differences are like the difference between talking about *black* and talking about *white.* Such differing selections belong in the metalinguistic area, and are not in the microlinguistic analysis at all.

It would be interesting to give semological examples from languages other than English; but not only have no appropriate studies been made, but it also would be necessary to give the reader an elaborate introduction and many preliminary data if he were to get anything out of it at all.

4.2. LINGUISTIC STRUCTURE AND THE OUTSIDE WORLD

4.20. When it was said (1.23) that language has sound, shape, and sense, the last characteristic implied that language and languages were in some sort of relation to the outside world, the world of reality. This implication not only makes sense, it is also common sense. Language is used to talk about the world, and we become aware of what we call the reality of the world we live in by means of language. It would seem, at first glance, that this is self-evident, and that it does not need extensive discussion. There are some implications, however, that can lead to dangerous misconceptions.

As soon as the users of any language begin to philosophize about the universe, they find that their language somehow does not correspond point for point with the world they live in. They then develop a logic, which is a series of linguistic statements aiming at an explanation of the lack of exact correspondence. If they discover other languages, they find that those, like their own, also do not correspond to the universe point for point; but, and more serious for philosophy and logic, the other languages do not correspond to their own language. Depending on the relative prestige of the languages (a metalinguistic matter), the logic is either expanded to take care of the differences, or the other languages are labeled "inferior" or "inexact" or "primitive", or by some other derogatory term.

When a modern linguistic analysis of a language has been made, it becomes clear that the language presents, in its semology, a unique basis for talking about the world its speakers live in, and that this basis is deeply involved with the details of the linguistic structure— not only the semological structure, but other structures as well. From this it follows that every language has its own logic, that every such logic, stemming from the structure of the language, presents a unique view of reality, and that there are few if any universal logical statements or appraisals of reality.

How then can one get at reality? Or, for that matter, what is reality?

The linguist answers these questions as follows: By examining and analyzing all the available levels of structure of a language, one gets at the reality that the speakers of that language are aware of. And by doing this, one arrives at the conclusion that reality is different for the speakers of each different language, and that no statement of a reality can be made without taking account of the linguistic structures being used. It follows further that there is no such thing as a universally valid logic, because a logic is a statement in a particular language of the particular relation of that language to the reality of which its speakers are aware.

The examples from different linguistic structures in the next section will make these conclusions more meaningful.

4.21.   The morphemic analysis of English showed that there is a class of words, nouns, which distinguish forms conventionally called

singular and plural (3.41). The definition of the class is based in part
on this distinction, and when we come to syntax (3.47) we find that
such structures as those of agreement (*It is* but *They are*) confirm
the dichotomy and extend it to higher levels. In the realm of semology also the singular-plural distinction is valid and important.
Speakers of English, whenever they use a word that is morphemically
a noun, MUST specify whether it is singular or plural: one has to say
boy if *one* or *a* precedes and *talks* follows; *boys* if *two* or *many* precedes,
and *talk* follows. This morphemic necessity and its syntactic corol-
laries lead to the semological possibility of pluralizing an abstraction,
such as *democracy*, and saying *The democracies of the United States
and of the Soviet Union are very different from each other.* We are also
led into the logical redundancy of indicating semological plurality
in several ways in a single sequence: *Two boys were running* has a
numeral that "means" more than one, it has the plural morpheme
indicated by the final *s* of *boys*, and it has the form *were* used with
plural subjects. All languages have such redundancies, however, and,
in fact, the large amount of redundancy in all cultural activity aids
in the process of communication. But our point is that whether we
are "logically aware" of redundancies or are not, there is nothing
we can do about them: the linguistic system requires them. In
English all aspects of the culture that can be referred to by nouns
or nominal phrases must, by virtue of that fact alone, be categorized
as singular or plural.

Let us look now at the nouns of the Taos language. The investigator,
starting from his own categories, asks for singulars and plurals, and
seems to get them. The word for 'mother' is *kána*; in response to the
question "How do you say more than one mother?" the reply is
kánemą; 'ax' is *kwóna*, 'axes' *kwóne*; 'eye' is *cínemą*, 'eyes' *cíne*. This
looks a little suspicious right from the start, and is complicated by
such instances as these: *p'ǫ́'óne* means 'water', but also 'rivers' as
the "plural" of *p'ǫ́'óna* 'river'; about *thǫ́na* 'house' it is said that it
does not have a separate plural, but *thǫ́nemą* means 'cover, shelter,
tipi', and has a "plural" *thǫ́ne*. In cross-reference in verb forms
further categories come out: *kána, mų́* means 'The mother saw it';
kánemą can be used with *'ąnmų́* and the phrase means 'The mothers
[the two of them] saw it'; or with *'imų́*, and then the phrase means
'The mothers [more than two of them] saw it'; the 'it' in each case
refers necessarily to a noun like *kána* itself (being then translated
her in English) or to a noun like *kwóna*. To say 'The mother(s) [one;
two; more than two] saw it [the house] or them [the houses]' the
sentences are: *kána, nąmų́*; *kánemą, 'ąnnąmų́*; *kánemą, 'inąmų́*. If

the "object" is *kwóne* 'axes', the verb forms are: *'ąwmų́*, *'ąnąwmų́*, *'iwmų́*. If the object is a word like *kánemą*, say *'ų́'únemą* 'sons, children', then 'saw them' is *'imų́*, *'ąpęnmų́*, *'ipimų́*. And, interestingly enough, if the object is a word like *cínemą* 'eye', the forms are the same as the last three cited. Clearly enough, whatever the confusion created by the forms as cited, the Taos notions of singular and plural do not coincide with those of English. On analysis of all the evidence, an entirely different categorization results. A Taos speaker must categorize a noun as "unitary" (*-na*), or "a set" (*-nemą*), or "an aggregate" (*-ne*); in referring to it as a verb object, by means of prefix complexes before the verb stem, he must categorize it as one of these three classes, or as one of the hidden (covert) class of "local" nouns like *thóna*. In the same prefixes the subject noun is referred to not by its class but by a threefold number division—"singular" if *-na*, "dual" or "plural" if *-nemą*. The relation of the noun classes to the number categories is semologically very special, and involves further reference, to the outside world (that is, the relation is partly metalinguistic). Nouns ending in *-na* are always singular: if they designate a person or an animal, then there also exists—with the same stem—a noun in *-nemą* (or *-ną*) referred to, when a subject, as dual or plural (another metalinguistic relation); nouns in *-na* that refer to inanimate objects have an accompanying form in *-ne*, and never occur as subjects, so that singular, dual, or plural reference to them is never specified except by numerals or quantity words; as objects, the nouns in *-na* are of the unitary class, and the accompanying noun in *-ne* is of the aggregate class. Further, the inanimate nouns in *-nemą* (or *-ną*) also have an accompanying form in *-ne*; the *-nemą* (or *-ną*) noun may be specified as singular in counting, and the *-ne* form as "more than one"; these also do not occur as subjects, but are either sets or aggregates when objects.

In the linguistic universe of speakers of English, the distinction between one and more than one seems simple and clear-cut (at least at first glance), and fits in well with such philosophical distinctions as the One and the Many. But in the Taos linguistic universe there is no such simple distinction: some things are indeed unitary, and others are multiple, but some unitary things can be multiple only in sets, while others are multiple as aggregates; moreover, a set can be unitary, if it is inanimate, or it can be multiple—but then only if it is animate; and there are aggregates which are uncountable, and units which cannot become multiple. Besides all this, there is cross-referencing in terms of being single, paired, or three or more.

Another example of different analysis of related notions may be taken again from English and Taos. In English, a verb like *dance* may have derived from it an agent noun *dancer* and an action noun *dancing*; the plural *dancers* is automatically formed, and there are situations in which the plural *dancings* might occur. In Taos the verb 'to dance' has the name form *t'ǫ́* 'he danced'; nouns derived from its stative stem *tò-* are *tò'óna* 'dancer', *tò'ónemą* 'dancers', *tò'óne* 'dancing'; the first is a unitary noun, with a set noun as its "plural", and the third is an aggregate noun, but is not plural and has no unitary singular. The English nouns are derived from the verb, one by the postbase *-er*, the other by nominalization of the inflected form containing the suffix *-ing*. The Taos affixes in the three items here considered may be called inflectional suffixes because they are cross-referenced to inflectional prefixes in certain constructions; but even if we called them derivational postbases, their relation to one another and to the verb base is semologically entirely different from the relations of the English words to one another. It is only in the metalinguistics that the two languages come at all close, and even there we find that the noun designating the action can be singular or plural in one language but can only be a nonnumberable abstraction in the other.

4.22. It is not necessary to go to languages as far apart as English and Taos, nor to the details of grammatical structure, as we have just done, to find instances of different analyses of the universe. English and Russian are fairly closely related languages. In English we *pour* both water and sand; in Russian one uses the verb *litĭ* /ljítj/ to say 'pour' of liquids, but the verb *sypatĭ* /sípatj/ of sand and other granular substances; this latter verb is actually cognate (see 6.1) with English *sift*. English and German are even more closely related. In English we *go*, on foot or by a vehicle; in German one uses *gehen* /géyen/ of going on foot, or being in motion in a general way, but *fahren* /fáhren/ of going for a ride or a drive; *fahren* is cognate with English *to fare* meaning 'to get along' (but compare the noun *fare* 'the cost of transportation'). English and French are more distantly related than English and Russian, but have had extensive cultural contacts in the last 900 years; yet in English we *know* people and facts, and *know how* to do things, while in French one uses *connaître* of knowing people and *savoir* of knowing facts or knowing how to do things; *savoir* has no English cognate (except the recent borrowing from Spanish, *savvy*), but *connaître* comes from Latin *cognoscere*, in which the *-gno-* is the cognate of *know*. In these examples areas of meaning have been differently distributed among words, and some of what were originally the same words have been differently distributed among meanings.

Another very widespread example of different metalinguistic analysis is in the area of color words. In English the basic color words are *red, yellow, green, blue*. Many of the modern languages of Europe have essentially the same system. French has *rouge* /ružə/, *jaune* /žoənə/, *vert* /veərə/, *bleu* /blø/; German has *rot* /rówt/, *gelb* /gélp/, *grün* /grüwn/, *blau* /bláw/; Russian has *krasnyi* /krásniy/, *žoltyi* /žóltiy/, *zelěnyi* /zjiljóniy/, *sinii* /sjínjiy/. But in Spanish *rojo* /róxo/ is not exactly 'red', for *rubio* /rúbyo/ and *colorado* /kolořádo/ are also used in this meaning; *amarillo* /amaříḷo/ is 'yellow' but with a brownish tinge; *verde* /bérde/ is 'green'; and *azul* /aθúl/ includes in its meanings that of our *azure* (with which it is cognate). In many other languages, however, the basic division of color is into three parts: 'red' (possibly extending a little into the kind of orange color we could call yellowish red), 'yellow' (extending a little into the greenish yellow), and all the rest—'green plus blue'. Many American Indian languages have this system; Taos says *pháywi* 'red', *c'úlwi* 'yellow', *cáḷwi* 'green-blue'. Asked how he would distinguish the color of the sky from that of the grass, a Taos Indian would say, "The sky is sky-*cáḷwi*", "The grass is leaf-*cáḷwi*"—as we might say *sky-blue* and *grass-green*. Physiological perception is clearly the same, but cultural classification is different. If the Taos wrote poetry, their imagery about skies and mountain meadows would have to be quite different from ours as regards colors at least.

4.23. As Western culture spreads over the world, and its several subdivisions become more alike technologically, the metalinguistic analyses of the universe become more and more alike, though the semologies of languages remain widely divergent in their structures. What happens is that equivalent terms are devised, so that intercommunication may take place with mutual intelligibility. Color terms, for instance, are expanded into a vast array of special words, each technically defined (by light waves or some other standard). Machines and their products get equivalent names. Government structures are made analogous, and the names applied to them are equated. But these processes of mutual accommodation, so to speak, are beset with numerous difficulties, because of the different linguistic structures with which they must operate, and the more so because in most cases the linguistic structures, especially at the semological level, are largely unanalyzed, and the cultural systems other than the language are at best known in skimpy ethnographic form.

In the remaining sections of this chapter we shall look at the expansion of vocabulary that occurs when languages take words from each other for new notions (4.3), how vocabularies are studied and recorded (4.4), and how equivalences between languages are established (4.5).

4.3. LOANWORDS

4.30. Whenever people who speak one language come into contact with others speaking a different language, there occurs the phenomenon of exchange of words and expressions for artifacts and notions new to one or the other of the groups in contact. In the technical language of linguistics this phenomenon is known as BORROWING, and the resulting terms are called LOANWORDS, or loans. The implication of such a terminology is that the "borrowed" items remain somehow apart from the main body of a language, and continue to exhibit their foreignness and apartness. Modern linguistics knows that this is not true except in some cases, and then only in special technical ways. But the terms *borrowing* and *loans* continue to be used.

The phenomena of borrowing have existed ever since the invention of language (1.12). If this invention took place only once, the learning of language by groups other than the inventors was a wholesale process of borrowing—sounds, words, sentences, structures, meanings. If language was invented more than once, every time two groups of speakers came in contact there was linguistic borrowing. The process has been going on ever since, and every language has elements—not only words, but whole structures—that have been taken over from other languages. If it were possible to recognize all the borrowed elements in a language, one would be able to tell its history in great detail. We shall examine some known examples of borrowing and draw some general conclusions from them.

4.31. Human beings are always thinking up new ways of doing things, new artifacts, new resultant behaviors and attitudes. Ways must be found of talking about these new things. Every language has ways of forming new words and expressions, and uses them constantly. When the new thing is something that some other group of people has invented, one way to name it is simply to take over the other people's term for it, that is, to "borrow" it. Most languages borrow terms readily, but there are some real differences in the ease with which this is done. These differences depend in large part on the structures of the languages involved: if the structures are similar, borrowing is easy; if dissimilar, it is difficult.

English and French are related languages, and have structures that are basically similar. When the Normans conquered England in 1066, it was relatively easy for Norman French words to be taken into English. The governmental structure of England was destroyed at that time and replaced by a different structure; the whole society was disturbed, and speakers of English found themselves displaced downward in the social hierarchy by the imposition of several layers of French speakers over them. To communicate with the French-speaking rulers, the English had to learn some French. The French, to communicate with their subjects, had to adapt their French language in various ways.

Thus it came about that English speakers had to learn that the French-controlled armed forces were an *army* (from *armée*), and not a *hera*; sheep were still *sheep*, but their flesh was called *mutton* (< *mouton*); calves were *calves*, but their flesh was *veal* (modern French *veau*); the flesh of cattle was now *beef* (< *boeuf*), that of pigs was *pork* (< *porc*). From these instances it is clear that the French overlords ate better than their subjects, and controlled what was produced in the way of meat. The French not only ate better, they lived better: their homes were *castles* (Norman French *castel*, modern French *château* < older *chasteau* < *chaste(a)l*), and the lords and ladies of the castles were addressed as *sir* (< *sieur*, cf. *monsieur* originally 'my lord') and *dame*; the castles were on *estates* (*estat*, modern *état*); the animals on the estate were principally *cattle* (Norman French *cattel* < Latin *capital* 'capital, property'), and some of the other items owned were *chattels* (the same word in a Parisian French form); people still *talked* and *spoke*, but they *addressed* their betters (< *addresser*, < (late) Latin *addirectiare* 'to direct [oneself] toward'). Time was now divided not only into *morning* and *evening*, and *day* and *night*, but technically into *hours* (< *heures*); and *space* was something different from *room*. But the directions in space, or at sea, remained *north, east, south,* and *west,* and came to be so named by the French and other peoples of northern and western Europe (modern French *nord* /nor/, *est* /est/, *sud* /sud/, *ouest* /west/). Learning now took place in a *school* (< Old French *escole*, modern *école*), and the teacher was a *master* (from a form with a different vowel nucleus from that in Parisian French—old *maistre*, modern *maître*).

The bulk of the population spoke the English *tongue*, but French was a *language*; after a while, English also was called a language, and the use of *tongue* in the meaning 'language' became poetic and unusual. All kinds of new artifacts were introduced by the French, and thousands of words for them came into the language: *table, chair, fork, collar, button, cap, chimney* are but a few examples. *Labor* was different from *work*, and *leisure* and *rest* (modern French *rester* means to 'remain, stay put, be inactive') were apparently practiced much more by French speakers than by English ones. *Music, art, literature* were new words for new organizations of activity (these last are actually LEARNED loanwords—see below). Kinship was restated in terms of the new social order: father and mother were, together, *parents*; their brothers and sisters became *uncles* and *aunts* (the Old English word for 'uncle' survives in the name *Eames*, cognate with German *Oheim* 'uncle'); certain kinds of relatives came to be known by the general term *cousin*; for two generations back from parents and two down from children the term *great* was used, but the parents' parents and the children's children were *grand*parents and *grand*children. The last term shows an interesting phenomenon of borrowing, change and adaptation in the new language: in French one says *grandpère* 'grandfather', literally 'big-father', and *petitfils* /pətifis/ 'grandson', literally 'little-son'; but in English only the *grand* was borrowed, and it was then extended to ascending and descending generations; moreover, it was then translated into 'great' and used for the further generations in both directions (this is LOAN TRANSLATION—see below). In government, law, and religion, the older English vocabulary was replaced by a new and expanded one from French: *rulers reigned* and had *subjects*; *judges, juries* dealt with *crime* and *criminals*, and even in America there are still courts of *oyer* and *terminer* ('hear' and 'decide, finish', and court sessions are announced by the command *oyez* [usually now pronounced /óyèz/] 'hear ye'); Old English *inwit*, 'inner knowledge' became *conscience*, and the holy ones were now called *saints*. We could continue this cataloging, and easily show that there is no vocabulary area in modern English that does not have large numbers of words of French origin.

Before the Norman conquest English had borrowed words from other languages. Some were from Latin, and may well have come into the common West Germanic spoken in what is now Germany before the English came to England; *wine, bishop, cheap* are examples; *cheap* has more of its original meaning in the London area known as *Cheapside*—an old marketplace; the word is originally from Latin *caupō* 'itinerant merchant' who followed the armies. Other Old English words undoubtedly came in from the Celtic languages of the inhabitants of England who preceded the English, but these were few, since the Celtic speakers largely fled (to Wales and Scotland, and across the Channel to Brittany). The Danes contributed some words too; one very interesting group are the modern personal pronouns: none of these correspond too well to the Old English forms, and some do not fit at all; Old English *ic* should have become something like /íč/ (or /íj/), and not *I* (modern Danish has /yǽy/); the Old English words for *he, she, they* all began with *h-* and would probably all have become /híy/, but instead the Danish forms were adopted for at least the feminine and the plural. Here is a case where a closely similar language provided words that continued an important grammatical distinction that might otherwise have been lost.

All the languages of modern Europe have many of the same kinds of loanwords as does English, though none has the heavy concentration of the particular kind of eleventh- and twelfth-century French that English has. At least one European language, Albanian, shows an even greater influx of foreign vocabulary than does English: speakers of Latin were so prevalent in the Illyrian-speaking area east of the Adriatic that the one group of Illyrians that survives—the Albanians—has retained only the basic structure and some vocabulary items of the old language, and uses words of Latin origin for nearly everything else.

4.32.   In all the languages of Europe a very important area of loanwords are the LEARNED (pronounced /lə́hrnid/) LOANS. These are technical words in all spheres—technology, religion, social structure, government, etc.—taken directly from Latin or from a Latin form of Greek, and introduced into the language with little modification. In the present paragraph the words *important, area, technical, spheres, technology, religion, social, structure, directly, Latin, introduced, modification, present, paragraph* are learned loanwords. Nearly all of these will be found in very similar form in most of the languages of Europe, as the following lists illustrate:

ENGLISH	FRENCH	SPANISH	GERMAN	RUSSIAN
important	*important*	*importante*		
area	*aire*	*área*		
technical	*technique*	*técnico*	*technisch*	*texnika* "technics"
sphere	*sphère*	*esfera*	*Sphäre*	*sfera*
technology	*technologie*	*tecnología*	*Technologie*	*texnologiä*
religion	*religion*	*religión*	*Religion*	*religiä*
social	*social*	*social*	*sozial*	*social'*nyi̥
structure	*structure*	*estructura*	*Struktur*	*struktura*

ENGLISH	FRENCH	SPANISH	GERMAN	RUSSIAN
directly	directe(ment)	derecho	direkt	
		"right"		
Latin	latin	latino	Latein	latinskii̯
introduced	introduite	introducido	introduziert	
modification	modification	modificación	Modifikazion	modifikaciä
present	présent	presente	präsent	
paragraph	paragraphe	párrafo	Paragraph	

Learned loans, as can be seen, are most often literary creations. They were used by someone who was literate in Latin, and were usually pronounced, at first, by reading the letters, rather than by imitating some speaker; this is especially true of French and Spanish, and to a large extent of German. In England, many learned words were taken from French and were heard as well as read. In Russian the learned words of the type listed are mostly modern introductions, created by transliterating German or other European forms into the cyrillic alphabet and then modifying the endings.

In the modern languages that are used as literary and official languages most new loanwords are essentially learned loans, because they are brought in by literate persons into the written language, and are pronounced in accordance with the spelling rules of this borrowing language. This is especially true of the languages that have only recently become official languages; in these, new loan-words are often introduced wholesale by commissions specially appointed for the purpose. The results are sometimes startling, as when the name *Iroquois* was adopted into Indonesian in recent years in the form *irok*; evidently somebody knew that *-ois* /wa/ was a French suffix (*chinois* 'Chinese', etc.), and decided to leave it off, not realizing that the word in question was a seventeenth-century spelling of a (probably) Algonkian name ending in /we/ or /wa/—cf. *Ojibway* or *Ojibwa*.

In many instances learned loans are disguised by being trans-lated into seemingly native material. When the telephone was in-vented the Germans took over the name as *Telephon* /tèlefówn/, but someone also invented the term *Fernsprecher* /férn+šprèxer/, literally "far-speaker", and this latter term is more widely used than the loan term. Fashions differ at different epochs about this matter: eighteenth-century German took over many learned loans, but nineteenth-century German preferred loan translations. English usually prefers the learned loans, but sometimes has both: *folklore* COULD mean the same as *ethnology*, but doesn't. In German there is *Linguistik* /liŋg-vístiyk/ 'linguistics', but also *Sprachwissenschaft* /špráhx+vĭsen+šàft/

(literally, 'speech-knowledge' [Wissenschaft 'knowing-hood']); Russian followed the German model and has *lingvistika* /ljingvjístjika/ and *äzykoznanie* /yazika+znánjiya/; in both of these cases, the two terms are virtually equivalent. Even within a language there may be borrowing of technical terms between dialects; American *zipper* is not unknown elsewhere in the English-speaking world, but *lightning fastener* is the technical term there; this was loan-translated into French as *fermeture-éclair* 'lightning closure' (the French word order is the reverse of the English, however); in German we have *Reiß-verschluß* /ráys+fer+šlùs/, where *Reiß-* is either 'draw' or 'rip', and *Verschluß* is 'closure'; Russian took this German phrase over as a technical loan, despite a resulting real phonemic cumbersomeness: rejsferšlüs /rjiysf(j)iršljús/.

Loan translation is not limited to literary languages. In some cases the structure of a language is such that ordinary loans are difficult to introduce. Navaho is such a language; there are very few loans from the adjacent Spanish or English, and the few that there are get restructured, so to speak. Spanish *americano* 'American' (in the United States sense) has become *bilagaana*; Navaho has few instances of /m/, so /b/ replaced it and the whole first part of the word was restructured into *bi-*, a common prefix meaning 'his', so that the word now means to a Navaho something like 'his *lagaana*', whatever *lagaana* may be! (For discussion of phonemic replacement and morphemic reanalysis, see 4.33). In the face of such pressure from its system, Navaho resorts to loan translation—*'adeii hooghan* 'upper house' = 'U.S. Senate', or even more to paraphrase: *'atah naaltsoos 'ahénil* 'I voted', literally, 'I was among those who put in papers'.

4.33. The process of taking over loans from one language to another—whether directly as words or phrases, or by loan translation, or by paraphrasing—always involves a degree of bilingualism on the part of a few speakers, at least. Someone knowing the term in another language must use it, in or outside of awareness, in his own language, and it must be heard by others who also in some way know the term; or else the introducer must explain or gloss the new term, often, in the process, devising a loan translation or paraphrase which may replace the loan term itself.

When these processes take place, there is always some departure from the original, in the phonology, in the morphology, in the semology; and in the metalinguistics. The first loanword noted above (4.31) was the English *army*. In Norman French the word was probably something like /arméhe/ phonemically, and we can

reconstruct the phonetics as, perhaps, [ærmˈɛ·ǝ̇ɛ̇]. This could come
into the English of the twelfth century as /arméh/ [armˈɛǝ]; the
complex nucleus /eh/ soon became /ih/, and the stress shifted to the
first syllable: /ármih/; like Middle English /ih/ in other positions, the
final one became /iy/ eventually, giving Early Modern /ǽrmiy/,
resulting in American /ármiy/ or /áhrmiy/, Southern British /áh(r)mi/,
and so on. Morphemically, the word came over as a noun, and even
brought its French plural (/s/ or /z/), since English too had some
plurals with a similar suffix. Semologically, the term was not too
different from the Old English word *hera*, but it referred, of course,
to the new French-controlled army. Metalinguistically, the new
word was quite different from the old; the French armed forces
were organized on a different basis with technically differentiated
ranks and a hierarchical system that has survived to the present day.

Before going on to the significance of such changes, a detailed
survey of some of the other English loans that have been mentioned
may be instructive. The Old French phonemic forms are reconstructions—informed guesses—from the spellings and from what is
known of the history of French as a whole; the Middle English
phonemicizations are again based on spellings, and are so reconstructed as to show the most probable course of the changes to
Modern English.

	Old French (Norman or other)	Middle English	Modern English
mutton	/mowtóhn/	/muwtúhn > mutúhn > mútun/	/mítin > métin/
veal	/vǽhl/	/véhl > víhl/	/víyl/
beef	/bǿhf/	/béhf > bíhf/	/bíyf/
pork	/pórk/	/pórk/	/póhrk/, etc.
castle	/kastél/	/kástel/	/kǽsil/, etc.
cattle	/katél/	/kátel/	/kǽtil/
chattel	/kyatél/	/kyátel > tyátel/	/čǽtil/
estate	/estáht/	/estáht/	/estǽyt > istéyt/
chair	/kyáyr/	/kyáyr > tyáyr/	/čǽyr > čéyr > čéhr/, etc.
uncle	/óhnkle/	/úhnkle > únkel/	/ínkil > ə́ŋkil/
cousin	/kowzíyn/	/kuwzíyn > kuzíyn kúzin/	/kízin > kézin/

A word like *cheap* went through a development that may be reconstructed thus: /káwpow/ > /káwp/ in Pre-Old English; then we get /kǽwp > kǽhp > kyǽhp/ in Old English, then Middle English /kyéhp > tyéhp > tyíhp/, and finally /číyp/.

The kinds of phonemic changes exemplified here are a small sample of the necessary changes and adaptations that come about when languages exchange material (borrow words). No two languages have identical phonemic systems. A word of another language is heard in terms of the phonemes of the hearer's language. The allophones that are perceived are those nearest the hearer's, and he restructures what is heard to fit his own pattern. In the process he may change the structure of the borrowed item very greatly, or he may actually change his own patterns by taking over something from the source language that fits into some part of his own system and, as it were, extends it.

The historical examples cited have to be guessed at and reconstructed, but in areas where languages are now in contact, the processes of borrowing, change, and adaptation can be observed. Very little such observation has actually been done with sufficient care to provide all the desirable information, but we can adduce some examples, and discuss them. In the Southwest of the United States, for instance, there are many speakers of Spanish who introduce English into their language, and whose English-speaking neighbors adopt some Spanish. In northern New Mexico speakers of English know the two Spanish words *primo* 'cousin' (in an extended sense, any relative) and *amigo* 'friend'. In the local Spanish these are phonemically /prímo/ and /amígo/; phonetically they are (from personal observation) something like [pr̃'į·mǒ], [ꞵm'i·gǎ]. In English they become /príymow, ə(+)míygow/, phonetically [pɹ'ivį^mǎ̈ṵ, ə(')m'ivį^gǎ̈ṵ]. The phonetic approximation is close enough, but the phonemic structures are quite different. When English words go into the local Spanish, the phonological changes are as great: *junior-high* becomes /junyařxáy/ [ɉⁱṵn̦iᵉr̃h₊'aị], with stress as in Spanish—two weaks and a primary, and no internal open transition, but with a new phoneme, /ǰ/, introduced from English. More often the English terms are morphemically adapted in whole or part, so that *gasoline* becomes *gasolina, Forest Service* becomes /fóres+serbísyo/; or there is loan translation, and we get *casa de cortes* for *courthouse*. In the kind of situation being discussed here, many of the Spanish speakers (and some of the English speakers) are more or less bilingual; the more they know of the other language, and the more use of it they make, the more likely they are to use the loanwords with little or no departure from the original phonology, switching from one language to another easily and, as it were, shifting gears as they go along. But even such speakers, when they have really completely adopted a word from the other language, adapt it phonologically. The author of this book speaks Spanish with a reasonably good pronunciation, but when he is speaking English and uses such words as *primo* or *amigo*, he adapts them as shown above.

The important point to be made from the preceding discussion is that a word or phrase has not been "borrowed" until it has been adapted—phonologically and in other ways. As long as such items remain reasonably similar phonologically to their originals, and are treated morphologically (morphemically and syntactically) in special ways, they remain foreign and unassimilated. Thus, in literary English such items as *double entendre* or *nonchalance* are still French as long as they are phonetically approximately [dublą̃tą̇'dʀ(ə); nǫ̇šǽlą̇'s⁽ᵠ⁾]; they become loans when the speaker says /dùwbəl+antándər/ and /nàn+šəláhns/.

Loans are morphemically adapted in many cases. One example that changed the morphemic system is the case of the -s plurals of French nouns taken into English. In Old English there were a few plurals in -s (which was undoubtedly pronounced /s/, but may very soon have become /z/ in some instances). As English acquired more and more of the French plurals, and as some of the older English plurals came to be the same as their singulars because of various changes that were taking place, the new and distinctive formation was extended to older nouns not of French origin. In present-day English there are only a few nouns that do not have the now regular plural in /-s, -z, -iz/. The borrowing of this morphemic item was easy, not only because there was already a similar native morpheme, but also because the system of singular versus plural was a strong part of the morphemic structure of English. For the same reason, and the additional fact that there are some irregular plurals, it is possible for English to adopt learned loans from Latin and retain the Latin plurals, giving both forms spelling pronunciations: *fungus* : *fungi*; *index* : *indices*, etc. Occasionally this practice leads to "overcorrectness", as when some speakers say /prásisìyz/ instead of /prásisiz/ for the plural of *process* (or, in some dialects, /prówsisìyz/ for /prówsisiz/). The Latin original of *process* is *prōcessus*, and its plural is *prōcessūs*, so the plural in /-ìyz/ has no Latin base at all.

4.34. Loanwords may bring with them rearrangements of the phonology at any level—new allophones, new distributions of phonemes, or even new phonemes. They may also change things in the morphology—new morphophonic relations, new morphs and morphemes, new syntactic arrangements.

The French loans and learned words of English, and similar phenomena elsewhere in Europe and in the rest of the world, may serve to illustrate all these phenomena briefly.

The reconstruction of Norman French phonetic details attempted in 4.33 suggests that sometimes French allophones were added to the phonetic repertory of a phoneme. When Old French /mowtóhn/ was introduced into English, the allophones of French /o/ may not have been identical with anything existing in the language; they were probably higher and more rounded than any English sound, and at first must have presented some difficulty of phonemic assignment. Our suggested reconstruction indicates that eventually they became members of the Middle English /u/ phoneme.

In the loans there occurred many new clusters and other distributions of consonants and vowels. Words like *pint, paint, point* had final /ynt/ in Middle English as they do now; this sequence was not found in Old English. Many French loans, and especially the learned ones, exhibited vowel phonemes of several qualities in places where Old English had only weak-stressed allophones like [ɪ] or [ɛ̇] or the like. French words with initial /v/ and /z/ helped to establish these items as new phonemes; in Old English they had been intervocalic allophones of /f/ and /s/; in Middle English they became phonemes early, but appeared only between vowels (except for dialect words like *vat* and *vixen*) or, later, in final position; the French loans made them fully represented phonemes in all positions. Compare with this the modern English phonemes /ž/ and /ŋ/; /ž/ is found in initial position only in foreign proper names; /ŋ/ is not found initially at all, except possibly in New Zealand English; there are no large numbers of loanwords coming in to establish these phonemes more strongly.

The vowel distributions referred to led to the development of the phoneme of tertiary stress, /ˈ/; in Old English there were primary and weak stresses in words, and also a medial (secondary) stress in phrases. Many of the weak stresses became no stress at all in Middle English, with loss of the vowel and consequently the syllable; others became phonetically much weaker than they had been. The medial stresses usually remained. The new nonprimary stresses were too strong to be weak, too weak to be medial. They ended up, in most cases, as the new tertiaries.

The French and learned loans established all kinds of new morphophonic relations; those exhibited in *public* /-k/ ~ *publicity* /-s-/, *sane* /ey/ ∼ *sanity* /æ/, and hosts of other examples, had not existed before. The spread of the /-s, -z, -ɪz/ plural morpheme has been noted. The learned words added new allomorphs of plural and other categories, and new morphemes in the form of postbases and prebases of many kinds.

The order of words, especially of various verb forms, changed in accordance with French practice. The spread of the indefinite and definite articles was fostered by French usage.

In semology we have such an instance as the development of *one* as an "indefinite pronoun". In Old English there were expressions parallel to modern German *man sagt* 'one says', where *man* is a weaker-stressed form of *Mann* 'man'—i.e., 'a man, some man, someone'. The Old English *man* with weak stress became /mə/, and went out of use. French used *on* (probably then pronounced /ŏhn/ in phrases) in this function; *on* is from the Latin nominative *homō* (whereas *homme* is from *hominem*). The Middle English word /óhn/ 'one' (Old English /ɔ́hn/, modern /wɔ́n/—instead of the expected /ówn/) was sometimes used in a way not too different from Old English *man* and French *on*. As *man* disappeared, English /ŏhn/ was equated to the French /ŏhn/ of such phrases as /ŏhn+dít/, modern *on dit* /on·di/. The semology of the French word was taken over, and the previously existing sememes connected with *man* were thus reinstated, or newly recreated.

4.35. Sometimes a word or other item is borrowed more than once, from different dialects, or at different times. These different forms of an originally single source are known as DOUBLETS. The presence of doublets leads to what are, in effect, new morphemes, and results in semological differentiation.

The English word *sample* is from Norman French /(ĕ)sámplĕ/, while *example* is from *exemple* already pronounced /ĕgzámplĕ/ (that is, a "popular" spelling pronunciation of a learned loan direct from the Latin *exemplum*); in *exemplify* the learned form is from Latin *exemplificare*. These are instances of doublet forms.

There are many other examples of doublets: *double* and *duplex*; *simple* : *simplex*; *reason* : *ration* : *ratio*; (*com*)*parison* : (*pre*)*paration*; *langu*(*age*) : *lingu*(*al*); *chattel* : *cattle* (mentioned above); *castle* : *chateau*; *cousin* : *consanguine*; (*man*)*euver* : *oper*(*ate*); *over*(*t*) : *aperitif*; *brief* : *brev*(*ity*); *-chester* : *-cester* : *-caster* in placenames; *renascence* : *Renaissance*; (*con*)*geal* : *gel*(*id*); *join* : *-junct*; *destroy* : *destruc*(*tion*); (*re*)*duce* : (*de*)*duc*(*t*); (*edi*)*fy* : (*edi*)*fic*(*ation*); *hour* : *hor*(*oscope*); *isle* : *insul*(*ar*); (*de*)*ny* : *neg*(*ation*); (*multi*)*ply* : (*multi*)*plic*(*ation*); *state* : *estate*; *fact* : *fait* (*accompli*); *beast* : *bête* (*noire*) :

besti(*al*); *disc* : *discus* : *desk* : *dais*; *rule* : *regul*(*ar*); the list could be greatly extended.

In the cases cited, there is in every instance some element of difference at some level in the different forms, and usually a resulting semological and/or metalinguistic difference. A *sample* is an *example* of something, but examples are not always samples; *to exemplify* is to cite or present an *example*, but here the two different base forms exhibit a morphophonic relationship of a kind found in the learned loans in English, thus putting these two forms together, while *sample* is apart from them. The three items *reason, ration, ratio* are now quite far apart semologically as well as in form. The three placename forms *-chester, -cester, -caster*, however, having no explicit metalinguistic reference, may quite possibly be semologically equivalent. The further apart the resultant forms are, the more likely they are to have become new bases with quite separate semologies.

Many of the doublet forms cited, and this is generally true, are recognizable as doublets only from knowledge of the historical changes involved. These matters are discussed in Chapters 5 and 6, which see. An extreme example is *loc*(*al*) and (*in*) *lieu* (*of*); Latin *locum* 'place' became something like */lúhw/* in pre-Old-French, which then became /líhw/, then /lyéw/, and finally modern French *lieu* /lyø/, taken over in a spelling pronunciation /l(y)úw/.

In addition to the doublets of the kind mentioned, there exist words of ultimately common origin which have become very different in form, but may retain a large part of the original meaning. One example must suffice: English *cow* /káw/ is from Old English *cū* /kúw/ by normal development; it goes back to an Indo-Hittite form with the base */gwow-/. English *beef* /bíyf/ is from Old French *buef* /bøhf/ < bↄhf/, which is from Latin *bov*(*em*) /bów-/. Latin *bōs* (nominative), *bovem* (accusative) is a form taken from some Italic dialect in which Indo-Hittite */gw-/ had become /b-/; so the word goes back to the same */gwow-/ as does *cow*; the real Latin development should have been */wow-/, but such a form was never recorded. At the present time, *cow* and *beef* certainly exhibit different bases, which have nothing in common; the fact that one can say *a beef* in the sense of a bovine animal (which should be a steer, but might be a cow) is a late development.

Forms like *cow* and *beef*, of which there are many in English because of its history of borrowing from related languages, are usually not called doublets, but are COGNATES; see Chapters 5 and 6.

In a strict sense, variant forms from different contemporary dialects are also cognates and doublets. They can be designated as doublets when some special difference of connotation or meaning develops. Thus *h'ist* /háyst/ is a variant of *hoist* /hóyst/; its special connotation (rustic simplicity to some, urban gangsterism to others) makes it a true doublet. A less clear case is that of the word *aunt* pronounced /áhnt/ by an American who normally says /éhnt/ or /ǽ(h)nt/. It may be that female relatives of this kind in general are /éhnts/, as are the insects, *ants*; but the speaker's Aunt Agatha is always /áhnt/; or /ǽntiy/ is used for an elderly colored woman, and /áhnt(iy)/ for a relative. These are stylistic or connotative doublets. The last instance brings to mind a special, artificial one: *fancy* is pronounced with /æ/ in both British and American speech, but Americans have produced a form /fáhnsiy/ in such an expression as "Fancy that", as a humorous or sarcastic pseudo-Britishism.

As has been indicated, doublets and other cognates, when introduced into a language, often result in there being created, as it were, new morphemes (and new allomorphs). This is the most usual way that languages expand their stock of morphemes and sememes. But there is also the possibility of the creation of new morphemes—chiefly bases—out of entirely new phoneme sequences or by apparently haphazard and deliberate changes from existing patterns.

It has become popular in certain industrial and commercial enterprises to invent names for new products by forming possible but otherwise nonexisting phoneme combinations. These then constitute new morphemes, with very specialized semological uses. A very widespread such form is *kodak*; this one is international by now, and is very well-known; how it came into existence has not been recorded. In English this gets analyzed as a base *kod-* and a postbase *-ak*, and new items like *recordak, muzak* get formed later. The postbases *-ex* and *-ol* have become popular in the names of products with hygienic or medicinal uses: *kleenex, tintex, cutex, oxydol, nujol*. Certain detergents have one-syllable names like *fab, dreft*. The ending *-on* (or *-tron*) has become a postbase in some scientific terms; *proton, photon, meson, positron, neutron*. Various parts of words—sometimes actually existing morphemes, but often arbitrarily cut-off portions—become new bases or postbases: *xerox* /zíhràks/, *verifax*. The advertising pages of popular magazines and technological journals are full of terms of this kind. The processes of formation have undoubtedly been used more frequently and more in awareness in recent years than ever before, but it seems certain that they must have existed even in preliterate times. This would explain the partial resemblances of many bases, and also the irregularities constantly encountered in instances with known historical sources.

In the newly invented items of the kind discussed, the semology may at first be very specialized, but the word may be widely extended by popular usage: *kleenex* was originally, and still is, a brand name of a particular make of cleansing tissue; in everyday American usage it is a term for any such tissue; there is even a semilearned joking plural *kleenices* /klíynisìyz/.

This discussion of the various new items in a language—borrowings, learned loans, newly invented forms, new postbases, new sememes—leads to the conclusion that a living language is constantly changing and growing. In language, as in other aspects of human behavior, there is constant change and development, and no system ever remains static.

4.4. DICTIONARIES

4.40. The making of dictionaries began very modestly some millenia ago. The Akkadian conquerors of Sumeria made word lists or glossaries of Sumerian for the use of scribes who spoke Akkadian and knew Sumerian only as a religious language; later the Hittites made glossaries of Akkadian and Sumerian for their own use. The ancient Greeks and Romans were constantly compiling glossaries of one kind or another, and similar lists were made in India in ancient times.

This kind of activity is one that cannot take place without literacy. In a preliterate society there are individuals who remember words from other languages, and who can translate them, but they have no way of conveying this knowledge except by word of mouth. As soon as a writing system exists, however, the word lists can be written down and used by many persons.

From what has been said so far, the first ancestors of dictionaries are seen to have been simple glossaries, lists of items in one language with equivalents or translations in other.

In all societies, literate or not, there has always been a need for explaining words of the native language: to children, newcomers, new workers in a specialty, and so on. These explanations are sometimes very elaborate, but at other times they may be simple glossing equivalents: a *palace* may be described as 'a large and elaborate dwelling of a royal personage', or it may be glossed simply as 'the king's house'. When writing came into use, and there began to be persons who composed various kinds of works in the literary language, it began to be desirable to compile dictionaries of the native language, with various kinds of glosses—full and detailed in some instances, succinctly equivalent in others.

4.41. There now exist one-language dictionaries in all the principal literary and official languages of the modern world. The English-speaking countries are probably best supplied with dictionaries of this kind; every literate person knows about Samuel Johnson and his dictionary, and when Americans speak of "the dictionary" they are most often referring to the works that are the successors of Noah Webster's nineteenth-century compilation.

A one-language dictionary can vary from an all-inclusive one to a short specialized one, with all kinds of intermediate stages. In theory the inclusive dictionary should contain every word that is used in the language, and should illustrate or exemplify all the uses of each word, so that there should be many phrases included. This kind of ideal goal is not only unattainable, but is also imprecise: it is not possible to record simultaneously all the words that may be in use at a given time, nor is it possible to set exact time limits within which usages will be recorded. In practice, then, an "all-inclusive" diction-ary will necessarily not include a good many recent usages, and may record many usages no longer current. The limits of inclusion must be defined by the compiler. The goal may be set as all words and their uses that are found in literary works, newspapers and magazines, technical works (usually excluding very specialized scientific mono-graphs and articles), children's books, and so on, that have been published between some starting date and the compiler's cut-off date (say, when the work begins). There are clear problems of definition in such a goal. What precisely is a literary work? Should one include all levels of fiction, from the best-seller to the 50-cent paperback with a lurid cover? Should country weekly newspapers and "little magazines" be included along with metropolitan dailies and magazines of large circulation (and among the latter, should one include the "true confession" type as well as the journals of political opinion)? Is a college textbook a specialized scientific mono-graph if it deals with biology, but an ordinary technical work if it is in the field of modern history? Do books for very young children contain lexical material worth recording?

When the goals have been delimited by answers to the questions above, and others, there arises a need for characterization and label-ing of different kinds of vocabulary items. Are *bad* and *evil* different kinds of words stylistically and connotatively? Should *arm* be listed while *humerus* is excluded, and if the latter is not excluded, how should it be labeled? Is *scram* a word in good standing at all levels, or does it have special limitations? Should an "all-inclusive" diction-ary include well-known but tabu words, or should it only have the technical and scientific equivalents of them? If *evil* is literary or religious, and *bad* is ordinary every-day usage, what is *wicked* in the two examples "The wicked shall be punished" and "Johnny, you're wicked for teasing your sister"? And should *lousy* and *rotten* as quasi-synonyms of *bad* be labeled "colloquial" or "slang" or "improper" or what?

Some of the problems and questions raised above are avoided or answered by limiting or otherwise specializing a dictionary. Thus there can be dictionaries of slang—modern American, British, or the like, if one can define slang—and of special jargons. The latter can be limited to an occupational group—advertising men, thieves, and so on; or to a profession or industry or technology—medicine, meat packing, nursing; or to a field of science—biology, chemistry, sociology. In such special dictionaries, the ordinary words of the language can be omitted unless they have some special usage in the field covered, and only the technical terms of the jargon need be included. Thus a dictionary of this kind can be a short glossary of special terms appended to an article or essay, or it can be a long compilation published separately.

In general dictionaries, and also in the special ones, there is always the necessity of giving at least some grammatical information. So-called irregular forms (*mice, went, took,* and so on) must be mentioned, at least after the basic word to which they belong, and often (as in the case of *went*) as a separate entry, with cross-reference. The question of how much grammatical information to include is variously answered at different times and by different compilers, and also for different languages.

The arrangement of items in a dictionary presents problems also. In modern times we are used to arrangement by alphabetical order. This principle of ordering arose a long time ago. In all writing systems, the various symbols used have to be ordered in some way. Alphabets seem to have fixed orders: they are recorded and presented as a series of letters: *a, b, c,* ...; α (alpha), β (beta), ...; and are often named from the first two or three letters: the *abc's*, the *alphabet*, Russian (older usage) *ázbuka* (from the Old Church Slavic names of the first two letters, *azŭ, buki*). (See Chapters 7 and 8 for discussion of writing systems and examples of alphabets.) The basic principle of ordering is easily applied to a word list. As soon as people learn to read and write they learn alphabetical order, and even the least educated usually have no difficulty with it.

But in dictionaries there are more problems than simply this ordering by alphabet. There is the question of whether different forms related grammatically by inflection or derivation should all be entered separately, or whether one should be chosen as a headword and others entered under it. This problem goes right back to that of the grammatical analysis and how much of it to include in a dictionary. In English and other European-language dictionaries, it is customary, in large dictionaries, to include as headwords even closely related derived forms, but to list inflected forms separately only when they are in some way irregular. Such listing often conceals similarities, and at other times hides differences. Thus listing *conceive, deceive, receive* separately from *conception, deception, reception* conceals the similar base forms *-ceive* and *-cep-*, and hides the morphophonic difference between the latter. It is easy to overcome this difficulty in a case like the present one: we can list *-ceive* and say "See *conceive, deceive, ...*", giving all the occurring prebase forms. And we can also list *-cep-*, cross-reference it to *-ceive*, and then list all the prebase forms having it, including different postbases, *-ception, -ceptive, -ceptual*.

In dictionaries of such a language as Arabic, it is customary to list as head entries the so-called roots—the bases, in our terminology —and to list under the roots all the individual derived words, no matter how complex the derivation and how remote the meaning from the supposed basic meaning of the root. Thus *k-t-b* would be an entry, with a paraphrase indicating that it means 'write'; under this would be found, in an order determined by a particular system of grammatical description, such words as *kita·bun* 'book', *maktuwbun* 'scribe', and so on. It is as if for English, we entered only such items as *-ceive* as a headword, and listed *conceive, conception, deceive, deceptive*, and so on, under it in a grammatically determined order.

In addition to the alphabetical and grammatical principles of ordering dictionaries, there is also the possibility of arrangement by subject matter, the so-called thesaurus type. This requires a list of subject headings under which are given all pertinent words and phrases. It calls for a system of classifying all knowledge, and obviously involves immense difficulties of organization and classification, since there is no agreement on any such system. To the anthropologically oriented user of a dictionary, the thesaurus approach is most appealing in principle, but most disappointing in practice.

It may be in point to suggest some possible ways in which dictionary making may be improved. An institution might be created for the centralized collection of examples of usage of the words and phrases of a language, utilizing the newest devices—computers and other machines—for storage and retrieval of the vast amount of data. A system of grammatical description and analysis could be agreed upon, and all the centralized data could be coded in terms of this system, which, ideally, would include semological as well as morphological coding and labeling. A system of description for other areas of culture could be elaborated, and all the linguistic data could be coded in terms of the pertinent cultural area of each item. Several kinds of things could be published as basic works of reference. First, a lexicon—a list of all the known morphemes of the language, bases, affixes, and so on, in alphabetical order of phonemic or, better, morphophonic constitution, with the briefest of semological and/or grammatical labels attached; this lexicon could have as an appendix a systematic presentation of the grammatical system (paradigms, rules of constructions, and the like). Then there could be a word list, containing all existing words, with a brief semological and morphological code, for reference back to the total original files. And finally there could be a master list of cultural subjects, with pertinent words listed under them. With such centralized files and basic reference works, all manner of dictionaries and glossaries for limited and specialized purposes could be compiled, and the data in each could be cross-referenced to others where pertinent, and could be full and informative without overlapping and without too much bulk and inconvenience in handling.

At present, no such organization or institution exists for any language. Existing dictionaries, with all their faults, should not be too harshly judged, therefore, since the attainment of the necessary completeness of basic data is as yet hardly begun, in terms of the above suggestions or any similar research procedures.

4.42. Translating dictionaries, usually from one language to another (and back again), involve all the problems of one-language dictionaries, and then the further difficulty of cross-cultural equivalences.

As was indicated in 4.40, it appears that the first dictionaries were translating glossaries. They were also limited and specialized. And their compilers probably knew intimately the area of knowledge they were dealing with. The problems of cross-cultural equivalences were thus minimal. One could list what looked like all-inclusive one-to-one correspondences, and exclude multiple choices.

As the distance—geographically and culturally—between two languages increases, and as the scope of a translating dictionary widens, the difficulties of finding equivalents grow immeasurably. In compiling the initial wordlist, let us say, one decides to limit the vocabulary to some fixed number of items. But no matter how the limit is fixed, there is trouble right from the start. Suppose the glossary is being prepared for French speakers who are reading English, and no previous knowledge of English is assumed. The compiler finds no difficulty, at first, in getting equivalents for such words as numerals, names of common household objects, buildings and their interiors, government institutions, schools and their teachers and subject matter. Soon problems present themselves, however. Among the numerals, one finds *billion*: this is easy, one might say—it means 'milliard'. But does it mean 'billion = a million million' as in Great Britain, or 'billion = a thousand million' as in the United States? A common household object in the United States is a pint jar. Since *pint* is a term in a system of measures that is not commensurate with the metric system used in France, how does one translate it? There are undoubtedly half-liter jars in France, which hold very nearly the same amount as a pint. But is the dictionary entry "pint-jar = bouteille qui contient un demi-litre" a translation or a paraphrase? Nor could one translate *pint* simply as "demi-litre": to many Frenchmen that immediately transforms itself into "un demi", meaning a large glass (a "stein") of beer. Or take the word *home*: in "He went home" the French equivalent is "chez soi", literally something like "at or to [the house of] himself". In "Home is where the heart is" the translator must pause; there simply is no easy way to do this one; one has to explain all kinds of things about what *home* is supposed to mean to an American before one can formulate even a long paraphrase. Then again, for *home* in "The home is the cornerstone of society" one puts down "le foyer"; but the French reader knows, or soon finds out that *foyer* also translates English *hearth*, and that hearths are usually no longer literal but figurative and connotative.

A conclusion to be drawn from the few examples just given is that the maker of translating dictionaries must know, or find out, a great deal about the metalinguistic structure of the societies speaking the languages before he can translate with any sort of accuracy. Then there is the further conclusion that the further apart the cultures are, the greater the difficulty of finding equivalents. And finally, the more specialized and limited a translating dictionary is, the easier it is to supply exact equivalents.

4.5. TRANSLATION AND INTERPRETING

4.50. The practical difficulties of translation have already been suggested in the preceding discussion of translating dictionaries

(4.42). Here we can consider some of the basic theoretical matters involved, and some modern developments toward practical solutions.

In 1.12 it was suggested that from the very beginning different groups of human beings had different languages, and that exchange between them took place. In 1.3 and its subsections linguistic diversity was discussed. In 4.23 reference was made to equivalences between different metalinguistic analyses. In 4.3 and its subsections we alluded to the kinds of language contact that led to the bilingualism which resulted in loanwords. All these are factors to be considered in any discussion of translation.

One very important element in translation problems is the translator. It is reasonable to suppose that there have always been persons, and quite possibly in all societies, who for one reason or another could, as it were, stand outside of the group sufficiently to observe, classify, analyze, and systematize some of the behavior events that were taking place. Such persons would be even more sensitive to the behavior patterns of other groups with whom there was contact. They were the precursors of the systematic observers who became the social scientists of modern times, and the appliers of sociological and other cross-cultural knowledge. It is from people like this that good translators arise. A translator has to be an observer and systematizer of some aspects of his own society, and a good listener to and observer of the behavior of members of other societies. He must also have a highly specialized and developed form of what is probably a general human characteristic, the ability to hear and imitate all kinds of sounds, and to recognize the recurrent patterns into which they fall. Along with this, the first translators (or interpreters—which is a better and more descriptive term) must also have been, at heart, tremendously courageous and adventurous. For they had to be willing to dare to look at strangers who might well be hostile, and to listen to them, and to learn their ways.

We can be sure that the average interpreter in all times has been relatively unaware of these high values that we have attributed to him. And in many societies he has been suspect, because the general populace was made uneasy by the nonconformity exhibited by him. But his usefulness has generally been recognized. In modern times, with the growth of cross-cultural knowledge and of the social sciences as sciences, the translator has found himself beset by all kinds of doubts. He can no longer simply enjoy knowing one or more languages other than his native one, and play with equating things in one to other and often quite different things in another. He is supposed to become a scientist, to study linguistic structures, to know about cultural differences, to understand beyond the words. And this task becomes increasingly difficult because he also finds his job threatened by machines, or by the threat of machines.

What we have said about the qualifications of translators or interpreters should indicate to the reader that translation has always been a kind of art, an application of out-of-awareness knowledge. Can it be made into a technology, an application of science? This question will be considered in the next section.

4.51. With the development of computers and other complex machines which can perform certain kinds of operations and calculations ever so much faster than human beings—once a human being has programmed them to perform the operations—the question began to be asked whether translation could not also be done by such machines.

The first asking of such questions was by persons who knew little or nothing of the nature and structure of language, or of the nature and art of translating. They wanted quick results for practical use; they thought it might be cheaper to develop the needed machines than to train, over long years, the needed number of human translators. And they figured that once the machines existed and were properly programmed, they would be easier to manage than human beings.

In attempting to answer such questions and demands, linguists found it necessary to investigate aspects of linguistic structure that had not been examined before, and to devise analytical tools according to new conceptual frames. In the years since 1950 there has developed a large amount of activity, among all the leading Western nations, in what is usually called mechanical (or machine) translation. There are journals devoted to it, and we find such terms being used as *mechanolinguistics* and *mathematicolinguistics*. Some success has been attained in actual machine production of usable translations in specialized fields, especially scientific works. And a good many insights have been attained into structures that could not easily be examined, because of the number of variables or the high incidence of occurrence, without machine assistance. The more such work is done, and the more successful the translations produced become, the more clear it is that translation is not and cannot be a mechanical product, that languages cannot be reduced to a set of quasi-mathematical rules, that leaving out the nonlinguistic culture is the surest way there is to insure failure in the resulting translation, and that before, during, and after the machine activity human translators are needed to add the art. Translation can be made an applied science, and machines are of much use in assisting in the activity, but any applied science requires artistry and skill on the part of its practitioners. The machine translation of today will perhaps someday be transformed by learning these precepts, and will then become cross-cultural interpreting with the aid of machines and any other available tools, under the direction of highly skilled and highly intelligent human beings.

Part II

LANGUAGES

Chapter 5

LANGUAGES THROUGH TIME

5.0. HISTORY AND LANGUAGE

5.00. It is generally held that language is ephemeral and fleeting; words can only be remembered, and sometimes not too accurately. But deeds are much more lasting, at least in their effects; and artifacts are thought of as enduring, tangible survivals from a past (near or remote).

It is true that tools, buildings, clothing, and other artifacts represent direct sources of information about something that has been made in the past. It is also true that the members of a society—the people—are tangible and enduring in their own persons and for the duration of their lives, and are direct descendants and ancestors of other tangible entities. And it is further true that institutions and ceremonies are tangible survivals. Until recording instruments (phonographs, tape recorders) were invented, language events could not be equally or analogously tangible.

But language nonetheless does have an actual persistence in time. For one thing, it is possible to observe differences between the speech of older and younger persons. Along with other forms of decrying the doings of the young, in many societies we find remarks about the misuse of the language by the young. Then further, it is realized that language is transmitted from generation to generation, and traditional texts are thought of as persisting unchanged, by contrast with evident changes elsewhere. For most of the years of human history, and for large parts of the world right up to the present, only such preservation of traditional sayings and observation of generation differences could throw any light on the history of a language as a linguistic system. Then writing was invented (see Part III, Chapters 7 and 8), and recordings of language could be made as material artifacts, and could be preserved.

129

5.01. With the coming into existence of writing, all kinds of records could be kept, and every recording in writing became a piece of evidence for something that had been spoken or could be spoken.

The written records are artifacts in themselves, or they are parts of other artifacts. They are inscriptions in stone, on pottery, on walls; they are written on palm leaves, or clay, or paper. If extensive, they may be rolled up in scrolls, or bound in books. Whatever form they take, they are historical sources: in their meaning content they reveal something about the cultural behavior of the people by whom and for whom they were written. In their linguistic forms, if we can read them, they tell, often in great detail, about aspects of linguistic structure at the time of writing.

If we have, for any language, a series of written documents whose absolute or relative ages are known, we can construct a series of historical statements. We can say that such and such items at period x changed into others by period y, and these changed in still other ways by period z. A systematic statement can then be made of the course of the developments as a whole, from x through y to z, or backward in time, to show how z came about.

5.02. The ordinary meanings of the word *history* are used in linguistics, as well as the special meanings implied in the last section. There is occasion to consider the extralinguistic history of languages —to discuss the location and migration of the peoples speaking them, the imposition of languages on new areas by invasion or by law, the changes in size of the populations speaking the language, and other general matters describing the background and situation. In some cases and where such knowledge exists, it can be shown how various parts of the linguistic structure have actually changed with the passage of time.

To illustrate the kinds of data that are involved in such historical studies, the rest of this chapter will present a survey of the history of English, a language for which historical sources abound.

In the next chapter, there will follow a discussion of how historical studies of languages have led to the discovery of relationships between them. This discovery has resulted in the kinds of studies most usually referred to as COMPARATIVE LINGUISTICS. For works dealing with the detailed development of English, and the methods of comparative linguistics, as well as presentations of known and putative language relationships and general historical data, see References and Notes.

5.1. THE HISTORY OF ENGLISH

5.10. In any strict chronological sense, the history of English, as of any language, begins with the invention of language, and goes through ages of unknown development and change. But the history of a language, in the sense in which we deal with it here, is con- structed from the data of written records. Some of these data are merely suggestive, especially for older periods and in respect to nonlinguistic history. The history of English begins, for us, with the coming to England of the people who spoke, in several closely similar dialects, the language which has turned into modern English by a continuous and uninterrupted development among their de- scendants.

It is known that there were inhabitants in the area now known as England before the coming of the people just mentioned, hereafter referred to as the Anglo-Saxons (see 5.11 for discussion of this term). The previous inhabitants were mostly speakers of Celtic dialects. Roman soldiers and administrators had come to Britain from the first century of the Christian era. Latin had been introduced as the official language, placenames had been Latinized, and there had come about a degree of replacement of the native dialects by Latin, an infiltration of Latin loanwords into them, and the incursion of a few Celtic words into the local Latin. Roman rule in Britain extended to the mountains of Wales in the west, and to the Scottish highlands in the north. But it was precarious over much of the territory out- side of the south and southeast of England; and it began to weaken in the fourth century. By about 450 the Roman Empire had been so weakened by incursions of various peoples from central and northern Europe, reaching to Rome itself, that Roman garrisons had been withdrawn from England, and law and order were collapsing.

About this time, some of the peoples who were invading various parts of the Roman empire began to strike out across the North Sea. In the period from 450 to 650, considerable numbers of these Anglo- Saxon invaders arrived, and they settled all of the country that had been controlled by Rome.

The Celtic inhabitants of these areas seem to have been unable to resist the invaders, and most of them apparently took flight. Some, we know, went across the English Channel to what has since been called Brittany (Latin *Britannia*); their place of origin, being larger, is now called *Magna Britannia* = Great Britain. Others retreated into the western and northern highlands, where their descendents are the Welsh and the Scots; the Welsh are even today only partly speakers of English, and the Scots began to become English-speaking some five or six centuries after the Anglo-Saxon invasions had stopped around 750.

5.11. The people we are calling the Anglo-Saxons were Germanic-speaking tribes from the areas of the continent that are now northern Netherlands and the eastward-stretching areas of northern Germany as far as Denmark. It may be pointed out that the dialects of the area we are talking about are known in historical linguistics as Anglo-Frisian, a branch of West Germanic; the other division of West Germanic, Continental, gave rise to German and Dutch (see References and Notes). The speakers of Anglo-Frisian in large part left the continent and went to England. But a few remained, and their descendents are the speakers of Frisian in the Netherlands and the nearby German islands to the north and east.

Tradition tells us that the invaders of England were of at least three kinds, the Angles, the Saxons, and the Jutes. The name *Jute* is now found also in *Jutland*, a part of Denmark. The Jutes must have been the farthest east of the Anglo-Frisians; and just possibly they may have been speakers of a Scandinavian variety of Germanic, and not Anglo-Frisian at all. The name *Saxon* recurs to the east and south, and the language whose remains are known as Old Saxon is Continental West Germanic rather than Anglo-Frisian. Possibly only those of the invaders who were known as Angles were actually speakers of an Anglo-Frisian dialect as such. They may have been somewhat more numerous or otherwise predominant, for the country they invaded came to be known as the land of the Angles—*Englaland*, modern *England*. But in some way these people also called themselves Saxons, for we have the names Essex, Middlesex, Sussex, Wessex—the east, central, south, and west Saxon territories, constituting much of England. Moreover, the West Germanic dialects of the time were all very similar, and must have been completely mutually intelligible. Whatever linguistic differences existed among the invaders were slight, and by the time their settlement in England had extended over several generations, there was a reshuffling and realignment of original groupings, and an elimination of many of the differences. We can speak of an English language from about 600 on. But we must realize that, like any language, it had local and social differences among its speakers.

5.12. The period from the settlement of English speakers in England until the Norman conquest in 1066 and its immediate aftermath is known as the period of Old English (abbreviated OE). It is often subdivided into Early (to 750), Middle (750–950), and Late (950–1100) OE. It is important to note that these chronological designations, and similar ones for other languages, never imply a sudden change. It is not as if people went to bed on some day in 750 saying "good night" in Early OE, and awoke next day to say "good morning" in Middle OE. The labels that are based on settlement and conquest do imply some sudden changes, but these changes were in the conditions of life of the persons involved, not in the language they were speaking.

During the EOE period, the various groups who were coming into England spread into the country, with the heaviest concentration of population in the east and southeast of England, and up the Thames River. It is probable that settlement was largely by these groups, though some mixing took place from the start. The foundations of subsequent dialect differences were thus present from the beginning, and persisted. The Celtic pre-English inhabitants were displaced during this early period. Those who fled to Brittany must have done so very soon after the first conquerors appeared, though it is not unlikely that there were stragglers over a generation or two. Those who went southwest into Cornwall and west to Wales may have moved more slowly, though we do not really have evidence on this matter. Those who went north did so last, and were the most reluctant to move.

With social, economic, and political conditions inevitably in turmoil as a result of the ongoing upheavals, it is reasonable to conclude that linguistic differentiation and adaptation were both going on all the time. As the social situation quieted down, settlement became more stable, people stayed put, the old towns were refurbished as habitations, and new towns sprang up. The varieties of language spoken became geographically more or less stabilized. Traditional lore had been retained (such as the *Beowulf* legends), and there was time for people to listen to it, to learn it, to repeat it.

It was during this early period too that the Irish monks who had been the leaders and propagators of Christianity in Roman Britain introduced Christianity to the new inhabitants and presumably devised a system of writing the new language (Columba is said to have come from Ireland in 565, and established a monastery in Britain). It should be noted that Christianity, like all the world's major missionizing religions, has always spread literacy while spreading its gospel. Pope Gregory sent Augustine and some monks to Britain in 597, to strengthen or replace the previous Christian teaching, and we can assume that these monks and their successors continued the system of writing. After writing had been introduced, a certain amount of literary activity other than religious came about, and some documents have remained. It is from these written records that our earliest direct knowledge of English comes. To the extent that traditional older materials were recorded, we are also able to get many hints about linguistic characteristics of an older, preliterate period.

During the MOE period, the social scene in England achieved a large measure of stability, and the society, though rent by political struggles, exhibited a fairly uniform culture. Not only were there the usual written documents pertaining to everyday affairs and to government, but there was also much creative literature being composed. It was toward the end of this period that King Alfred fostered the collection and preservation of English writings. Because of this activity, much that is left of these writings is in the West Saxon dialect that Alfred favored, probably because that was the way he spoke.

It was also during this period that London, situated at the meeting place of several dialect areas, became a focal point for the growth of a standard and generally accepted form of the language. From that time on it was the English of London that set the style for the proper way to speak and write English.

In the ninth century the last invasion of Germanic-speaking people into England took place. Various Scandinavian groups, the Vikings, were moving about the north of Europe at the time, sailing the seas and attacking coastal populations. One group of these people occupied Normandy, which gets its name from them—the land of the North-men; after little more than a century of Francization, these Normans—as Frenchmen—invaded England (see 5.13). The invasion we are dealing with here is that of the so-called Danes, who settled in the northeast of England. Their appellation does not necessarily equate them with the Danes of modern times. They were a Norse-speaking (i.e., Scandinavian) group, and very probably little different from those who went to Normandy. These Danes had a considerable influence on the English language, a fact which would seem to indicate that their language may have been almost mutually intelligible with English. The linguistic influence shows up in what is called the LOE period. In this period there began certain developments which were intensified in the years immediately preceding and following the Conquest, and led to a restructured language labeled Middle English, known from the documents in English which reappeared after 1100.

5.13. In 1066 (October 13) the Normans under Duke William defeated the English in the battle of Hastings, and took over the rule of the country. The English nobles, the English churchmen, and, indeed, all Englishmen of any social position above the peasants and economically lower artisans were displaced down to the lowest economic and social stratum, and were replaced by Normans. These Normans were speakers of a French dialect, and were members of French (i.e., French-speaking) society. Their culture was a sub-culture of the medieval European descendent of Roman culture that was then flourishing in western Europe. English culture from the fifth to the eleventh centuries, however, had developed along rather different lines politically, legally, and in all other ways. English culture was not Roman-derived, although, as a West European culture, it had experienced Roman cultural influences in one way or another for a thousand years. When the Normans took over, there was thus a very great amount of change in the detail of all aspects of social activity. Cultural changes of such magnitude can violently upset a society; there are cases in history in which the new ways have so changed the cultural system that the society has literally ceased to exist, though the people may have continued to live as members of or on the fringes of other societies. In England, however, the number of French overlords in proportion to the total population was small, the cultures of the two groups had a basic European common core, and the changes were imposed from the top down, at first affecting, or so it seemed, chiefly political and legal structures. In such a situation a, very apparent mark of change will be the use of the conquerors' language, and the introduction of loanwords into the language of the conquered.

From the date of the Conquest until about 1100 so little was written in English that nothing has been preserved. If one were to judge only from the documents that have survived, one would conclude that the language of England was French. But of course the bulk of the population kept right on talking English. The changes in the structure of the language that had become evident in the LOE period went on developing, and when material written in English began to appear again, these changes and others were clearly evident. This language we now call Middle English.

In the earliest ME period there are large numbers of French loanwords for all kinds of technical things—artifacts, institutions, laws, religion. As the use of French diminished, with the absorption of the French ruling class into the general population, some of these loans went out of use. But large numbers of them remained, as has already been shown (4.3).

The ME material that appeared after 1100 was written by scribes who were literate in French, and it exhibits an orthography that has been greatly modified from that of OE. A few examples are: The word for 'house' was written *hus* in OE, and the complex vocalic nucleus ("long vowel") was sometimes indicated by some special mark, so that in modern printed OE texts it is customary to normalize the spelling and write *hūs* (or *hús*). We may conjecture that the OE phonemic structure of this item was /húws/. When the word reappears in ME, it is written *house*. Does this represent the same pronunciation, or a changed one? And if the latter, how much changed? The detailed answer depends on what one thinks the pronunciation of Norman French was like. We can be certain that *ou* did not, in the twelfth century, represent the same sound as it does in modern French. We conjecture here that *ou* in Old French regularly meant some kind of complex vowel nucleus which may be written phonemically as /ow/. In Norman French the first element of the complex may have been a rather high, tense, well-rounded vowel, say [o^w]. The complex [o^wu̯], if it was that, would have been the nearest in sound to the vocalic nucleus of LOE *hús*, even if the first element of that nucleus had already begun to change in the direction that we know it to have taken—from [ʊ] to [ʊ<] or [ʉ] and eventually [ɨ] in MME. So as far as the vocalic nucleus is concerned, we can be fairly sure that in the new French spelling of English *ou* represented very much the same thing as the fifty-year earlier spelling *u* or *ú*. As for the final /s/ of the English word under discussion, it may have appeared to the scribes that they had to affirm that it belonged integrally to the word, and was not a plural ending or the like, so they added an *e* on the end of the word. At the period when such spellings of a presumably "silent" *e* began, the actual complete disappearance of the final weak-stressed /e/ (or /ə/) in ME had not yet taken place. But there are early spellings with an apparently silent final *e*, and it is not unlikely that in both Norman French and ME of the twelfth century the final vowels of this type appeared or were omitted in terms of various grammatical forms, phrase structures, and the like.

So we get *hús* transformed into *house*, a spelling whose persistence into modern English reflects the way in which English-speaking people have always chosen to muddle through a bad orthography rather than do anything about it.

The entire appearance of the written language was transformed by analogous changes. So *īs* /íys/ became *ice* (hence *mice* from *mȳs*, but *mouse* from *mūs*); *mētan*, with OE /eh/ changing to /ih/, became *mete* or *meet*; *āc* /óhk/ became *oak*, *fōt* became *foot*. All the spellings of complex nuclei were changed to some degree, though some of the simple nuclei remained as they had been.

Consonant spellings were also changed, though less drastically in most cases. In OE, *c* was the regular spelling for /k/, and also, in some positions, for /ky/; the latter soon became /ty/, with a sound like that represented by *ch* in French, and the *ch* spelling came into English. In loanwords from French, *c* before *e* and *i* represented /s/, so the letter *k*, not used in OE, came to be employed for /k/ before a front vowel; *k* also came to be used instead of *c* in final position— alone after a complex nucleus, as in *oak*, after *c* elsewhere, as in *back*. The sequence /kw/, OE *cw*, came to be written in a Latinized form, so *cwic* became *quick*. The sequence /hw/, OE *hw*, was perhaps not heard accurately by the French, but in any case they wrote it *wh*; the lip rounding of the /w/ was possibly most prominently heard.

A complete study of the history of English spelling has never been made; if it is ever done, there will probably result from it some new insights into the phonological changes in English, and some corrections of present views on some of the details.

For the first generation or two after the Conquest, there was little or nothing written in English, with only French being used in documents. But a large amount of written material in English persisted. There were manuscripts in the monasteries, and in various official depositories of records, and there was undoubtedly a small but continuing amount of private writing in English. After 1100, the ruling class seems to have established itself securely enough to interact more with those they ruled, and the need for writing English became urgent: personal names had to be recorded, taxes assessed, placenames written down, graves marked, contracts signed. The scribes were at first French-speaking and wrote in the French orthography discussed above. But before long many of them were native speakers of English, and the flood of writing in English gained momentum. This reflects the growing anglicization of the Norman-French ruling class. For a long time French was to continue to be the language of law courts and of elegant discourse, but more and more it became a denatured kind of French, cut off from its roots in France, spoken with an increasingly marked English accent, and written that way too, as it were.

5.14. During the twelfth century the English language had recuperated in England. By the thirteenth century it began to spread north and west. The border regions with Scotland became English-speaking during this time, and English dialects became native in southern Scotland itself. In the southwest of England the persisting

Celtic dialects retreated slowly, so that in Cornwall there were still a few speakers of Cornish in the eighteenth century. In Wales, English became the official language in the fourteenth century, but there are still many people there whose first language is Welsh, and who do not learn English until later in life. In recent years, in fact, school instruction in Welsh has been introduced, and English is taught as a foreign language.

In the other Celtic-speaking regions of the British Isles, the spread of English has gone on inexorably. After 1300, more and more of Scotland became English-speaking, so that by the end of the eighteenth century there were only a few peripheral regions that were still monolingual in Gaelic (as the Celtic speech there is usually called). During the nineteenth century, all of these areas became bilingual, and Gaelic is now maintained as a sort of subordinate, family-and-home language in a few places, with its speakers also knowing English. It should be noted that in the southern and southeastern areas of Scotland, which were anglicized early, there developed varieties of English which are considered to be, in effect, a separate language, called Scots. This language was often written in the official records of Scotland from the fourteenth to the seventeenth centuries, and some vocabulary items from it are used to the present day—and have been recorded in nineteenth-century literary works, usually in a form that has been modified to insure its being understood by readers of ordinary English. Spoken Scots persists today in the same areas, and the population learns Standard English as a second language, acquired in school. Scots and English are structurally similar, and are probably mutually intelligible to those accustomed to their use.

In the regions of Scotland that remained Gaelic-speaking after the political union of Scotland with England, Gaelic was gradually replaced by the official English. In these areas the language today is Scotch English, that is, various English dialects differing in some degree from standard English, but not as Scots differs from English.

On the Isle of Man, Manx, a dialect of Gaelic, persisted until the nineteenth century, but is now kept alive only as a sort of conscious remembrance of things past. The common children's ditty beginning "Eeny-meeny-miney-moe ..." is said to have been introduced by tinkers (traveling hardware salesmen) from Man, and the first item in it, *eeny*, could well be the numeral one, spelled *aoine* in Gaelic, and pronounced /íynə/.

In Ireland, English was introduced by the conquerors from England in the thirteenth century. In northern Ireland it soon became the only language, there being many settlers from England. Elsewhere it spread slowly, and even today there are areas in southwestern Ireland in which English is only known as a second language.

As the English language was carried all over Great Britain and into Ireland by conquest, it was the English of the court in London that became the model to be learned and used by the people of all of the British Isles in their dealings with government and law and in commerce. From 1400 on there was an increasing uniformity in the written language, and an increasing manifestation of the linguistic characteristics of modern English. It is usually said that Middle English turns into Modern English during the fifteenth century. By this time French had completely disappeared as an ordinary spoken language, but persisted in legal and other special terminology for a considerable time.

5.15. The age of exploration and discovery by Europeans of the rest of the world began in the late fifteenth century, with voyages around Africa, to India and China, overland travel across central Asia to the Pacific, and finally the discovery of America. Under Elizabeth I, England began to assume the proportions of an important European power. With the defeat of Spain in 1588, England became a world power and colonization of the new lands began in the seventeenth century. The settlement of English speakers in America from 1607 on started English on its career as a world language. In the eighteenth century English was brought to India, and spread more widely in North America. In the nineteenth century English came to various parts of the Pacific, and to the commercial coast cities of the Far East; and at the end of the century to several parts of Africa.

The English that was exported to the areas of settlement was Modern English, with the local and class characteristics of the speakers who did the settling. These settlers often constituted groups of fairly homogeneous origin, so that in the areas settled we find continuation of the dialects that existed in England. But the groups always had some dialect mixture and also a large contingent composed of persons sufficiently literate to write a standard kind of English and to speak a language approaching the standard literary English centering around London. As has been the case with all the European languages that have been exported to colonial lands, it was generally a more or less uniform and standardized form of the language that was established; this standardization occurred especially in those areas where the colonizers were few in number or were chiefly officials.

There is one kind of historical development that has been different from the picture of uniformity just suggested. In a few areas the number of English speakers was apparently too small to introduce the language as it then existed, and a special form—Pidgin English—grew up. Pidginized or creolized forms of other languages have arisen also, and the process whereby a pidgin comes into being is not really known. English in this form developed in the Pacific and on the coast of China and in the Caribbean—the latter in the eighteenth century, the former two in the nineteenth century.

In the twentieth century English spread to new regions, and into new uses, but also lost ground in some ways. The United States introduced English into the Philippines and in Puerto Rico at the turn of the century. After World War I the use of English as an official language was extended to some territories that had been under German or Japanese administration previously. Between the two world wars the use of English as an auxiliary language in commerce and science grew. After World War II, English as an auxiliary language spread even more widely, and it is one of the five official languages of the United Nations.

Certain colonial countries, in securing independence, have tried to replace English by some native language. In Ireland the fostering of the Irish language (a Celtic language, also called "Gaelic"—the Gaelic of Scotland consisting of closely related dialects) has not stopped the use of English and its spread to the few remaining non-English-speaking areas. In the Republic of South Africa, on the other hand, the fostering of Afrikaans has interfered with the learning of English both by white Afrikaners and by Negroes of various linguistic affiliations. Elsewhere in Africa the most recently independent countries formerly under British rule have retained English as the language of contact with the Western world, and some former French colonies have decided to introduce English in the schools. In India English was toppled from its official position after independence, but the realities of the situation are such that it has been necessary to retain it as a teaching medium at all higher levels and as a generally widely used language for the country as a whole. With less disturbance, the same course has been followed in Pakistan. In the Philippines there was an attempt to replace English by Tagalog, but English has come back stronger than ever. In the Melanesian areas in the Pacific some areas have set up Pidgin English, under the name of Neomelanesian, as an official language, but even if this succeeds for a while, it will eventually be replaced by ordinary English. In Indonesia, English has replaced Dutch as the language of Western contact. In

French Canada the spread of English is held back by political and ecclesiastical forces, but it becomes more widely spoken anyway.

5.16. From the language of a few thousand people in the forests and marshes in what is now northwestern Germany, English has in 1500 years become the world's most widely spoken unified language. This is said despite the claims of Chinese: in China there are at least five different languages and the official North Chinese language (Mandarin), while spoken by perhaps two-thirds of the population, exists in widely divergent dialects, and is known as a written language by not more than 10 to 15 per cent of the people.

In the countries where the bulk of the population speaks English— Great Britain and Ireland, the United States, Canada (except Quebec), Australia, New Zealand, parts of the Republic of South Africa, and a considerable number of island and other territories in various parts of the world, there are nearly 300 million people; all but a few millions of the adults in these areas are native speakers of English as their first language, and over 90 per cent of the adults are literate in the one standard and highly uniform written language.

Besides the native speakers, there are about 250 million more persons in the world who know English to a greater or lesser degree. Quebec, the Philippines, India and Pakistan, various western, central, and southern African countries, and the remaining colonies of the British Commonwealth form the first ranks of this group, with English as an official or second language. Japan is a country where many people know or learn English as the road to contact with the Western world. Indonesia is supposed to consider English in the same way. In Scandinavia, France, Germany, the U.S.S.R., and other countries, English is the preferred foreign language taught in the schools.

There are thus over 500 million people for whom the predominant values of their Western culture are stated in English, the language whose over-all structure was sketched in 2.4 and 3.4, and which has been the chief source of illustrations of theory and analysis presented in this book.

5.2. LANGUAGES WITHOUT HISTORY

5.20. It was possible to present the history of English in the preceding section because there is documentation concerning the historical events that have taken place in the British Isles over the past 1500 years. Except for the earliest of these events, those occurring in the fifth, sixth, and seventh centuries, the documents were for the most part locally produced by participants and observers on the scene. Of these locally produced documents, which exist in increasing quantities as the centuries pass, all except a few early ones written in Latin and those written in French in the eleventh to thirteenth centuries are in some form of English. This means that they not only inform us about the activities of people, the things that happened to them, and the goods and artifacts they produced and used, but they also give us direct evidence of the linguistic forms that were employed in talking about the activities, events, goods, and artifacts dealt with.

This direct linguistic evidence has many uses. We can determine more or less accurately how the words employed sounded, and how they behaved grammatically. By comparing documents of different dates we can see how the sounds and forms changed with time. We can see vocabulary items go out of use, and others come into the language. From this study, we can make statemants about cultural systems at different times, and about how they changed. (The References and Notes indicate where the reader may find a survey of the most important facets of the historical changes and developments that can be determined from documents for the English language.) It should be noted, however, that no one has yet taken full advantage of the available documentation, for English or any other language, to try to produce even an approximation to a picture of the total culture at any one period, or of cultural changes over time.

5.21.   What about the thousands of languages for which there are no historical documents? Can we learn anything about their histories, and about the development of the cultures of the peoples who speak them? The history of languages without written documentation can be reconstructed, but only partially. It depends on the kind of contemporary evidence available.

If a language exists in a number of dialects, comparison of the varying forms makes possible the reconstruction of the probable originals that gave rise to the variation (see Chapter 6). The linguistic forms thus reconstructed make it possible to formulate reconstructions of other kinds of cultural data. Most usually this sort of reconstruction is done for languages that have grown far apart. An example would be the datum that English and some other languages of Europe and Asia have words for the beech tree which all stem from a single original term. Besides pointing to the relatedness of these languages, such a datum also tells us that the speakers of the ancestral language inhabited a region where beech trees grew. Botanical and silvicultural data can be used to identify such regions, and thus to tell us something about the ancestral homeland.

Examination of Finnish and various related languages discloses a number of words that closely resemble certain Germanic words. An example is *kuningas* 'king'. This shows us that at some time in their unrecorded past the ancestors of the speakers of Finnish encountered speakers of Germanic. More than that, it tells us that the encounter was at a time when the Germanic word had the form **kuningaz* (the asterisk denotes a hypothetical reconstruction), a form not completely reconstructible from the existing forms *king*, German *König*, and so on. The further knowledge that the Russian word *knäzĭ* /knjazj/ 'duke, prince' also goes back to the Germanic form **kuningaz* throws still more light on the history of contacts between peoples in prehistoric eastern Europe.

The examples adduced here are obtained by the methods of linguistic reconstruction and the determination of language relationships that are discussed in Chapter 6 of this book. The methods are mentioned here to point out that they are available, though it is unfortunately true that only the most superficial use of such data has been made to reconstruct ethnohistory.

Other clues to the history of unwritten languages can be found in archeological remains and in traditional lore (folklore and mythology). These methods involve much guesswork, however, and give little certainty, as yet.

Chapter 6

RELATED LANGUAGES

6.0. CONTRAST AND COMPARISON

6.00. The data of different languages, as items or as systems, can be considered side by side, two or more at a time, and the differences and similarities can be examined and noted.

When the materials compared are historical documents in a single language tradition, the results are the statements of HISTORICAL LINGUISTICS in the narrow sense of the term. This kind of historical investigation of language data was alluded to in 5.1 (see also References and Notes). Wider comparisons were also mentioned, indicating relationships between languages that are not considered as being one and the same language (say English and German). This wider comparison is the province of what was named COMPARATIVE LINGUISTICS in 5.02 (see also 5.21). Comparative linguistic studies result in historical statements, but where there are no historical documents, these statements are reconstructions and are often tentative and inexact, so that the term *historical linguistics* is best restricted to the cases where there is documentary evidence. Implied in all comparative linguistics is also what may be called CONTRASTIVE LINGUISTICS. In this kind of study, lack of similarity and specific differences and contrasts in structure are noted. Contrastive work may be the first step to a comparative statement indicating relationship. Or it may have other purposes: it may be aimed at constructing adequate pedagogies for teaching differing languages, or at the examination of different parts of the language systems as structures differing or being similar in type. Contrastive studies of this last kind are TYPOLOGICAL, and are sometimes part of the approach to comparative studies that show linguistic relationship.

Comparative linguistics thus includes contrastive and typological studies, and historical studies, which may be of either of these kinds.

Its aims are to find related languages, to determine the nature and extent of the relationships, to indicate development of typological and specific structures, and to determine possible or probable courses of historical change. Comparative linguistics is possible, and is a scientifically profitable activity, because of the essential structural similarity (see 1.23) of all human language (and its quite probable single origin as the first cultural invention—1.11–1.12), and also because of the diversity of existing languages (1.3). Because people can learn one another's languages, and because in doing so they evaluate structures and subsystems as similar or not, typological and contrastive conclusions have been arrived at by human beings at all times and in all places. Where, as in the Western world, there exist documents of recent as well as remote origin, and where there is a lively interest in group and individual history, people go beyond contrastive and typological conclusions; they formulate historical conclusions also, and subsume the whole in comparative statements of relationship.

6.01.   The first persons who thought about the structure of their language—its grammar—were typologists of a kind. The structures they found or imputed to their languages were set up by their followers as types, and other languages were described as near or far, similar or different, in relation to these theoretical types. In the case of the explicit grammars for which historical records exist—Sanskrit, Greek, Arabic—the types were taken to be universal, and all other languages were thought of as having to fit into the established types or be considered as lacking in perfection. Given the well-nigh universal ethnocentrism of human societies, it is probable that all grammars—explicit or not—expressed this attitude.

The Ancient Greek grammarians did a reasonably good job of analyzing their own language, and they set up its type as the universal model not only for language description but also for "logic". All speakers of languages other than Greek were 'babblers'—*bárbaroi* (whence our word *barbarian*). When the Romans began to write grammars of Latin, they put them into the same form as the Greeks used; the two languages are sufficiently similar in type to make this transfer possible, but some important differences in structure were overlooked until later. Following ancient times in Europe, the revival of classical learning brought back the Greco-Latin grammatical type as the universal model, and comparative linguistics suffered from this blight until the nineteenth century. Even today much linguistic analysis is still cast in this basic mold, for even the most enlightened anthropologically oriented linguists are still in many ways part of their culture in this respect.

The Sanskrit grammarians implied that their typology was universal and universally applicable. Their techniques were more like those of modern linguistics than were those of the Greeks, and had in them the possibility of valid contrastive linguistic study. Their successors, however, in most cases merely followed the model, and described all Indic languages, and the Dravidian ones as well, as if they were a kind of Sanskrit.

The medieval Arab grammarians knew both the Greek and the Sanskrit models, apparently. They used some of the best features of both, and came up with a valid grammar of Classical Arabic. As a typological model this was useful for descriptions of Hebrew and other Semitic languages. But it was too rigid to be useful for comparative linguistics in the wider sense.

In China a grammatical tradition of the Sanskrit or Greco-Latin type never developed. Chinese is of a structure quite different from other languages with which there was contact. The Chinese ethnocentrism about language simply took the form of not feeling any need for grammatical description in the ordinary sense. There is thus no native Chinese grammar, and modern linguistics has yet to come up with a satisfactory model for description of a very interesting typological structure.

The traditional grammars, having set up their typology as a rigid universal, did not give rise to systematic contrastive studies. The contrastive remarks are always in terms of specific noting of departure from a norm. In the Sanskrit tradition the notion of historical continuity and causality of development (in the Western sense of history) is absent, and no idea of historical relationship of languages ever developed; the contrastive data were simply noted as such, or were ignored. In the Arab world the easy applicability of the grammatical model to Hebrew gave rise to the notion of historical relation, and this fitted in with the theological tradition stemming from the Old Testament. In the European world, Greco-Latin grammar gave a good start to contrastive descriptions, but the Old Testament tradition proved a great impediment; reconciling the Hebrew Semitic structure with the Greco-Latin one was not possible, even though the two have some basic structures that are similar; and much energy was wasted on the task. Nonetheless, with its strong interest in history, and the Greek and Roman traditions of at least reporting on the doings of barbarians, including the way they talked, the Western world began providing linguistic descriptions with large amounts of contrastive detail. And from these descriptions grew historical speculations.

In the Western world, beginning with the Renascence, there began to appear, from time to time, a venturesomeness and exploratory fervor that showed itself also in scholarly activities. The Classical languages—Greek and Latin—were restudied, but when they were compared and contrasted with the living languages of Europe, a few scholars began to see the differences not as corruptions or departures from perfection, but as developments over time. The presence of large numbers of historical documents led to the growth of historical perspective.

Concern with the spoken languages of Italy, Spain, France, and Germany grew with the centuries of the Renascence. There began to appear speculative or other works describing the languages, and even attempting to account for their form by historical change. It was soon seen that the various languages and dialects of Italy, Spain, and France resembled each other greatly, and also bore a special resemblance to Latin. Latin was known to resemble Greek. It was concluded that all these languages were somehow related, and there was even some systematic statement of the way in which the three modern languages differed from Latin. How Latin and Greek differed or were similar was never systematically worked out at that time. No one could go beyond Greek. Theology called for a connection with Hebrew to be shown. Much time and effort was expended on the task, but of course without success.

In the eighteenth century, European powers began to extend their colonial rule to southern Asia. In India they found the Sanskrit literary and grammatical tradition, which had been virtually unknown in Europe. After the English had established their rule in India, numbers of European scholars began to study Sanskrit and other languages of India, and learned societies were established dealing with many phases of Indic studies. Sir William Jones, who was a British official in India, and who has been called the first great European Sanskrit scholar, having acquired the methods of grammatical analysis developed in India while learning Sanskrit, was able to see that Sanskrit greatly resembled Greek and Latin in structure. From the similarity he drew the conclusion, in 1786, that the resemblances were too great to be the product of chance, but must be due to the fact that the three languages "have sprung from some common source which, perhaps, no longer exists". It is usual to date comparative Indo-European linguistics from this statement; and since it was with Indo-European that comparative linguistics started, all modern comparative linguistics began at this point.

As will be seen in the next sections, this point of view led to the development of strict methods of comparison and reconstruction. From these, it became evident that languages are patterned and systematic, that they are systems of human behavior that, like other systems in the universe, are observable and predictable. In the nineteenth century the scholarly world was looking for measurement and consistent systems in the fields of learning that were being called sciences. Language had been thought of only as concerned with imprecise, unscientific activities of human beings; it was one of the "humanities". The comparative study of languages was an indication that scientific observation could be carried out on at least some aspects of human behavior. Comparative linguistics became, by this development, the first SOCIAL SCIENCE, in the modern meaning of that term. Unfortunately, knowledge was scanty, and over-enthusiastic outsiders eagerly, but usually mistakenly, started citing linguistic evidence to prove almost anything. So comparative linguistics became more and more philological and less and less observational in the direct sense. Its social-science components were overlooked, and it was almost a hundred years before linguistics and anthropology were once again considered as being intimately connected.

The early comparative linguistics of the nineteenth century had been concerned with anthropological data in that it had considered languages spoken by peoples whose cultures had come to differ profoundly despite the linguistic relationship. The comparativists were interested in these cultural differences—in kinship systems, social structure, reactions to the ecology of the areas where the languages were spoken, technical terms, and all the other things that anthropologists concern themselves with. Anthropology as a field of science hardly existed at the time, however, and the linguistic observations and conclusions were often made by methods and from premises which would not be considered properly anthropological today. Nonetheless, they were often not only valid in themselves, but also valuable as auxiliaries to anthropological activity in the narrower sense.

After the middle of the nineteenth century, anthropology developed as an independent scientific discipline, and the linguistics of the languages spoken by the peoples whom anthropologists studied became explicitly part of the science. Most of this kind of linguistic study was purely descriptive, but from time to time linguistic anthropologists made comparative studies of various languages for which there were no written historical records. Such comparative studies were, in America, made by anthropologists who were also trained in the Indo-European comparative methodology. Elsewhere—as in Africa—the studies were done by persons with other training, such as philological, historical, sociological, or, and principally, by linguists untrained in anthropology.

Work in anthropologically oriented historical linguistics of American Indian languages has been done since about 1880. Gradually more and more such work has become known to linguists in other areas, and the lessons and findings of traditional historical comparative linguistics have become available to linguistic anthropologists. By the middle of the twentieth century, the mutual interdependence of these various specialties was clear.

Much study in historical linguistics is done by linguists who in their descriptive work use few if any anthropological approaches. Some linguistic anthropologists are unaware of historical and comparative linguistic findings that are pertinent to their special interests. Further, both within and outside of these fields, there are persons who accept findings from them uncritically or without proper understanding. Nonetheless, historical and comparative linguistics is properly to be considered one of the activities within anthropological linguistics.

6.1. LANGUAGE RELATIONSHIPS

6.10. The search for language relationships has been carried on, as indicated in 6.01, for a long time in the Western world because of an interest in history. It was also in the Western world that a science of anthropology developed. The study of the languages of many peoples, both "civilized" and "primitive", led to their comparison as systems, and to the stating of the similarities and differences in their systems. Systems of sounds were compared, and systems of grammar.

The statement cited from Sir William Jones may be taken as the first explicit realization that comparison of languages to establish relationships had to be done systematically. It also indicated that the systematic comparisons had to result in systematic resemblances, not merely haphazard ones. And it further implied that related languages were the product of change over time in some original language which ceased to exist as such.

It was no longer possible to cite chance resemblances and have them accepted as proof of relationship. To give a well-known example, consider the fact that *máti* is Modern Greek for 'eye', and that *mata* is the word for 'eye' in Malay. Are Greek and Malay related because of this similarity? The answer can be given only after systematic comparison. There are very few other such striking vocabulary resemblances between the two languages, and their grammatical structures are wholly different. Further, it is possible to show that *máti* goes back to an older form *ommátion*; this came to be pronounced /ománti/; the definite article for this word was *to*; the phrase came to be said as /to(+)máti/, with the two *o*'s coalescing; so the word became *máti*. The word *ommátion* is a derivative, by the addition of several postbases, of Ancient Greek *óps* 'face, eye': this can be shown to be related to Latin *oc(ulus)* 'eye', Old Church Slavic *oko*, German *Auge*, and English *eye*. On the other hand, other Malayan languages point to a Proto-Malayan form like **mata* (the asterisk means reconstructed, but not attested in a written document) existing at a time when the derivative *ommátion* did not exist.

Many such chance resemblances exist. One even more striking can be given. In the Indo-European languages various words for 'tongue' or 'language'—English *tongue*, Latin *lingua* (for expected **dingua*), Old Church Slavic *ęzykŭ* (pronounced approximately [yæ(ᵈ)zʻiˑku], phonemically perhaps /yənჳíykí/)—may go back to a reconstructed (see 6.22) form something like **dengú-*. In the languages of the Azteco-Tanoan family, of which Aztec (in Mexico) and Taos (in New Mexico) are widely separated examples, the reconstructed form for 'language' or 'speaking' turns out to be something like **duŋw-*. But at any plausible former time when the similar forms **dengú-* and **duŋw-* may have existed—say, more than 5,000 but less than 10,000 years ago—Indo-European and Azteco-Tanoan were separated by many thousands of miles, and by many thousands of years of separate development even if they ever had a connection in space and time. If we could reconstruct back another 5,000 years—which can't be done for lack of evidence—it is not improbable that the forms would be quite different.

To replace chance resemblances, linguists began to use systems of correspondences. These correspondences were at first—and to a large extent have continued to be—phonological ones only. We shall see later what use can be made of morphological and semological correspondences. Systematic correspondences were found by taking word lists in two or more languages that were to be compared and by determining the correspondences for each phoneme from the beginning of the word, as far as one could go. Then if several words showed the same sets of correspondences, these were considered to be systematic—at least tentatively—and further details were sought.

We shall now illustrate sets of systematic correspondences in phonology, with some instances of other kinds of correspondences. **6.11.** It was said above (6.01) that it became apparent in the Middle Ages that French, Spanish, Italian, and Latin were languages that resembled each other greatly. Any list of words may be drawn up for any one of the languages, and the words of the same or similar meanings in the other languages can be compared with them. The following list will serve as an example (English meanings are given first):

ENGLISH	FRENCH	SPANISH	ITALIAN	LATIN
'father'	*père*	*padre*	*padre*	*patrem*
'beautiful'	*beau*	*bello*	*bello*	*bellum*
'land'	*terre*	*tierra*	*terra*	*terram*
'tooth'	*dent*	*diente*	*dente*	*dentem*
'hundred'	*cent*	*ciento*	*cento*	*centum*
'related'	*germain*	*hermano*	*germano*	*germanum*
'field'	*champ*	*campo*	*campo*	*campum*
'joy'	*joie*	*gozo*	*gaudio*	*gaudium*
'whom'	*que*	*quien*	*chè*	*quem*
'when'	*quand*	*cuando*	*quando*	*quando*
'fire'	*feu*	*fuego*	*fuoco*	*focum*
'salt'	*sel*	*sal*	*sale*	*salem*
'today'	[aujourd']*hui*	*hoy*	*oggi*	*hodie*
'mother'	*mère*	*madre*	*madre*	*matrem*
'new'	*neuf*	*nuevo*	*nuovo*	*novum*
'milk'	*lait*	*leche*	*latte*	*lactem*
'king'	*roi*	*rey*	*rege*	*regem*
'it is worth'	*vaut*	*vale*	*vale*	*valet*
'game'	*jeu*	*juego*	*giuoco*	*jocum*

As given here in their ordinary spellings, nearly all of these words clearly show close resemblances. The Latin forms are the accusative singular of nouns, adjectives, and pronouns, and there is one 3rd person singular present verb form (for details of Latin structure, and for the changes from Latin to Romanic, consult the works mentioned in References and Notes). When we examine the actual phonemic structure of the words given, the resemblance is in some cases even greater, but in others less:

/peərə/	/pádře/	/pádre/	/pátrem/
/bo/	/béḷo/	/béllo/	/béllum/
/teərə/	/tyéra/	/térra/	/térram/

/dan/	/dyénte/	/dɛ́nte/	/déntem/
/san/	/θyénto/	/čɛ́nto/	/kéntum/
/žermen/	/ermáno/	/ǰermáno/	/germá·num/
/šan/	/kámpo/	/kámpo/	/kámpum/
/žwa/	/góθo/	/gáwdyo/	/gáwdium/
/kə/	/kyén/	/kɛ́/	/kwém/
/kan/	/kwándo/	/kwándo/	/kwándo·/
/fø/	/fwégo/	/fwɔ́ko/	/fókum/
/selə/	/sál/	/sále/	/sálem/
-/ẅi/	/óy/	/óǰǰi/	/hódie·/
/meərə/	/mádře/	/mádre/	/má·trem/
/nøf/	/nwébo/	/nwɔ́vo/	/nówum/
/leə/	/léče/	/látte/	/láktem/
/rwa/	/réy/	/rɛ́ǰe/	/régem/
/vo/	/bále/	/vále/	/wálet/
/žø/	/xwégo/	/ǰwɔ́ko/	/yókum/

The French pronunciation is that of standard Parisian French. The Spanish is Castillian (central Spain); in all American Spanish /θ/ is replaced by /s/, and in most American Spanish /ļ/ is replaced by /y/. The Italian is standard central Italian. The Latin is late Classical (around the beginning of the Christian era). All the Latin initial consonants are illustrated, as well as the cluster /kw/.

From this short list it is seen that French, Spanish, and Italian, if they are considered historically as products of Latin, have diverged from Latin in systematic ways. Most of the initial consonants have remained, but Latin /k/ and /kw/, and /g/, have undergone various changes. Latin /h/ has disappeared; Latin /w/ and /y/ have changed in various ways. Going beyond the initial consonant, it is seen that vowels and internal consonants have changed, and that the final consonants /m/ and /t/ have disappeared. Moreover, within each of the later languages we can see systematic differences from each other as compared to Latin: *père* and *mère* as contrasted with *padre*, *madre*; *tierra*, *diente* contrasted with *terra*, *dente* (also French *terre*, but *dent* is special because of the /n/); *feu*, *jeu* against the others; and so on.

If we now look for other Latin words beginning with the Latin initial consonant phonemes, we shall find that wherever such words have survived in French, Spanish, or Italian, the consonants have remained or changed in the same manner as above. (There are a few instances where this is not so; they are explained by special circumstances applicable to the specific items—see 6.21.) Thus *pontem* 'bridge' is French *pont*, Spanish *puente*, Italian *ponte*; *vīvum* 'alive' is *vif*, *vivo*; *sitem* 'thirst' is *soif*, *sed*, *sede*; *factum* 'done' is *fait*, *hecho*, *fatto*; and so on.

6.12. What do the examples just studied show us? And how do they exemplify language relationships?

First of all, there is seen to be a large measure not only of resemblance but of actual coincidence between languages that are thought to be related. Not only do French, Spanish, and Italian show hundreds of vocabulary items in common, but they also exhibit marked grammatical similarities: to French *écrire* 'write', *écrit* 'written' correspond Spanish *escribir*, *escrito* and Italian *scrivere*, *scritto*; all three languages have verbal phrases like *j'ai écrit* 'I've written', *he escrito*, *ho scritto*; pronominal forms like *il* 'he', *le* 'him', *lui* 'to him'—*él*, *le*, *le*; *egli*, *lo*, *lui*; vocabulary items like *la main* 'the hand'—*la mano*, *la mano*; "idioms" like *il s'en va* 'he goes away'—*se va, si ne va*. French, Spanish, and Italian also exhibit similar meaning developments: *chef* 'chief, chef', *cabo* 'head, leader', *capo* 'head, beginning'; but French *tête* 'head' (of body), Italian *testa* (Spanish, however, has *cabeza*).

Second, it is seen that Latin, the presumed original language, has ceased to exist as such. It has survived only in the form of the several modern languages. And the changes have been similar or identical, and they have been systematic.

On these two factors we base our notion of related languages. Two OR MORE LANGUAGES ARE SAID TO BE RELATED IF THEY EXHIBIT SYSTEMATIC CORRESPONDENCES in phonology, as well as in morphology and semology, AND CAN BE SHOWN TO BE THE PRODUCTS OF REGULAR CHANGE FROM A PREVIOUSLY EXISTING SINGLE LANGUAGE. The techniques by which systematic correspondences are arrived at have been illustrated in part by the examples in 6.11. They will be considered further in the next sections, where historical reconstruction in its various aspects will be examined.

6.2. HISTORICAL RECONSTRUCTION

6.20. The most important consideration in the evaluation of language relationship is regularity of correspondence. Whatever may have happened to a phoneme of an original language in two languages surviving from it, and no matter how great the difference between the resulting sounds, there is no difficulty if the correspondence is regular. Given an initial list like the one above, one looks for more examples, until one is assured of regularity of correspondence. When the languages being compared are not very far apart, this examination is easily done. But suppose we have languages where there are fewer resemblances? The same principle still holds.

To Latin *sex* 'six' and *septem* 'seven' correspond Greek *héx* and *heptá*. Even if there were only these two examples, they would constitute strong evidence for regularity of the correspondence Latin *s-* = Greek *h-*. In Modern Greek the *h-* has disappeared, but the correspondence still holds, in the form Romanic *s-* = Greek 0- (zero). Examination of the Greek and Latin vocabularies shows many items with the same correspondence. Further, there are many instances of Latin *-em*(-) or *-en*(-) corresponding to Greek *-a*(-): *centum* 'hundred'—*[he]katón* is but one example. This last item may be used to illustrate greater divergence: Old Church Slavic has *sŭto* (/sĭtó/) for 'hundred', Russian has *sto*; many Latin forms in *-um*, such as neuter nouns, Greek in *-on*, have Russian correspondences in *-o*; and many Latin and Greek /k/'s correspond to Russian /s/: *cor* 'heart', *kardía, serdce*; Greek *kálamos* 'reed', Russian *soloma* 'straw'; *canis* 'dog', *kúōn (kun-)*, *su[ka]* 'bitch'; *ac[idus]* 'sour', Greek *óxos* 'vinegar' and *oxús* 'sharp' (both with *x* /ks/), Russian *os[tryį]* 'sharp'; and so on.

There are instances where regularity of correspondence does not occur, and yet the forms are clearly similar. For 'five' Latin had *quīnque*: French, Spanish, and Italian show, respectively, initial /s-/, 0-, č-/. These are the regular correspondences to Latin /k-/ before a front vowel; but Latin /kw-/ regularly becomes /k-/ in this situation. This is then some kind of special case. As we shall see, instances of this kind strengthen the notion of regularity because of their infrequency, and are explainable by special situations. In the instance cited, it is believed that Latin *quīnque* came to be pronounced /kí·nkwe/—an instance of DISSIMILATION (see below, p. 161)—and this went on to change regularly; Spanish *cinco* also points to a form like /kí·nkum/, but this form had to come into existence AFTER the dissimilation of the first /kw/ to /k/ under the influence of the second /kw/.

The regular correspondences lead to the establishment of statements about them—so-called "sound laws" (see 6.21)—and to the formulation of plausible explanations for the seeming irregularities. These sound laws and explanations make possible reconstruction of original forms, and the ascertainment of degrees or closeness of relationship—see 6.22.

6.21. When two or more languages have been compared, the statements about the relationships of the various sounds in the compared items can be made in various forms. If, as in the examples above, it is determined that one of the languages is ancestral to the others, it is customary to make the statements in this form: "original *x* becomes *y* in language A and *z* in language B". But it is also common to say "*y* of language A corresponds to *z* of language B". In the case of languages being compared for which no ancestral language is known or is being set up, only the second kind of statement is possible. In the latter instance, if, on the basis of the statements of relation, it is possible to conjecture what an original might have been like, the conclusion is called a reconstruction (marked by *). See 6.22 for reconstructions.

In order to clarify and exemplify the notions of regular correspondences, the principal statements of sound laws will be given for the list in 6.11. The statements will be made mostly in the second way just described, but will imply the first procedure by comparison of the French, Italian, and Spanish forms with Latin. The discussion will be based on the phonemic forms, rather than on spelling.

The word for 'father' shows initial /p/ in F, S, and I, corresponding to L /p/, indicating no phonemic change. S and I show /á/ corresponding to L /á/, but F has /eə/. S /dř/ and I /dr/ go with L /tr/, while F has only /r/. F /ə/, S and I /e/ correspond to L /em/.

L /béllum/ has corresponding to it I /béllo/, where /b/, /ɛ/, /ll/ seem unchanged (L /e/ was [ɛ], it is believed), and /um/ has become /o/. In terms of the previous item also, it would appear that nothing corresponds to a final L /m/. S also has /b/, /e/ (S does not distinguish [ɛ] from [e] phonemically), and final /o/, but has /ļ/ (or /y/ in many dialects) for L /ll/. F has initial /b/, but everything else seems different; however, there is a form *bel* /bel/ occurring before a word beginning with a vowel, and there is the feminine form *belle*; it would appear that in French special statements are needed for some items occurring in final position, or before consonants, or in isolation.

F /teərə/, S /tyéra/, and I /térra/ 'land' have /t/, as does the L /térram/. L final /m/ is again not represented in F, S, I. The L prefinal vowel /a/ is found as /a/ in S and I, but F has /ə/. I has /rr/, as does L, but S seems to show /r/; however, it must be noted that in the phonemicization being used here /r/ is [r·], which is phonetically the same as I /rr/ and presumably L /rr/. I has /ɛ́/ corresponding to L /é/, as in /béllo/—/béllum/, but S has /yé/, and F has /eə/. In F, 'father' and 'land' rime, which must be a late development in F itself. The S /yé/ as contrasted with /é/ in /bélo/ needs further evidence before it can be explained.

In the item for 'tooth', initial /d/ shows everywhere, and internal /nt/ show in S and I. The correspondences S /yé/, I /ɛ́/, L /é/ are as in 'land'; the L final /m/ is missing in S and I, but the vowel preceding it seems to stay put. F once more is different, with no /t/, and /a/ for the only vowel left, the end of the word having nothing corresponding to the vowels of the other languages; this was also true for 'beautiful'.

In 'hundred', the vowel correspondences, and the end of the word, are as for 'tooth'. The initials are varied: F /s/, S /θ/ (but /s/ in many dialects), I /č/, L /k/. We can conjecture that the original /k/ was palatalized before the front vowel L /e/. The processes involved may have been as follows: /k/ became [ky], then [ty]; in I this became [ty₍ₐ₎], then [tš], then [ǽš] = /č/; in S, [ty₍ₐ₎] became [ts], then [tθ], then [θ] (in the dialects which have /s/, the [tθ] stage may not have existed); in F, the [ts] stage led to [s] = /s/.

The L *germanus* (accusative *germanum*) meant '(truly) related' in speaking of brothers and sisters, or of cousins. In English we have *cousin german*, a phrase taken from medieval French; in French the word is now used almost entirely as a literary word, in the sense of English *germane* (which is itself a learned loan direct from Latin). The Italian word is also learned, or it may be a learned word of different history, meaning 'Germanic' (our 'German'). In Spanish, however, the term survived and became the ordinary word for 'brother'. The F and I words show correspondences to L that are found in many other items: /ž/, /ĵ/, /g/ before a front vowel; F /en/ for I /án/, L /á·n/; internal consonants unchanged. In S we have nothing corresponding to L /g/; there are words in Spanish with /x/ for L /g/, such as *gente* 'people' (*gentem*); the conditions governing these differences require more evidence before they can be stated.

For 'field', we have the exact correspondences in S and I to L /k/, /á/, /m/, /p/, and the correspondence of /o/ to /um/, as before. In F the end of the word has disappeared, the nasal is represented by /n/, which in the phonemicization used here means phonetic nasalization of the preceding vowel; and the initial is /š/; we can conjecture /k/ becoming [ky], then [ty], then [tš] (in Old French), and finally /š/.

For 'joy', the I word, which shows exact correspondences to the L, with the final /o/ for /um/, is a learned loan with the meaning 'contentment', rather than a direct development from L (we might expect something like /*góżżo/ in the latter case); I *gioia* 'joy' is a medieval loan from F. S shows the initial /g/, but /ó/ for /áw/, and /θ/ for /dy/; there is evidence that the development of the internal consonant cluster was approximately this: /dy/ > [dz] > [dð] > /ð/ (in Old Spanish), then /ð/ > /θ/. In F we have initial /ž/, and this parallels initial /š/ in *champ*; that is, /g/ became [gy] before the /a/ of /áw/, then [dy] > [dž] > /ž/. The internal /dy/ must have become something like /ðy/, then simply /y/; meanwhile /áw/ had become /ów/, and the sequence /ówy/ resulted in /óy/. English *joy* is from the Old French /ǰóyĕ/ (where weak-stressed /ĕ/ was probably phonetically [ɨ] or [ə]); later in F /oy/ became /oe/, then /we/, then /wa/.

The correspondences to L /kwém/ show /k/ in F, S, and I, the expected /yé/ and /ɛ́/ in S and I (cf. *terram, dentem*), and /ə/ in F; S retains a final nasal, as /n/. It is interesting here to compare F *rien* /ryen/ 'nothing', which comes from L *rem* /rém/, accusative of *res* /re·s/ 'thing' (*ne . . . rien* 'not a thing', i.e., 'nothing'); *rem* gave a F result parallel to S *quién*, and this suggests that *que* is due to special conditions (the unaccented position of the item in phrases).

The correspondences to L /kwándo·/ show /kw/ in S and I, but /k/ in F. S and I retain /nd/, and have /o/ for /o·/. In F the end of the L item has been lost; but in syntactic phrasing *quand* shows a "linking *t*"—as in *quand il est arrivé* 'when he arrived' /kan+til·e·ta-rive/; this /+t̮/ is a development of Old French final /t/ from L /d/: OF /kánt/ became /kán/ except before vowels, where the internal transition arose in the same position, after /n/, as under other circumstances, but the /t/ was joined to the following vowel in normal transition.

The comparison of the correspondences to L *centum, campum, quem, quandō* shows that before an original L /e/, L /k/ was palatalized in F, S, and I; but before L /a/, L /k/ was retained except in F, where a different kind of palatalization took place. On the other hand, L /kw/ became /k/ before /e/ in F, S, and I; but before /a/, /kw/ remained in S and I, but became /k/ in F.

In the item for 'fire', the initial is /f/ everywhere. S and I show final /o/ for /um/, while F shows nothing in that position, as in previous examples. For the first vowel, S has /wé/ and I has /wó/ corresponding to L /ó/. We know L /ó/ was phonetically about [ɔ]; here, in a syllable ending in the vowel, the vowel was lengthened and "diphthongized"; the phonemic development may have been /o/ > /oh/ [ɔ·] > /uh/ [uə], from which S got /ue/ > /we/, and I /uo/ > /wɔ/. For the internal /k/, S has /g/, but I retains /k/. In L, *focus* meant 'hearth' (whence modern English *focus*), but in the modern Romanic languages it is 'fire'.

For 'salt', the initial /s/ is found everywhere, and the internal /l/; final /em/ corresponds to /e/ in I, as in previous examples, but S has nothing (this turns out to be the case regularly after /l/); as in some of the previous items, S and I have /a/ for L /a/, but F has /e/. The final /ə/ of French is in terms of the phonemicization adopted here, where F has no final /l/s, but only cases of /lə/.

The F, S, and I words for 'today'—originally a phrase in L, *hoc die 'on this day', with closing up of open transition to give hodie /hódie·/—show nothing corresponding to L /h/. There is evidence that L /h/ became silent, as we say, during the post-Classical period in everyday speech. Contrary to the situation in the word for 'fire', S and I have /ó/ and /ɔ́/, not /wé/ and /wó/ corresponding to /ó/. In I, there is /ĵĵ/ [d>·ž] for L /di/ before a vowel, and S has /y/; the difference of these items from S gozo and I gaudio has to be explained by special circumstances. In F the /d/ has disappeared, as in S, but the resulting vocalic nucleus is different; it is probable that in French the L /ó/ had first become /ʉh/ [üə]; the sequence /ʉhy/ was then simplified to /ʉy/, resulting in modern F /ẃi/. The modern F term for 'today' is a phrase, aujourd'hui, literally 'on the day of "today"'.

The word for 'mother' shows initial /m/ everywhere, and otherwise the same developments as the word for 'father'. The correspondences to both L /a/ and /a·/ are the same in F, S, and I.

For 'new', we find initial /n/ in all four languages, and final /o/ in S and I for L /um/. The L /w/ has become /v/ in I, and /b/ (here as [β]) in S; the F /f/ is a development from /v/ (the feminine is neuve, and neuf is pronounced /nø+v‿/ before a vowel in a few old phrases). The F /ø/ is as in the word for 'fire'.

In the item for 'milk', the initial /l/ is found everywhere, S and I have /e/ for L /em/, as before, and F has nothing. For L /kt/, I has /tt/, which is found in all other such cases also. The S /č/ is probably the result of some such development as [kt] > [xt] > [x̣t] > [x̣t_y] > [ty] > [č]. S shows /e/, which is the result of the following palatal sounds. In F, the development was probably /ákt/ > /áyt/ (with intermediate steps like those in S); then /áy/ eventually became /eə/, and the final consonant disappeared.

For 'king', initial /r/ is found everywhere, though the actual pronunciation is quite different today: [R] in most F dialects, [r³⁺] in S, [r²] in I. The I [ɛĵ] is expected on the basis of the previous examples, and S has /e/ as in /béĺo/ (before a palatal) and /y/ for /g/. The F /wa/ developed from /ey/: /ey/ > /oy/, and then as for /žwa/ above.

In 'it is worth', the initials in F, S, I, and L are like the internal consonants in the words for 'new'. The L final /t/ has disappeared. For L /ále/, I has /ále/ as in /sále/, but S also retains the vowel /e/, which is not found in /sál/; this retention is to be attributed to the fact that the final /e/ is a regular verb ending (see below). The F form represents a development from pre- OF *valt, where /al/ > /aw/ > /ɔw/ > /o/; in F the final /t/ lasted a long time, and is still found in such a situation as vaut-il "is it worth?" /vo+til/.

In the word for 'game', the developments of everything after the initial are the same as for 'fire'. The correspondence of F /ž/ and I /ǰ/ is as for *germanum* above. The S /x/ is also one of the regular correspondences (see *gente* under *hermano* above): /y/ > [dy] > [dž] = /ǰ/; then /ǰ/ > /ž/, which fell together with /š/ in the sixteenth century, giving modern /x/ ([š] > [x̣] > [x]).

The statements made above can also be given in formulaic form. The L phoneme will be given first, then the equivalents in F, S, and I. The previous order could be used just as well. The various correspondences would need to be grouped by position in the words. The sample is too small to give all the formulas, so only those for initial consonants are presented:

LATIN	FRENCH	SPANISH	ITALIAN
p	p	p	p
b	b	b	b
t	t	t	t
d	d	d	d
k before e	s	θ	č
g before e	ž	θ before weak vowel and	ǰ
		x before stressed vowel	
k before a	š	k	k
g before a	ž	g	g
kw before e	k	k	k
kw before a	k	kw	kw
f	f	f	f
s	s	s	s
h	θ	θ	θ
m	m	m	m
n	n	n	n
l	l	l	l
r	r	r	r
w	v	b	v
y	ž	x	ǰ

These formulas do not include all the statements about initial consonants. In S, for instance, original L /f/ in most cases before a vowel has become θ, passing through the probable stages [f] > [φ] > [h]: *fīlium* 'son': *hijo* /íxo/. The clusters of two consonants other than /kw/ sometimes show special developments also: in I, L *pl*- and *cl*- have become /py/, /ky/: *planta* 'plant': *pianta*, *clarum* 'clear': *chiaro* /kyáro/. In S, *cl*- has become /ḷ/: *clamare* 'to call': *llamar* /ḷamár/.

At this point attention may be called to seeming exceptions. The last example, S *llamar*, seems to be contradicted by *claro* 'clear'; an examination of all the available evidence indicates that the correspondence /kl : l/ is regular, and that words with /kl/ in S are later introductions—that is, learned loans—from Latin. Another example is S *fé* 'faith', L *fidēs*; the initial *f* indicates that this is a partly learned loan.

Besides the loanwords, there are also other disturbances of regular development. Compare the S forms *sal* and *vale*: L *salem* and *valet* became, in early Spanish, *sale* and *vale*; then there occurred the loss of final *-e* after *l*, and the form *sal* came into being, and *vale* should have become *val*; but this was a verb form, part of a paradigm in which such forms as *vales*, *valen* remained; and there was pressure from other verbs with some consonant other than *l* before the *e*, which was not lost in these cases; so, since *dices*, *dice*, *dicen* remained unchanged, *vale* too was preserved, or restored. This sort of resistance to phonological change is called ANALOGICAL change. There are many instances of this phenomenon in the historical development of languages, and many seeming irregularities are explained by analogy.

Another kind of deviation from the expected changes is found when a change takes place in the original form. The L *quinque* 'five', according to other items which developed regularly, might have been expected to result in */kínke/ in I and S, and */kenk/ in F; the actual forms are I /čínkwe/, S /θínko/, F /senk/. Leaving aside for the moment the endings /kwe/ in I and /ko/ in S, we see that the initials show developments that could have been expected from L /k/, but not from /kw/. We can assume that people started saying /kí·ŋkwe/ at some time in L (perhaps by the fifth or sixth century A.D.); such a change is one of DISSIMILATION (two phonemes or phoneme sequences which are originally the same are changed so that one or the other becomes something else). The I /kwe/ shows retention of /w/ before weak-stressed /e/, which turns out to be regular. The S /ko/ shows that some people must have been saying /kí·ŋkum/; after the original initial /kw/ had been dissimilated to /k/, the ending was changed by some analogy (analogies are often hard to trace) from /e/ to /um/, whereupon the second /kw/ became /k/ automatically, because L at this stage had no sequence /kwu/. F /senk/ could come from either /kí·ŋkwe/ or /kí·ŋkum/.

Dissimilation may be further exemplified from the Romanic languages by changes in words having two /l/s or two /r/s: L /peregrí·-num/ 'wanderer' resulted in F /pelərən/ 'pilgrim', with the first /r/ changed to /l/. In S /pelígro/ 'danger' = L /perí·kulum/, the /l/ and /r/

seem to have changed places; this transposition is called METATHESIS, and is probably a form of dissimilation combined with ASSIMILATION (a phoneme becomes more like, or the same as, some neighboring phoneme): first /r...l/ assimilates to /l...l/, then /l...l/ dissimilates to /l...r/.

Other cases of assimilation may be illustrated from Italian. Latin *factum* 'made, fact' results in I /fatto/: /kt/ becomes /tt/ by assimilation of the /k/. In S, we have *hecho* /éčo/; here /kt/ became something like /yt/, then /t/ became /ty/ by assimilation, and /ay/ became /ey/ by a similar process, which was carried further so that /ey/ became simply /e/; /ty/ resulted in /č/ by further assimilation also. (The change of /f/ to /h/ is late, and regular.)

It can plausibly be argued that all linguistic change in phonology results from the operation of the simple factors of assimilation and dissimilation in various combinations and to various degrees. OE *hlāf-weard* gave rise to ModE *lord* by the following processes, most probably: in *hl-*, the initial /h/ was voiced to [н], by assimilation to /l/, which is voiced, then [н] became assimilated in articulatory position to /l/, resulting simply in initial /l/; internal /f+w/ became /fw/, whereupon /f/ was assimilated to /w/; the resulting /ɔhwə/ sequence became modern /oh/ by a series of mutually adapting assimilations. In ModE, American intervocalic /t/ pronounced [ṭ] is a case of assimilation of voiceless [t] to the surrounding voiced environment; but the British intervocalic [tʻ] is perhaps due to dissimilation of earlier [ṭ] by devoicing.

The loss of the final consonants or syllables of L in the Romanic languages can be considered as assimilation to silence following a word. The loss of internal syllables, as in *insula* /íʻnsula/ 'island' = S /ísla/, is dissimilation from the relative loudness of the first and last vowels.

6.22. The term *reconstruction* has been used in the preceding discussions. The comparisons and correspondences that have been discussed make it possible for us now to define what reconstruction is, and to delimit how much can be learned from reconstruction about the historical development of the sounds and forms of a language. This will lead to the formulation of degrees of language relationships in a precise way. Then, in the next section, we will set forth a theory of the methodology of comparative linguistics.

Let us go back to the list of examples given in 6.11 and discussed in detail in 6.20 and 6.21. We take the three existing languages, French, Spanish, and Italian, for which direct spoken evidence is available, and forget that Latin exists in written records or that we know anything about it. All we have, let us assume, are the three known living languages. Cursory examination has shown that F, S, and I are in many ways similar. It seems reasonable to suppose that they are related. If this supposition is valid, they are the results of change from a single original language which we can call Proto-Romanic (PR). Can we find out what this language was like? And how much of the original form of that language can we determine? These problems are basic in reconstruction.

We can start from the basic assumption that where the languages being compared show complete agreement, the original language had the same sound. This assumption is quite possibly not entirely valid, because it is conceivable that in some situations an original sound may have changed in the same way everywhere; but where the original language is unknown and is being reconstructed, such a situation would not be ascertainable. All the Germanic languages, for instance, show initial /f/ in the word for 'father'; if the other Indo-Hittite languages were unknown, there would be no way to find out that this /f/ results from some kind of original stop, usually written *p (this is reconstructed from the fact of L *pater*, Greek *patér*, Sanskrit *pitá*, and so on). Actually, the assumption is confirmed by this example: from English, German, Swedish and other Germanic words for 'father' with initial /f/, we can only reconstruct Proto-Germanic /f/. Additional evidence is necessary to go back to the ancestor of Proto-Germanic and the other languages mentioned, Proto-Indo-Hittite. This example shows one of the limitations of reconstruction: only the available evidence can give a basis for reconstruction, and reconstruction must be done stage by stage if it is to have meaning.

After the first basic assumption, we then assume that where one language or group diverges from others in a correspondence, the original form must have been more like what the majority of surviving languages show. In the example cited (or other items for the same correspondence), Germanic has /f/, Celtic has nothing, and Armenian has /h/, but all the other languages have /p/. The conclusion is that the original was *p. This assumption may also, in some cases, prove invalid, but needs to be made. One conclusion that can be made for the postulated *p is that it was perhaps [ph], which might possibly have been phonemically a cluster of labial stop, say /b/, with /h/.

Further, it has always been assumed that phonological change was not haphazard, but followed systematic rules: a labial changed, if at all, to another labial; a stop changed to another stop; changes took place one at a time; etc. This has not usually been explicitly stated as to mechanisms involved, but the assumption has occasionally been made explicit.

To exemplify the possibilities and some of the problems of reconstruction, we will now reconstruct the initials of the examples previously discussed, in the manner suggested above—i.e., as if Latin were unknown; the reconstruction will be starred, and written as orthography (in italics), since in such a preliminary survey we cannot be certain of its phonemic nature:

	FRENCH	SPANISH	ITALIAN	RECONSTRUCTION
'father'	/p/	/p/	/p/	*p
'beautiful'	/b/	/b/	/b/	*b
'land'	/t/	/t/	/t/	*t
'tooth'	/d/	/d/	/d/	*d
'hundred'	/s/	/θ/	/č/	*c [tˢ] (see discussion below)
'related'	/ž/	Ø	/ǰ/	*ǰ—or *y? (see discussion below)
'field'	/š/	/k/	/k/	*k—or *ky? (see discussion below)
'joy'	/ž/	/g/	/g/	*g—or *gy? (see discussion below)
'whom'	/k/	/k/	/k/	*k (see discussion below)
'when'	/k/	/k/	/kw/	*kw
'fire'	/f/	/f/	/f/	*f
'salt'	/s/	/s/	/s/	*s
'today'	Ø	Ø	Ø	*Ø
'mother'	/m/	/m/	/m/	*m
'new'	/n/	/n/	/n/	*n
'milk'	/l/	/l/	/l/	*l
'king'	/r/	/r/	/r/	*r
'it is worth'	/v/	/b/	/v/	*v
'game'	/ž/	/x/	/ǰ/	*y

The first four reconstructions call for no special comment; given the data, they are the only ones possible. Then we come to the problem of reconstructing /s/, /θ/, and /č/ into a single original. We know there is a following front vowel, and a knowledge of phonetics suggests some kind of sibilant as a starter; if we postulate *c, a dental or alveolar affricate, we can explain I /č/ by palatalization before a front vowel, S /θ/ by dentalization of the [s] element and elimination of the stop onset, and F /s/ by the loss of the stop onset. As far as S and F are concerned, there is good evidence that there was a [tˢ] stage, but that is as far as we can go in those two languages. Postulating *c for I, however, is simply not right in this case; where /c/ does appear in I, it corresponds to F /s/ and S /θ/, as in the postbase I -*ezza* /ecca/, S -*eza* /éθa/, F -*esse* /esə/. An examination of distributions of other correspondences and of the distribution of the items set up by the preliminary reconstruction might lead us to notice the skewed and limited occurrences of *k and *kw, and then we might guess that it was *k before e that gave rise to F /s/, S /θ/, I /č/. In the Romanic case, we can check the guess against Latin, and find out that we are right. In the case of other languages, where the original is unknown, we might still, in a parallel situation, make the same guess because we know about the Romanic development. But in the latter instance, there would be no certainty. When, or if, further evidence is adduced, the situation changes. If we happen to find Sardinian *kentu* 'hundred', then we can restore the original *k with virtual certainty, because it is quite unlikely that [k] would result from [č], whereas the opposite seems to be an easy and frequent change.

The next reconstruction, from /ž/, ϑ, /ǰ/, is a difficult one: F /ž/ and I /ǰ/ could easily be reconstructed to *ǰ, but for a sound like [dž] to disappear completely, even in a relatively weak syllable, seems strange; the intermediate steps would be hard to guess at. If we reconstruct *y, the problem is a little less difficult; *y could have become /ǰ/ easily, and /ž/ either directly or through earlier /ǰ/, and in S it could have been reduced to ϑ by assimilation in tongue-height position to the following vowel. The actual original, L /g/, could hardly be guessed at except from a thorough study of distribution of phonemes, as for the preceding reconstruction.

In the case of /š, k, k/ the reconstruction *k is pretty certain, but the F /š/ (even without a knowledge of Old French, we would guess it had been /č/ earlier) suggests a palatalizing element. Only thorough study of distribution of phonemes could confirm the guess at an original *k.

The details for /ž, g, g/ are exactly parallel to those for /š, k, k/, and need not be separately discussed.

The three /k/s in the next reconstruction pose a new kind of difficulty. Is the reconstructed *k different from that in 'field', or are the accompanying conditions different? Only after reconstructing *kw, examining all the distributions of k-like sounds and clusters, and guessing at possible instances of *k in 'hundred' and 'field', would we be able to guess that here the three identical results do not go back to a similar original, but to L /kw/.

The reconstructions *f and *s are easy, though the preceding example should be kept in mind as a caution.

The reconstruction of initial *θ is the best we can do. Only from existing spellings could anyone ever think there was an original /h/.

The reconstructions *m, *n, *l seem to offer no difficulty. That of *r is also easy in the light of European spelling habits; but if these were unknown and "exotic" languages, we might record [γ] in F, [ᵈr³] in S, and [r²] in I; the last two are similar enough to suggest an original *r ([r³] or [r²]), but the [γ] would be hard to get into the picture.

The reconstruction of /v, b, v/ as *v is sound enough, though the S /b/ might suggest bilabial [β], or even [w].

The final reconstruction would probably result from reasoning somewhat similar to that for the item 'related', with S /x/ resulting from depalatalization of an older /y/ before a back vowel. If the data for Old Spanish, indicating /ž/ there, were known, there would be little problem, though we might decide on *$ž$ as the original in any case.

From the reconstructions and the discussion of them it is evident that much guessing has to be done about the kinds and directions of phonetic development. What is reconstructed is a phonemic system, or a part of one. Usually it is a partial system, with only vowels and consonants reconstructed. Accentual systems are often ignored, or only partly treated in comparative work; and transitions, which were unknown until recently, have hardly been considered in reconstructions as yet. However, we are not limited to phonemic reconstruction alone, even though discussion of phonological reconstruction has most often been put in purely schematic terms.

It is possible, wherever there are good descriptions of the languages being compared, to make statements about the phonetic nature and probable allophones of the reconstructed phonemes, both as separate entities and as part of a system. This is done, as has already been said at the beginning of 6.22, by postulating an original sound which is most likely to result in the actual sounds found in the languages being compared. In the Romanic examples, for instance, all present t's and d's and all prevocalic n's and l's are dental; it is quite easy to say that Latin must have had dental t, d, n, l. For the Germanic languages (see References and Notes) it is harder to determine the place of articulation of the original t, d, n, l: German, English, and Danish have alveolars; Dutch has dentals; Norwegian and Swedish have dentals in most positions, but retroflex sounds where an original *r* preceded. The geographical location of Dutch suggests Romanic (French) influence. The rest of the evidence leads to the conclusion that the Proto-Germanic *t, *d, *n, *l were probably postdental or actually alveolar, with retroflex allophones after *r, and dental allophones perhaps in other positions. There is, however, further evidence to be considered. The Germanic languages are part of the Indo-Hittite family of languages, and are thus related to the Romanic languages (see References and Notes). In all the known other branches of Indo-Hittite, the *t*'s, *d*'s, *n*'s, and *l*'s have dental sounds as their principal or only allophones. The Proto-Germanic sound that corresponds to other Indo-Hittite *t*'s is /θ/, a dental, and it is Proto-Germanic *d*, which probably had [ð] as its principal allophone, which corresponds to Slavic *d*, Sanskrit *dh*, Ancient Greek *th* (which has become [θ] in Modern Greek). There is thus good reason for supposing that Indo-Hittite had dental sounds of the nature of *t, d, n, l*, and that the Germanic alveolars, if they were that, developed from the dentals by shift of point of articulation.

A further instance of phonetic reconstruction may again be placed in terms of Germanic. The Indo-Hittite sounds represented by the initials of Latin *pater* 'father', *tenuis* 'thin', and *cornu* 'horn', are represented in Proto-Germanic by /f/, /θ/, and /h/ (originally /x/), as in the English glosses of the three Latin examples. If we postulate the stops as original, as we do, then we can suppose that to have become the Germanic spirants they most probably must have been, in a pre-Germanic stage, affricated and before that aspirated: /f/ < [pf] < [ph], etc. This development is generally accepted, but is thought of as having taken place entirely after the Indo-Hittite stage, in which the stops are thought to have been unaspirated. It is quite possible, however, to suppose that the original stops were [ph, th, kh], and that change took place not only in Germanic but also everywhere else. The argument would be: in Germanic (and Armenian) these stops eventually became spirants of some sort, while elsewhere they became deaspirated (and in Greek, apparently, even lenis rather than fortis as in Latin). (The References and Notes mention discussions of the bearing of this kind of phonetic reconstruction on the phonemic reconstruction of Indo-Hittite.) In further discussions of reconstruction, evidence of protophonetics of this kind will always be noted.

When the phonemic system of the original of a group of related languages is reconstructed, the data used are words of the compared languages, so that morphemes are being reconstructed at the same time. If *father*, Latin *pater*, Greek *patér*, Sanskrit *pitar-* are used to reconstruct Indo-Hittite phonemes that are traditionally written *p, *ə, *t, *e, *r, we get a resulting reconstructed form *pəter- which is meant to represent an Indo-Hittite stem meaning 'father'. The result of reconstruction based on comparison of vocabulary items is always at least a stem and/or a base. But where there is much detailed historical material, it is often possible to reconstruct whole inflectional systems too. We have seen that the Romanic languages do not preserve the Latin -m of the singular accusative of nouns. But comparison of Latin -Vm with Greek -Vn and Sanskrit -Vm and certain older Slavic forms usually written as a nasal vowel -ǫ makes possible the reconstruction of an Indo-Hittite accusative ending in -m. So also other inflectional forms can be reconstructed, and for many items we can be pretty sure of what the actual protoform of a word may have been: for 'father' in the accusative, Indo-Hittite must have said something like *pəterem; but note that a stress has not been marked; also, the exact nature of *ə cannot be determined without much further discussion. The stem was *pəter-, and the suffix was probably -m, with a vowel necessarily appearing before it in some cases.

Because of what are often extremely thorough rearrangements of morphemic systems, reconstruction here is usually less complete and less exact than for phonology. Thus, the study of linguistic relationships always depends on phonological reconstruction of bases and of some parts of the morphemic system. The morpheme reconstructions help in establishing a protosystem, and are used whenever they can be made.

It has been said that comparison starts with items that have the same or similar meanings. This statement must be understood first as implying a very broad generalization as to what is the same. When we reconstruct an Indo-Hittite term for 'father', we can assert that the reconstructed item had that semological meaning, allowing for cultural change in the metalinguistic applications. Among the speakers of Indo-Hittite there were persons who were biological fathers and who had a position in the social structure that was indicated by their being called or designated by the reconstructed term. As cultural conditions changed and the role of fathers changed, the term changed its exact connotations. When Christianity came in, for instance, it was extended to priests. An item like this, despite time and such details as that last mentioned, retains the "same" meaning, for purposes of reconstruction.

A somewhat different situation is found in reconstructing the word that gave rise to English *mere* 'pool', German *Meer*, Latin *mare*, Russian *more*—the last three meaning 'sea' (but German *Meer* also means 'lake'). The English meaning seems to be the older one in Germanic, and it is conjectured that if, as supposed, the Indo-Hittite peoples dispersed from an original inland continental location, they knew no seas but only lakes and ponds. Here there is change of meaning, but within a general semantic area, and the meaning 'body of water' holds.

When we come to such a case as English *deer* and German *Tier* 'animal', identification may be more difficult. The correspondences are right, but the meanings are rather different. However, when we recall the old expression "such small deer", meaning small animals, it is easy to see that in English the word has been specialized in recent times.

In the case of names of trees and animals, the same original item may come to be applied to new entities that were unknown before, especially if the old referent is not found in the new environment.

The most difficult instances to deal with are those in which the correspondences are regular, but the meanings seem entirely different. Such a case as English *wit* originally 'knowledge', German *wissen* 'to know', compared with Latin *vidēre* 'to see', might cause doubt if the correspondences were more complex. Another example is Indo-Hittite **gen-* ~ **gon-* ~ **gn-*, reconstructed from words meaning 'to know' (*know*, Latin *cognoscere*, Russian *znati*), and also 'to beget' (*generare*, *kin*); the speakers of Indo-Hittite may actually have used 'to know' in respect to sexual intercourse, or the two expressions may have been homonyms.

In the absence of a generally accepted theory and methodology of semological analysis, the reconstruction of meanings is done chiefly in metalinguistic and extralinguistic terms. But it works well enough for comparative purposes. Eventually it may be possible to reconstruct semological entities. It is possible that many more relationships will be discovered then.

6.23. When a series of relationships between languages has been established, it is customary to call the related group a language family. It was soon discovered, however, that there were many kinds of groupings, and that as reconstruction proceeded, successive stages were established for which a single term like language family did not suffice. No system of terms has been agreed upon, however, for the steps in a hierarchy of linguistic relationships.

One set of terms, following a long-established tendency to use biological analogies, designates a large group like Indo-Hittite as a PHYLUM. Then the groups under it like Germanic, Celtic, Slavic, etc., are FAMILIES. There is room for SUBPHYLA, SUPERFAMILIES, and SUBFAMILIES. Then come LANGUAGE GROUPS, then LANGUAGES, then dialects. East Coast American (see 1.3 and subsections) is a dialect of the English language, which belongs to the Anglo-Frisian language group, which is part of the Germanic family, which belongs to the Indo-Hittite phylum.

Once a language family or similar grouping has been established, it is often graphically presented as a FAMILY-TREE DIAGRAM. In older publications this was often a stylized tree, with branches, the temporal axis being from the bottom up to the contemporary top. More usual is a diagram that looks like a genealogical chart, except that it shows no marriages. Various other styles of presentation are also found. Implicit in such diagrams is the notion that branching is always binary, but in practice this notion is often overlooked. We shall now examine this idea and come to a conclusion about useful graphic representations of a theory of comparative linguistics.

It has been said (6.12) that related languages are the result of change from a single original language that no longer exists. It is necessary to make more precise the notions "single" and "no longer".

At any particular moment in time there is no language that is spoken completely the same by all its speakers, no matter how small the community. If the community is an isolated family, the members of it will have sex and age differences. But so long as the interacting members of the community consider themselves as speaking the same language, the linguistic analyst must include all the usages of all the speakers in his observations. If he is able to observe sufficiently to describe the whole as a coherent system, then we can say there is a single language. If then at a moment in time and place a single language, in this sense, is in existence, and the community is divided as some part of it leaves to live somewhere else, without further contact, there exist, from that moment, two communities instead of one; and if there is no further reinforcing mutual influence, there are, by virtue of that fact, two languages, even though the two may remain virtually identical in system for a long time to come. It is theoretically possible, and has probably happened, that the members of a community split into several groups simultaneously. But in order to compare the languages of such groups it would be necessary to take them two at a time in any case. As a working principle of comparative linguistics, then, it is stated that A LANGUAGE ALWAYS DIVIDES INTO TWO, and EACH OF THESE DIVIDES INTO TWO, and so on, so that it is always A SINGLE LANGUAGE that GIVES RISE TO or is reconstructed from TWO LANGUAGES that are being compared, and that furthermore AS SOON AS A BINARY SPLIT HAS OCCURRED THE ORIGINAL SINGLE LANGUAGE NO LONGER EXISTS, but there are then two contemporary languages in existence.

The best way to diagram this procedure is the following:

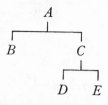

The form of the diagram may be this:

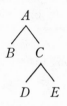

Such diagrams, carried down through time, can show accurately the exact time of a split if known, or the relative time in terms of the preceding and following developments. And by constructing each succeeding split carefully, closeness or distance of relationship can be depicted on the chart by the amount of space between items.

It should be noted that a diagram of the following kind DOES NOT meet the requirements of the principles we set down:

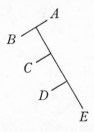

Here there are binary splits, but the points at which the split takes place are not labeled. By reconstructing *D* and *E*, one would get what? This ambiguity can be eliminated by saying that one would get *C'*, and then that *C'* and *C* reconstruct into *B'*, and *B* and *B'* into *A'*:

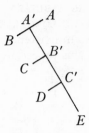

For some purposes this kind of labeling will be more instructive than that on the first diagram above. But the important point is that there should be a label for each place where a split occurs.

In actual practice it has not been possible to make complete reconstructions at any such points, but the partial reconstructions that are made are always in binary terms. As soon as a third language is brought in, there must be comparison of it with each of the other two separately. Suppose we have the following languages:

$$D \quad E \quad F \quad G \quad I \quad J$$

It is suspected that they are related. How do we proceed? We could take any pair at random and work it back, and so on. Often this has to be done. But suppose there are sufficiently good descriptions to make us suspect that some of the items are more alike than others, say D and E, and F and G, and I and J. We could reconstruct D and E to *C'; then we could reconstruct F and G to *C; and then I and J to *H. This would give:

It then appears that C and C' are more alike than either is like H. So we reconstruct them to B, thus:

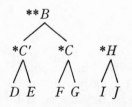

How do we attach *H to the group? We shall have to postulate a **B', and then reconstruct **B and **B' to ***A. In practice, rarely more than one asterisk is used, but theoretically the several reconstructions are of different orders of realism or exactness. The completed diagram is then:

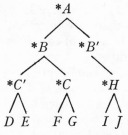

One question presents itself. How is *B' to be arrived at? *B' will have to be postulated, rather than reconstructed. We shall have to say: *H is one product of a stage *B'; that stage was closer to *B than is *H, and we may be able to indicate some of the details. In practice this means that we shall be comparing a kind of modified *H with *B, and establishing *B' in terms of needed points in the system to take care of things in *H that are not found in *B as based on *C and *C'. It might be useful to use two asterisks for such a stage as **B', which is postulated and then extrapolated, rather than reconstructed in the ordinary way.

It should also be made clear that often enough at the beginning of the reconstruction of a language group or family, it is convenient and sometimes even necessary and expedient to take all the data into account at once, to make preliminary comparisons. It may be that the relationship is first suspected by a confrontation of D and J. Then G is found, and is perhaps put with D as against J, though the closer relationship may not be apparent at this time. If I is then examined, it is seen to belong with J, and this confirms that G is closer to D. *H can be reconstructed in part and a kind of *C'', and after that it may be possible to begin to reconstruct *A without the B stages being explicitly set up.

This discussion shows that the principle of binary comparison is often impossible to carry out in detail, for lack of data. But once the outline of the scheme of stages is established, all refinements and corrections are then aimed at filling in the stages that are needed to provide a full set of binary comparisons. For no group of languages so far studied has this theoretical principle been fully carried out, but it is usually evident from the discussion of problems of comparison that what is being done is precisely the implementation of the principle of binary comparison.

When, as in the case of the Romanic languages (see References and Notes), there are historical data that tell us the time of settlement and separation of peoples, statements about time depth can be made with considerable accuracy. Even for a single language, such as English, where there are historical documents, dating can be done on an accurate basis from comparison of dated texts, which are evidence of dialect differences and change through time. But is there any way to determine time depth in other cases?

There have been estimates made on the basis of known time for development. If we know that French and Spanish have been going their own way, as it were, since about 700, and that English and Frisian have been separated since about 600 (and possibly 100 years earlier), then, if we inspect two related languages X and Y and guess that they are about as different from each other as the two pairs of languages just mentioned, we may decide that X and Y separated from 1100 to 1300 years ago. But of course such an estimate depends on subjective judgment, and the subjectivity is determined by the depth of knowledge and insight of the estimator. It would be nice to have some more accurate way of measuring the separation of languages in time. Differences in phonetics, or in phonemic systems, cannot necessarily be used as measuring devices: for one thing, it depends on how one phonemicizes; for another, phonemic systems change suddenly, and changes seem often to be rapid. The author of this book phonemicizes all the Germanic languages as having vocalic-nucleus systems with simple nuclei (three, five, nine, twelve vowels at various stages and in the various languages), and with complex nuclei of the /VS/ type. But even if the systems are thus all typologically alike, the details are different. If Proto-Germanic had three vowels, let's say, and Gothic, some five to ten centuries later, also had three vowels, this doesn't help determine rate of change at all. But, perhaps 600 years after our Gothic records, Norse is found to have nine simple vowels. It is usually said that Norse and Gothic are more closely related to each other than either is to West Germanic. Reconstructed West Germanic has five simple vowels, and can be dated at about the same time as Gothic.

If time depth is not determinable from phonological data, can morphology help? Possibly, but here again there seem to be differences in rate of change. It is known that Latin inflections were still functioning quite well around 500, but by 800 they had apparently been largely changed or eliminated. The new inflection of the future found in French, Spanish, and Italian seems to have already existed by about 800, but in Portuguese the forms are still separable into a phraselike entity more than 1000 years later (see References and Notes).

Semological analysis has not progressed far enough to be usable as a base for historical reconstruction and dating. But vocabulary is something for which we have records, and the procedure of comparative linguistics has always been to start by comparing vocabularies. There thus arises the question: Can change in vocabulary be examined so as to give clues to rate of change, and if this rate can be established, can time depth of separation of languages be calculated from the rate? In the 1950s, a method of calculating separation in time was devised on the basis of some known or supposedly known dates of separation of some European languages, and the determination of percentage of cognates left in a basic vocabulary of 200 words. It came to be known as GLOTTOCHRONOLOGY, and later as L E ICO-STATISTICS. It was seized upon by nonlinguistic anthropologists, archeologists, and historians as a wonderful aid in their attempts at dating tribal movements, artifacts, and historical sequence of events. After less than ten years of sometimes violent polemic and equally violent enthusiasm, it has been shown that the mathematical basis of the method is untenable, that the original test dates are mistakenly interpreted, and that the supposed "acultural" and universally usable basic vocabulary (at first 200 items, but later only 100) is, anthropologically speaking, a chimera, and is often unusable. As lexicostatistics—a determination of the statistical relationship of two lexicons—the method has whatever usefulness any statistics has in certain contexts.

As a determiner of time depth in linguistics, the method is useless, and indeed misleading. Where it has been taken seriously, it has sometimes led to ridiculously long or ridiculously short periods of separation; where examined critically, it has turned up cases in which the same speaker is separated from himself by several centuries on two different recording occasions, or in which two mutually intelligible languages, A and A', are several centuries further apart than language A and language B, which is clearly very much more differentiated and is not mutually intelligible with A. The powerful appeal of "exact" numbers has led some archeologists or other anthropologists to revise well-established sequences based on more tangible kinds of evidence. Ambitious attempts have been made to tie together language groups that show so little resemblance that the time depth comes out at 10,000 years or more; and this despite the fact that sound comparative techniques have nowhere established sure relationships further back than 6,000–8,000 years, and that the percentage figure for 10,000 years is so small as to be just as likely to result from chance resemblances as real relationship.

The absurdity of these wide-ranging efforts has been shown by a comparison of English and certain American Indian languages (see References and Notes); a Macro-Mixtecan was arrived at by a kind of free-running inspection, with a time depth for the reconstructions of over 6,000 years. Then, deliberately ignoring the known history of English, certain vocabulary items were compared with the Macro-Mixtecan, and English was found to be more closely "related" than some of the languages used to construct Macro-Mixtecan. Even if all the world's languages do stem from one ultimate source, the ancestors of the speakers of English and of Macro-Mixtecan have not had any possibility of being one people for at least the period from several millennia before the peopling of America to the present, which may be as much as 50,000 years. Accordingly, any resemblances can be attributed to chance. Other resemblances of this order are just as devoid of real meaning.

There is, then, NO SOUND METHOD OF DATING LINGUISTIC CHANGE. Relative chronology can be determined by kind and extent of differences and resemblances between languages shown to be related by standard comparative techniques. Absolute chronology can be established only where there is historical documentation. Extent of difference between languages is the result of many factors of a historical nature—all involving change in the whole of the culture through time. No single aspect (vocabulary) of a single cultural system (language) could possibly give significant insights of the kind supposedly derivable from lexicostatistics.

One final remark must be added to this chapter on language relationships. Although it is possible to prove many linguistic relationships by the methods of comparative linguistics, and to suggest many more by guesswork and other unsound methods, IT IS NOT POSSIBLE TO PROVE THAT TWO LANGUAGES ARE NOT RELATED. Over time, all resemblances may have disappeared, and there are no doubt now in the world unrelated languages that have some resemblance to each other and related ones that have no resemblance at all.

Part III

WRITING AND WRITING SYSTEMS

Chapter 7

WRITING

7.0. THE NATURE OF WRITING SYSTEMS

7.00. Human beings have been talking for perhaps a million years (1.11). But there is no evidence that anyone, anywhere in the world, did any writing before about 10,000 years ago. Until recently, there were no societies in which more than a small percentage of the population could read and write; and even now the majority of human beings—even counting only adults—are illiterate, and the majority of languages do not have regular systems in which they can be written. Chapter 1, sections 1.40–1.43, discussed in general terms the relation of writing to language. The present chapter will consider in some detail what is known of how writing came about, and discuss the history and development of the various writing systems of the world. In Chapter 8, writing systems of the kind that are called alphabets are presented in tables, with extensive commentary and discussion.

It can be surmised that human beings learned early to make marks on the surfaces that were available to them—stone walls, smooth sand, packed earth, snow, ice, bark, large leaves, animal skins, their own skins—with various kinds of marking materials—pigments whose color would contrast with the surface, sharp stones whose edges could cut into the surface, the ends of fingers or of sticks that could produce a more or less permanent disturbance of the surface, and so on. Paintings have been found on cave walls that must be 50,000 or more years old. The excellence of the techniques of representation of some of these paintings is such as to make it certain that the graphic arts of design and representation were invented a very long time ago. Drawing and painting pictures may be as old as modern man, *Homo sapiens*, himself. The making of artifacts—figurines—that looked like people or animals, or like things in nature, is perhaps even older. These activities produced symbols of a kind; a statuette is a symbol—of a human being, a god, a notion of fertility, a value, a payment, an order; a picture is in the same way a symbol of the same things, but goes further—it tells a story, it relates symbols to each other, it represents more complex things than does a single artifact.

The making of symbolic artifacts, the drawing of pictures, the use of conventional signs to blaze a trail (or to direct traffic)—all these have not only been present for a long time, but they are also very widespread in the world. There is not sufficient evidence to enable us to say that all societies have used at least some of these means of nonverbal communication across the barriers of time and distance. But we can hazard the guess that in all societies for the last 100,000 years, and perhaps more, there have been individuals who invented such symbols and signs *ad hoc* as the need arose; and most societies possess rather well-established systems of such activities, even if only on a small scale and practiced by few individuals. But a special development is necessary to produce writing from any system of making artifacts and drawing pictures.

7.01. For the purposes of this discussion we can define a writing system simply and precisely. A WRITING SYSTEM IS ANY CONVENTIONAL SYSTEM OF MARKS OR DRAWINGS OR ANALOGOUS ARTIFACTS WHICH REPRESENTS THE UTTERANCES OF A LANGUAGE AS SUCH; it must be so constructed as to make possible the writing of any utterance of the language, and in such a way that any reader instructed in its conventions can read the utterance that was intended. A set of pictures cannot pass the test of depicting all the possible utterances of a language, and there is no way to be sure that a picture will be interpreted in the same way—that is, in the same words—by two successive observers.

Let us consider some examples: any literate speaker of English will read the symbol 7 as "seven hundred" in the sequence 723, as "seventy" in the sequence 73, as "seven" when it is by itself, and as "sevenths" in the arrangement $\frac{3}{7}$; in the last instance, he may also have learned to say "three over seven", but this is known to be equivalent to "three-sevenths". Similarly, such a reader knows that in "*X* marks the spot", the symbol *X* is to be read /éks/. He knows that the symbol *A* is to be read in "the letter *A*" as /éy/, but in "A little more" as /ˀəʹ+/, and in "HAT" as [ˈæ˙]. If the English reader knows no French, he cannot read the French sequence "723 hommes"; he can say, "It says seven hundred twenty-three something or other", but he cannot READ the French to produce the utterance "sept cents vingt-trois hommes".

These examples suggest some others: the reader who has not learned algebra may not know how to read the sequence of symbols $(a + b)^2 = a^2 + 2ab + b^2$; once he has been instructed, he can read it as "*a* plus *b*, the quantity squared, equals *a*-square plus two *a*-*b* plus *b*-square". It is true that the French reader who knows algebra receives the same algebraic message from the equation as does the English-speaking reader. But—and this is the crux of the matter— the French reader READS IT IN FRENCH, according to instructions he has received. The author of the present book, though he speaks French with considerable ease, never learned mathematics in French, and does not know how to read even simple arithmetic in French, much less an algebraic formula. Moreover, neither the English nor the French reader of the formula knows what it "means" in the metalinguistic sense unless he has learned something more about algebra than how to read the symbols, any more than he knows what *evolution* or *évolution* means unless he knows more than how to pronounce the word. Mathematical symbols are part of writing, and they have to be read conventionally, as do any other written symbols: they "mean the same thing" in English and French only in the same sense that *mother* and *mère* mean the same, or that *Paris* may mean the same whether said as [p'ˈæɹɪs] or as [pæʀˈi].

Further, consider the way in which the reader of this paragraph must behave when confronted with this drawing:

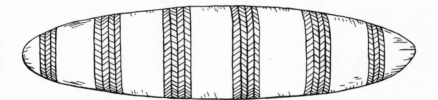

Without a caption, he can only begin by describing it in terms of shape, ornamentation, etc. He can say, "This is a drawing of some kind of object; it looks like a long ellipse, and is not quite regular. The shadings along the edges suggest that this is perhaps a drawing of something that is a solid body, an elongated ovoid. Or possibly it's just a partly ovoid shell, hollow on the other side. The bands around it may be something made of another material—leather or cloth; but they could be painted. I wonder what it is." No two readers would say exactly the same thing. An anthropologist might say "artifact" instead of "object", and might try to guess that it was a boat, or a container for liquids. It is not likely that anyone who was not a specialist would guess that it is a picture of a shield made by Australian aborigines. But even the specialists who would recognize the picture would not use the same words in describing it. It is a PICTURE, not a piece of writing.

Now let us consider the next drawing:

This picture is, for an American at least, easier to describe and identify. It is clearly part of a street and road map. There are some city streets, one at least (horizontal) a principal thoroughfare, and some others seemingly dead-end residential streets; there is a divided highway passing under the main street (there is the conventional indication of a bridge), and there are so-called cloverleaf access roads to the main street from the highway and *vice versa*. This kind of drawing is "read" by many people in almost the same terms, if they have learned the conventions of highway maps in the United States. But there is no exact identity of the descriptions; and those who have not learned what a highway map is like may not understand the drawing at all.

Finally let us look at the following chart:

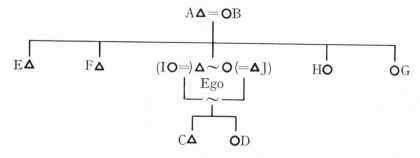

This picture is part of a chart of a kinship system. Anyone who has studied enough anthropology to have read about kinship terms and systems of relationship will recognize it as such. The triangles indicate males (the symbol is easier to draw than the more formal one, ♂) and the circles females (♀); the double bond, =, indicates marriage, single lines indicate descent and consanguineal relationship. Without the letter labels, all that could be said is that the chart shows Ego (the anthropologist's informant, who supplies the terms for his relatives) at the center, as usual; that Ego is either male or female—that is, the terms are the same whether a man or a woman is speaking, and that Ego's parents, brothers, sisters, and children are shown. That there are two brothers and two sisters indicates that probably there are different terms for older and younger siblings. It is also clear from the chart that brothers and sisters are designated by different terms, and that sons and daughters are known by different terms. Also shown are the spouses of male and female Egos, so that there must be different terms. When the labels for the particular system being studied are added, then all these surmises are confirmed. There are terms for 'father' (A), 'mother' (B), 'son' (C), 'daughter' (D), 'older brother' (E), 'younger brother' (F), 'older sister' (G), 'younger sister' (H), 'wife' (I), 'husband' (J). The double bond, =, and the single lines are, to begin with, signs of relationship; they can be made into writing symbols if the convention is established that = is to be read 'married to', a vertical line is 'descended from' and a horizontal line is 'consanguineally related to'; the symbol ~ is a piece of writing if it is agreed that it is to be read 'or'. If, however, =, |, —, ~ can be read in various equivalent ways, as is usually the case, then they are signs and not writing symbols. The letter labels are real writing, but they are secondary written symbols, referring to the written form of the words designating the various relationships. When the labels are found in a list, and the terms are noted, then writing is being read.

The diagram is part of one showing the kinship terms of the Indians of Taos Pueblo, New Mexico. (See References and Notes for material on the Taos language.)

The three kinds of graphic material just examined should make clear how writing differs from pictures and diagrams. Writing is a symbolization of language. Whenever there is a systematic representation of LINGUISTIC ELEMENTS—specific morphological (words, phrases) or phonological (phonemes, syllables) items—then there is writing. It may be sporadic and occasional, and subsidiary to pictorial representation, or it may be central and ubiquitous, with pictures in a subsidiary role, but it is writing when it meets the tests indicated.

Given the widespread phenomenon of representational art in the world's cultures, it can be understood that writing might have been invented many times and in many places. The present author believes that this is indeed what happened. Many human beings have hit upon various aspects of the analysis of language, and there have even been grammatical analyses without writing; it follows that there must have been many instances of spontaneous application of graphic labeling to the linguistic analyses. But, like any invention, writing had to have a proper cultural environment in which to grow and flourish and be used. Not enough is really known of the nature of culture to enable us to be precise about these fostering and nurturing conditions. But it is significant that writing appeared in societies that had acquired agriculture and had established fixed settlements. In such circumstances there were individuals who had time to do other things than provide food and shelter and defense. To these individuals fell the tasks of governing, of performing religious ceremonies, of knowing and keeping the whole complex of the lore of the society. Among them, those who had inclinations to develop artistic skills found the time to do so, and here and there some of these individuals hit upon the idea of representing specific linguistic items by specific graphic symbols.

In Mesopotamia, among the Sumerians, an invention of writing took place perhaps six thousand years ago (4000 B.C.). Social and material conditions were such that this invention could be implemented and could become an active part of the culture (see 7.10). In the Indus valley, a similar invention took place, but apparently somewhat later (after 2500 B.C.); for some reason it lasted only about 500 years. In Egypt, in the valley of the Nile, perhaps a millennium later than, but possibly at about the same time as, in Sumer, the elaborate decorative use of pictures was turned into a writing system (see 7.11). In China, not later than 2000 B.C., we find a writing system coming into being (7.40). And, before the beginning of the Christian era, another elaborate decorative technique became a writing system in Yucatan, among the Mayas (7.51).

The inventions in the three Old World centers mentioned could all be connected, though the distances are great and there is no reason why the inventions could not have been independent. The New World invention was certainly independent. In the Near East there are also some undeciphered ancient writing systems that may or may not be connected with the others mentioned.

The question of the ultimate beginnings of these four writing systems cannot be answered; but their subsequent developments are known. And they are the only writing systems that survived long enough and spread far enough for us to have such knowledge. Sumerian writing in one form or another continued until after the beginning of the Christian era. Chinese writing is still in active use today in the Far East. Mayan writing lasted until the coming of Europeans to the New World. And Egyptian writing gave rise to Semitic writing; all the other writing systems of the world—in Europe and Asia—that have been used or continue to be used are outgrowths from the latter.

Among the Polynesians there were navigational charts which were analogous to our maps. They showed islands, stars, and wind and water currents, but apparently the identity of the various objects was a matter of memory. It is possible, of course, that some of the makers of such charts actually used conventional labels for some of the things represented; if so, then they were *ad hoc* inventors of writing. It was the Polynesians also who carved the stone statues on Easter Island, but it is not known whether the marks on them are really writing.

The Australian aborigines often depicted genealogies in the sand, it being very important to identify the kinship relations of strangers. Those charts were analogous to the one given above for the Taos Pueblo Indians. But it is probable that the positions had no graphic labels, but were named from memory or from the relationship indicated. If so, then these charts were a sort of cross-cultural sign system which elicited linguistic items but did not necessarily represent them. This would not be writing, though it is close to it.

American Indians of various tribes used pictures to record historical events. Some of the pictures, especially those of historical date, are accompanied by special conventional signs, or are themselves such signs. In this case, we have again elementary writing systems, though they may be largely *ad hoc*.

Further study of pictographs, especially as they continue to be used by illiterates and so-called primitives, may throw more light on the history of the major writing systems. But the essential nature of writing must not be forgotten: it represents specific items of specific languages.

We shall next examine the different kinds of writing systems and the ways in which they have been applied to languages, and the general history of the spread of writing and what it does to a society and to the culture of the society. Then, the rest of the chapter will consider the known writing systems in their geographical and culturo-linguistic contexts.

7.02. If writing is a symbol system that represents language items, it follows that it may conceivably represent any level of linguistic unit: articulation, sound, phoneme, morphophone, morpheme, syntactic operator, sememe, unit of occurrence, unit of discourse. Depending on the perspicacity of the native analyst of the language, any one of these might be recognized and selected for the unit of the writing system. And there are also aspects of paralanguage that could be represented.

Examination of the known writing systems shows that only some of these aspects of language have ever actually been recognized in writing systems. This is not surprising, since some of them have only recently come to be recognized by linguistic analysts.

We can conjecture that the individuals in various cultures and through the ages who drew pictures that represented whole scenes were—at least sometimes—trying to "write down" whole units of occurrence and/or discourse. But no system of writing has ever been developed from such all-inclusive pictures. Some of the pictographs that we have, however, especially the stylized and conventional ones of some American Indians, seem to have been on the way to becoming writing systems with such highly complex units.

Writing systems that use sememes—or some prescientific analog of sememes—as units are common, however. In fact, it appears that writing sememes may have been the first stage in all the known writing systems. If one had been using pictures to convey messages, and one hit upon the idea of making a particular picture represent a specific linguistic unit, it followed that the picture of the sun, say, represented the word for 'sun' in all its sememic variety; when it became necessary to devise a symbol for 'to rise', and one could find no appropriate picture, one might get the idea of taking the sun picture, and arbitrarily modifying it to represent 'it [the sun] rises'; the sememe of *sun* was thus abstracted, consciously or outside of awareness. Other sememic identifications followed. The so-called LOGOGRAPHIC (word writing) systems are actually in many cases SEMEMOGRAPHIC. However, since sememe analysis has never yet been done to any great extent, and prescientific sememe analysis is likely to run into all kinds of difficulties resulting from the difference between the linguistic categories and various kinds of physical realities, no writing system could consistently use sememes as its basic unit. But languages have easily perceivable units, words, that may be taken to be the possessors or havers of sememic content. So the first writing systems became logographic in theory; in practice this led to sememographic writing part of the time, and to the other developments about to be discussed. The sememographic content of the logographs—the symbols for words—made it possible for a system to be applied to other languages: if a circle with a dot at its center was the symbol for *sun*, then it could also be the symbol for *soleil* (French), or *solnce* (Russian), and so on.

Sememographic logographs had some disadvantages. If the language had inflection, questions arose as to how to write various members of a paradigm, especially those dealing with relations whose sememes were not easily apprehended. If ⊙ is *sun*, then perhaps ⚭ can be written for *suns*, but how does one write the case form *sun's*? When problems like this became pressing, some new inventions were needed.

The most important development at this stage is the idea of phonological equivalence of parts of utterances. This is inherent in the structure of language, and many persons are aware of it; but to come upon this idea in developing writing seems not to have been easy. However, the realization that the phonological analysis of words can lead to ways to write parts of them did come about, and apparently came about repeatedly in various parts of the world. So, if one says *suns* for the plural, and has a symbol to write that plural, one can also write the possessive *sun's* in the same way. Or if one writes the numeral 2 as two lines, say ‖, then one can write *to* and *too* in the same way. Such writing is now no longer directly sememographic, but is still entirely logographic. The words being written here are, however, phonemic entities, and so the writing is PHONEMO-GRAPHICALLY logographic; perhaps the term PHONEMOLOGOGRAPHIC can be used.

Once this step is reached, another discovery can be made. The terms *suns* and *sun's* are morphemically different but phonemically the same; by writing them the same we are writing morphemes phonemically; let us call this PHONEMOMORPHEMOGRAPHIC writing. If these developments and discoveries and inventions take place with a language that has mostly short words, and most of these of one syllable, and especially if the syllable structure is a simple one, say predominantly CV and CVC, then the writing system may rather quickly become SYLLABOGRAPHIC. This kind of syllabographic writing is apt to be rather consistent in its representation of phonemes: that is, each sequence of CV or CVC is usually written in the same way every time, regardless of its morphophonic or morphemic structures. Once phonemosyllabographic writing has been achieved, the step to a PHONEMOGRAPHIC system, in which an individual phoneme is represented by a single symbol—at least in theory—is easy.

The four main streams of writing that have been mentioned have all produced various kinds of systems. The Sumerian system originally was sememographic and logographic. It developed some phonemomorphemographic aspects, and gave rise to systems that were syllabographic (Akkadian), and eventually to phonemosyllabographic (Hittite, Old Persian) and phonemographic (Ras Shamra) systems. The Chinese system started as a sememologographic system, and remained such, with only a few phonemomorphemographic aspects; it gave rise to phonemosyllabographic systems (Japanese), and also to phonemographic ones (Korean, modern Chinese "phonetics"). The Egyptian system again was sememologographic, developed some phonemomorphemographic aspects, and very early gave rise to phonemosyllabographic systems (the Egyptian syllabic writings); from it followed the basic Semitic systems, which were phonemographic in a special way, and from these followed a host of phonemographic systems of various kinds. The Mayan system was logographic, with the sememographic aspect less emphasized than in the Old World systems; from it developed some phonemomorphemographic systems, and possibly even some phonemographic practices.

Of the aspects of language that could be written (see the beginning of this section), a combination of morphemes and sememes, in words, was the first to be represented by the main known writing systems. Later, representation extended to syllables and separate phonemes; but all the writing systems kept some of the earlier types of representation, and have even in some cases expanded them.

It was not until modern times, with the invention of phonetic alphabets, that representation of sounds as such came to be practiced. Some linguists have also devised symbol systems for articulations, but these are not really writing, at least not in the form that most of them take. Much phonetic writing, however, when it uses diacritic marks, is representing articulations. See 2.23, and 7.61.

The phonemographic systems that are called ALPHABETS (see below, and 7.12) all represent phonemes, though sometimes only partially, and often not consistently. Moreover, there are many situations in which allophones are represented, or in which the phonemic analysis is mistaken and the symbols are, accordingly, misleading or confusing. Established alphabetic systems usually represent some of the morphophones of a language, and morphemic writing is common. Syntactic operators are sometimes shown, by hyphens, lack of spacing, or the like. Sememes are often represented by certain words, and by other devices. Punctuation, which is mostly modern, attempts to indicate some sememes (capitals for proper nouns, for instance), and marks off units of occurrence and discourse (capitals for the beginnings of sentences, indentation for paragraphs, and the regular punctuation marks).

The symbols of logographic writing systems are called by such names as HIEROGLYPHICS (Egyptian, Mayan), GLYPHS (Mayan), CHARACTERS (Chinese); some call many of these kinds of symbols pictographs, and do not believe they are really writing.

Systems whose symbols represent mostly syllables are called SYLLABARIES (Akkadian, Japanese *kana*, Cherokee).

Systems whose symbols represent phonemes are called ALPHABETS, and the symbols are called LETTERS.

All the known writing systems actually mix several of the basic principles, and there is no purely alphabetic or purely syllabic or purely logographic system in existence. Details will be found in sections 7.1–7.6 and their subsections. Here we may mention the following characteristics of our own writing system:

The numerals we use are logographic, and also sememographic (by position): 7 'seven'; 7[3] 'seventy [...]', 7[23] 'seven hundred [...]', etc. When the spelling of strange words or names uses such devices as "Saigon is pronounced 'SIGH-gone'", it is phonemologographic. The capitalization of the first syllable is actually a late phonemographic device, to show the phoneme of primary stress. The spelling of *meat* 'flesh' to distinguish it from *meet* 'to encounter' is phonemologographic and morphemographic at the same time, and our phonemographic principles are being strained by our use of two different graphs for the same phonemic entity—*ea* and *ee* for /iy/. When we write "He X-ed out that clause", reading "X-ed" as /èkst/, we are writing syllabographically; and this particular instance is also phonemosyllabographic, because X is read only as /éks/.

In books that are printed in special type, with decorative initials and other devices of that kind, we are representing metalinguistic considerations of various types. Similar considerations also pertain to cases such as the comic-strip "Pogo", where some of the characters have their speeches written in black-letter type, suggesting the paralanguage—pompous, orotund tones; and even the ordinary remarks have some words or syllables emphasized by heavier lines than others to indicate prosodic and paralinguistic characteristics. Analogies with these comic-strip devices, as well as the balloon coming out of the characters' mouths to contain their speeches, are found in Aztec manuscripts, having been independently invented by the Aztecs long before our modern use of them.

Even pictographs are present in our everyday writing. It is customary to indicate profanity by a collection of unpronounceable symbols: "He went away swearing loudly: 'I'll be &§⫼/%□ if I ever talk to that ?!#* again.'" Many readers will say "blankety-blanked" for the first set of symbols, and "so-and-so" for the second, but since those readings are not predictable, and are not conventionally stylized, the sequences of symbols can only be of the nature of pictographs. They present a situation, but each observer furnishes his own linguistic material to interpret the symbols.

The next section treats the spread of writing in the world.

7.03. The oldest known writing systems, those of the Indus valley and of Sumer, have not survived. The spread and influence of the Indian one are not known; it is probable that the system died out for lack of proper cultural environments, and left no traces, unless it gave rise elsewhere to the idea of writing. The Sumerian system and its descendents flourished in Mesopotamia and the adjacent parts of the Near East—ancient Palestine and Syria, parts of Arabia, and ancient Persia—for some 1500 years or more; it almost certainly influenced Egyptian and Egyptian-derived writing in one way or another.

Egyptian writing spread to the Semitic world after 2000 B.C. The Semitic alphabets gave rise to the alphabets of the Mediterranean world after 1000 B.C., and also to the alphabets of India about the same time. The Semitic-derived Greek alphabets gave rise to the Italic alphabets between 800 and 500 B.C.; and in Christian times Greek produced Coptic around 200 A.D., Gothic after 300 A.D., Armenian and Georgian around 500 A.D., and the Slavic alphabets after 800 A.D. Latin writing conquered the whole of western and central Europe during the first half-millennium of the Christian era, and after the age of discovery—1500 and on—it spread to America and other parts of the world. It is now the leading alphabetic system, with Russian Cyrillic in second place but far behind it.

Mayan writing spread to the Aztecs and other peoples of the valley of Mexico, but was wiped out by the Spanish after 1500.

At the present time, the efficient functioning of Western culture is highly dependent on literacy—the knowledge of reading and writing. Statistics on literacy are not very accurate, and in any case are somewhat misleading. In the United States of today, everybody's life is governed by the necessity of being literate: the infant's food and health are taken care of by written prescriptions and directions; and by the time a child learns to talk he is already aware that the marks on paper, on jars of food, or on public buildings are symbols of language and are to be read; long before a child can read himself he asks, "What does it say?" Note the term "say"; he does not ask "What is written there?", but "What does it *say?*" This is functional literacy.

Despite their misleading nature, a few statistics on literacy are in order. Usually they are concerned with the ability to read and write of persons 10 years of age and over, and record the percentage of such persons in a nation or some other political entity. The figures do not, and cannot, tell us how well people read and write.

Literacy of 95 per cent or more of the population is found in most of the United States (all the states except Arizona, New Mexico, Texas, Arkansas, Louisiana, Mississippi, Alabama, Tennessee, Kentucky, Virginia, North Carolina, South Carolina, Georgia, Florida, Alaska); in Canada except Yukon Territory, the Northwest Territories, Quebec, Labrador and Newfoundland, New Brunswick, Nova Scotia, Prince Edward Island; in all of Australia except the Northern Territory; in New Zealand; and in Europe in Iceland, Great Britain, Ireland, Norway, Sweden, Finland, Denmark, Germany, Belgium, northern and northeastern France, and Switzerland.

Literacy from 90 per cent to 95 per cent is found in Texas, Arkansas, Tennessee, Kentucky, Florida, Georgia, Virginia, Quebec, Labrador and Newfoundland, Nova Scotia, New Brunswick, Prince Edward Island; in Europe in Estonia, Latvia, Austria, Hungary, the Netherlands, and parts of France; and in Japan.

In the range from 80 per cent to 90 per cent literacy, we find

Arizona, New Mexico, Louisiana, Mississippi, Alabama, North Carolina, South Carolina, Northern Baja California; northern Argentina and also in the southern pampas of Argentina, in northern Chile and the area around Santiago, in the area around Lima in Peru; in most of European Russia and in Siberia; in northcentral Spain.

From 70 per cent to 80 per cent of the population is literate in Alaska, Yukon, the state of Nuevo León in Mexico, central Argentina, Uruguay, some parts of Chile, Colombia around Bogotá, some parts of northern Spain, eastern White Russia, Rumania, central Italy, central Asian U.S.S.R. (except the Kirghiz and Tajik republics).

From 60 per cent to 70 per cent literacy is found in northern Mexico, Southern Baja California, Guyana, the state of São Paulo in Brazil, Poland, Lithuania, Greece, Kirghizia, Tajikistan, central Italy, southern Spain.

From 50 per cent to 60 per cent literacy is found in Yucatan in Mexico, the Republic of South Africa, Portugal.

Between 40 per cent and 50 per cent literacy is found in the Northwest Territories of Canada, in central Mexico, in interior central Brazil, in Siam, and in the Philippines.

Most of Africa, the interior of China, and the interior of India are counted as having less than 10 per cent literacy.

It will be noted that high literacy is found in a few languages only —English, French, the Scandinavian languages, Finnish, German, Dutch, Estonian, Latvian, Hungarian, Japanese, Spanish, Russian. Somewhat lower is literacy in Italian and Portuguese. The lowest literacy rates are in the new countries of Africa, in South America and south Asia, and in China. Except for China, these are countries in which until recently formal schooling was largely in nonnative languages, and no attempt was made to achieve literacy in the native languages.

It is said that learning to read and write Chinese is harder than to achieve literacy in a language written in an alphabet. But in Japan, where the Chinese writing system is complicated by the special adaptations to Japanese, there is nonetheless high literacy. It may be true that some writing systems are harder than others, but it is the educational system and the rest of the culture that really determine the extent of literacy.

One final thing must be said: regardless of the percentages of literates, all the countries of the world that are participants in Western culture are, or are becoming, highly literate. Populations with low literacy are mostly outside Western culture—Indians in South America, Africans of all kinds, Arabs in the Near East, and non-Moslem and non-Christian Asians. It is likely that in the next few decades literacy in all the Western-culture countries will be over 90 per cent—in the Latin or the Cyrillic alphabets mostly—and that in Africa and Asia there will be growing literacy in various native languages, but also in the established world languages, especially English.

7.1. WRITING IN THE ANCIENT NEAR EAST

7.10. The oldest writing system in the Near East seems to be the Sumerian. It is described as CUNEIFORM, meaning 'wedge-shaped' (Latin *cuneus* 'wedge'), from the shape of the strokes which form the symbols. This shape was a secondary result of the writing materials used: the surface for writing was smoothed soft clay, and the writing instrument was a stylus that had a narrow triangular or rectangular cross section; one end was pressed into the clay to produce the marks. The original pictures from which the system was elaborated were replaced by combinations of wedge-shaped marks, with the curves replaced by lines at angles to each other. Most of the symbols came to have little or no resemblance to any possible original picture. It should be added that the wedge shape and the finished system were the result of specific developments and inventions long after the idea of writing had begun among the Sumerians. Two examples must suffice: an old symbol for the word for 'ox' is ৬ ; this eventually became �; 'fish' was at first ⇒ , then 𝕎.

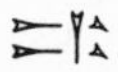

It is not certain what the date of the earliest Sumerian writing was. Some place it around 4000 B.C., others as much as nearly a thousand years later (3100 B.C.). Considering the many changes that had to take place before the system reached the stage found in the numerous Sumerian documents after 2500 B.C., the longer period of development seems reasonable. The earliest inscriptions seem to involve labels indicating ownership of objects, and quantities: the symbols were word signs, representing numbers, names, artifacts. The idea of using the signs which derived from pictures as representations of phonemic sequences arose fairly early among the Sumerians, and after 3000 B.C. the writing system was largely syllabic. The symbols represented words, mostly of one syllable (that being the nature of the language), and then syllables of the forms CV, CVC, VC; the device of combining a CV and VC to spell out a CVC syllable was used, and it thus became unnecessary to devise too many CVC signs. There were about 600 word signs in Sumerian, and about 150 syllabic signs.

Around 2500 B.C. the Akkadians, speakers of a Semitic language (see References and Notes), came into contact with the Sumerians, and adopted Sumerian writing. They adapted it by turning it into a real syllabary, retaining only a few word signs for names of divinities, persons, and places. Many of the word signs were spelled out in the syllabary, and most of our knowledge of Sumerian comes from these phonemic indications. At about the same time as the Akkadians, another people, the Elamites, adopted and adapted Sumerian writing. The Elamite language is not known to be related to any other, and we do not have the kinds of clues to reading it that we have in Akkadian because of its relationship to other Semitic languages which are well known.

After 2000 B.C., the Hurrians adopted writing from the Akkadians, and by about 1700 B.C., the Hittites, speakers of an Anatolian (Indo-Hittite) language, had learned to write, using Akkadian and Hurrian models. Almost a thousand years later, around 800 B.C., the Urarteans, a people in present-day Armenia, began to use cuneiform writing.

About 1400 B.C. there was devised in what is now Syria an alphabet of 30 letters, in cuneiform shape, for writing a Semitic language of the time, Ugaritic. It was also used to write Hurrian. It is possible that this was simply a Semitic alphabet transformed into a cuneiform style, since none of its symbols seem traceable directly to Akkadian ones, but some of them resemble Canaanite letters. This system is known as the Ras Shamra alphabet, having been discovered in a Syrian village of that name (see 8.30, end).

Another cuneiform writing system is that of Old Persian, dated at 600 to 400 B.C. There are four word signs ('king', 'province', 'country', 'Ahuramazda'), a word separator, three vowel symbols (*a, i, u*), and the rest are symbols for a consonant and a following vowel, in most instances, *a* (the symbols for combinations with *a* are also used for the consonant alone); and in a few instances, *i* or *u*. It is a sort of cross between a syllabary and an alphabet of Semitic type. The style is clearly based on the Mesopotamian writing systems, as is the representation of syllables with different vowels by different signs. It was probably a sudden invention, perhaps by an individual who knew about other writing systems but did not actually control the use of any of them. It has also been suggested that Babylonian and Royal Achaemenid Elamite writing, as well as the Ras Shamra alphabet, served as models for this special invention. The symbols used in Old Persian are:

The Old Persian Writing System

𒀀	𒄿	𒌋								
a	i	u	b(a)	č(a)	ç(a)	d(a)	di	du	f(a)	g(a)

gu	h(a)	x(a)	ya	ǰ(a)	ǰi	k(a)	ku	l(a)	m(a)	mi	mu	n(a)

nu	p(a)	r(a)	ru	s(a)	š(a)	t(a)	tu	t̠(a)	w(a)	wi	z(a)

The order here is that of our source (Gelb—see References and Notes, 7), and is approximately alphabetical in the Latin alphabet. The symbols transcribed $b(a)$ etc. were used for consonants alone and for consonants plus /a/; and with the symbols i and u they represented /Ci/ and /Cu/ where there were no special symbols for the latter.

By the time of the beginning of the Christian era, writing was so well established in the Near East and efficient materials for it were so widely known, that cuneiform writing on clay was simply too old-fashioned and cumbersome to continue. Cuneiform writing, which may have been the first of all writing systems, went out of use, leaving no direct traces anywhere.

All the cuneiform writing systems seem to have been arranged in horizontal lines starting at the left and going to the right, from the top of a tablet down. There are, of course, instances of decorative labeling where the lines may run around a vase, or surround a picture, but apparently the left-to-right, top-to-bottom order was established almost from the beginning in picture writing.

7.11. Egyptian writing is called hieroglyphic (Greek *hierós* 'sacred', *glúphein* 'to incise [on stone]') because it was thought that it was used chiefly for sacred purposes, and was always carved on stone. But of course it has been found to be used for all kinds of purposes—practical, commercial, political, literary, scientific—and to be written on any suitable surface, including paper. Egyptian writing was a long time undeciphered, but in 1822 François Champollion deciphered it, after he discovered the famous Rosetta stone on which parallel Greek and Egyptian inscriptions were written.

The Egyptian writing system developed in an atmosphere of technical excellence of pictorial representation. The symbols were well-carved or drawn pictures, conventionally stylized, but unmistakably pictorial in form. Moreover, like Mayan writing, they were an integral part of the total picture, and were a part of the total art of decorating buildings and other public artifacts. As in other writing systems, the symbols were at first logographic, and largely remained so. There eventually developed a restricted number of signs (about 100) that had phonemic value, representing a single consonant or two consonants; there were about 700 word signs. These symbols were technically syllabic, as a vowel was read with each consonant. But because of the nature of the language, vowels were, in large part, morphophonically determined by the grammatical function of a word; thus the idea never arose of representing the vowels separately, nor of varying the representation of a consonant according to the vowel that followed. The Sumerian writing system and those derived from it always represented the vowels of syllables to some extent; but the Egyptian system did not. This being the case, the symbols really became alphabetic letters, representing consonants or sequences of consonants (our x is an instance of the latter practice). For this reason, and the lack of comparative material of sufficient extent to throw light on the vowel patterns of Egyptian, the writing can be said to be technically imperfect and inadequate; and knowledge of the language is limited in respect to actual pronunciation. The patterns of consonants are known; even the logographs are, in most cases, also written out in parallel symbols somewhere and sometimes; and the grammatical relations are usually clear. No one has ever sufficiently studied the late surviving Egyptian dialects known as Coptic to arrive at a reconstruction of vowels; and no comparison with Semitic has been possible since one of the terms of comparison was missing.

The pictorial signs were used on public monuments, but for other uses script forms were developed. One, still quite close to the pictures, is called HIERATIC ('priestly'), and was used in literary and official documents. The other, called DEMOTIC ('popular'), was used in everyday writing of all kinds, and eventually became the most widely used form. As systems, these were merely variant styles of each other. Two examples may be given (the transcriptions are those traditionally used by Egyptologists):

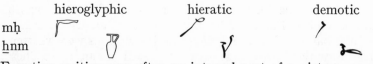

	hieroglyphic	hieratic	demotic
mḥ			
ḫnm			

Egyptian writing was often an integral part of a picture, or of a building, or the like. The symbols were arranged artistically, and often seem to be in no particular order. They start anywhere and run up, then across, then down, and so on. As the writing developed and began to be used for ordinary documents, on paper or similar materials, the symbols were arranged in horizontal lines, running usually from right to left, and from top to bottom. The symbols face in the direction of the writing: ⎩ or ⎧ *i*, ⌐ or ⌐ *d*, etc.

We may mention here in passing the so-called "hieroglyphic Hittite" writing. An Anatolian language close to the Hittite written in cuneiform characters was in use in the Hittite empire from about 1500 to 700 B.C., and was written in a pictorial sign system (with cursive forms developing later) of the same type as Egyptian, but apparently not in any way connected with or derived from the latter. The material has been only partly deciphered, and not much can be said about it with certainty. There seem to be around 500 word signs, and perhaps 50 syllabic ones. They are written more or less regularly in left-to-right horizontal lines from top to bottom.

Other pictorial and syllabologographic writing systems will be mentioned in 7.20 and 7.30, though very little is known about them.

The guess may be hazarded here that all the writing systems of the ancient Near East and adjacent Aegean areas were interconnected in terms of theory, but were independent creations by local inventors who had gotten the idea from traveling or meeting travelers; the process is the one that anthropologists call "stimulus diffusion". Writing was, in my opinion, a cultural trait all over the area, and it would be profitless to try to guess more than this in the absence of data which will probably never be available.

7.12. The Egyptian syllabary was the source of the writing system that we consider to be the first alphabet—the Semitic system of writing. But it must be pointed out that the term "source" here does not necessarily mean that the Semitic symbols can be directly traced to Egyptian symbols. Attempts to do this have been made, and some of the connections are plausible enough. But it is not at all impossible that no one of the Semitic symbols is really based on any of the Egyptian symbols at all. It was the idea and the manner of writing that developed in Egypt that was learned by some one individual, with possibly a few associates, and which was the inspiration for the invention of the Semitic alphabet. The possible connections between symbols will be noted below (8.30), but the important point of departure is the notion of a writing system that represents the consonants of the language. The 100 or so symbols used in Egyptian writing to represent one consonant or two consonants were, in effect, alphabetic letters, because they really were intended to represent only the consonants, and were thus phonemographic units, and not syllabographic devices. The vowels were simply not represented, just as in our own writing system some of the phonemes—stresses, pitches, transitions (in part)—are not represented. In Egyptian writing after 2000 B.C. there was increasing use of the symbols for /y/, /w/, and / ʾ / to indicate the vowels /i/, /u/, /a/ respectively. This use was common especially in spelling out foreign names; it indicates that the nonsememographic symbols in Egyptian writing were really used alphabetically, and makes clear why Semitic writing is the way it is.

Some time around 1700 B.C. someone in the area of the Sinai peninsula devised a simple system of keeping records of names and activities of people. This person—or group of persons, perhaps—was probably a speaker of whatever Semitic language was being spoken in that area (a language of the Phoenician-Hebrew type probably), was literate or partly literate in Egyptian, and had the analytic ability to determine the main lines of the structure of his language. This inventor of the Semitic alphabet figured out that the language had 22 consonant phonemes; he also knew that the vowel patterns were the indicators of grammatical function, and that they came out automatically, as it were, from the structure of a phrase or clause (it is for this reason that we conjecture that he was a native speaker). An alphabet that marked the consonant phonemes of the language was sufficient to write the basic structure of the words, and was what the inventor created. The idea of consonant writing was already known in Egypt, and our unknown inventor simply thought up or copied or adapted a number of simple combinations of lines and curves and got his alphabet. The new alphabet was written solely from right to left; Egyptian hieratic and demotic were usually written in this way also, but not exclusively; perhaps the inventor was left-handed.

One characteristic of the Semitic alphabet perhaps indicates that our speculative account of its origin is too simple—the order of the letters. There is certainly nothing in Egyptian that necessitates the order of Semitic. Yet the Semitic order has been preserved in most of the alphabets derived from it later. Those alphabets which have not preserved the order may, paradoxically, contain the answer to the question. Just possibly the Semitic order of the letters is purely accidental and haphazard. But we do not know. There are also some alphabets which have no established order of letters, or else use varying orders. It is possible that some magical formula or some other mnemonic device was involved, with the letters being the initials of the words.

The original Semitic order of letters was: ʾ (glottal stop, also associated with the writing of the vowel /a/), *b*, *g*, *d*, *h*, *w* (also the vowel

/u/), *z*, *ḥ* (a pharyngal voiceless spirant), *ṭ* (a velarized *t*), *y* (also the vowel /i/), *k*, *l*, *m*, *n*, *s*, ' (a voiced laryngal spirant), *p*, *ṣ* (a velarized *s*), *q* (a postvelar voiceless stop), *r*, *š*, *t*. Of the later Semitic alphabets, Arabic started with this order, but added six letters by modification of existing letters with similar sounds (*ð* < *d*, *x* < *ḥ*, *ẓ* < *ṭ*, *ḍ* < *ṣ*, *γ* < ', *θ* < *t*); then the letters were rearranged so that similar shapes came together, distinguished only by diacritical marks; the resulting order, that of the Arabic alphabet as known since the spread of Islam, is: ', *b*, *t*, *θ*, *j* (= original *g*), *ḥ*, *x*, *d*, *ð*, *r*, *z*, *s*, *š*, *ṣ*, *ḍ*, *ṭ*, *ẓ*, ', *γ*, *f* (= *p*), *q*, *k*, *l*, *m*, *n*, *h*, *w*, *y*. In Ethiopic the order was rearranged also: *h*, *l*, *ḥ*, *m*, *š*, *r*, *s*, *q*, *b*, *t*, *x*, *n*, ', *k*, *w*, ', *z*, *y*, *d*, *g*, *ṭ*, *ṣ*, *f*. For the actual symbols, added symbols, and other details, see 8.3 and its subdivisions.

The Semitic alphabets at first had no way of representing vowels. The letters ', *w*, *y* were used in writing complex vocalic nuclei, but these were originally phonemically /V', Vw, Vy/, and continued to be so morphophonically, so that the writing was proper in terms of the system. Later, after vowel writing had been developed elsewhere, special symbols were devised, in the form of diacritical marks, to show vowels. They have never become a real part of the writing system, being used mostly in writing sacred texts or materials for beginning learners. In Ethiopic, however, the vowel symbols have been incorporated into the writing system (see 8.33).

In the writing of Hebrew sacred texts, prosodic characteristics were also indicated in late writing, but these may have been musical rather than linguistic indicators.

7.2. MEDITERRANEAN WRITING SYSTEMS

7.20. The area at the eastern end of the Mediterranean—Egypt, Syria, Palestine, Arabia, Mesopotamia, as well as Greece and the Greek islands—was one in which writing seems to have been known to all the cultures from 2000 B.C. on, if not earlier.

In Crete, a hieroglyphic pictorial writing appeared around 2000 B.C.—the so-called "class A"; this writing was followed in the next few centuries (to 1700 B.C.) by "class B" hieroglyphics, which look not unlike Egyptian. Between 1700 and 1400 B.C. appeared a cursive writing, "linear A", followed by another set of cursive forms, "linear B", used up to about 1200 B.C. These forms are all thought to be related and successive, and "linear B" has been deciphered. The language of "linear B" was Greek, but the others were probably one or more pre-Hellenic languages. The writing system, with syllabic signs indicating /CV/, was badly adapted to Greek, with its consonant clusters and consonant finals, and went out of use rather quickly.

About 1000 B.C. or a little later, the Phoenician alphabet was brought to Greece, and adapted for the writing of Greek. In the process the writing of vowels was invented. This invention improved the Semitic alphabet and made it really usable for languages with structures in which the vowels were not morphemically patterned, as they are in Semitic. The process of adaptation involved the use of the Semitic consonant symbols for Greek phonemes that were similar to Semitic ones phonetically; the several signs for glottal phonemes (', h, ') were made into vowel signs, as was y. The order of letters was maintained, and new letters were added at the end; these two characteristics have been kept by all Greek-derived writing systems. The Greeks also took the Semitic names of the letters; in Semitic these names have meanings, and were perhaps given because of real or fancied resemblance to pictures of objects—*'aleph* 'ox', because the symbol A might be thought of as a picture of an ox-head turned over, $\forall$; *bēth* 'house', because B is an inclosing symbol, $\sqcap$ or $\sqsupset$, developing into $\boldsymbol{\mathsf{B}}$ or the like; etc. In Greek the names were only names for letters, with no other meaning; *alpha, beta*, etc.

It is sometimes said that the Greeks turned ' and h into vowel symbols because they had no similar consonant sounds. This conclusion is probably incorrect. The following explanation is more plausible linguistically. In the Greek of the tenth century B.C., the original Indo-Hittite laryngeals were still retained at least in the form of an initial vowel onset, say /'/, which was in complementary distribution with some instances of "vowel length", and which had various allophones before different vowels—perhaps a glottal stop, [ʔ], before /a/; a palatalized glottal stop, [ʔ$_y$], with voiceless palatal glide from [ʔ] to the vowel, before /e/; some velar glide, [ʔ$_x$], before /o/; labialization before /u/, [ʔ$_w$]; before /i/ the palatalization was stronger than before /e/. An initial syllable /'a/ would be written, in Semitic fashion, by the symbol A, and a "long vowel" /a·/ would be written, it is likely, also as A, after a consonant symbol. A syllable /'e/ might have sounded like [he] to a Semitic speaker, and got written as E; initial /'o/ was perhaps interpreted by the Semitic speaker to be like his /'o/ (if he had an /o/ phoneme, otherwise as /'/ with a back allophone of /a/, [ɒ]), and written O; "long e" and "long o" would also be written E, O respectively. Initial /'i/ and earlier /y/ before a vowel had probably already fallen together into /'i/, and the letter I was clearly appropriate for it. In the Greek of those days, /w/ was still clearly consonantal in function, so the letter F was appropriate only for /w/. To the Greek speaker, /'a/, /'e/, /'o/, /'i/ all began with the same phoneme, and /a·, e·, o·/ all ended with the same phoneme, and /'/ and /·/ were probably allophones of one phoneme. If the inventor of the Greek alphabet (if we wanted to personify him, we could call him by the traditional name Cadmus) found his Semitic-speaking teachers writing different letters, A, E, I, O, he either misunderstood the practice and thought they were writing the vowels, or, more likely, arrived at the brilliant insight that since he did not need to write four different consonants, he could use the four letters as vowel symbols, with the initial onset /'/ not separately written, since word separation by a space made the initial onset automatic before a vowel. Vowel writing was thus invented as one single intellectual achievement, which immensely improved the few attempts at vowel writing made by Semitic alphabetizers previously. This speculative explanation also suggests why /u/ came to be written with a new letter; /w/ still existed, and /'u/ may already have been [ʰu]; once the letters A, E, I, O became vowel symbols, and F and H were retained as consonants (the latter for a good strong [h⁺], probably), it was a simple matter to invent one new vowel letter, V (or Y), perhaps in origin a modified F. Further details of Greek writing will be found in the next section.

The invention of vowel writing completed the development of the kind of writing system that we still use in the Western world. Vowels and consonants are indicated by single letters, and sequences of phonemes are represented by sequences of letters. Further improvements in details of phonemic representation—writing of vowel length, accents of various kinds, pitches, and transitions—took place much later in the history of writing systems, and have hardly affected the system established by the Greek alphabet about 3000 years ago. For these developments see the various sections following, and Chapter 8.

The Semitic alphabet from which the Greek alphabet was derived was written from right to left in horizontal lines. The Greeks adopted it in this way. But the prealphabetic writing systems used in Greece (see above) were written from left to right, or else indifferently in either direction, and other writing systems that may have been known to the inventor of the Greek alphabet went from left to right. In any case, a change of direction seems to have taken place soon. There are some old inscriptions that run in both direction alternately; they are called *boustrophēdon* 'ox-turning', from the motion of oxen in plowing furrows, first in one direction, then the next one in the other, and so on. The right-to-left direction lasted long enough to be taken to Italy and used in some of the alphabets there (see 7.22). When the direction was changed, some of the letter forms changed also, and mirror images were used: B and Ꮭ, < and >, etc.

7.21. The Greek alphabet shows two principal varieties. East Greek is the alphabet that has come down as the alphabet in which Classical Greek was written. West Greek was used to write various Greek dialects in ancient times, and gave rise to the alphabets of Italy.

The Classical Greek alphabet (see 8.10) had 24 letters, transliterated thus: *a, b, g, d, e, z, ē, th, i, k, l, m, n, x, o, p, r, s, t, u, ph, kh, ps, ō*. The letter *ē* was originally a sign for /h/, but in the Ionic dialects this phoneme disappeared early, and the letter was left around without function; however, the name of the letter had been *hēta*, and then became *ēta*; this clearly paralleled other names for vowel letters, and by the acrophonic principle (the head sound, that is, the first sound, of the name is the value of the letter) the symbol began to be used for *ē*. The letter *x* went back to the Semitic sign for *ṣ*; this latter being velarized, and /ks/ being a frequent combination in Greek, it was no doubt considered an appropriate choice for a two-consonant sequence; moreover, *z* must originally also have represented two phonemes in Greek—/dz/ or /dy/?—so the pattern was not unique; the invention of a letter *ps* was following out this analogy. Since the Semitic *ṭ* was used for /th/, it seemed reasonable to invent letters for /ph/ and /kh/ also. After H had become the symbol for *ē*, *ō* was invented; these two long vowels were probably phonetically more different from the short ones than was the case for *ī, ā, ū*, which is why special letters for them found favor.

The East Greek alphabet, when adopted for the *koinḗ*, the standardized literary language of ancient Greece (see References and Notes), was perfected by the accent marks ´, `, ^ or ˜ (= ^), by the so-called breathings, and by punctuation marks. For later developments from the Greek alphabet, see 7.24.

In the West Greek alphabet, the symbol H continued to indicate /h/; X was the symbol for /ks/, and the symbols for *th, ph*, and *kh* (this latter often in the form of East Greek *ps*) were sometimes not used, or not used consistently. There was also no *ō*. The West Greek alphabet went out of use in Greece before the accents and other improvements were devised, and the Italian descendents of West Greek writing never used these devices.

In Italy various forms of the West Greek alphabet were introduced from about 800 B.C. on. Some of them at least were written from right to left. Etruscan was the principal language to be written in this alphabet (from right to left), and because Etruscan phonology was quite different from Greek, various letters came to be used in new ways, or went out of use altogether (see 8.11). The Oscan and Umbrian alphabets (see References and Notes) were taken directly from Etruscan (see 8.12), including the symbol 8 for /f/; and the Latin alphabet was based on Etruscan, though apparently not as directly as might be expected. See the next section for details on Latin.

It is not known whether the Greek names of the letters were brought to Italy with the alphabet, but there is no record of their being used to name the letters in the local alphabets that arose in Italy.

7.22. The Latin alphabet would certainly be expected to show Etruscan influence, but in fact shows very little of it. A couple of very early Latin inscriptions are written from right to left, but after that they all go from left to right. Except for the use of C for /k/ and /g/, and then the later creation of the new letter G for /g/, and the almost complete disuse of K, the Latin alphabet might go straight back to West Greek without any intermediary. The letters B, D are used in the traditional way; F (from earlier FH) is used for /f/ and not for /w/; Q is retained in QV /kw/; I and V are used for both vowel and consonant (/i, y; u, w/); X is /ks/. Z was originally at the place after F, and had the value [z] which was not needed in Latin (this is attested by the Latin-letter writing of Oscan, whereas in the Oscan alphabet the letter after F had the value /ts/). When G was created, it replaced Z in position (the symbol may really be a sort of blend of C and Z—that is, the assignment to Z of the phoneme value originally held by C, and modification of the symbol to look like a slightly changed C). Only much later were Greek Υ and Z added at the end of the alphabet. The letters corresponding to Greek Θ, Φ, Ψ were never used.

The Latin alphabet of 23 letters (without modern J, U, W) replaced all the other alphabets of ancient Italy—Etruscan, Oscan, Umbrian, Greek—as Roman political power was extended. When the Roman dominions were extended beyond Italy, the Latin language and its alphabet went with them (see References and Notes). Most of the areas conquered had no native writing systems, and whatever non-Latin material was written down by the Romans— names, words for local products, etc.—was written in the Latin alphabet, and necessarily adapted to Latin phonology and morphology. For their own use, the Romans transcribed Greek words in their alphabet also (see References and Notes); but in the Greek-speaking parts of the Roman empire Latin never took over, and the Eastern church used Greek and the Greek alphabet in its missionizing.

Latin used the following names for the letters: *ā, bē, cē* (i.e., /ké·/), *dē, ē, ef, gē, hā, ī, kā, el, em, en, ō, pē, cū, er, es, tē, ū, ix* (/íks/). The acrophonic principle was dropped for *f, l, m, n, r, s, x*—two spirants, the liquids, and the one two-phoneme letter—and the sound came at the end of the name; this is understandable for *x*, since /ks/ was not an initial cluster in Latin, but is harder to explain for the other letters, especially for *f*, since /f/ did not normally occur in final position in Latin. When *y* and *z* were added, the Greek names went with them—*ȳpsilon* (probably /úwpsilon/ or /íypsilon/, with [ʉ·] in the first syllable used only by speakers who knew Greek); and *zēta* (/zé·ta/, or with various native replacements of [z], say [s] or [dy]). When /h/ > 0, the name of the letter seems to have been changed to *acha* /ákha/—with a Greek-imitating learned pronunciation retaining a vestige or imitation of the traditional sound. The names of *j, v, w* developed after the Middle Ages.

When the western Roman empire began to break up politically, in the fifth century, there was introduced into the Roman world for the first time the possibility of writing extensively in some language other than Latin. Very little such writing was done, however, so that the Gaulish, Iberian, Illyrian, and Germanic dialects of the fifth to eighth centuries have hardly survived. In the late seventh century, the writing of non-Latin languages in the Latin alphabet began in a serious way—in Ireland, in England, in Germany, and possibly elsewhere. See the next section for an account of these extensions of the Latin alphabet.

7.23. All the languages of western Europe began to be written in the Latin alphabet as Christianity was extended beyond the area of the Roman empire. Old Irish, various Germanic dialects, the developing Romanic languages, the more western Slavic languages—all these began to acquire orthographies from the sixth century A.D. on. The general practice from those times to the present day was to maintain the basic order of the 21 or 23 letters that constituted the starting alphabet, to add a few digraphs as necessary, and to put the digraphs and any new letters at the end of the alphabet or wherever it seemed most convenient. Digraphs were formed with *h*, which had no other function in late post-Classical Latin, and new letters were minor modifications or combinations of old ones. Nowhere was there the idea that a new alphabet was being created. Accent marks were used to some extent, mostly with vowel letters.

Old Irish used an alphabet consisting of the letters *a, b, c, d, e, f, g, h, i, l, m, n, o, p, r, s, t, u; c* was used in the value /k/; digraphs with *h—bh, ch, dh, fh, gh, mh, ph, th*—were used for various sounds morphophonically related to those shown by the first letter; later the custom arose of writing a dot instead of *h*, and that is done in modern Irish—ḃ, ċ, etc. (but only when the old style of letter is used; modern Roman type is written with *h*). Long vowels were indicated by the acute accent—*á, é*, etc. Vowel digraphs like *ea, ai*, etc., usually indicated some quality of the following consonant (velarization, palatalization).

The Germanic languages needed a symbol for /w/, and the letter *w* was devised, by writing two *v*'s or two *u*'s; in German *w* is called /véy/ (spelled *we*), but *v* is called /fáw/ (spelled *vau*). In German *z* came in from French as a symbol for /ts/, and has remained so. In Dutch *z* is /z/, in a later tradition. Old English writing was more systematically created, probably by Irish monks; only the letters used in Irish were employed, but the runic letter Ƿ (*wen*) was adopted for /w/; and the runic thorn, þ, was used for /θ/. The Irish probably heard the difference between the allophones [θ] and [ð], and this difference probably brought about the creation of the letter *edh*, ð, but the English mixed up the two until both were dropped in Middle English. The writing of the vowel nuclei may have reflected some attempt to indicate allophones, and was perhaps partly based on Irish practice. On the continent, the Germanic languages had trouble writing long nuclei, and still do.

In Icelandic, þ and ð were retained, as also the acute accent for length. The letter ø ("o-slash", as it has been called in English) was created, and other diacritics were used inconsistently. The modern Scandinavian languages do not need þ or ð, but they use ø, and å (or *aa*).

In German the vowels /ɛ/, /ø/, and /ʉ/ were denoted by *ae, oe, ue* when they came into existence after the umlaut changes from Old High German. The abbreviations *ä, ö, ü* began to be used early, but were not made the regular and only usage until about 1900.

From German, Finnish borrowed *ä* and *ö*, and Hungarian used *ö* and *ü*. The latter language used ' for length—*i, é, á, ó, ú*—and then wrote "long" *ö, ü* as *ő, ű*.

In French, *z* was used in the old language for /ts/, but after /ts/ > /s/, *z* was restricted to new loanwords, mostly Greek, and was pronounced /z/, that being a phoneme already in the language and represented by single intervocalic *s*. In French the use of the accents ' (acute), ` (grave), and ^ (circumflex) grew up in a haphazard way;

after the Middle French change of /s/ to /h/ before a consonant (with final change to length or ɵ), the use of ^ to replace the old s became quite consistent: *teste* > *tête*, *hoste* > *hôte*, etc. The writing of front rounded vowels and of the "diphthongs" gave rise to many problems in French, and there are still inconsistencies: *eu* or *oe* or *oeu* for modern /ø/ (and also *ue* in *cueillir* /køyir/); *o* or *ou* for older /ow/, now always *ou* /u/; *ai, ay, ei, ey* for /ey/ > /e/. The letter *ç*, with the mark, called *cedille* 'cedilla'—a Spanish word meaning 'little *z* (zeta)'— came to be used regularly in French; the sequence *o e* came to be printed *œ*; but neither *ç* nor *œ* is considered as a separate letter. In French *y* is called *y grec*, 'Greek *y*'; *j*, separated from *i* in the eighteenth century, is called *ji* /ži/, while *g* is *gé* /že/. In the late nineteenth century, the custom was introduced of calling the consonant letters by names beginning with the consonant and followed by /ə/: /bə, sə, də/, etc. But this practice brought about homonymy of *c* and *s*, *g* and *j*, and had other difficulties; the most usual names now are: *a, bé, cé, dé, e* /ə/ (or *é*), *èfe, gé, ache* /ašə/, *i, ji, ka, èl, ème, ène, ô, pé*, /kə/ for *q*, because /kʉ/ is also the form of a tabu word, *ère, esse, té, u, vé, double vé, ixe, y grec, zède*.

As has been recounted in 5.21, English spelling since the twelfth century has been based on French. The Old English letter *wen*, Ⴤ , was replaced by *w*, and *þ* and *ð* both came to be gradually replaced by *th*; *k* and *qu* were introduced. The various accent marks and diacritics have never become part of English spelling, although attempts are made to retain *ç* in *façade*, *ê* in *fête*, and the like. English letter names have undergone the regular sound changes, and are now: /éy, bíy, síy, díy, íy, éf, ǰíy, éyč, áy, ǰéy, kéy, él, ém, én, ów, píy, kyúw, áhr, és, tíy, yúw, víy, dábəl(+)yùw, éks, wáy, zíy/. The name /zíy/ is American, /zéd/ being used elsewhere. The name /ǰéy/ is probably by analogy with /kéy/; /áhr/ represents change from /éhr/ as seen in *sergeant* /sáhrǰint/, *clerk* and *Clark*, *Berkeley* and *Barclay*, etc. The name /wáy/, from an early Middle English /wíy/ or /wíy/, may represent an attempt to imitate an older French */ʉy/ or the like; /éks/ instead of */íks/ is unexplained.

In Spanish the use of *ç* has gone out, and the only diacritics are tilde, ~, with *n*—*ñ*; the acute accent (*acento*) with vowels to show irregular stress, or occasionally to differentiate homonyms; and the dieresis (*trema*), ¨, with *u*—*ü*—to indicate /w/ after *g* before *e* and *i*. The digraphs *ch*, *ll*, and the letter *ñ* are given separate alphabetical position, but *rr* is not. The letters are called: *a, be, ce* /θé/, *de, e, efe, ge* /xé/, *ache* /áče/, *i, jota* /xóta/, *ka, ele, elle* /éle/, *eme, ene, eñe, o, pe, cu, ere, erre, ese, te, u, ve, doble ve, equis* /ékis/, *i griega, zeda* /θéda/.

Since *be* and *ve* are both pronounced /bé/, they are sometimes distinguished as /bé/ *de burro* '*b* of *burro* "donkey"' and /bé/ *de vaca* '*v* of *vaca* "cow"'. The names of *h, w, x* are probably from French; *jota* is the Greek *iota*. The use of *sh* for /š/ in South America is a recent innovation, the traditional letter for /š/ being *x*, as in *México*, originally /méšiko/.

In Portuguese, *ç* is used; and the tilde, ˜ (called *til*), is written in *ãe, ão, õe* to indicate nasalization—/əyN, əwN, oyN/. Modern Portuguese spelling also uses the acute accent and the dieresis; and the digraphs *ch, lh, nh* have separate alphabetical places.

In Italian the only diacritic regularly used is the grave accent, ˋ, to show stress on final vowels—*città, perchè*. The letters *j* ("*i* lungo" = 'long *i*') and *w* are not considered part of the regular alphabet; and *x, y* are not really in the alphabet either; *h* is used only in the digraphs *ch* and *gh* (/k/ and /g/ respectively before *e* and *i*), and in the forms of *avere*—*ho* 'I have', *hanno* 'they have'.

The Slavic languages have made most changes in the use of Latin letters. The use of *c* for [ts], and of *k* for /k/ and *j* for /y/ consistently, began early, as well as of *y* for a nonpalatalizing /i/, and of *z* for /z/. As diacritics, *h* was used with *c*—*ch* /x/, and *z* with *c* and *s*—*cz* /č/, *sz* /š/. Early in the fifteenth century *cz* and *sz* were replaced by *č* and *š* in Czech, *ž* was introduced, and the use of the wedge (ˇ) spread generally in the Slavic languages except in Polish, where the digraphs were retained. To a large extent South Slavic spellings, and also Czech in part, are transliterations of Cyrillic, rather than independent adaptations of the Latin alphabet.

In the nineteenth century and since, the Latin alphabet has been extended to numerous languages in Asia, the Pacific, and Africa. After the Russian revolution in 1917 there was talk, off and on, of replacing Cyrillic by the Latin alphabet; but this was culturally unfeasible, and after 1930 the idea was no longer thought about.

In Africa, an "African alphabet"—a Latin alphabet with new letters taken from the International Phonetic Association alphabet— was adopted by various agencies interested in literacy for the native Africans. In the half-century since this alphabet was first proposed, very little use has been made of the alphabet's new letters, though its general principles are being employed. These principles are those of alphabetic writing in general—one letter to one phoneme where possible; and of the Latin alphabet historically—use of digraphs as long as these are unambiguous, and employment of letters not otherwise needed as diacritics in the digraphs. In this African usage, *y* is the palatal semivowel, *j* is /ǰ/ or /ž/, *c* is used for /č/ or for a click, *x* is used for a click or for /x/; long vowels are usually shown by doubling; tones are shown by the usual accent marks, but often are simply omitted. It may be that in the next half-century some of these orthographies may be elaborated and perfected, but for the most part at present they are inadequate and not well thought out, and do not lend themselves to use alongside of the orthographies of the European languages which continue to be used for outside contacts.

In Asia, Vietnamese—formerly called Annamese—was provided with a Latin-letter orthography in the seventeenth century by Roman Catholic missionaries, and this is now the only writing used in Vietnam. It was originally entirely phonemic, and still remains a good spelling system. The tone marks are omitted outside of Vietnam, but seem to be used regularly and consistently there. No other Asian official language uses the Latin alphabet. There have been proposals for romanization of Japanese, and various transliteration systems for Japanese, Chinese, and Indic languages are in use (see 8.02), but only a few have any official sanction.

The discussion of equivalence of alphabets (8.01) and of transliteration (8.02) will summarize what seem to be, at this time, the basic usages followed in extending the Latin alphabet to new areas.

At some time early in the Christian era the Latin alphabet was used as the basis of the so-called runic writing for Germanic languages. And in Ireland there developed the ogham writing, with entirely new letter forms, but obviously based on the Latin alphabet. See 8.24 for these alphabets.

7.24. The Greek alphabet was first extended to non-Greek languages in ancient times. In Asia Minor Lycian and Lydian (Anatolian languages—see References and Notes) were written in modified Greek alphabets in the last few centuries before the Christian era. And, of course, the extension of West Greek writing was what brought about the Latin alphabet.

After the introduction of Christianity, Greek missionaries began to extend the alphabet in the eastern Mediterranean area and the Near East. In the third century A.D. the Coptic alphabet (see 8.21) was formed for writing the Egyptian of that time—Coptic. It contains the 24 letters of Greek, with seven additional letters taken supposedly from demotic writing: *š*, *f*, *ḫ* /x/, *h*, *ǰ*, *č*, and a letter for the syllable *ti*. In Coptic, Greek *theta*, *phi*, *khi* represent /th, ph, kh/. The supposed demotic origin of the seven last letters is quite possibly a myth; the letter forms are such that quite different origins are possible: *š*— ϣ —from Semitic (Hebrew or Syriac) *š*; *f*— ϥ —from Semitic *p* or Greek *phi*; *ḫ*— ϧ —from Latin *h*; *h*— ϩ —un-

known; ǰ— ꙩ —from Coptic d— ꙗ ; č— ꙍ —from Greek σ;
while Coptic s— ꙅ —is from Greek ς; ti— ꚋ —is from Greek τ
with ι over it.

In the fourth century, the Gothic alphabet was based on Greek
(see 8.21).

In the fifth century, Greek missionaries brought Christianity to
the Caucasus, and the Armenian and Georgian alphabets were
devised. See 8.22 for the Armenian and Georgian alphabets (see
References and Notes for material on the Armenian and Georgian
languages).

In the eighth and ninth centuries the Slavic alphabets were perfected. See 8.24 for the alphabets.

In the early eighteenth century Russian Cyrillic was simplified
and modified to look more like Latin letters. In the nineteenth
century the several other languages using Cyrillic adopted the
Russian forms of the letters, with each language omitting unneeded
letters and adding a few new ones. Early in the nineteenth century
this activity brought about the Serbocroatian elimination of the
Cyrillic preiotacized vowel letters (denoting /ya, yu/), and the introduction of the symbol j from the Latin alphabet. The Russians extended their alphabet to Aleutian, Yakut, and Ossetic during the
nineteenth century, with new letters added and others omitted (see
References and Notes for these languages). After the Russian revolution in 1917, for about ten years efforts were made to introduce
Latin-letter orthographies for all the non-Russian languages of the
Soviet Union; then, after 1930, all these new orthographies were
replaced by Cyrillic equivalents—Kirghiz, Uzbek, Tajik, Buryat
Mongol, and others; in these Cyrillic variants, all the Russian letters
are used, so that Russian loanwords remain unchanged except for
grammatical endings, but new letters or letters with diacritics are
introduced as needed. There are also, however, instances of the use of
arbitrary digraphs, such as оǐ (i.e. об) for /ø/. In these new practices,
Russian Cyrillic is being used in about the same way as the Latin
alphabet has been extended, rather than the way Greek was originally modified (see 8.23, end).

7.3. WRITING IN INDIA

7.30. It has been indicated above (7.01) that one of the known
inventions of writing may have taken place in the Indus valley.
However, that writing system did not survive, and apparently left
no traces. The writing that is found in India in modern times has
developed from the introduction of some form of the Semitic alphabet.

India had two types of early writing, going back to an origin, in India, perhaps as long ago as 500 B.C. The oldest inscriptions are attributed to the king *Aśoka*, third century B.C., and indicate that writing was well developed then. Interestingly enough, the Aśoka inscriptions show both of the early types: the *brāhmī* ('pertaining to Brahma'), which goes from left to right, and the *kharoṣṭhī* ('pertaining to Kharoṣṭha'—presumably the inventor), which goes from right to left. Kharoṣṭhī went out of use by the second century A.D., and all the modern writing systems are developments from brāhmī.

The Semitic origin of the system of writing is clear, but it would be difficult to trace in detail the development of the form of any particular symbol. At first used for general secular purposes, as in the Near East, the writing came to be applied to the sacred literature that had been orally transmitted for perhaps a thousand years. When this application took place, the writing system was remade into an instrument for preserving in great detail, and unchangingly, this ancient literature. It is the codified and rigidly regulated language and writing systems of these later documents that have come down to us.

7.31. The Sanskrit writing system is known as *devanāgarī* (this may be pronounced, in English, /dèyvǝ+náhgǝriy/), a name which does not make much sense when literally translated: *nāgarī* means 'pertaining to the city', i.e., 'urban'; *deva* means 'god' or, interpreted, 'Brahman'; the *devanāgarī* is then the 'god-city' or the 'divine-urban' writing. The devanagari is usually called a syllabary with a consonantal base: its symbols represent, when unmodified, an initial consonant followed by the short vowel /a/: *ka*, *ga*, etc. But there are 14 letters that are said to represent initial (and postvocalic) vowels: *a*, *ā*, *i*, *ī*, *u*, *ū*, *ḷ*, *ḹ*, *ṛ*, *ṝ*, *e*, *ai*, *o*, *au*. Phonetically or phonemically, these are syllabic signs, but they are alphabetic in terms of a writing system. It is true that to write *ka* one simply uses the unmodified symbol (see the list below); to write *kā*, another symbol follows, so we have *ka* with an added symbol, interpretable as a length mark. There is a symbol for initial *a*; for *ā* the marker of length is the same as in *kā*. Let us now compare the "initial vowel" signs with the writing of internal "vowels":

Initial and Internal Vowel Signs in Devanagari

a अ	*ā* आ	*ka* क	*kā* का
i इ	*ī* ई	*ki* कि	*kī* की
u उ	*ū* ऊ	*ku* कु	*kū* कू

$ṛ$	ऋ	$ṝ$	ॠ	$kṛ$	कृ	$kṝ$	कॄ
$ḷ$	ऌ	$ḹ$	ॡ	$kḷ$	कॢ	$kḹ$	कॣ
e	ए	ai	ऐ	ke	के	kai	कै
o	ओ	au	औ	ko	को	kau	कौ

In Sanskrit there was probably a phonemic initial onset of vowels, /'/, as was postulated above for Greek. The so-called "initial vowel" symbols were, in my opinion, symbols for the initial consonant phoneme /'/ followed by some vocalic: three of them, *a*, *ṛ*, *o*, in fact, start with the same symbol, a symbol which may go back to the same original as our letter A; most of them also exhibit some portion that is like the vowel symbols used with other consonants. It may be speculated that in this writing system which was worked out with great precision for a specific purpose, the Semitic habit of writing consonants was retained as the basis, and vowel symbols were developed in somewhat the same way as for Greek. Some have argued that since the letter without a vowel symbol represents /Ca/, this is a syllabary and not an alphabet. I do not accept this categorization. The letter अ meant /'a/, so it was perfectly logical to construct the rest of the system on this basis, and to modify for other vowels. Then, in writing a consonant without /a/ or any vowel, the original way was probably simply to write the letters together, blending them into each other, and completing only the last one. If that one did not have a vowel, a special sign, "no vowel", was devised. In my opinion, then, the devanagari is an alphabet, with the peculiarity that it omits writing one of the vowels, the commonest one, and has a symbol for vowellessness, as well as the device of combination of letters. See 8.40 for further details; the "exact" transliteration suggested there shows the difference in principle of the devanagari from the Greek or Latin alphabets.

The Semitic names and order of letters are completely lost in India. The letters are called, in Sanskrit, *akāra*, *kakāra*, etc. ('a-maker', '*ka*-maker'), or simply *a*, *ka*, etc.; *r* is never called *rakāra*, but only *ra*, or else *repha* 'snarl'; the nasalization sign is called *anusvāra* 'after-sound'; the sign of vowellessness is called *virāma* 'stop'; and the final *ḥ* (replacing original *s*) is called *visarga* 'out-breathing'. The order of symbols used in Sanskrit dictionaries and glossaries compiled by Western scholars is the phonetic order of sounds devised by the Sanskrit grammarians, and not the order of letters in an alphabet, though it has become that in modern usage. (This fact makes all the more unreasonable the practice of some Western scholars of arranging Sanskrit transcribed into Latin letters by the supposed Sanskrit order.)

7.32. Once the devanagari writing system was established, there was no other basic writing used in the whole of the Indian subcontinent until the Muslim invasions in the fourteenth century, when the Arabic alphabet was introduced.

The devanagari alphabet is used for writing modern Hindi, and has been used ever since its inception for various Prakrits (Middle Indic languages) and modern Indic languages. In various parts of India, divergent styles of writing developed, and some of these have become very different in appearance from the original. Generally speaking, however, these different writing styles do not constitute separate alphabets. All the letters are there, and all the writing practices are observed, at least in theory. In some cases, Sanskrit itself is written in these variant styles. One thing may be noted: as applied to the modern languages, Indic writing is completely alphabetic, though it is often inconsistent and irregular.

Bengali (developed after 1000 A.D.) is most like devanagari in appearance; Panjabi is written in *gurmukhī*, which is also very much like the original; more scriptlike are the Gujerati and Orissa writing systems. In southern India, the Dravidian languages Kanarese and Telugu are written in cursive forms of the alphabet that only distantly resemble devanagari; and Tamil uses a very much elaborated cursive form. In some cases the elaborations and changes of form of these alphabets are attributed to the writing materials (palm leaves, with the veins used as lines from which the letters depend). See 8.41 for some examples of these alphabets.

7.33. The devanagari alphabet was used for writing various Prakrits, and the Buddhist religious texts were written in it. As Buddhism was carried out of India, the writing system went along, as always with missionizing religions.

In Tibet the alphabet is from a north Indian variety of devanagari, and developed about 700 A.D. In appearance it is not very different from devanagari. At first, some of the original letters were not used, but were added later for writing Sanskrit words. The alphabet is used in new ways in Tibet, adapted to the structure of the language; there is only one "initial vowel letter", and some of the letters, originally with phonemic values not needed in Tibetan, are used to mark differences of tone (see 8.42). (See References and Notes.)

Going east out of northern India, Buddhism was carried by the Pali language (a Prakrit), and the alphabet has developed three main varieties in southeast Asia: Burmese, Cambodian, and Siamese (see 8.43). Burmese uses highly cursive forms: nearly all original straight lines are replaced by curves that are circles or parts of circles; the general principles of Indic writing have been retained, but various new uses of the letters have developed to show tones. Cambodian employs a style of writing not very different from Burmese. Both the Burmese and the Cambodian alphabets have retained the original number of letters and, in large part, the original distinctions in sound. Siamese has modified the alphabet considerably; new letters have been added, and an elaborate system of indicating tone by the use of different consonant letters has been worked out.

Indic writing even went into the East Indies. The Malayan languages Batak in Sumatra, Buginese and Macassar on Celebes, and Javanese on Java developed original alphabets on an Indic base. As Hinduism was replaced by Islam, these writing systems largely went out of use and were replaced by the Arabic alphabet. In modern times all these languages have been written in the Latin alphabet—first in terms of Dutch spelling, and recently in the pattern established for the new over-all (and artificial) language called Indonesian. Javanese writing developed an interesting elaboration: the basic letters were written on the line, the combining forms below the line, and vowels and diacritics above the line.

7.4. WRITING IN THE FAR EAST

7.40. The Chinese writing system is an independent invention of writing that has survived and grown. The evidence of the earliest writing in China is that the system began in a series of pictures that were established as word symbols. In this beginning it seems to have been like all the other original writing systems. As the system expanded, the number of symbols grew, but did not really go beyond a fairly small number. That is, new characters, as they are called, were formed by combinations of parts of other characters. It is in the manner of combining these parts, and the fanciful mythology that grew up about it, that Chinese writing differs from other writing systems.

Like all writing systems, the Chinese one had to come to a point where new pictorial symbols could no longer be devised. The writing then had to become phonemosyllabographic: that is, the sounds of syllables had to be indicated. Here it should be mentioned that in Chinese all native morphemes are monosyllabic, that all of these monosyllables can, at least in theory, be uttered alone as words, and that there are no inflectional or derivational affixes or processes (at least none that are productive). This means that the grammar of the language involves the syntactic combination of monosyllabic words into phrases by means of a limited number of phrase superfixes. The monosyllables themselves are of fairly simple structure: an initial (single phoneme or certain limited clusters) followed by a medial (vowel, or semivowel followed by vowel) and ending with the medial, or in a final (semivowel or certain single consonants, or semivowel and one of these consonants); each syllable also has as part of its intrinsic structure one of a limited number of tones. (See References and Notes for a fuller description of Chinese.) To write such a language it is basically necessary only to have a means of writing each monosyllable distinctively. The sequence of the distinct monosyllables can be read by the native speaker even if no indication of phrase superfixes or other combinatory devices is present. Given the phonemic structure of Chinese syllables, the number of different syllables, even in the phonologically most complex dialects, is relatively small. For modern so-called Mandarin (the North Chinese standard language), the actually existing syllables number little over 1300. An adequate syllabic writing could be made to have just this number of different characters. But it must be remembered that the writing started out to be logographic, and even alphabetic systems such as ours continue to be partly morphemographic. The Chinese enhanced the logographic (which also means morphemographic, in this case) nature of the system; any homonymous words had to have different characters for the different meanings. The writing system finally worked out some 1500 years ago established a group of basic characters—called "radicals"—each with a reading and a meaning. The radicals as they are now used vary in complexity from one stroke (line, curve, dot, or the like) to 17. They are combined with other elements, often called "phonetics", to make up the total character. The radical is supposed to indicate the general area of meaning of the word, while the phonetic is supposed to give a clue to the pronunciation. Determining the meaning and pronunciation involves at times much fantasy, pointing to the conclusion that individual inventors with creative imaginations developed the system, though there are no records to prove it. A few examples will illustrate the processes.

Many basic characters are described as remodeled pictures:

rì 'sun, day': 日; originally ⊖

ywè 'moon, month': 月; originally ☽

hwě 'fire': 火 in combination ⺍; < 火

srwěy 'water': 水 , in combination 氵; < 巛

ywǐ 'rain': 雨 < 雨, 'drops of rain falling from heaven'

srān 'mountain': 山 < 山

mǎ 'horse': 馬 < 馬

yáng 'sheep': 羊 < 羊

rén 'man': 人 < 人

thyán 'field': 田

Then there are some symbols that are iconic:

yī 'one': 一

èr 'two': 二

sān 'three': 三

sràng 'up, above': 上

syà 'down': 下

Some symbols are supposed to represent a word with an abstract meaning by picturing something concrete connected with it:

kāw 'high': 高 < 高, supposedly a picture of a tower

pěy 'north': 北 < 北 two men standing back to back, because the north is in back of a person, and one habitually faces south

Then there are the characters that are labeled "combined sense"— two or more pictures combined to bring their meanings into "logical" relationship:

hǎw 'good': 好, formed of 女 'woman' and 子 'son', because having a wife and child is good

khū 'to cry': 哭, formed of 犬 'dog' and two 'mouths', 口

kǔ 'ancient': 古 formed of 十 'ten' and 口 'mouth', because that which is ancient has come down by word of mouth for ten generations

Most numerous are the characters with a radical and a phonetic:

kūng '[physical] work' is 工, a picture of a carpenter's square; serves as a common phonetic

húng 'red' is written 紅, where the radical is 'silk', and the phonetic *kūng* indicates something that has to do with silk and sounds something like *kūng*

cyāng 'river' is written 江, with the radical for 'water'—something that has to do with water and sounds something (remotely!) like *kūng*

Chinese writing originally was incised or scratched on bones and shells. As it became more widely used, it was written with ink on bamboo strips, which were held vertically. After paper began to be used, and the writing instrument—a camel's hair brush—was perfected, the lines were still written from top to bottom, beginning at the right edge and moving to the left. The characters themselves are always written beginning at the top left, vertical strokes before horizontal ones. (The most common modern arrangement of radicals and phonetics is based on the number of strokes.) Before Western influence began, Chinese books were always printed in vertical lines from right to left, and thus began with what we would call the last page. However, the fact that each character is drawn from the top left has made it possible to turn the page, as it were, through 90° to the left, so that the lines of characters run horizontally from left to right. This new style is used for modern books that include citations from Western languages. (See the Japanese text given in 7.41 for an example of the modern arrangement of characters of Chinese origin.)

Some idea of the effect of reading texts in these two ways may be obtained by noting that in the Western world writing is sometimes arranged in vertical lines, as on public buildings, theater marquees, and the like. A building known as the "Central Auditorium" may very well have its name arranged vertically on a wall, with or without neon lights:

                        C   A
                        E   U
                        N   D
                        T   I
                        R   T
                        A   O
                        L   R
                                 I
                                 U
                                 M

Another variation of usual order is sometimes found in traffic markings on roadways; the approach to a school crossing, for example, may be painted on the pavement so that it is to be read from bottom to top (that is, from nearer to further as one moves):

WATCH FOR CHILDREN
SCHOOL CROSSING
15 MILES PER HOUR
SLOW

This is to be read, of course, as "Slow. 15 miles per hour. School crossing. Watch for children." This arrangement, from bottom to top, is harder to get used to than the vertical-line arrangement, probably because this really goes counter to the systematic patterns of the writing system.

Chinese writing has been so elaborated, and has become so deeply imbedded in the entire culture, that no suggestions for change or reform have been successful in modern times. In the nineteenth century a transcription system was devised by two Englishmen, Wade and Giles, and most of the Chinese material—chiefly names of persons and places—appearing in the Western world is in the Wade-Giles transcription. German and French transcriptions are different, and the Russians have one in Cyrillic. In recent years a number of other transcriptions have been proposed, and are used in some textbooks. Before the Chinese revolution in 1911, the Wade-Giles system had been adopted by the Chinese government for postal and telegraphic communication. Since the Chinese Communists took over in 1949, a new Latin-letter transcription has been adopted as official; it is a transliteration of a previously used transcription in Cyrillic. (For the relation of this and other transcriptions to the phonemes of Chinese see References and Notes.)

There is no prospect of the characters being displaced in the immediate future. In China there are not only numerous dialects, but actually several different languages. Throughout history they have all been written in the same way. The writing is in a literary language that is about 1500 years old, and everybody reads the material in his own dialect or language, the structures being sufficiently alike so that there is little difficulty. However, what is read usually has to be expanded or glossed to be fully comprehensible. Until such time, if ever, when a single standard language is spoken in China, it is not likely that a phonemographic writing of any kind will be adopted.

Various forms of cursive writing have developed in China. In these the characters often become very different from their original form. A few examples:

	Usual form	Running hand	Grass character (a kind of shorthand)
mǎ 'horse'	馬	馬	乃
mén 'door'	門	门	⁀
cyēw 'bird'	隹	隹	乃

In a writing system that has accumulated perhaps 40,000 characters over the centuries, and in which as many as 10,000 to 15,000 are in regular use, it would obviously be impossible to offer a transliteration. All one can do is provide an approximate transcription, which is only as good as the analyst's phonemic system.

7.41. Chinese was the vehicle for civilization in all of what we call the Far East—China, Japan, Korea, the southeast Asian mainland. With Chinese technology, government, art, and literature went the Chinese language in the form of loanwords, and the Chinese writing system. Since the writing system is logographic, it can be read, in a manner of speaking, in any language, just as our numerals are read in any language. Of course, if the structures of the languages differ greatly, there have to be special rules for reading. The Chinese sentence equivalent to the English 'I want to buy a book' is *wě yàw mǎy ī-běn srū*, whose literal translation is 'I want buy one-copy book'. It is written with six characters, which we can represent as A B C D E F. The literal translation of the Japanese equivalent is *I*-(as topic) *book*-(as goal) *buy* [subordinate] *want* [finite, present]; the Japanese reader of the characters A B C D E F has to read "A F C B", and has to supply the particles indicating the grammatical functions of *I* and *book*, and the endings of *buy* and *want*, omitting D and E entirely. This practice is somewhat similar to the German one of reading the number 123 as "hundred three-and-twenty"; but it is rather difficult for a whole text.

From an early period attempts were made in Japan to devise a system of writing that would represent the actual sounds and words of the language, rather than alluding to them, as it were, by a logographic code. By the eighth century, there had developed a syllabary, now used in two styles, by means of which Japanese can be written quite accurately without recourse to any Chinese character. However, the nature of Chinese writing is such that it constitutes an integral part of many aspects of the culture; with Chinese culture, Chinese writing also came to Japan, and no one has ever seemed to want to separate out the elements and get rid of some or any of them. The syllabary, known as *kana*, has thus been used only as an auxiliary writing system in Japan: inflectional endings, particles, and derivational affixes are written out in *kana*, but the base of a word, except for some recent technical loanwords, is written with a Chinese logographic symbol. Depending on the kinds of affixes, the Chinese characters—called *kanji* in Japanese—may have various pronunciations. The resulting writing system is thus one of great complexity.

To illustrate the nature of Japanese writing, we shall use some English examples and treat them as if we had to write them in the Japanese manner. Let us suppose that the character for 'man' in the source writing system (Chinese) is *X* (the actual character is 人 , pronounced *rén* in Standard Chinese). The Japanese word for 'man' (*hito*) is then written *X*. The derivative *manly* is written *Xly*; the verb form (*he*) *mans* is written *Xs*. This much is simple enough. But then we want to write *human*; we do it thus: *Xan*. Then *humanity* is *Xanity*; and *hominid, hominoid* are *Xid, Xoid*. *Anthropology* is written *Xology*. But how shall we write *anthropoid*, to differ from *hominoid*? We differentiate by writing *Xpoid*. Then there is *androgynous*: we write *XYous*, where *Y* is *woman*. The science-fiction word *android* becomes *Xroid*. What is the pronunciation of *X*? There are many: *man, hum-, homin-, anthrop-, anthro-, andro-, and-*.

The *kana* syllabary is used in teaching children to read, for transcribing foreign names, and for indicating the pronunciation of *kanji*; but no serious movement has ever existed to replace *kanji* by *kana*. The two styles of *kana* are: *katakana*, used to spell out loanwords and as a kind of "italics" for emphasis, and generally a formal writing system with relatively simple forms; *hiragana* (g < k is a regular morphophonic change in some Japanese "compounds"), used to write grammatical suffixes and in handwriting (thus informal as compared with *katakana*), and having cursive forms of some complexity. The symbols are based originally on Chinese characters. There are 50 basic symbols, and with the addition of certain diacritics, the number is 72. The *katakana* symbols, in traditional order, with the most usual transcription, are:

The Katakana Symbols

イ	ロ	ハ	バ	パ	ニ	ホ	ボ	ポ	ヘ	ベ	ペ
i	*ro*	*ha*	*ba*	*pa*	*ni*	*ho*	*bo*	*po*	*he*	*be*	*pe*
ト	ド	チ	ヂ	リ	ヌ	ル	ヲ	ワ	カ	ガ	
to	*do*	*chi*	*(d)ji*	*ri*	*nu*	*ru*	*(w)o*	*wa*	*ka*	*ga*	
ヨ	タ	ダ	レ	ソ	ゾ	ツ	ヅ	子	ナ	ラ	
yo	*ta*	*da*	*re*	*so*	*zo*	*tsu*	*(d)zu*	*ne*	*na*	*ra*	
ム	ウ	ヰ	ノ	オ	ク	グ	ヤ	マ	ケ	ゲ	
mu	*u*	*wi*	*no*	*o*	*ku*	*gu*	*ya*	*ma*	*ke*	*ge*	

フ	ブ	プ	コ	ゴ	エ	テ	デ	ア	サ	ザ	キ
fu	*bu*	*pu*	*ko*	*go*	*e*	*te*	*de*	*a*	*sa*	*za*	*ki*

ギ	ユ	メ	ミ	シ	ジ	エ	ヒ	ビ	ピ	モ
gi	*yu*	*me*	*mi*	*shi*	*ji*	*we*	*hi*	*bi*	*pi*	*mo*

セ	ゼ	ス	ズ	ン
se	*ze*	*su*	*zu*	*n*

The *kana* writing system is phonemosyllabographic. The use of a diacritic to indicate syllables beginning with /p/ is indicative of a historical change; it can be assumed that the symbol *ha*, for instance, originally denoted some kind of labial spirant, probably [φ], as the initial; in certain cases, this probably assumed the allophonic form [p‘]; when [φ] changed to [h], and /h/ and /p/ became phonemically separate, the device of writing the basic symbol for /h/, and the same symbol with the diacritic ° for /p/, was invented. The fact that the voiced stops, affricates, and spirants are denoted by the voiceless symbols with the diacritic ‘‘ probably results from the early recognition of morphophonic alternation between the two sets. Symbol economy was achieved in this way.

In modern times the *kana* symbols are often arranged in ten columns, in an order based on the devanagari alphabet:

a	*ka*	*sa*	*ta*	*na*	*ha*	*ma*	*ya*	*ra*	*wa*
i	*ki*	*shi*	*chi*	*ni*	*hi*	*mi*	—	*ri*	*(w)i*
u	*ku*	*su*	*tsu*	*nu*	*fu*	*n*	*yu*	*ru*	—
e	*ke*	*se*	*te*	*ne*	*he*	*me*	—	*re*	*(w)e*
o	*ko*	*so*	*to*	*no*	*ho*	*mo*	*yo*	*ro*	*(w)o*

The details of this arrangement (*shi* with *sa*, *chi* with *ta*, *fu* with *ha*, etc.) depend on the phonemics of Japanese.

Examples of *kana* used for transcribing foreign names are:

ワシントン = wa-shi-n-to-n 'Washington'

トレーガー = to-re-‾-ga-‾ 'Trager' (the symbol ‾ is a new one used for showing "long vowels")

スミス = su-mi-su 'Smith'

In the Japanese translation by Akira Ota of Trager and Smith's *An outline of English structure* (see References and Notes) there are many passages illustrating the complexity of the modern Japanese writing system. The following is a passage from the Introduction, p. 1:

更に本書を　Kenyon　や C.

K. Thomas などのアメリカの学者, あるいは Jones, Firth などのイギリスの学者,

それからプラーグ学派やコペンハーゲン学派などと比較すると単に細部だけでなく

根本的考え方に相当の開きが見られる。

In this sentence there are Chinese characters, *kanji*; *hiragana* affixes, always belonging to the *kanji* or *katakana* preceding them; names in the Latin alphabet; *katakana* transcriptions of foreign names; and the Western punctuation marks comma and period. The Chinese characters are of two kinds as far as the Japanese reading is concerned: those with *kun*-readings represent regular Japanese words; those with *on*-readings represent Chinese loanwords (there are two kinds of these also—*go* readings for early Chinese loanwords from the Wu [= *go*] dialects, and later "Classical" loans with *kan* [= Han 'Chinese'] readings; only the latter are found in this passage). In the transcription that follows, the rendering of each character or symbol above is separated from the next one by a space; KUN readings are in roman capitals; *ON* readings are in italic capitals; *hiragana* symbols are in italics; KATAKANA symbols are in small capitals; and Latin-letter items are in ordinary capital and lowercase roman type. The transcription is followed by a running text, with interlinear translation, and then a free translation.

SARA *ni HON SHO o* Kenyon *ya* C.

K. Thomas *na do no* A ME RI KA *no GAKU SHA, a ru i wa* Jones, Firth *na do no* I GI RI SU *no GAKU SHA,*

so re ka ra PU RA⁻GU *GAKU HA ya* KO PE N HA⁻GE N *GAKU HA na do to* HI KAKU *su ru to TAN ni SAI BU da ke de na ku* KON PON TEKI KANGA *e* KATA *ni SŌ TŌ no* HIRA *ki ga* MI *ra re ru.*

	Sára-ni	hónsho-	o	Kenyon-ya C.
	moreover	*book-this*	*(object)*	*K. and C.*
K. Thomas-nado-no	Amerika-no	gakusha,	arúiwa	Jones,
K. T. etc. 's	*American*	*scholar(s),*	*or*	*J.,*
Firth-nado-no	Igirisu-no	gakusha,		
F. etc. 's	*English*	*scholar(s),*		

so-re-kara　　　Purágu-gakuha-ya　　　Kopenhāgen-　　gakuha-
and- then　　　*Prague school and*　　　*Copenhagen*　　*school*

nado-to　　hikaku-　　　suru-　to　　tán-ni sáibu-dake-de náku
etc.   with   comparison   do　　when   merely details only in not

konponteki-	kangae	káta-ni	sōtō-no	hirakíga
basic	*think*	*way in*	*considerable*	*divergence*

miraréru.
is seen.

'Moreover, when we compare this book with [the works of] the American scholars Kenyon, C. K. Thomas, *et al.*, or the English scholars Jones, Firth, *et al.*, as well as the Prague school and the Copenhagen school, we see that it is not [a case of] mere [differences in] detail—there is a considerable divergence in the fundamental thinking [of its authors]'.

It is evident that the Japanese writing system is able to include in the actual appearance of the writing itself a great deal of information that is extralinguistic. It is this aspect that gives rise to the ardent defense of it exhibited by nearly all those who have learned to use it properly. An analogous reaction is found among literate English-speaking people when spelling reform is mentioned. It can be argued that the bulk of a population can never appreciate the possibilities of such a system as the Japanese one, but the fact remains that in Japan even those who are not well educated take a certain pride in the complexity of the writing system. This is an anthropological fact, and it suggests that there is more to a writing system than merely representing the bare facts of a language in the simplest possible way. In 7.52, there will be occasion to point to another writing system, the Aztec, that had also gone far beyond our relatively simple phonemography.

Another writing system derived from the Chinese is that of Korean. This alphabet was devised about 1445. It was originally used only to supplement Chinese characters, in the manner of Japanese *kana*. But it soon came to be quite regularly employed to write Korean, and is now the only writing system in regular use in Korea. Originally written in vertical lines from right to left, it is now written horizontally from left to right. The symbols for a syllable are combined into a unified graph, as if *cat* were written $^c a_t$ or the like; this is still done in modern typing and printing. Going from left to right, the symbols are combined from top to bottom.

The symbols of this alphabet (called *onmun*) are:

ㄱ	ㄴ	ㄷ	ㄹ	ㅁ	ㅂ	ㅅ	ㅇ	ㅏ	ㅑ	ㅓ	ㅕ
k	*n*	*t*	*r*	*m*	*p*	*s*	*' or ng*	*a*	*ya*	*e*	*ye*

ㅗ　ㅛ　ㅜ　ㅠ　ㅡ　ㅣ　ㅈ　ㅊ　ㅋ　ㅌ　ㅍ　ㅎ

o　yo　u　yu　ï　i　j　jj　kk　tt　pp　h

The title of the textbook "English for Koreans" is written thus:

$$영 \quad 어 \quad 학 \quad 본 \; = \; \begin{smallmatrix}'\text{ye}\\\text{ng}\end{smallmatrix} \; '\text{e} \; h_k a \; \begin{smallmatrix}\text{p}\\\text{o}\\\text{n}\end{smallmatrix}$$

This spells *yenge hakpon* 'English textbook' (*hak* is most nearly equivalent to the English '-ology', and *pon* is 'book').

In Vietnam, before the introduction of the Latin-letter orthography in the seventeenth century, there was a system of writing which combined the use of Chinese characters as such with adaptations of Chinese characters to the writing of Vietnamese. This system was called *chữ nôm* 'southern writing' (*chữ* 'letter, word, writing'; *nôm* < *nam* 'south'); written Chinese was called *chữ hán* 'Han [= Chinese] writing'.

Chinese characters first came into use in Vietnam around 900 A.D. Each character had a Vietnamese pronunciation which was close to the Chinese pronunciation of the time. As loanwords, these Chinese characters are called *Hán-Việt* 'Sino-Vietnamese'. By 1300 A.D., the use of the characters to write Vietnamese had developed, and there is an inscription in *chữ nôm* dating from 1343.

The various ways that Chinese characters were adapted to Vietnamese are:

1. The character is used sememographically; *mùi* 'odor' is written by means of Sino-Vietnamese *vị* 'flavor, taste';
2. the character is pronounced the same as a Vietnamese word of the same meaning: *tài* 'talent' is written by Sino-Vietnamese *tài*;
3. the character is pronounced as a Vietnamese word, but has a different meaning in Chinese: *một* 'one' is written by *một* 'no, not';
4. the character suggests the pronunciation and meaning of the Vietnamese: *đời* 'life' is written *đại* 'generation, time';
5. two Chinese characters—a "radical" and a "phonetic"—represent a Vietnamese word: *đến* 'to reach' is written *chí* 'to arrive' and *điển* 'code';
6. two "radicals" are put together: *trời* 'sky' is written by *thiên* 'sky' and *thượng* 'up, above';
7. a Chinese "radical" is combined with a *chữ nôm* "phonetic": *lời* 'words, speech' is written *khẩu* 'mouth' and Vietnamese *trời* 'sky'.

This complex and haphazard system was never fully developed, and had no prestige. Official and literary material was simply written in Chinese characters, and was presumably decoded in the way that is used for reading the various non-Northern Chinese languages in China itself, and as has been alluded to for Japanese. The *chữ nôm* system was complicated, ambiguous, and difficult. It did differentiate homonyms: *năm* 'year' was written *nam-niên* 'south-year', while *năm* 'five' was written *nam-ngũ* 'south-five'; but the phonemic adequacy and simplicity of the Latin-letter orthography proved to be much stronger than the minor advantages of *chữ nôm*.

The characters for the examples above, with Standard Chinese pronunciation, are (see References and Notes for the Chinese phonemic orthography):

1. *mùi* 'odor': 味 Chinese /wə̀y/ [u̯ᴇ̀ɪ̯] 'taste, odor, smell'
2. *tài* 'talent': 才 Chinese /cháy/ [c'áɪ̯] 'talent, ability, material'
3. *một* 'one': 没 /mə́y/ 'not, yet, to die'
4. *đời* 'life': 代 /tày/ 'to replace, represent'; also 'generation, era' in 上代 /ˈˈsràng+ˈtày/ 'older generation'
5. *đến* 'to reach': 𦤾 not a possible Chinese sequence; 至 /crɨ̀/ [c̣ɨ̀] 'to reach, extreme', as in 至上 /ˈˈcrɨ̀+ˈsràng/ 'the highest'; 典 /tyăn/ [tɪ̯ɛ̆n] 'regulation, law, tale'
6. *trời* 'sky': 𡗶 not a Chinese combination; 天 /thyān/ [t'ɪ̯ɛ̄n] 'sky, heaven' in 天上 /ˈthyān+*srăng/ 'sky, heaven'; 上 /sràng/ [ṣàŋ] 'to ascend' in 上天 /ˈsràng+ˈˈthyān/ 'to ascend to heaven'
7. *lời* 'words, speech': 口𡗶 not possible in Chinese; 口 /khə̆w/ [k'ɔ̆u̯] 'mouth'; 口味 /ˈˈkhə̆w+ˈwə̀y/ 'breathe, favor, interest'; 口才 /ˈˈkhə̆w+ˈcháy/ 'speech talent'

7.5. WRITING IN THE NEW WORLD

7.50. One of the known inventions of writing took place in America; also the subsequent development of an elaborate writing system—that of the Mayas—occurred there. From Mayan writing several other systems developed. These systems are treated in the next two sections.

Elsewhere in America, there were many instances of prewriting, in the form of so-called pictographs. Some of these show evidence of sporadic true writing, but none of them carried these accidental beginnings any further.

In Peru, among the Incas, there developed a system of using knotted cords of various colors and lengths to record quantities of material and other numerical data. Such uses make these *quipus* analogous to the abacus, notched sticks, and the like. But it has also been said that the quipus were used to convey nonnumerical messages; if so, they were at least an analog of writing. There are also legends that some kind of writing may actually have been in use among the Incas, but no evidence has ever been found.

7.51. Around the beginning of the Christian era, the Mayan civilization existed in what are now southern Yucatan, Campeche, Tabasco, Chiapas, in Mexico, and the adjoining areas in Guatemala. There were many cities, with some temples and other structures. These structures were covered with inscriptions; also all kinds of other records, on paper and other materials, have been found. It is clear that centuries of development preceded this flourishing condition of the society. The Mayan society flourished for some centuries more. In the fifth century A.D., the Mayas moved north into Yucatan, and the southern cities declined. Several centuries of development of the new areas followed; and from about 1000 A.D. there was an era of political unity and extensive cultural development. By the thirteenth century, political dissension began, and the Mayan cities engaged in destructive wars, during which Aztec allies were brought in by some of the parties. When the Spanish arrived, there was at first strong resistance to them, but in 1541 the Mayas were defeated, and the Spanish took over.

Mayan society was developed around a strong ceremonial system, and involved much calendrical calculation. The numerical and writing systems which accompanied these activities were highly elaborated, and present some very interesting aspects of writing and calculating which were not found elsewhere in the world. Mayan texts were mostly a part of the decoration of various stone structures, but were also carved in wood, molded in stucco, scratched on shells, etched on bones, engraved on metal, drawn on plaster walls, and painted in fiber-paper books. All of these except the stone and paper were rare and occasional. The stone structures have largely survived, but the large number of books known to have existed was almost entirely destroyed, and only a few are known to have come down to us.

The characters (glyphs) of Mayan writing are most often so made as to fit within a square with rounded corners— ☐ ; in the paper books, the codices, the shape is more rhomboid or even oval— ▱ , ◯ . But these are merely minor differences in style. In the stone inscriptions the glyphs are arranged in parallel columns which are read two columns at a time, from left to right, and top to bottom:

ab   gh   mn
cd   ij   op
ef   kl   qr

The glyphs are often very elaborately carved or drawn, and there seem to be very many of them, but closer analysis reveals a limited number of basic and fairly simple elements. It can be conjectured that these elements were phonemographic or syllabophonemographic in nature: they identified the word structure and facilitated the reading of glyphs whose other parts were sememographic. Recent Russian studies of Mayan writing indicate that this is indeed the case, as was suggested by Morley early in the twentieth century and by Whorf around 1940. The Russian results are said to be very extensive, but have not yet been published to any extent. Most Mayan research in the United States has concerned itself with analyzing the numerical portions of the writing (see below), and has treated the rest of the material as a kind of puzzle in which a few glyphs—names of gods and important personages, and of places, months, and other periods of time—were known, and the meaning was to be guessed at from these clues and the numerous illustrations. It is this treatment that has led some students of writing to conclude that the Mayas did not have true writing. The facts of the matter seem to be that the Mayas not only had true writing, but had actually worked into it the representation of aspects of style and of special semological and even referentially semantic detail that have not been found in any other writing system. It will take publication of the studies now being made, and analysis and translation of many Mayan documents, before a real description of this remarkable writing system can be made.

The names of the months of the year and various other names of a calendrical nature have been preserved, and the glyphs for them are known. They will serve here as minimal illustrations of Mayan writing. There were 18 months of 20 days each, and a five-day period at the end of the year. The names were (in the usual Mayan orthography devised by the Spanish): *pop, uo* /wo/, *zip* /sip/, *zotz, tzec, xul* /šul/, *yaxkin* (*k* = /q/), *mol, chen* /čen/, *yax, zac, ceh* /keh/, *mac, kankin, muan, pax, kayab* (b = /p'/), *cumhu*; the five-day period was called *uayeb* /wayep'/.

The names *pop, uo, zip, zotz,* and *uayeb* are written as follows (the top row gives the forms used in inscriptions; the bottom row, those used in codices):

pop   uo   zip   zotz   uayeb

The best understood Mayan characters are those for numbers. The
system of numbers, based on 20, and with a zero symbol, was very
elaborately worked out, and any numeral, into the millions if
necessary, could be written. Although this was a positional system
of writing numbers, and had a zero symbol, the use of the zero was
different from that in our system; some details will be given below
in 7.62, where the writing of numbers is discussed.

7.52. The Aztecs got the idea of writing from the Mayas, but did
not, it appears, directly borrow any of the highly elaborate and very
complexly specialized Mayan symbols. This is easy to understand;
Mayan writing was the province of a few specialists, who worked it
out long before the Aztecs arrived in Mexico and preserved it practically unchanged over the centuries. The Aztec priests and others who
practiced writing were similar specialists; once they got the idea of
writing, they developed it on their own, and probably never had
knowledge of the actual Mayan system.

The Aztecs wrote on deerskin, fiber paper, and woven cotton
cloth, and used many colors of writing materials; the colors were
actually painted on the surface. The codices were sometimes rolled,
but more usually were folded in the manner of our scenic-postcard
strips. There was no single order of reading; one could go from bottom
to top, from right to left, or in any other combination. But within
any codex, the same order was followed.

The codices were in effect illustrated books, with varying amounts
of writing. Some of the drawings were pictures, others mnemonic
pictographs; then there were logographic sememographs, and finally
various kinds of phonemographic symbols. Some of the codices
picture persons with balloons containing written symbols issuing
from their mouths, as in our comic strips. Another device that the
Aztecs used was to indicate what we would call paralanguage by
various kinds of modifying symbols added to the ordinary writing.

A few examples of Aztec writing will have to suffice. The word for
'water' was *atl* (where -*tl* is a nominal affix); the symbol for the word

atl was also used for the syllable *a-*. The word for 'flag' was *pantli*, and the symbol was also used for *-pan*; the word for 'teeth' was *tlantli*, and the symbol could be used for *-tlan*. The name of the towns of *Apan* and *Atlan* could be written *a(tl)-pan(tli)*, *a(tl)-tlan(tli)*:

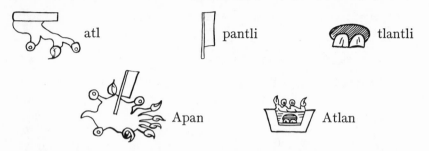

In the Aztec codices, the symbols that represent names and single words are clearly distinguished from the pictures. But it is interesting to note that certain pictures were completely conventionalized also. It is tempting to speculate that they may have been attempts to write whole sentences or even larger sections of discourse; if the linguistic material attached to, say, a representation of a baby in a cradle-basket was always the same, then the symbol was a phrasographic one, and not pictorial. If a conventionalized picture of a woman with words coming out of her mouth was always read by the equivalent of "The woman said . . .", or if the picture of a man with a name glyph attached to his neck was read "The man named X"—then these symbols were really writing. The symbols referred to above are:

Another very interesting aspect of the Aztec codices is that sometimes the "speech scroll"—the balloon issuing from the mouth of a character depicted —is specially elaborated to indicate what we may call the paralanguage of the speaker. In one instance ambassadors delivering speeches are shown with knives coming out of their mouths, indicating harsh, unfriendly words; in another, a Spaniard is shown talking to Aztecs, and his speech scroll is decorated with feathers, indicating the soft, smooth words he used.

It is clear that the Mayan and especially the Aztec writing systems had been developed with great imagination and artistry, and quite possibly had invented ways of representing aspects of language which our own writing can only approach with special descriptive verbal assistance. It is interesting to speculate on what might have come from these systems if they had not been destroyed by bigoted conquerers.

There are indications that the Toltecs (predecessors of the Aztecs in the Valley of Mexico), the Otomis, the Tarascans, and possibly other pre-Conquest groups in Mexico, also used writing; but the evidence is very scanty. Otomi, Tarascan, and many Aztec speakers survive, but there is no record of their having retained any traditions about their one-time knowledge of writing. That only the Aztecs took on the habit of writing their language in Latin letters does not prove that only they had writing; Aztec was the language of the rulers of Mexico at the time of the Conquest, and the Spaniards dealt officially mostly with speakers of Aztec.

7.53. In the Americas after the arrival of Europeans various Indian languages began to be written in the Latin alphabet. The Spaniards devised fairly standardized orthographies for Aztec and Mayan in Mexico, and for Kechuan in Peru. Elsewhere the Spaniards did what other Europeans—mostly speakers of Portuguese, French, and English—did; they wrote down, as well as they could according to their own spelling habits, names of people and places, and terms for indigenous fauna, flora, and artifacts. As the study of American Indian languages in the Americas progressed through the eighteenth and nineteenth centuries into the twentieth, many orthographies were devised, and came to be used to some extent by native speakers.

One writing system devised in America by an Indian—the Cherokee syllabary—can be called a new invention. It was not an invention of the idea of writing, of course, but the symbols, even those that looked like letters of the Latin alphabet, were made up arbitrarily and given entirely distinct values; and the system was syllabic, not alphabetic.

The syllabary was invented by a Cherokee Indian named Sequoya (*Sikwâyi*) in 1821. Sequoya had started a few years earlier by trying to devise a logographic system, using pictographic signs. Then he abandoned this clearly too complex device, and began using letter forms that he found in English books and other material, as well as modifications of them. Sequoya could not read English, so he used the letters in an arbitrary fashion, and he used them to denote syllables, mostly of the form CV. At first he had about 200 symbols, but this was reduced to 85 in the form Sequoya presented to his people in North Carolina. The syllabary was learned by many of the Indians, was taken along by those who migrated to Oklahoma after 1830, and was widely used there to publish official documents of the Cherokee nation, newspapers, and other materials (type for the symbols having been first made in Boston in 1827). After extensive use in the nineteenth century for all kinds of ordinary writing purposes, the Cherokee syllabary became more and more a private writing system, limited largely to correspondence between individuals, to reading of the Bible in Cherokee, and to Indian medicine—conjuring, charms, warding off harm, and the like.

Recent experiments have been carried out to extend literacy in the syllabary, in an attempt to bring about more favorable conditions for the integration of Cherokees in both Oklahoma and North Carolina into the general American culture.

Our source (see References and Notes) gives the syllabary in two ways: lists of symbols, as for learning, appear in printed form (resembling letterpress reproduction); and words and connected text are in hand-printed form (reproduced from pencil or ink drawing). In the newsletter published by the project (see References and Notes), the title and page headings are given as if in letterpress, and there is a table of the syllabary, in what is presumably the preferred order, on the last page of each issue, in the same style, with printed Latin-letter equivalents. The text of the newsletter, however, is hand-printed and reproduced photographically. Type was not used for printing the syllabary because of cost and lack of trained persons to compose it, but a typewriter with the symbols has been prepared.

The table referred to is reproduced here. In the last column, in the Latin-letter equivalents, the letter v is the usual symbol for the sixth Cherokee vowel, phonetically [ə]. The syllabary does not distinguish voiced and voiceless stops and affricates except as shown; accordingly, syllables transcribed with initial g, d are sometimes to be read as having k, t, while those with kw, tl, ts may need to be read with gw, dl, dz. The symbols are nearly all primarily read as representing /CV/, but are also used for /CV·/ (some write /CVV/), and those for /V/ also represent /V·/ (/VV/). Syllables beginning with /hC/ are written with the corresponding /CV/ symbol, except that /hna/ has a special symbol. The symbol *nah* (some write *hno*) seems never to have been used in actual Cherokee texts. There is one symbol for a consonant alone—syllable-final *s*. Originally there was a symbol for the end of a word or sentence, but now modern punctuation is used.

Cherokee Syllabary

G W Y J ꮝ G Ꮧ ꮄ J
[tsa la gi di   de lo kwa s di]

D a		*R* e	*T* i	ꮈ o	*O* u	*i* v			
ꮝ ga	Ꭷ ka	*F* ge	*y* gi	*A* go	*J* gu	*E* gv			
Ꮂ ha		*?* he	*Ꭿ* hi	*F* ho	*Γ* hu	*Ꮁ* hv			
W la		*d* le	*P* li	*G* lo	*M* lu	*Ꮙ* lv			
ꝺ ma		*Ol* me	*H* mi	*ꮐ* mo	*y* mu				
* Θ* na		*Ʌ* ne	*h* ni	*Z* no	*ꝺ* nu	*O* nv			
ꝉ hna		*G* nah							
Ꭲ kwa		ꭴ kwe	*ꝑ* kwi	*Ꮽ* kwo	ꭤ kwu	*Ɛ* kwv			
Ʊ sa	ꮠ s	*4* se	*Ꮖ* si	*f* so	*Ꮑ* su	*R* sv			
l da		*ꮝ* de	*J* di	*V* do	*S* du	*Ꮷ* dv			
W ta		*Ꮏ* te	*J* ti						
ꭴ dla	*ꮬ* tla	*L* tle	*C* tli	*ꝺ* tlo	*Ꮺ* tlu	*P* tlv			
G tsa		*V* tse	*h* tsi	*K* tso	*d* tsu	*C* tsv			
G wa		*ꮿ* we	*Θ* wi	*ꮼ* wo	*ꮄ* wu	*6* wv			
ꮎ ya		*ꮄ* ye	*ꮑ* yi	*ꮁ* yo	*G* yu	*B* yv			

A sample text, a conjuration against burns, follows:

D	ℰ	Oᴼ	B	ℬ	Oᴼ	Λ	ℛ	ℓ	W	Oᴼ	B	ℬ
a	ma	u	vv	dla	u	ne	s	da	la	ıı	yv	dla

ı	Oᴼ	ℏ	Oᴼ	B	ℬ	Oᴼ	ℓ	႒	ℛ	J	Oᴼ	B	ℬ
v	nv	tsi	ıı	yv	dla	u	hna	nu	s	di	u	yv	dla

Oᴼ	ℏ	ℓ	Ǥ	Ƴ		h	E	⅃	ℛ	Ⱶ	ℛ	J
u	tsi	hna	wa	kwo		ni	gv	di	s	ge	s	di

This is to be interpreted phonemically (according to our source) thus:

/ama uhyv́:dla une:sdala uhyv́:dla v:n(v)tsi uhyv́:dla u:hnanu:sdi
water cold   ice   cold   snow   cold   to rime

uhyv́:dla utsi:hna:wagwo nigvdi:sge:sdi/
cold   relief, just   I will be saying to

Another syllabary used in North America was invented in the 1840s by an English missionary for the use of the Cree, and other Algonkian Indians in Canada. The inventor, J. Evans, seems to have thought that the "simple natives" would learn a syllabary more easily than an alphabet. To the extent that the syllabary ignored phonetic detail and represented cross-dialectal phonemic differences by cover symbols, it really was "easier" for the native speakers. About 1885 the Reverend E. J. Peck introduced a modified version of the Cree syllabary to the Eskimos of the eastern Arctic. This orthography has spread widely, and, precisely because of its cross-dialectal character, is known to many Eskimos and is accepted by them with considerable enthusiasm. The Canadian government has recently begun to simplify and unify the various Latin-letter orthographies also in use among various Eskimo groups, and is replacing the syllabary by a standard morphophonically correct cross-dialectal orthography in the Latin alphabet.

For its historical as well as practical interest, we present the syllabary here, with equivalents in the new standard orthography:

The Eskimo (Cree) Syllabary

▽	*ai*	△	*i*	▷	*u*	◁	*a*		
∨	*pai*	∧	*pi*	>	*pu*	<	*pa*		
∪	*tai*	∩	*ti*	⊃	*tu*	C	*ta*	ᶜ	*-t*

ᑫ	*kai*	ᑭ	*ki*	ᑯ	*ku*	ᑲ	*ka*	ᒃ	*-k*
ᒉ	*gai*	ᒋ	*gi*	ᒍ	*gu*	ᒐ	*ga*		
ᒣ	*mai*	ᒥ	*mi*	ᒧ	*mu*	ᒪ	*ma*		
ᓀ	*nai*	ᓂ	*ni*	ᓄ	*nu*	ᓇ	*na*	ᓐ	*-n*
ᓭ	*sai*	ᓯ	*si*	ᓱ	*su*	ᓴ	*sa*		
ᓓ	*lai*	ᓕ	*li*	ᓗ	*lu*	ᓚ	*la*		
ᔦ	*jai*	ᔨ	*ji*	ᔪ	*ju*	ᔭ	*ja*		
ᕓ	*vai*	ᕕ	*vi*	ᕗ	*vu*	ᕙ	*va*		
ᕃ	*rai*	ᕆ	*ri*	ᕈ	*ru*	ᕋ	*ra*		

As originally applied, the three small raised characters were used to denote the first elements of various internal clusters of consonants, and also as finals. The latter usage was fluctuating because of varying pronunciations, and in some recent writing in the syllabary the final consonants have been omitted. In Latin-letter spelling also there have been attempts to omit final *p*, *t*, *k*, *q* (the only possible finals—the syllabary represents *p* and *t* by *t*, *k* and *q* by *k*). But the Eskimos themselves prefer to write these, as they are morphemically significant.

It should be noted that the syllabary does not show all the possible phonemic distinctions. The alphabetic orthography for consonants is as follows: *p*, *t*, *k*, *q*, *m*, *n*, *ng*, *rng*, *v*, *s*, *j*, *g*, *r*, *l*. The sequence *rng* is for /ŋ̇/, while *ng* is for /ŋ/; *v* is [β] or [v]; *j* is [ɟ] or [ʲy]; *g* is [ɣ]; *r* is [ɣ̇]. Internal clusters are: *pp*, *tt*, *kk*, *rq* (= /qq/ ~ /ɣ̇q/), *mm*, *nn*, *nng* /ŋŋ/, *vv*, *ss*, *jj*, *gg*, *rr*, *ll*. Vocalics are: *ii*, *i*, *ai*, *a*, *aa*, *au*, *u*, *uu*. In the syllabary /k/ and /q/ are not distinguished; /ŋ/ is written *-ngV*; the geminate clusters are shown by various combinations (morphophonically determined) of *-t*, *-k*, *-n* and following *CV* symbols; long vowels are usually not written.

The publication *Inuktitut* ('Eskimo Way') is printed in the syllabary. Its title appeared first in this form:

ᐃ ᓄᒃ ᑎ ᑐᑦ = *i-nu-*^{k}*-ti-tu-*^{t}

A 1965 issue omits the internal ^{k}, and the title is printed thus:

ᐃ ᓄ ᑎ ᑐᑦ = *i-nu-ti-tu-*^{t}

This and other spelling variations point up the difficulties of applying writing systems to languages other than those for which they were devised, and cross-dialectally within a language, regardless of the symbols used.

There are reports on various other nineteenth-century and more recent inventions of alphabets and syllabaries for various languages of North and South America.

There have also been such inventions in Africa, one, the Vai syllabary (Sierra Leone and Liberia), having been invented around 1850 by a native.

The Cherokee and Vai syllabaries, as well as the other writing systems alluded to here, in some ways share the nature of the special symbol systems discussed in the next section (especially those in subsection 7.61).

7.6. SPECIAL WRITING SYSTEMS

7.60. One of the early characteristics of writing systems, and one that has in some ways survived to this day, is that they were esoteric, unknown to the generality of people, the property of some special class—priests or the like—and used for special purposes. The attitudes stemming from these situations survive even in literate cultures like our own: if something is written, it has greater value than the spoken word—"put it in writing"; the usage of the written language is "correct"; written documents guarantee legality (courts accept transcripts made by court stenographers, but reject or forbid tape recordings of what is actually said!); "the book says so"; and so on.

When writing began to be more widely used, the old secrecy could be restored by the invention of codes and ciphers. A code is defined as a set of signals representing letters—special marks, flags, flashes of light, and others; or as a system of secret writing where letters and other signs are given special meanings; in this last meaning, code and cipher are equivalent. In the present connection, we shall not go into a detailed discussion of codes and ciphers, but will consider some as examples.

The ogham writing of Old Irish (see 8.24) was a cipher, based on the Latin alphabet, and using a very simple system of lines to represent the original letters. As it developed, it became a writing system, but was eventually replaced by the alphabet. Ogham exhibits one kind of cipher: the original writing is replaced by a much simplified set of symbols.

A modern instance is the telegraph code: there are only two symbols, a dot and a dash, corresponding to a momentary and a prolonged electric impulse; all the letters and figures of ordinary writing are replaced by combinations of dots and/or dashes. The code is not secret, but it is known largely only by persons who have an occupational need to know it; and it is adapted to transmission by telegraph wires. Material to be sent by telegraph has to be encoded, and the message then has to be decoded. Modern machinery encodes directly from a typewriterlike keyboard, and decodes directly to such a keyboard; but originally these processes had to be carried out by a human being carefully writing out and then sending by instrument, or sending the dots and dashes directly from ordinary writing, and then taking down the dots and dashes as received and putting them back into letters. Such a system, involving transliteration at both ends of a message, is not a primary writing system, though it could be used as such.

The Braille system of writing for the blind is another example. The letters are represented by arrangements of raised dots which are read by being felt by a fingertip. This is a tactual instead of a visible writing system.

The other kind of code—a cipher—involves replacement of ordinary letters by others—either other letters used in different values, or special symbols. Thus one can encipher a message by replacing every letter, let us say, by the fourth letter following it: A by E, B by F, etc.; a message written in this way is usually not read directly, but is deciphered; in order to do this, one has to know the rule for the cipher. The same is even more true when other kinds of symbols are used: one could arrange 26 symbols like *, †, ‡, §, +, etc., so they represent the letters of the alphabet and then encode a message; the message has to be decoded, though of course one thoroughly accustomed to the cipher could read it right off. For real secrecy such ciphers involve complicated rules, with many steps for encoding, and only those provided with the key can decode easily.

Some codes and ciphers are constructed to involve special keys consisting of word lists or the like. One can use a specific dictionary, for instance, and encode by indicating page and line number where the word will be found.

Writing systems like the Chinese can be coded by representing characters by sets of numbers. The numbers can be simply assigned in order to a list (arranged by some standard procedure), or they can consist of four or five digits that represent characteristics of the actual original symbol.

All codes and ciphers that involve complex encoding and decoding are definitely secondary as writing systems, and have special and limited uses. The simple codes—the telegraph, light flashes (heliograph), and signal flags—are useful for transmission of visual and auditory or electric signals over distances. With modern electronic devices, actual sounds or complete pictures can be transmitted, and the older kinds of codes are no longer needed as much as they once were.

7.61. Another special kind of writing that has developed in the modern world is that known as phonetic alphabets. All ordinary writing systems, and especially all alphabets, are intended to represent, at least in part, phonemic entities. So called phonetic alphabets, however, are supposed to represent all speech sounds in general, and not the phonemes of any one language.

In 2.23 the tables of phonetic symbols that are used in this book were presented. As was discussed there, many phonetic alphabets are in use. They all start from some basic alphabet, usually the Latin alphabet, add new letters from other alphabets or by invention, and supplement the list of symbols by various kinds of modifying symbols called diacritics. The devices involved are extensions of those used in applying alphabets to the writing of previously unwritten languages.

Extensions of alphabets that have come to be used as parts of ordinary writing systems are punctuation marks. These marks have a partly phonemographic base, as when they represent terminal or other transition phonemes. But they also, and more often, represent different kinds of discourse, and are then sememographic at various levels.

The devices of special styles of letters, decorative letters, unusual arrangements of words on a page (as in advertising), etc. are all special kinds of writing conveying messages that often go beyond language and involve the communication of aspects of other cultural systems. Scientific studies of such devices from an anthropologico-linguistic point of view have not been made.

7.62. At various points in the discussion of writing in this chapter, allusion was made to the writing of numbers.

All writing systems have devised ways to write numbers. The Sumerians and Egyptians had logographic symbols that wrote out the simple numbers, say 1 to 10, the tens (20 to 90), the hundreds, perhaps one or more thousands. The Semites and the Greeks (and also the Goths) used letters of the alphabet, usually with some diacritic to indicate the special use; in this use the letters were logographic. The numerical values of the letters of various alphabets are given in the tables in Chapter 8.

In Latin, numbers were represented by logographic symbols which look like letters of the alphabet, but have a different origin. The letter I for 1, then II for 2, and III for 3 are instances of a single stroke written one or more times as needed. V for 5, X for 10, L for 50, D for 500, M for 1000 represent Etruscan symbols that were replaced by letters that resemble them. The numbers between are represented by a system in which position counts: a symbol for a smaller number is subtracted from a following larger number, but is added to a preceding one: IV is '1 subtracted from 5' = 4; VI is '1 added to 5' = 6. The system is ingenious, can be used to write numbers up into the thousands, and is esthetically well matched with the alphabet. This is undoubtedly why we continue to use it for special purposes and as a variation from our ordinary number-writing system.

The success and value of the so-called Arabic numeral system is due to the small number of symbols, the use of zero, and the strict adherence to positional values. The symbols 1, 2, 3 clearly show their origin as one, two, three strokes; the symbols 4 to 9 are arbitrary logographs of unknown origin. The zero is the great invention that made possible easy calculations of all kinds. This system of numerals was introduced into Europe by the Arabs in the Middle Ages. The Arabs got it from India. In India, it came into use in the early centuries of the Christian era. The invention of zero took place at some time before 500 A.D., but the date and place are unknown.

The Mayan system of writing numbers, based on counting by 20s, was theoretically as good as the Arabic system, having symbols for zero, and for 1 to 19. In practice, it was tied in with the calendar calculations, which introduced a number of complications—special symbols for time units of 20 and multiples of 20, use of 18 instead of 20 in the second order or position in counting time ($18 \times 20 = 360$, instead of $20 \times 20 = 400$, in the place analogous to 100 in our system, but then by 20s again—7200, 144,000, etc.), and counts beginning with zero; then when 19 was reached, it was equated to the special sign for 20 at that level. We do not know how these higher numbers were said, so the actual use of these special devices is unknown.

The zero in Mayan writing was invented long before zero appeared in south Asia. There are vague reports in Chinese documents of voyages to what might have been Mesoamerica, in the first centuries of the Christian era. It is perhaps possible that such voyagers, if they ever made contact with peoples in the interior or east of Mexico, might have learned about the idea of a zero symbol from the Mayan practice. In the manuscripts (codices), the Mayan zero symbol is an oval shell, ⬬ , so that even the symbol we use might have come along with the idea. But this is speculation, and there will probably never be any positive evidence for such an early instance of transmission of an American culture trait to the Old World.

This chapter concludes with a selection of various forms of the so-called Arabic numerals now in use:

European: 1 2 3 4 5 6 7 8 9 0

Sanskrit: १ २ ३ ४ ५ ६ ७ ८ ९ ०

Arabic: ١ ٢ ٣ ٤ ٥ ٦ ٧ ٨ ٩ ٠

Burmese: ၁ ၂ ၃ ၄ ၅ ၆ ၇ ၈ ၉ ၀

Japanese: 一 二 三 四 五 六 七 八 九 〇 (the Chinese numerals 1 to 9 with zero added, and used decimally)

Chapter 8

ALPHABETS
OF THE WORLD

8.0. INTRODUCTION

8.00. The present chapter is intended to exemplify further those parts of Chapter 7 which deal with alphabetic writing systems, chiefly 7.21–7.24 and 7.31–7.33. The tables and commentaries may also be used to supplement treatments of alphabets to be given elsewhere in connection with the discussion of the phonological systems of specific languages and the representation of the phonology in traditional writing systems (see References and Notes).

Below, the following alphabets are presented: the alphabets of the ancient Western world, principally Greek and Latin; the alphabets derived from Greek and Latin, devised originally for the spread of Christianity; the old Semitic alphabets from which Greek writing came, and their later and modern descendents; and the Indic alphabets. Finally some modern special writing systems are shown.

Each table shows the alphabet under discussion, in the various forms known or in the styles used, indicates what is known of the history and origin of the letters, and gives one or more transliteration equivalents (see 8.02). Numerical values of letters in older writing systems (cf. 7.62) are also given. Each table is followed by explanatory notes and discussion of diacritics and other supplementary symbols used with the alphabet. Where pertinent to the history of an alphabet, the alphabet from which it is derived is given in the table for ease of comparison, even if it is presented separately elsewhere.

8.01. All the alphabetic writing systems presented below are ultimately of the same origin (cf. 7.12, 7.21, 7.22, 7.30). They are for this reason partly equivalent, show actual resemblances of form despite the extensive changes during their separate developments, and can be transliterated into one another (see 8.02).

But, given the nature of an alphabet, a language can be represented adequately by any available alphabet, and, if more than one alphabet is used, the several systems can be made equivalent to any degree desired. There are a few instances in the world where a language is regularly written in two alphabets, and it is of interest to examine these situations.

Serbocroatian is a language regularly written both in Cyrillic and in Latin letters. In the Roman Catholic parts of Yugoslavia the Latin alphabet has always been used, whereas in the Orthodox areas the Cyrillic has been used since the tenth century. The two alphabets were at first used for different dialects, and independently of each other. With the beginnings of Yugoslav nationalism (in Serbia and also in Croatia) in the nineteenth century, conscious efforts were made to bring the literary dialects together, and the two writing systems were brought into direct equivalence. One result was that Cyrillic as used for Serbocroatian became an alphabet of the same type as the Latin alphabet; originally Cyrillic had represented /yV/ or /jV/ (/j/ is here used for palatalization of a preceding consonant) by special "preiotacized" vowel letters; the Cyrillic spelling of Serbocroatian, however, was reformed by eliminating these special letters, introducing the letter *j* from the Latin alphabet as a symbol for /y/, and combining the old palatalization sign, ь, with four letters to produce four new letters for the remaining palatal consonants. The two alphabets equate as follows:

а б в г д ђ е ж з и ј к л љ м н њ о п р с т ћ у ф х ц ч џ ш
a b v g d đ e ž z i j k l ļ m n ń o p r s t ć u f h c č ǧ š

In actual Croatian common usage, the symbols *đ, ļ, ǧ* are replaced by *dj, lj, dž*; when this is done, the two orthographies still remain completely equivalent, but the Latin-letter alphabet is not exactly equivalent to the Cyrillic, having three letters less and using three digraphs.

Another language regularly written in two alphabets is Hindi-Urdu. Hindi is written in devanagari, and Urdu—its Pakistani version—is written in Arabic letters. The devanagari letters used in Hindi and their Arabic-letter equivalents follow (the Latin-letter equivalents are the usual phonemicized values):

The Hindi-Urdu Alphabets

अ आ इ ई उ ऊ ऋ ए ऐ ओ औ

آو ‎ َ ‎ آ ‎ ‎ ‎ ‎ ‎ ‎ ‎ ‎ ‎ ‎ ‎ ‎ ‎ ‎ ‎ ‎ ‎

a aa i ii u uu ri e ai o au

क ख ग घ ङ च छ ज झ ञ ट ठ ड ढ ण

كَ كِ گَ گِ ن چ چِ ج جِ ن ٹ ٹھ ڈ ڈھ ن

k kh g gh n č čh j jh n ṭ ṭh ḍ ḍh n

त थ द ध न प फ ब भ म य र ल व श ष स ह

ت تھ د دھ ن پ پھ ب بھ م ي ر ل و ش ش س ه

t th d dh n p ph b bh m y r l w š š s h

The Urdu is a transliteration of devanagari, using digraphs for stop
plus /h/. Urdu also uses additional Arabic letters in unassimilated
words of Arabic origin. As has been indicated in 7.31, the devanagari
alphabet is of a special type in its treatment of vowels, whereas
Arabic is of the general Semitic type. Equating the two alphabets
involves some adaptation of one or the other; in this case Arabic
has been adapted to devanagari, but has also retained its own alphabetic character by sticking closer to the phonemic analysis.

In the Soviet Union during the 1920s, a good many languages
were provided with Latin-letter orthographies, using diacritical
marks or special new letters, and these orthographies were replaced
by Cyrillic ones in the 1930s; only the latter are now in use. The
Cyrillic orthographies are usually close transliterations of the previous Latin ones: *c* /č/ and *ç* /ǰ/ were replaced by ч and џ; ҁ /γ/
was replaced by г; *ө* /ø/ and *y* /ʉ/ were replaced by ѳ, ү; but the
old Cyrillic habit of preiotacized letters was retained to facilitate
introduction of Russian loanwords in their usual visual form, so
that *ja* /ya/ became я, *jo* became ё, and so on.

8.02. The basic equivalence of alphabets just demonstrated has
made possible TRANSLITERATION, the process of rewriting a language
in another alphabet by equating the original with the new alphabet
letter for letter. This was done by the Romans in taking over Greek
words into literary Latin, and is done in modern times in writing,
say, Russian names in Latin letters for use in English text.

It should be noted that TRANSCRIPTION as used in this book denotes
writing a language so that its phonological system is represented
with some approach to accuracy and completeness. A transcription
may have no connection with the way a language is ordinarily
written, and may be devised for a language that has no ordinary
writing system. *Transcription*, then, means 'writing down' the
sounds (phonemes) of a language; *transliteration* means 'writing over
the letters' in which a language is ordinarily written.

Transliteration differs from transcription in that it involves representing a source alphabet in such a way that each letter of the source is represented by a letter or by an unambiguous sequence of letters in the target alphabet. In theory, transliterations can be purely arbitrary, paying no regard either to the pronunciation of the original or to the phonemic values usually attributed to the target symbols. In practice, however, both sets of phonemic values are taken into account, since most transliterations are meant to be read as words in the target language, and are intended to at least suggest the original pronunciation.

Transliteration in modern times becomes a practical matter, since usually a supply of type for any but the locally used alphabet is not available, and readers would not know how to read any other alphabet. In the parts of the world where the Latin alphabet is used, transliteration applies principally to the Cyrillic, Greek, and Arabic alphabets. Each of these involves its own set of problems.

The Cyrillic alphabet as used for Russian has 32 letters. It would be easy to use the 26 Latin letters and add six numerals or arbitrary signs to complete the list. In recent machine-translation work with computers, such transliterations have been used; an example is: A, B, V, G, D, E, J, Z, I, 1, K, L, M, N, O, P, R, S, T, U, F, X, Q, C, W, 5, 7, Y, 6, 3, H, 4. But such a system, with spellings like OB5I1, SOVETSKI1 SOHZ, OBLAST6, and so on, would be so contrary to ordinary reading habits as to be unusable in popular material and uncomfortable in scholarly literature. The more acceptable practice is to use digraphs or letters with diacritical marks for the additional letters. But then spelling habits of the target language cause problems: in French, *j* is a good equivalent for ж, but is not so good in English, and is no good at all in Spanish or German; for ш, *sh* is good in English, but in French *ch* would be better, in German one should use *sch*, and not all Spanish readers know what *sh* means; the letter щ, phonemically /šč/ in Russian, can be written *shch*, or *chtch* for French, or *schtsch* for German, but the last, especially, is cumbersome; if ц is transliterated as *ts*, then the sequence тс, which also occurs, may cause ambiguity. These problems have given rise to two styles of transliteration: popular—where some details of the source alphabet may be unrepresented, and where the pronunciation habits of the target alphabet's users are always respected; and scientific—where the attempt is made to represent each source letter unambiguously, and the reader must learn the values of letters with diacritics, and other strange usages. Transliterations are exact if they are reversible, so that the transliterated material can be put back into the original mechanically. Popular transliterations may be exact and reversible, but only if certain rules are followed; the less exact ones are not reversible. In a reversible transliteration, there may be multiple use of symbols; in a widely used transliteration of Russian, the Russian letter e is transliterated by *ye* initially and after certain other letters, otherwise by *e*; *y* also occurs elsewhere in the transliteration, but the rules for its use are exact, and there is no ambiguity. See 8.23 for the Russian alphabet with various transliterations.

The transliteration of Greek used by the Romans was exact and reversible, although it had some multiple use of symbols. The Greek accents were not transliterated, however (they were devised late in the history of Greek-Roman contact). Modern transliterations of ancient Greek may differ from the Latin one in choice of symbols, but are otherwise equivalent. In many scholarly texts, moreover, Greek is retained as such. Modern Greek, however, presents a problem. One can transliterate as for ancient Greek, and learn the complex reading rules of the orthography; or one can try to adapt the transliteration to the modern pronunciation. In the latter case, there will always be ambiguities, unless one devises a really complicated system. Consider the place name *Euboea*: this is the traditional Roman transliteration of Greek Εὔβοια; however, in Modern Greek the name is pronounced /évya/, and the question arises as to how it should be transliterated. Shall we write *Evvia*, as one system has it? This is good as far as pronunciation goes, and is partially reversible. Or should we simply write *Euboea*, and let those who don't know Modern Greek say /yùwbíyə/? The spelling *Euboea* (or, for some purposes, the modern transliteration *Eúboia*) is preferred in the present book. See 8.10 for Greek transliterations.

With Arabic, transliteration problems arise mostly from the fact that it is a Semitic alphabet which does not regularly indicate vowels. The consonants themselves also offer some difficulty, in that there are so many more of them than there are letters available in the Latin alphabet. Scholarly transliterations have been developed which are reasonably exact, and which fill in the vowels from knowledge of the linguistic material. Popular transliterations of Arabic leave out all diacritics, use vowels supplied in various ways, often incorrectly, and are generally highly inexact. In Egypt a Latin-letter transliteration was once formulated by the government, but it has not been followed consistently.

Other alphabets are transliterated more or less haphazardly and in an *ad hoc* manner. In a few countries, the governments have devised Latin-letter transliterations (Israel, Thailand, Japan), but these are not always followed even in the country itself. The Japanese system is a transcription, since there is no alphabet there.

The Soviet government uses various Latin-letter transliterations, but no one of them has been set up as official. As to transliteration into Cyrillic, this is usually done as transcription because of the vagaries of spelling of the various European languages. There are some well-established traditions for this kind of transcription, but they do not lead to exactness either in rendering pronunciation or transliterating original spellings. One peculiarity of older Russian transcriptions is the use of *g* for Latin *h*, even in learned words (*hygiene* comes out as *gigiyena*), but this is not done consistently (*history* is *istoriya*). In more modern practice, *x* is used for *h*, but also not consistently. And there are always some transliterations mixed in with the transcriptions. A few examples will illustrate the various usages (see 8.23 for Slavic alphabets; the examples are in the popular transcription given there): *Washington* > *Vashington*, *New York* > *N'yu York*, *New Jersey* > *N'yu Dzhersey*, *Mexico* > *Meksiko*, *Hamilton* > *Gamil'ton*, *Chicago* > *Chikago*, *San José* > *San Khozè*, *San Francisco* > *San Frantsisko*; these transcribed forms are given spelling pronunciations in Russian, of course.

8.1. ALPHABETS OF THE ANCIENT WORLD

In this section the following alphabets are presented: 8.10, Greek; 8.11, Etruscan; 8.12, Oscan and Umbrian; 8.13, Latin.

8.10. The alphabet used for Classical Greek (*koinē*) follows, with the names of the letters (as usually written in English), the exact transliteration used in this book, and the old Latin transliteration. The text supplements the information in the table, discusses accent marks and other signs, and contains remarks on variant transliterations and some historical matters. The numerical values of the letters in Ancient Greek are given in a separate column. See 7.20 and 7.21 for the history of the Greek alphabet.

The diacritical marks used in Greek are: the accents—acute, $\acute{\alpha} = \acute{a}$; grave, $\grave{\alpha} = \grave{a}$; circumflex, $\hat{\alpha}$ or $\tilde{\alpha} = \hat{a}$; the breathings—rough, $\dot{\alpha} = ha$; smooth, $\dot{\alpha} = a$ (not transliterated); iota subscript—ᾳ, ῃ, ῳ = a_i, $\bar{e}_i$, $\bar{o}_i$. The Romans transliterated the rough breathing as *h*, but did not show the smooth breathing or the accents; they wrote *iota* subscript as *i*, on the line. In both transliterations here given $\dot{\rho} = rh$.

The accents and breathings were written together thus: ἄ, ἂ, ἆ or ἅ, ἃ, ἇ or ᾅ = *á*, *à*, *â*, *há*, *hà*, *hâ*. Since circumflex never occurs on ε or o, ῆ and ῶ are transliterated simply *ê* and *ô*, the macron being

The Classical Greek Alphabet

Letter	Name	Transliterations		Numerical value
		Modern	Roman	
A α	alpha /ǽlfə/	a	a	1
B β	beta /béytə/	b	b	2
Γ γ	gamma /gǽmə/	g	g, n	3
Δ δ	delta /déltə/	d	d	4
E ε	epsilon /épsilàn/	e	e	5
[F, ϝ	digamma /dày+gǽmə/	w	-]	6
Z ζ	zeta /zéytə/	z	z	7
H η	eta /éytə/	ē	e	8
Θ θ	theta /θéytə/	th	th	9
I ι	iota /àyówtə/	i	i	10
K κ	kappa /kǽpə/	k	c	20
Λ λ	lambda /lǽm(b)də/	l	l	30
M μ	mu /myúw/	m	m	40
N ν	nu /n(y)úw/	n	n	50
Ξ ξ	xi /záy/ (/ksíy/)	x	x	60
O ο	omicron /ámikràn/	o	o	70
Π π	pi /páy/ (/píy/)	p	p	80
[- ϙ	qoppa /kópə/	q	-]	90
P ρ	rho /rów/	r	r	100
Σ σ, ς*	sigma /sígmə/	s	s	200
T τ	tau /táw/	t	t	300
Υ υ	upsilon /yúwpsilàn/	u	y, u	400
Φ φ	phi /fáy/ (/fíy/)	ph	ph	500
X χ	chi /káy/ (/kíy/)	kh	ch	600
Ψ ψ	psi /sáy/ (/psíy/)	ps	ps	700
Ω ω	omega /òwméygə/	ō	o	800
[- ϡ	sampi /sǽmpiy/	ś	-]	900

* The symbol ς is used at the end of a word, and σ elsewhere.

unnecessary. In diphthongs the accents are written on the second letter: αί, οî; we transliterate accordingly—*aí, oî*.

The Romans transliterated γγ, γκ, γξ, γχ as *ng, nc, nx, nch,* as the pronunciation was /ŋg, ŋk, ŋks, ŋkh/; but they wrote *g* for γ before *m, n,* where it was also pronounced /ŋ/, as was *g* before *n* in Latin. The Romans wrote *u* for υ in the diphthongs (*au, eu, ou,* etc.), but *y* for the vowel, pronounced [ʉ] in Classical Greek; ου was usually transliterated by the Romans simply as *u.*

The internal sequence ρρ is transliterated *rrh* even if the rough breathing is omitted in the original.

When used as numerals, the letters were followed by a raised mark (only one being used for a sequence): $\alpha' = 1$, $\rho\alpha' = 101$. For the thousands one began with *alpha* again, using a lowered mark, $,\alpha = 1\,000$. The letter *digamma* (originally called *wau*, and out of use by Classical times because prevocalic /w/ had been lost) was usually written in later times as ς, and ς' = 6.

For Modern Greek the present author prefers to use the same transliteration as for Classical. The only satisfactory alternative would be a phonemic transcription. Attempts at combining transcription and transliteration are cumbersome and inexact.

The 22 letters of the older Greek alphabets from *alpha* to *tau*, including *wau*, *qoppa*, *sampi* (which belonged after *nu*), were directly taken from Semitic forms (given in 8.30). The letters *upsilon*, *phi*, *khi*, *psi*, *ō* were Greek additions. For a conjectural explanation of how some of the Semitic letters came to be used for vowels, see 7.20 (where other historical details are also given). For the differences between the East Greek and West Greek alphabets see 7.21.

8.11. The Etruscan alphabet was discussed historically and in relation to the Latin alphabet in 7.21 (end) and in 7.22. It was written from right to left, and in its earliest form consisted of the following letters:

Υ Φ Χ ΥΤ϶ϙ Ρ Μ ꓶ Ο⊞ Ϻ Ϻ Ϳ Ͱ Ι ⊗ Ϧ Ι ꓶ Ϟ Ϙ ꓭ Ϡ Α
kh ph x u t s r q ś p o ṣ n m l k i th h z w e d g b a

The Etruscan language had no voiced stops, and *b* and *d* soon went out of use, though the forms were known and went into Oscan and Umbrian (see 8.12) and Latin (8.13). The letter *g* also was not needed, but an early form, $>$, was taken as a variant of Ϳ , and it came to be used for /k/ (and Ϳ was later dropped), whence the Latin usage; it is thus usually transliterated as *c*. ꓶ is usually transliterated *v* [w] or [ß]?), and is the source of the Latin *f*. The letter Ι = *z* was used for [ts], whence the Oscan usage. The letters ṣ, *o*, *q*, *x* also were not needed in Etruscan, and were dropped. The late ("classical") Etruscan alphabet, about the fifth century B.C., was:

Ϧ Ϳ Φ Ϝ Τ϶ ꓭ Μ ꓶ Π Ϻ Ϳ Ι ☉ Ϧ Ι ꓸ Ͽ Α
f kh ph u t s r ś p n m l i th h z v e c a

The retention of *z* may mean that [ts] was a unit phoneme, /c/; the aspirates *th*, *ph*, *kh* were phonemically different from *c*, *p*, *t*, but could have been clusters. The sound of *ś* cannot be determined; perhaps it was /š/. The shape ⊂ of the letter *r* shows confusion of original *d*, no longer used, with original *r*. The letter 8 = *f* is of unknown origin.

(For a treatment of the Etruscan language, see References and Notes.)

8.12.   In discussing the Oscan and Umbrian languages, the alphabets can be treated by giving transliterations and a few phonological symbols (see References and Notes). Here we are interested in the two alphabets as such; they are listed in columns in the table below; additional columns give West Greek, Etruscan, and Latin. Some comments on the comparisons follow.

In the West Greek column, the arrows indicate forms that developed later from the original ones; a comma separates contemporary variants; the symbol in brackets is East Greek for *x* /ks/, but seems to have been in some West Greek alphabets also.

The Etruscan column combines the early and late alphabets given in 8.11; symbols in parentheses are those that were dropped because there was no further use for them.

The Oscan letters **í** and **ú** were late developments from **i** and **u**.

The last Umbrian letter, **ç**, is of unknown origin.

In the Latin column, Z is in its original place, and the letters that developed later are in brackets.

The transliterations of Oscan and Umbrian are the usual ones, printed in boldface letters, as is customary.

It is clear from the comparison of these alphabets that Oscan derives from a relatively early form of Etruscan, Umbrian from a slightly later form; Latin probably comes from a very early form of Etruscan (before 8 = *f* was introduced), but its left-to-right direction may indicate some direct late West Greek influence. The differences of these alphabets from one another are perhaps not surprising in view of the relatively small use of writing at the periods involved. That there are these differences suggests that writing was introduced to the various peoples of ancient Italy by individuals and at different times, and that the introducers were not too expert in the use of writing and were possibly fairly ignorant of the language being written.

8.13.   Some of the technical aspects of the various forms that the Latin alphabet has assumed in modern times will be considered in the present section. (For the Latin alphabet as the vehicle for

Oscan and Umbrian Alphabets

West Greek	Transliteration	Etruscan	Transliteration	Oscan	Transliteration, Latin-letter equivalent	Umbrian	Transliteration, Latin-letter equivalent	Latin
A	a	A	a	A	**a,** a	A	**a,** a	A
B–B	b	(B)	(b)	B	**b,** b	B	**b,** b	B
Γ,>–Γ,Γ,<	g	Γ–Ͻ	c	>,Ͻ	**g,** g	—		C, [G:?←C+Z]
Δ,D	d	(D)	(d)	Я	**d,** d	q	**ř,** rs	D
Ⴇ–E	e	Ⴇ–Ⴈ	e	Ⴈ	**e,** e	Ⴈ	**e,** e	E
Ⴈ,Ⴈ–F,Ⴈ	w	Ⴈ–Ⴈ	v	Ⴈ	**v,** v	Ⴈ	**v,** v	F
I	z	I	z	I	**z,** ?	⾮	**z,** ?	Z [?+C→G]
Ⴖ,H	h	Ⴖ	h	Ⴖ	**h,** h	ⵔ	**h,** h	H
⊗,⊙	th	⊗,⊙	th	—		—		—
I	i	I	i	I,–I	**i (i),** i	I	**i,** i	I, [→J]
Ⴟ–K	k	(Ⴟ)	(k)	Ⴟ	**k,** c	Ⴟ	**k;** c, g	K
Λ,Ⴑ–Ⴑ	l	Ⴑ	l	Ⴑ	**l,** l	Ⴑ	**l,** l	L
Ⴏ–M	m	Ⴏ	m	Ⴏ	**m,** m	Ⴏ	**m,** m	M
Ⴔ–N	n	Ⴔ	n	Ⴔ	**n,** n	Ⴔ	**n,** n	N
[Ⴥ]	[x]	(Ⴥ)	(ś)	—		—		—
O	o	(O)	(o)	—		—		O
ᕴ–P	p	Ⴈ,Ⴈ	p	Π	**p,** p	Ⴈ	**p,** p	P
Ⴏ–λ	ś	Ⴏ	ś	—		—		—
Ⴓ	q	(Ⴓ)	(q)	—		—		Q
◁–P,R	r	Ⴓ–Ⴓ	r	ᑎ	**r,** r	ᑎ	**r,** r	R
Ϛ	s	Ϛ–Ϛ	s	Ϛ	**s;** s, z	Ϛ	**s,** s	S
+–T	t	T	t	T	**t,** t	Ⴤ	**t;** t, d	T
Y,V	u	Y–V	u	V,–V̇	**u, ú;** v = u	V	**u;** v = u	V, [U, W], Y
X	x	(X)	(x)	—		—		X
Φ	ph	Φ	ph	—		—		—
Ⴤ	kh	Y–V	kh	—		—		—
—		8	f	8	**f,** f	8	**f,** f	—
—		—		—		d	**ç,** ȝ	—

writing the Latin language, see References and Notes.) The late spread of this alphabet to become the world's leading writing system was taken up in 7.22.

The original Latin alphabet of 21 letters added Y and Z during the first century B.C., and the 23 letters were perfected in the artistically elegant shape of the so-called lapidary capitals—the letters as carved in stone. In writing on other media, the shapes were often simpler and less elegant, more like our modern sans-serif type. However, the use of serifs, and the varying thicknesses of the lines, could only have developed by the use of a penlike instrument and a paperlike surface. The serifs are the start of the penstroke, the thicker lines are the downstrokes, and the thinner lines the result of lesser pressure in approaching and departing from the heavy downstrokes. Let us look at a few examples: **A** : start at the bottom left: _ ; then round back half way: ⌐ ; then up at an angle, thin stroke: **/** ; then down at an angle, heavy stroke: **Λ** ; then finish by half-rounding to the left and a horizontal light stroke to the right: **Λ** ; finally the cross-stroke is written as a horizontal thin line: **A** .

B : start at the top, vertical downstroke, heavy: **I** ; back to starting point, horizontal light stroke, to right past the vertical stroke, curve down, increasing thickness, then curve back to heavy vertical stroke, decreasing thickness: **P** ; repeat for lower curve: **B** .

All the roman capitals are made by these same kinds of strokes; in some type designs, Z has the upper and lower horizontal strokes heavy, and the reverse-slant downstroke is accordingly light.

There can be no doubt that these letter shapes first were drawn before being carved on stone. Earlier inscriptions show no serifs, and lines are of equal thickness. The Latin alphabet, then, in its accustomed form, was the result of an elaboration, a perfecting invention, in the pre-Classical period of Rome. It is the sort of thing that could have been begun by one scribe, and followed by all the others very soon.

The roman capital letters were stately and dignified; they were inscribed on monuments and buildings, and produced official texts which were handsome and eminently readable. But they required care and time to write or carve. It was inevitable that most writers would continue to use the earlier simpler forms. It was also inevitable that as the number of scribes increased, and writing became more and more used by individuals for personal rather than public purposes, even easier means of forming the letters would be sought. It is known that there were early cursive forms in Rome. Forms of shorthand existed, which must have started as cursive script, then went beyond it. A very few examples of the early cursive writing have survived. During the first centuries of the Christian era, several new forms of script developed in western Europe. The uncial style, with well-rounded forms very well suited to calligraphy, had developed by the third century. In the next two centuries—when Christianity gave impetus to writing all over Europe—new and localized styles of letter forming came into use. As these styles developed, there grew up the consistent use of letter forms which were simpler, more rounded, and more easily written with continued strokes of the pen; these forms were preferred in all except prominent positions such as the beginning of a page, or a sentence, or for headings. These minuscule cursive forms gave rise to the letters we now use as "small" letters, while the old capitals became more and more restricted to special uses. By the sixth and seventh centuries the various letter forms we now use had been invented, and were sorting themselves out into majuscule and minuscule pairs. From the ninth century on all writing in the Latin alphabet, in whatever style or hand, used capital and small-letter pairs as we do now. It is interesting to note that the Latin alphabet has developed the greatest amount of difference in form between majuscule and minuscule letters of any of the world's alphabets. In fact, most alphabets do not have this characteristic; Greek has it, but the minuscules are largely cursive forms of the majuscules. The various alphabets derived from Greek (see 8.2 and subsections) have in most cases not elaborated the dichotomy and usually show merely a difference in size rather than in form between majuscule and minuscule letters. It is interesting to speculate that the Latin alphabet never really added letters, precisely because of the tendency to consider new letter forms simply as variants. The forms u, j, w; æ, œ, ø, ð were all late additions, used only locally, or were not separate letters at first. On the other hand, the other alphabets—those derived from Greek—added new letters with new values as needed, rather than creating mere variations of form.

In central Europe the heavily decorated style of letters known as black letter developed and was used more than any other. When printing was invented (or brought to Europe), this style was the first one used in casting type. Such is the conservatism of literate people that in Germany this style of printing continued in use until after the Second World War.

As handwriting became more widespread, script forms developed which were based on the majuscule and minuscule pairs. When printing was introduced, some typefaces were based on several of these forms, producing italic type. In the nineteenth century the typewriter was invented, bringing into being typefaces that were adapted to the requirement that all the letters be of the same width. In the 1950s typewriters with variable spacing were invented, making it possible to type in a form resembling printing.

At the present time hundreds of Latin-letter typefaces exist in the countries of the world where the alphabet is used. These typefaces vary in height and width of the characters, in the proportions of different parts of the letters, and in other details of design—serifs or their absence, relative roundness or squareness, and so on; but they all belong to a very few basic types:

roman: ABCDEFGHIJKLMNOPQRSTUVWXYZ
  abcdefghijklmnopqrstuvwxyz

italic: *ABCDEFGHIJKLMNOPQRSTUVWXYZ*
  abcdefghijklmnopqrstuvwxyz

sans serif: ABCDEFGHIJKLMNOPQRSTUVWXYZ
  abcdefghijklmnopqrstuvwxyz

boldface: **ABCDEFGHIJKLMNOPQRSTUVWXYZ**
  abcdefghijklmnopqrstuvwxyz

boldface italic: ***ABCDEFGHIJKLMNOPQRSTUVWXYZ***
  abcdefghijklmnopqrstuvwxyz

black letter: 𝕬𝕭𝕮𝕯𝕰𝕱𝕲𝕳𝕴𝕵𝕶𝕷𝕸𝕹𝕺𝕻𝕼𝕽𝕾𝕿𝖀𝖁𝖂𝖃𝖄𝖅
  abcdefghijklmnopqrstuvwxyz

Besides the 26 letters in the samples above, with 26 capital forms, and 19 lowercase forms that are conspicuously different, there are some additional symbols in wide general use. Many typefaces have special pieces of type for the combinations fi, fl, ff, ffi, ffl; æ and œ are common units; the numbers 1, 2, 3, 4, 5, 6, 7, 8, 9, 0 are designed to fit with the various typefaces. The symbol "ampersand", &, is in most sets of type: it is a logograph, read 'and' or its equivalent. The symbols $ 'dollar(s)', £ 'pound(s)', ¢ 'cent(s)' are also logographs. The symbols † "dagger", ‡ "double dagger", § "section", ¶ "paragraph", % "per cent" are common sememographs. Outside of the English-speaking world, there are numerous letters with diacritics, and they exist for all the typefaces that are used to print materials in languages requiring these symbols. A sampling follows: á, à, â, ä, ã, ç, é, è, ê, ě, ë, í, ì, î, ï, ñ, ó, ò, ô, ö, õ, ú, ù, û, ü, č, đ, ǧ, ł, ř, š, ţ, ž, å, ø.

The punctuation marks now used developed during the Middle Ages. They have spread to other alphabets and writing systems, being largely sememographic. The most common are: , . ; : ? ! " " ' ' - — ( ) [ ].

Mathematics and other special disciplines have required special symbols, and these are usually styled to fit in with various styles and sizes of roman type: $+ - = \times \div$.

Finally, with the development of phonetic alphabets, which are almost entirely based on the Latin alphabet, a large number of special letters has been developed. See 8.50.

8.2. CHRISTIAN ALPHABETS

8.20. As has already been indicated, the spread of Christianity carried with it the spread of writing. Where the missionaries used the Latin alphabet for their own language, they merely adapted it slightly to the sounds of the new language, added an occasional diacritic or digraph, and let it go at that. The world is full of numerous Latin-letter orthographies which are more or less unsuited to the languages for which they are used.

But where the missionaries used the Greek alphabet, they usually modified some letters and introduced new ones. The modified Greek alphabets that have survived are Coptic, Gothic, Armenian, Georgian, and the various forms of Cyrillic. Coptic and Gothic are presented in 8.21, Armenian and Georgian in 8.22, and the Slavic alphabets in 8.23.

The old Germanic alphabet known as the *futhark*, though pre-Christian, is at least in part an offshoot of the Greek alphabet, and is given in 8.24.

8.21. When Greek Christianity came to Egypt in the third century, the Greek alphabet was adapted for writing various Egyptian dialects then in use. Collectively these dialects are known as Coptic, and a single modified Greek alphabet is used for them. Since the sixteenth century, the use of Coptic has survived only in the Ethiopic Christian church and the few Coptic Christian churches left in Egypt. The alphabet is the Greek alphabet in majuscule and minuscule form, with seven added letters that are commonly said to be derived from demotic writing (cf. 7.11); see 7.24 for the history of the Coptic alphabet.

The letter forms of the Gothic alphabet (see References and Notes for a discussion of the invention of the alphabet and the origin of

Coptic and Gothic Alphabets

Greek or other originals	Coptic			Gothic		
A α	𝕬 ⲁ	a		ⲁ	a.	1
B β	Ⲃ ⲃ	b		Ⲃ	b	2
Γ γ	Ⲅ ⲅ	g		Ⲅ	g	3
Δ δ	Ⲇ ⲇ	d		ⲁ	d	4
E ε	Ⲉ ⲉ	e		Ⲉ	e	5
[see text]	—			u	k^w	6
Z ζ	Ⳛ ⳛ	z		Z	z	7
H η	Ⲏ ⲏ	ē		ⵀ	h	8
Θ θ [see text]	Ⲑ ⲑ	th		ⲫ	θ	9
I ι	Ⲓ ⲓ	i		ι, ï	i	10
K κ	Ⲕ ⲕ	k		Ⲕ	k	20
Λ λ	Ⲗ ⲗ	l		ⲗ	l	30
M μ	Ⲙ ⲙ	m		ⵞ	m	40
N ν	Ⲛ ⲛ	n		ⵠ	n	50
Ξ ξ [see text]	Ⳃ ⳃ	x		Ⲅ	y	60
O o [see text]	Ⲟ ⲟ	o		ⲡ	u	70
Π π	Ⲡ ⲡ	p		ⲡ	p	80
[see text]	—			ⵕ	[q]	90
P ρ [see text]	Ⲣ ⲣ	r		Ⲣ	r	100
Σ σ, ς [see text]	Ⲥ ⲥ	s		s	s	200
T τ	Ⲧ ⲧ	t		Ⲧ	t	300
Υ υ [see text]	Ⲩ ⲩ	y		Ⲩ	w	400
Φ φ [see text]	Ⲫ ⲫ	ph		ⵂ	f	500
X χ [see text]	Ⲭ ⲭ	kh		X	x	600
Ψ ψ [see text]	Ⲯ ⲯ	ps		Θ	h^w	700
Ω ω	Ⲱ ⲱ	ō		Ⲋ	o	800
[see text]	—			↑	[š]	900

Demotic section (Greek or other originals column), with [see text]:

Demotic	Coptic	
ⲩ (𓏴)	Ϣ ϣ	š
ⲩ (⌣)	Ϥ ϥ	f
ⲋ (𓊪)	Ϧ ϧ	ẖ
ⲋ (or)	Ⳅ ⳅ	h
ⲩ (𓈖)	Ϫ ϫ	ǰ
ⲥ (⌣)	Ϭ ϭ	č
ⲭ (or○)	Ϯ ϯ	ti

the letters) exhibit some difference in style from those of Coptic, but both alphabets are based on the same kind of Greek writing of about the same period. Greek letter forms in the early centuries of the Christian era were written in much the same styles as were those of Latin (capitals, uncial rounded forms, various scripts); Coptic and Gothic are both based on uncial forms. See 8.22 for Armenian and Georgian, based probably on cursive forms of somewhat later date with very different letter shapes, and 8.23 for the two Slavic alphabets—Glagolitic, based on very much elaborated cursive forms, and Cyrillic, based on late post-uncial styles and showing many characteristics of letter shapes in common with Coptic and Gothic.

The table on the preceding page lists the Coptic and Gothic alphabets, with a column of Greek (or other) letters that are the originals of the other two; numerical values of Gothic are given.

A glance at the table shows that the Coptic alphabet is evidently composed of the Greek letters, with some additions at the end. The use of majuscule and minuscule letter pairs, sometimes rather different in form, was preserved from the Greek alphabet also. The Greek names of the letters were also taken over, but as recorded in our source (*Alphabete und Schriftzeichen*; see References and Notes) they reflect the rather different phonology of Coptic, as well as the phonology of Greek of the third century; *alfa, vida* (/v/ or /w/?), *gamma, dalda, ei, zita, hida* (was the *h* there? why *zita* with *t* but *hida* with *d*? was *hida* already a symbol for *i* rather than *ē*?), *thida, yoda, kappa, lola* (origin?), *mi, ni, exi, o, bi* (does this mean [b̭], contrasted with φ /ph/?), *ro, sima, dau* ([ḓ]—cf. θ /th/?), *he* (what phonemic value?), *phi, khi, epsi, o* (same as omicron?), *šai, fai, ḫai, hori, ǰanǰa, čima, di* = *ti*. The last seven letters certainly bear non-Greek names, and could, at least in four of the cases, come directly from the demotic Egyptian (which differs considerably in five instances from the older hieroglyphic forms). But letter shapes can change so much from a common source, and can look so much alike even when of different origins, that this purported provenience of the seven letters may not be true for any or at least most of them. Possible alternatives are:

ϣ : from Semitic (Hebrew) שׁ, probably influenced by the demotic symbol

ϥ : a possible modification of φ

ϧ : a possible modification of Latin *h*

ϩ : ?

𝒳 : a modification of 𝔏 *d*
𝜎 : from Greek σ, while Coptic C is from the form ϛ
Ꞇ : ligature of *t* and *i*

The Gothic alphabet is just as clearly taken from the same general style of Greek writing as Coptic, but there has been much inventiveness in adapting it to the Gothic language. Also there is no distinction between majuscule and minuscule. The alphabet was invented by Wulfila ('Little Wolf'), who was born in Cappadocia (eastern Asia Minor) about 311, the descendent of Goths brought to the area as captives about 75 years earlier. He became a bishop, and died about 383. He invented the Gothic alphabet for the purpose of translating the Bible into Gothic; practically all we know about the language is to be found in the one surviving manuscript (see References and Notes). The letter here transliterated as k^w (most usually written q) is in the place of *digamma* or Latin f; there is no accepted explanation of its form, however. Wulfila may have invented what was in effect a combination of Greek *digamma* (of whose traditional value as /w/ he might somehow have been aware) and Latin *qu* (the two-letter sequence), using the position and numerical value of the former, and the shape of the second part of the latter. He did not use the shape of q because Greek had retained that form as a numeral, and he took it over as such into Gothic. That Wulfila knew the Latin alphabet seems certain from the value he assigned to *h*—retaining the position of Greek *eta*—and from other evidence. The apparent reversal of the positions of θ and ψ, so that the latter shape appears between *h* and *i*, but with the value /θ/, while the former goes to the place of Greek *psi*, though with the new value h^w, may be more apparent than real: it is imaginable that either shape could result in the other, and that the value of /θ/ was assigned to the same place as in the Greek alphabet. The letter after *n*, transliterated *y* here (often *j* elsewhere), looks like Latin G, but is in the place of Greek *xi*; perhaps, like Gothic k^w, it is a kind of blend of the position of *xi*, and possibly even part of its shape (the upper part of the form ξ), with a value of Latin G known to Wulfila; or it could be an arbitrary assignment of value. It may be pointed out that Gothic *u* and *o* look like the Runic letters (the *futhark*, see 8.24), and they probably are those letter forms put into appropriate places in the alphabet (*u*, a short vowel, where *o* belonged, and *o*, a long vowel, where *omega* belonged). The symbol for 90 is the old *qoppa*, in its proper place, but with no letter value. The forms of *r* and *s* look as if they were taken from the Latin shapes, but could have developed from Greek *rho* and *sigma*. W has the shape of Greek *upsilon* but also of Runic *wen*; this may be another blend of position and value. The form *x* is Greek in position and in value—though not needed in Gothic. The Gothic *f* looks like Latin, but is where Greek *phi* belongs. Just possibly the best explanation for the Gothic letters that we transliterate as *θ, f, h^w* is this: when the easy equivalences between Greek and Gothic had been established, these three letters were, in a manner of speaking, left over, and were then assigned haphazardly. The symbol for 900 was not used as a letter. There is no evidence for the names of the Gothic letters, which might have helped in determining origins.

8.22.   In the fifth century Greek missionary efforts in the Caucasus area produced two alphabets of similar appearance and with similar differences from the Greek original. The Armenian alphabet seems to have been the earlier, and was probably the model for the Georgian one. Though the languages are not related, their phonological systems seem to have much in common. Over the years Armenian phonology has produced widely varying dialect results, and the eastern and western dialects, which have become literary languages, exhibit two seemingly contradictory uses of a number of the letters (see References and Notes for material treating the Armenian language). The Armenian alphabet of 38 letters is probably based on some form of Greek cursive writing; most of the letter forms are very different from their Greek originals—so much so that for many of them the originals can only be guessed at. The table below presents the most common printed forms of the alphabet, both capitals and lowercase, with a transliteration that follows the traditional Old Armenian values; two columns of transcriptions, for modern East and West Armenian, are appended. The old numerical values are also shown.

The form of the Georgian alphabet that shows its origin from the same kind of cursive as does the Armenian is now practically out of use, occurring only for decorative capitals and headings, and the like; there are majuscule and minuscule forms. The common alphabetic form in use now has made the letters extremely cursive—no angles or straight lines, but smooth curves almost everywhere; there is no distinction between capitals and small letters in this form of Georgian. The table below shows the older and the newer forms, with a transliteration that seems to fit the modern phonology as well as it did the older one. Numerical values are shown. (The Georgian language is Caucasic—see References and Notes.)

Possible Greek (and other) originals are given in the first column.

Armenian and Georgian Alphabets

	ARMENIAN					GEORGIAN				
Probable or possible Greek or other originals	Letter	Transliteration (Old Armen.)	Modern East Armen.	Modern West Armen.	Numerical value	Letter (Modern)	Letter (Old)	Transliteration	Name of letter	Old numerical value
A α	Ա ա	a	a	a	1	ა		a	ani	1
B β	Բ բ	b	b	p	2			b	bani	2
Γ γ	Գ գ	g	g	k	3			g	gani	3
Δ δ	Դ դ	d	d	t	4			d	doni	4
E ε	Ե ե	e	ye-,-e-	ye-,-e-	5			e	eni	5
(digamma —γ?)										
Z ζ	Զ զ	z	z	z	6			w	vini	6
H η	Է է	ē	e	e	7			z	zeni	7
(? η)	Ը ը	ə	e	e	8			ē[ei]	he)	8
Θ θ	Թ թ	th	th	t	9			th	thani	9
(? ζ)	Ժ ժ	ž	ž	ž	10					
I ι	Ի ի	i	i	i	20			i	imi	10
(? Lat. l)	Լ լ	l	l	l	30					
(? Lat. h)	Խ խ	x	x	x	40					
(? τ ς)	Ծ ծ	c[ts]	c	ç[dz]	50					
K χ	Կ կ	k	k	g	60			k	kani	20
(? Lat. h)	Հ հ	h	h	h	70					

Armenian and Georgian Alphabets (continued)

Probable or possible Greek or other originals	ARMENIAN					GEORGIAN				
	Letter	Transliteration (Old Armen)	Modern East Armen.	Modern West Armen.	Numerical value	Letter (Modern)	Letter (Old)	Transliteration	Name of letter	Old numerical value
(modified ζ)	Ձ ձ	ǰ[dz]	ǰ	c	80					
Λ λ	Ղ ղ	ł[łẋ]	y	y	90	ლ	Ⴊ ⴊ	l	lazi	30
?	Ճ ճ	č̌	č̌	ǰ	100					
Μ μ	Մ մ	m	m	m	200	მ	Ⴋ ⴋ	m	mani	40
(replacing ξ ?)	Յ յ	y	h-, -y-	h-, -y-	300					
Ν ν	Ն ն	n	n	n	400	ნ	Ⴌ ⴌ	n	nari	50
(modified ξ ?)						(ჲ)	Ⴢ ⴢ	y	ye)	60
(modified s?)	Շ շ	š	š	š	500					
Ο ο	Ո ո	o	o	wo-, -o-	600	ო	Ⴍ ⴍ	o	oni	70
(cf. Arm. ǰ)	Չ չ	č̣	č̌h	č̌	700					
Π π	Պ պ	p̌	p	b	800	პ	Ⴎ ⴎ	p	pari	80
(replacing qoppa)	Ջ ջ	ǰ	ǰ	č̌	900	ჟ	Ⴏ ⴏ	ž	zhani	90
(modified ρ ?)	Ռ ռ	r̄	ṙ	ṙ	1000	რ	Ⴐ ⴐ	r	rae	100

					Greek equivalents	value		name	trans.	Georgian	Georgian	value
Σ σ,ς		s	s	s	Ս ս	2000	ს	s	sani		Ⴊ ს	200
?		w	w	w	Վ վ	3000	ტ	t	tani		Ⴐ ტ	300
T τ		t	t	t	Տ տ	4000						
P ρ		r	r	r	Ր ր	5000	უ	u	uni		Ⴍ უ	400
(cf. Arm. y) Υ υ		c[c']	ch	c	Ց ց	6000	(ჳ	wi	vi)			—
?		u	u	u	Ւ ւ	7000	ფ	ph	phari		Ⴔ ფ	500
?							ქ	kh	khani		Ⴕ ქ	600
Φ φ		ph	ph	ph	Փ փ	8000						
X χ		kh	kh	kh	Ք ք	9000	ღ	γ	ghani		Ⴖ ღ	700
Ω ω		ō	o	o	Օ օ	10000	ყ	q	qari		Ⴗ ყ	800
?		f	f	f	Ֆ ֆ	20000	შ	š	shini		Ⴘ შ	900
(? Arm. t')							ჩ	čh	chhini		Ⴙ ჩ	1000
?							ც	ch[ts']	tshani		Ⴚ ც	2000
?							ძ	ʒ[dz]	dzili		Ⴛ ძ	3000
(? Arm. č)							წ	c	tsili		Ⴜ წ	4000
(? Arm. ç)							ჭ	č	chari		Ⴝ ჭ	5000
(? Arm. ǰ)							ხ	x	hhani		Ⴞ ხ	6000
?							ჰ[qx]	h'ari			Ⴟ	7000
?							ǰ	jani			Ⴠ	8000
(? Arm. b)							(ჯ	h	hae			9000
?							ō	hoe)			Ⴢ	10000
(? Arm. ǰ)												
(? Arm. h)												
?												

The above table shows that Armenian inserted new letters into the alphabet and rearranged old letters quite freely, whereas Georgian pretty much retained the Greek order, and added new letters only at the end of the alphabet. In either alphabet, it is not easy to identify even the forms of the letters that maintain the traditional order; the letters that have been moved to other places are difficult to trace, and the new letters that have been added are almost impossible to identify as to origin.

It should be noted how different an alphabet can look after the passage of time. One example of such difference is the first letter of the Armenian and Georgian alphabets:

Greek A α, Armenian Ա ա, Georgian Ⴀ ა replaced by Ⴆ.

For still further elaborations, see the Slavic alphabets in the next section.

8.23. In 7.24 the extensions of the Greek alphabet that resulted in Cyrillic were presented. This section will list the Glagolitic, older Cyrillic, and modern Cyrillic alphabets. The latter will be shown as used in Russian, Ukrainian, White Russian, Bulgarian, Macedonian, Serbocroatian, and several of the non-Slavic languages of the Soviet Union. The origins suggested for the non-Greek letters are speculative in some cases, but no consensus has been reached because of the dearth of assured historical data. (For material on the Slavic languages, see References and Notes.)

The first table gives the Glagolitic and Old Church Slavic (OCS) Cyrillic alphabets, with their numerical values, a transliteration (of the "exact" or "scientific" type), the known Greek originals, and the possible origins of the non-Greek letters.

It is known that Glagolitic was based on a late Greek cursive style of writing, but it seems clear that much inventiveness or plain fantasy was exercised in forming the letter shapes. Some of them seem to have been deliberately distorted or turned around or made different from any existing model. Capital letters are found in Glagolitic manuscripts, but they are simply larger versions of the letters that are given in the table. The order of the letters $ī$ and i is puzzling; in Cyrillic it is reversed, which is the way it is in Greek. The letter j has no Cyrillic equivalent; it is perhaps in the same tradition as Gothic Ⱪ $= y$. The letter u seems to be made up of two instances of o; in Cyrillic it was always originally two letters, like Greek—ou; the later symbol ȣ is a digraph of o and u, and the modern Cyrillic y probably represents this digraph. The letter which looks like *theta* is either used only to transcribe Greek *theta*, or is modified and is an

Glagolitic and Old Church Slavic (Cyrillic) Alphabets

Greek or other originals	Glagolitic		Transliteration	Cyrillic	
α	Ⰰ	1	a	А а	1
(Latin b?)	Ⰱ	2	b	Б б	—
β	Ⰲ	3	v	В в	2
γ	Ⰳ	4	g	Г г	3
δ	Ⰴ	5	d	Д д	4
ε	Ⰵ	6	e	Є є	5
(? ζ ς)	Ⰶ	7	ž	Ж ж	—
(? δ ς)	Ⰷ	8	ẑ [dz]	Ѕ ѕ	6
ς	Ⰸ	9	z	З з	7
ι	Ⰺ	10	ī	І і	10
η	Ⰹ	20	i	И и	8
(Latin g?)	Ⰼ	30	ǰ		—
κ	Ⰽ	40	k	К к	20
λ	Ⰾ	50	l	Л л	30
μ	Ⰿ	60	m	М м	40
ν	Ⱀ	70	n	Н н	50
o	Ⱁ	80	o	О о	70
π	Ⱂ	90	p	П п	80
ρ	Ⱃ	100	r	Р р	100
σ	Ⱄ	200	s	С с	200
τ	Ⱅ	300	t	Т т	300
ου	Ⱆ	400	u, ou	Ѹ оу, ȣ	400

Glagolitic and Old Church Slavic (Cyrillic) Alphabets (continued)

Greek or other originals	Glagolitic		Transliteration	Cyrillic	
φ	Ⱚ	500	f	Ф ф	500
θ	⊕	—	ꜰ (θ)	Ѳ ѳ	9
χ	ᚼ	600	x	Х х	600
ω	Ο	700	ō	Ѡ ѡ	800
(š plus t?)	Ⱎ	800	ś	Щ щ	—
(t plus s?)	Ⰲ	900	c	Ц ц	900
(t plus s? Latin q?)	✚	1000	č	Ч ч	90
(σσ?; cf. Semitic ꟙ)	Ⱎ	—	š	Ш ш	—
(modified ĭ?)	Ⱚ	—	ŭ	Ъ ъ	—
(ŭ plus ī or ĭ)	Ⱚ Ⱚ	—	y or ŭī, ŭĭ	ЪІ (ъи)	—
(modified ĭ?)	Ⱚ	—	ĭ	Ь ь	—
(modified A?)	Ⰰ	—	ě	Ѣ ѣ	—
(i plus o[u]?)	Ⰱ	—	ü	Ю ю	—
(i plus a)	—		ä	Ꙗ ꙗ	—
(i plus e)	—		ë	Ѥ ѥ	—
(modified E?)	Ⱗ	—	ę	Ѧ ѧ	900(?)
(o plus ę?)	Ⱘ	—	ǫ	Ѫ ѫ	—
(modified ę?)	Ⱙ	—	ę̈	Ѩ ѩ	—
(modified ǫ?)	Ⱚ	—	ǫ̈	Ѭ ѭ	—
ξ	—		k^s	Ѯ ѯ	60
ψ	—		p^s	Ѱ ѱ	700
ꙋ	Ⰲ	—	ẏ	Ѵ ѵ	400(?)

The Russian Alphabet

Roman	Italic	Script	Transliteration	Name of letter
А а	A a	*A a*	a	a /á/
Б б	Б б	*Б б*	b	bè /bé/
В в	В в	*В в*	v	vè /vé/
Г г	Г г	*Г г*	g	ge /gé/
Д д	Д д, д	*Д д*	d	dè /dé/
Е е	Е е	*Е е*	e (ye and e)	e /yé/
Ё ё	Ё ё	*Ё ё*	ë (yë and ë)	ë /yó/
Ж ж	Ж ж	*Ж ж*	ž (zh)	že /žé/
З з	З з	*З з*	z	zè /zé/
И и	И и	*И и*	i	i /í/
Й й	Й й	*Й й*	ĭ (y)	i kratkoe /ĭ+krátkaya/ 'i short'
К к	К к	*К к*	k	ka /ká/
Л л	Л л	*Л л*	l	èl /él/ (or èlĭ /élj/)
М м	М м	*М м*	m	èm /ém/
Н н	Н н	*Н н*	n	èn /én/
О о	О о	*О о*	o	o /ó/
П п	П п	*П п*	p	pè /pé/
Р р	Р р	*Р р*	r	èr /ér/

The Russian Alphabet (continued)

Roman	Italic	Script	Transliteration	Name of letter
С с	С с	C c	s	ès /és/
Т т	Т т, т	Т т,т	t	tè /té/
У у	У у	У у	u	u /ú/
Ф ф, Ф	Ф ф, Ф	Ф ф	f	èf /éf/
Х х	Х х	Х х	x (kh)	xa /xá/
Ц ц	Ц ц	Ц ц	c (ts)	cè /cé/
Ч ч	Ч ч	Ч ч	č (ch)	čè /čé/
Ш ш	Ш ш	Ш ш	š (sh)	ša /šá/
Щ щ	Щ щ	Щ щ	šʹ (shch)	ša /šča/
Ъ ъ	Ъ ъ	ъ,ъ	ŭ (ʹʹ)	tvërdyj znak /tvjórdiy+znák/ 'hard sign'
Ы ы	Ы ы	ы	y	ery /yirí/
Ь ь	Ь ь	ь,ь	ĭ (ʹ)	mägkij znak /mjáxkiy+znák/ 'soft sign'
Э э	Э э	Э э	è	è /é/
Ю ю	Ю ю	Ю ю	ü (yu)	ü /yú/
Я я	Я я	Я я	ä (ya)	ä /yá/

equivalent of *f*. It should be noted that the form of *f* in both Glagolitic and Cyrillic could be confused with Greek *psi*, but should be
phi. The letters following *omega* were all new inventions, and it is
difficult to determine their origins. A restatement of the phonemicization of OCS proposed by the present author (see References and
Notes) suggests the basis for some of these letter forms.

The Cyrillic forms, based on Greek uncial majuscule forms, are
much more readable than the Glagolitic ones. As the alphabet became
widely used, it developed some clear differences between capital and
small letters. As given here, the capitals are those used in printing
OCS texts (the Bible and others) in modern times. The numerical
values of Glagolitic were assigned in the order of the letters, but
Cyrillic kept pretty well to Greek numerical values; 6 was assigned
to *ž*, and this letter, despite its value as /ʒ/ [dz] may actually owe its
shape to Greek *digamma* (especially as written ϛ′ = 6). The order of
i as 8 and *ī* as 10 corresponds to *eta* and *iota* respectively; in Russian
the letters—when both were still used before the spelling reform
inaugurated in 1917—were sometimes called 'i eight-saying' and
'i ten-saying'. The number 9 was assigned to *theta*, which was not
used except in transcribing Greek, and which was probably always
pronounced [f]. The number values of this letter and others indicate
that originally all the letters were kept in their Greek order; but
later the unneeded or Greek-transcribing letters were put at the end.
The value 60 of *xi* (*kˢ*) is another instance like that of *theta*. The value
90 of *č* may have been assigned because this letter looked like Greek
qoppa, used only as a numeral, 90; just possibly the letter form was
actually that of *qoppa*, arbitrarily assigned to /č/. The origins of most
of the Cyrillic letters following *omega* seem clear, but it is not at all
certain that their Glagolitic equivalents were derived in the same way.

Printing was introduced into Russia in the late fifteenth century
(after 1480). The type was cast in the form of OCS Cyrillic. In the
early seventeenth century the letter forms were made over to look
like Latin letters. Since then all the Slavic languages using Cyrillic
have adopted the new forms, and the former OCS forms are used
only in printing the Bible in OCS, or occasionally for decorative
titles and headings. All the variations—roman, italic, capitals,
small letters—have been developed, and are used in about the same
ways as in the world of the Latin alphabet. Even small capitals are
used occasionally, though there are only five letters for which the
lowercase shape is different from the capitals, so that small capitals
are not very distinctive. As stylistic equivalents of our black letter,
the Russians use OCS Cyrillic. In recent years, Cyrillic and Latin

typefaces have been cast to match and blend completely. Cyrillic handwriting is also in the same styles as are used in Europe and America for the Latin alphabet, and individuals transfer their handwriting style completely from one alphabet to the other. The table above gives the Russian alphabet in roman, italic, and script form, with the scientific transliteration used in this book and also a widespread popular one (see References and Notes) in parentheses where it differs from the scientific; the names of the letters are in the scientific transliteration. For the history of Russian Cyrillic see 7.24. The use of the dieresis with *ë* is not consistently followed, though it is supposed to be standard; and *ë* is not counted as a separate letter. The following four letters were removed from the alphabet in the reform of spelling promulgated in 1917, and accepted by the Academy of Sciences in 1924:

I i *I i* 𝒥 *i* ї *i s točkoi̦* /î+s+tóčkay/ 'i with dot'; followed й; replaced by и

Ѣ ѣ *Ѣ ѣ* Ӗ̃ *ě* *ěti* /yátj/; followed ь; replaced by e

Ѳ ѳ *Ѳ ѳ* Ѳ *ɵ* F *fita* /fjitá/; followed я; replaced by ф

V v *V v* 𝒴 *ꙋ* Y *ižica* /ížica/; last letter; replaced by и

The letters I and V are used in Roman numerals as equivalents of Latin I and V. In present-day typing, V is usually replaced in this usage by У, the old letter not being put on most typewriter keyboards; II and III are often typed and sometimes printed as П and Ш.

The second transliteration, where there are two in the table, is that of the U.S. Board on Geographic Names (BGN) (see References and Notes). In that system, the letter e is transliterated as *ye* initially and also after the letters а, е (and ё), и, о, у, ъ, ы, ь, э, ю, я; otherwise as *e*; the same is true of ë = *yë*, č. The sequence of letters тс may be distinguished from ц by writing *t.s* and *ts* respectively; the rare sequences шч, ыу, ыа may similarly be written *sh.ch, y.u, y.a* to distinguish them from щ, ю, я. The letter э initially may be written *e* instead of *è*, since Russian e in that position is *ye*. The use of ' over *e* for э, and the dots in *t.s, sh.ch, y.u, y.a* are not parts of the BGN system as officially adopted.

In Ukrainian, the alphabet takes the following form: а, б, в, г, ґ, д, е, є, ж, з, и, й, і, ї, к, л, м, н, о, п, р, с, т, у, ф, х, ц, ч, ш, щ, ь, ю, я, '. The scientific transliterations for ґ, ï, ' are *ḡ, ï, "* respectively. A popular transliteration system, differing from Russian, is as follows: *a, b, v, h* for г, *g* for ґ, *d, e* always for e, *ye* always for є, *zh, z, y* for и and й, *i* for i, *yi* for ï, *k, l, m, n, o, p, r, s, t, u, f, kh, ts, sh, shch, '* for

Serbocroatian, Macedonian, and Bulgarian Cyrillic Alphabets

SERBOCROATIAN		MACEDONIAN		BULGARIAN	
Letter	*Transliteration*	*Letter*	*Transliteration*	*Letter*	*Transliteration*
А а	*a*	А а	*a*	А а	*a*
Б б	*b*	Б б	*b*	Б б	*b*
В в	*v*	В в	*v*	В в	*v*
Г г	*g*	Г г	*g*	Г г	*g*
		Ѓ ѓ	*g' (gy)*		
Д д	*d*	Д д	*d*	Д д	*d*
Ђ ђ	*đ or dj*	——			
Е е	*e*	Е е	*e*	Е е	*e*
Ж ж	*ž (zh)*	Ж ж	*ž (zh)*	Ж ж	*ž (zh)*
		Ѕ ѕ	*ż (dz)*		
З з	*z*	З з	*z*	З з	*z*
И и	*i*	И и	*i*	И и	*i*
				Й й	*ĭ (y)*
Ј ј	*j (y)*	Ј ј	*j (y)*	——	
К к	*k*	К к	*k*	К к	*k*
		Ќ ќ	*k' (ky)*		
Л л	*l*	Л л	*l*	Л л	*l*
Љ љ	*ļ or lj (ly)*	Љ љ	*ļ or lj (ly)*	——	
М м	*m*	М м	*m*	М м	*m*
Н н	*n*	Н н	*n*	Н н	*n*
Њ њ	*ń (ny)*	Њ њ	*ń (ny)*	——	
О о	*o*	О о	*o*	О о	*o*
П п	*p*	П п	*p*	П п	*p*
Р р	*r*	Р р	*r*	Р р	*r*
С с	*s*	С с	*s*	С с	*s*
Т т	*t*	Т т	*t*	Т т	*t*
Ћ ћ	*ć (tch)*	——		——	
У у	*u*	У у	*u*	У у	*u*
Ф ф	*f*	Ф ф	*f*	Ф ф	*f*
Х х	*h*	Х х	*h*	Х х	*x (kh)*
Ц ц	*c (ts)*	Ц ц	*c (ts)*	Ц ц	*c (ts)*
Ч ч	*č (ch)*	Ч ч	*č (ch)*	Ч ч	*č (ch)*
Џ џ	*ǧ or dž (dzh)*	Џ џ	*ǧ or dž (dzh)*	——	
Ш ш	*š (sh)*	Ш ш	*š (sh)*	Ш ш	*š (sh)*
——		——		Щ щ	*ś (sht)*
——		——		Ъ ъ	*ŭ (ă or ŭ)*
——		——		Ь ь	*ĭ (')*
——		——		Ѣ ѣ	*ě (ye or ya)*
——		——		Ю ю	*ü (yu)*
——		——		Я я	*ä (ya)*

ь, *yu, ya, " for '*. The letter sequences зг, кг, тс, сг, шч, иу, иа may
be distinguished from ж, х, ц, ш, щ, ю, я respectively as *z.h, k.h, t.s,
s.h, sh.ch, y.u, y.a*. In present-day Ukrainian spelling, ï seems to be
replaced by i, ґ is often replaced by г, and ' seems to be simply
omitted.

The White Russian language is officially written in the following
alphabet: а, б, в, г, д, е, ё, ж, з, й, i, к, л, м, н, о, п, р, с, т, у, ў,
ф, х, ц, ч, ш, щ, ы, ь, э, ю, я, '. The letter ў may be transliterated *u̯*
in the scientific transliteration. In a popular transliteration of White
Russian these equivalents hold: г = *h*, е = *ye*, ё = *yo*, й = *y*, i = *i*,
ў = *w*, ы = *y*, э = *e*, ь = *'*, *'* = *"*.

Outside of the Russian sphere of influence, Serbocroatian and
Bulgarian are the old languages traditionally written in Cyrillic.
Macedonian has recently been added as a separate language with its
own Cyrillic orthography. The alphabets with their transliterations
are given in the table above (Serbocroatian is transliterated by the
official Croatian Latin-letter orthography, but popular alternatives
are given in parentheses).

Bulgarian ѣ is sometimes now replaced by е or я according to
pronunciation; the old letter ѫ ǫ is now regularly replaced by ъ *ŭ*.

In the Cyrillic alphabets devised in the Soviet Union for the
various non-Slavic languages, the Russian alphabet is followed
consistently, and any new letters, or letters with diacritics, or digraphs, are so arranged as not to interfere with the Russian orthography in Russian loanwords. The several orthographies all follow
more or less the same principles: all the Russian letters are retained
for loanwords; the letters е, ё, и, ю, я are used for /ye, yo, yi, yu, ya/;
vowels of the /ø, ʉ/ type are usually rendered by the modified letters
ө and ү; /γ/ is written ғ or ҕ ; ж, з are used for /ǰ, ʒ/ if /ž, z/ do not
exist, or new letters are devised—Җ or Ч̡ for /ǰ/ and some modification
of з for /ʒ/; Ң or Н̡ are used for /ŋ/; a few other special characters are
less widely employed. Digraphs and even trigraphs are also common,
especially for glottalized and labialized consonants and for long
vowels and vowel clusters. The letters ъ and ь are sometimes used
for the glottal stop, /ʔ/, after back or front vowels respectively, as in
Bashkir.

The list (below) of special letters and letters with diacritics added
to the Russian alphabet for the languages indicated is taken from
the latest source (Gilärevskiĭ—see References and Notes). The
phonemic values sometimes have to be guessed at (indicated by a
question mark), as they are not given in the source; suggested

scientific transliterations are given in parentheses. The capital forms of the special letters are usually the same as the lowercase ones—for example, h, h.

Cyrillic Letters Added for New Soviet Alphabets

ä	/æ/?	(á)	Hill Mari, Kalmyk, Khanty
ă	/ʌ/	(ă)	Chuvash
æ	/æ/	(æ)	Ossetic
ғ	/ɣ/	(g)	Azerbaydzhani, Bashkir, Karakalpak, Kazakh, Khakass, Tajik, Uygur, Uzbek
ҕ	/ɣ/	(ĝ)	Abkhaz, Yakut
h	/h/	(h)	Azerbaydzhani, Bashkir, Buryat, Kalmyk, Kazakh, Kurdish, Tatar, Uygur, Yakut
ĕ	/ə/	(ĕ)	Chuvash
ҽ	?	(ɛ)	Abkhaz
ҿ	?	(ɛ̧)	Abkhaz
Җ	/ǰ/	(ž̧)	Dungan, Kalmyk, Tatar, Turkmen, Uygur, Uzbek
Ӝ	?	(ž̌)	Udmurt
ҙ	/ð/	(ẓ)	Bashkir
ӟ	?	(ż)	Udmurt
ҙ	/ʕ/	(ẕ̧)	Abkhaz
ӥ	?	(ï)	Udmurt
ӣ	?	(ī)	Tajik
i	/i/, ?	(ī)	White Russian, Kazakh, Khakass, Komi, Komi-Permian, Ukrainian
ï	/yi, ji/	(ï)	Ukrainian
j	/y/	(j)	Altay, Azerbaydzhani
Қ	/q/?	(k̦)	Abkhaz, Karakalpak, Kazakh, Tajik, Uygur, Uzbek
Ҝ	?	(k̉)	Azerbaydzhani
Ҡ	/q/	(k̂)	Bashkir
қ	?	(ƙ)	Abkhaz
Ҟ	?	(ḳ)	Chukchee, Khanty
q	/q/	(q)	Kurdish
Ң	/ŋ/	(n̦)	Bashkir, Dungan, Kalmyk, Kazakh, Kirgiz, Tatar, Turkmen, Tuva, Uygur
Ҥ	/ŋ/	(n̂)	Altay, Mari, Yakut
Ӈ	/ŋ/	(ṇ)	Chukchee, Khanty
ö	/ø/	(ö)	Altay, Kalmyk, Khakass, Khanty, Komi, Komi-Permian, Kurdish, Mari, Udmurt

ө	/ø/	(ø)	Azerbaydzhani, Bashkir, Buryat, Kalmyk, Kazakh, Kirgiz, Mongol, Tatar, Turkmen, Tuva, Uygur, Yakut
ӫ	?	(ö̇)	Khanty
ҽ	?	(ð)	Abkhaz
п̢	?	(p̌)	Abkhaz
ҫ	/θ/	(ş)	Bashkir, Chuvash
т̡	?	(ţ)	Abkhaz
ӱ	/ʉ/	(ü)	Altay, Kalmyk, Khakass, Khanty, Mari
ӯ	?	(ū)	Tajik
ў	/w/	(u̯)	White Russian, Dungan, Uzbek (= /o/)
ӳ	/ʉ/	(ü̯)	Chuvash
ŷ	?	(ú)	Karachaev
ү	/ʉ/	(ü̇)	Azerbaydzhani, Bashkir, Buryat, Dungan, Kalmyk, Kazakh, Kirgiz, Mongol, Tatar, Turkmen, Tuva, Uygur, Yakut
¥	?	(ü̇)	Kazakh
w	/w/	(w)	Kurdish
х	/h/	(x̣)	Abkhaz, Karakalpak, Tajik, Uzbek
ҵ	?	(c̣)	Abkhaz
џ	?	(ǰ)	Abkhaz
ҷ	?	(č̣)	Abkhaz, Tajik
ҹ	?	(ç)	Khakass
ӵ	?	(č̈)	Udmurt
ҷ	?	(ç̇)	Azerbaydzhani
ӹ	?	(ẏ)	Mari
ə	?	(ə)	Abkhaz, Azerbaydzhani, Bashkir, Dungan, Kalmyk, Kazakh, Khanty, Kurdish, Tatar, Turkmen, Uygur
ӛ	?	(ə̇)	Khanty
I	/'/	(:)	Abaza, Adygey, Avar, Dargwa, Ingush, Kabardinian, Lakish, Lezgian, Tabasaran, Chechen (This letter, though it looks like the older Cyrillic I i, is clearly modelled on the Arabic alif, ا, used as a sign of glottalization; only the one form, I, is used, without distinction of capital and lowercase.)

Digraphs are: long vowels—аа, ээ, ыы, оо, уу, өө, үү, ии; diphthongs—уо, үө, ыа; digraphs in place of special letters—оь /ø/, уь /ʉ/, нг /ŋ/, нь /ñ/, ль /ļ/, дь /ǰ/.

From such evidence as is available, the special letters and letters with diacritics are not used in representation of these various non-Russian linguistic materials in an otherwise Russian text. In English practice *façade, élite, cañón, Čestmír, Łódź* are apt to appear as *facade, elite, canon* (or *canyon*), *Cestmir, Lodz*. In other cases there will be Russian transcriptions: җ or ҷ will be replaced by дж, y by ю, and the like.

8.24. Two alphabets that were, strictly speaking, not Christian, may be included here. One was the ogham alphabet, used for Irish before the introduction of Latin letters, and the other the Germanic alphabet known as the futhark (or the runes, runic writing).

The oldest Irish material in the Irish language (see References and Notes) consists of grave inscriptions written in a special alphabet, known in Middle Irish as *ogom* (modern *ogham*). This was a very simple writing system made up of short and long strokes; the short strokes are perpendicular to and on one or the other side of a straight line (usually vertical); the long strokes are written across the line, some perpendicular to it, others at an angle; a single stroke, or sequences of up to five strokes, make up the symbols. The line for writing was a vertical groove cut into wood, or an edge of a squared post, or occasionally a horizontal edge or groove. The symbols are:

    b l f s   n h d t c   q mg ng z r   a o u e i

The order of the letters is thought by some to have been determined by their names, which were words for trees and shrubs; these plants had sacred significance in Irish lore, and their names were always arranged in a certain order. The actual forms bear no relation to Latin letters, but are a code, like Morse or Braille signals (see 7.60). The letter transcribed *f* represented at first the ancestral sound of Irish *f*—a [v] or [w]; *c* was [k], *q* was [kw]; *h* occurs only in newer inscriptions; and *z*, though found in representations of the alphabet and traditionally so transcribed, has not been completely identified in inscriptions. Ogham inscriptions, especially on stones, are found in Wales and in Scotland. The oldest ogham material may go back to the third century A.D., and the system continued in use after the introduction of Christianity and the Latin alphabet.

Various allusions to the *futhark* have been made previously. The Old English letters *thorn* and *wen* were taken from this alphabet, a form of which had been used to write down some very early Old English. In devising the Gothic alphabet, Wulfila seems to have used some of the old letters or at least been influenced by them. The origin of this Germanic alphabet is unknown, but it may have come into use near the beginning of the Christian era. It is clearly based on Latin, the changes in form being the result of carving on wood. These runes, as they are often called, were not a general writing system, but were a special or priestly writing. The letters were arranged in the order given as initials of what may have been a formula of mystic significance. There were originally 24 letters, in three groups of eight, as follows:

ᚠ ᚢ ᚦ ᚨ ᚱ ᚲ ᚷ ᚹ ᛬ ᚺ ᚾ ᛁ ᛃ ᛈ ᛇ ᛈ ᛉ ᛊ ᛬ ᛏ ᛒ ᛖ ᛗ ᛚ ᛜ ᛟ ᛞ

f   u   þ   a   r   k   g   w   h   n   i   j   ᴇ   p   z   s   t   b   e   m   l   ŋ   o   d

The usual name of the alphabet comes from reading the first six letters as a word. The transliteration here given is the usual one employed by Germanic scholars; *θ* might be used for *thorn*, *þ*; *y* for *j*; and *ng* for *ŋ*. The letter *z* is sometimes transliterated as ʀ. It is not known for which Germanic dialect this alphabet was devised, and the phonemic nature of ᴇ, *e*, *o* is not known, nor why *ŋ* was made into a separate letter; nor is it certain that *z* represented a separate phoneme. In England the runic writing seems to have been used, with some added letters, for some time after the Latin-letter orthography was introduced. In Scandinavia the runes were used until the thirteenth century; at first the number of characters decreased (in 850 A.D. there were only 16, several with multiple values); then new letters began to be added again. In Germany the runes went out of use early.

Some of the Old English runes are mirror images of older forms, and nearly every letter appeared in several forms: ᚠ and ᚥ (*f*), ᚷ and ✷ (*g*), ᛒ and ᛦ (*b*), and others. Modified symbols were: ᚣ for *a* and ᚪ for *æ*, ᚤ for *y*, ᛇ for *ea*, ✳ for *io*, ⋔ for *c* (*ċ* ?),✹ for *ġ*. (See References and Notes—Woolfson.)

The runic alphabet could have been perfectly adequate for the Germanic languages. But conditions were such as not to foster its wide use, and it was not until Christianity was imposed that writing really became a constant activity (even though the number of literate persons was small); then it was writing in the Latin alphabet, and only in out-of-the-way places did the runes survive for a time.

8.3. SEMITIC ALPHABETS

8.30. The present section is concerned with the external form and the history of the letter forms of the various Semitic alphabets. (For the actual use of these alphabets in terms of the phonological systems of the languages written in them, see References and Notes.) General historical considerations in regard to the connection of Egyptian writing and the Semitic alphabets have been taken up in 7.11 and 7.12.

Although we agree with the theory that the Semitic letters were not directly taken from Egyptian symbols as such, some of them do coincide in form (in part) and can perhaps be considered as coincidentally of direct Egyptian origin.

The Old Canaanite letter forms, written from right to left, from which all Semitic alphabets and all the later derived alphabets came, are listed below, with a Semitic-language type of transliteration. Suggested or possible Egyptian symbols from which the Canaanite forms might be derived are also given.

The Old Canaanite Letter Forms

Possible Egyptian originals	Old Canaanite	Trans-literation	Possible Egyptian originals	Old Canaanite	Trans-literation
🐦	⟨	'	[?]	V	l
🔲	◁	b	🐦	⌐	m
🔺	⟨	g	∿∿∿	Y	n
◡	◁	d	⊣⊢	‡	s
🔲	⅄	h	▭ [?]	O	'
🐦 [?]	Y	w	▭	⌐	p
[?]	I	z	[?]	⌐⌐	ṣ
🔺 [?]	H	ḥ	◿ [?]	ϙ	q
◡ [?]	⊗	ṭ	◡	◁	r
4	⅂	y	◻	W	š
◡	⅄	k	◠	+	t

The Canaanite forms given could have originated from the Egyptian ones shown, which were used with about the same values as the Semitic letters. But there were other Egyptian forms with the same values; and some of the suggested originals do not fit very well (these are followed by a question mark in brackets).

The Ugaritic Ras Shamra alphabet is cuneiform, and runs from left to right, but may be based on a Semitic alphabet like the Old Canaanite. The forms are in the list below.

The Ras Shamra Alphabet

'a	'i	'u	b	g	d	ḏ	h	w	z	ḥ	ṭ	y	k	l

m	n	s	s_2	'	ġ	p	ṣ	ẓ	q	r	š	ś	?	ż	t

The Old Persian writing system (see 7.10) may have been a special invention which used the above alphabet as a model, at least in part (see References and Notes).

8.31. The Hebrew alphabet was based directly on the oldest Canaanite symbols. The Syriac alphabet is a later version, in the Aramaic tradition. The connections with the Old Canaanite are clear. No variant forms of these alphabets are given here (see References and Notes). The manner of writing vowels, invented much later, is discussed after the table, as are other diacritical marks.

Hebrew preserved a distinction of two shibilants that the language for which the alphabet was first formed—Old Canaanite— did not have; hence the next-to-the-last letter, ש, was differentiated by dots: שׂ *śin* (now simply /s/), and שׁ *šin*. The letters for the stops— *b, g, d, k, p, t*—were also used for the corresponding spirants developed from the stops (at first allophonic, then phonemically separate, but in morphophonic alternation); when diacritical marks were invented to facilitate reading, the stops were marked with a dot, called *dageš*—כ ג ד ב פ ת; the dotted letters were also used internally to show gemination (doubling—*bb*, etc.); the undotted letters, representing the spirants /v/ (or /β/), /ɣ, ð, x, f/ (or /ɸ/), /θ/, are usually transliterated *bh, gh, dh, kh, ph, th*. In printing Hebrew (and in the old manuscripts), words are not divided at the end of a line, and five of the letters have stretched-out forms to fill up the space: א ', ה *h*, ל *l*, מ *m*, ת *t*.

The sounds represented by ', ḥ, ṭ, ', ṣ, q were probably [ʔ, ḥ, t_x, ʕ, s_x, q] respectively.

As in all Semitic writing, vowels were originally not written in Hebrew; but the letters ', h, w, y were used as symbols for some

The Hebrew and Syriac Alphabets

HEBREW				SYRIAC			
Trans-literation	*Letter*	*Name*	*Numerical value*	*Initial*	*Medial*	*Final*	*Name*
'	א	'āleph	1	ܐ	ܐ	ܐ	'ōlaph
b	ב	bêth	2	ܒ	ܒ	ܒ	bēth
g	ג	gimel	3	ܓ	ܓ	ܓ	gōmal
d	ד	dāleth	4	ܕ	—	ܕ	dōlath
h	ה	hē	5	ܗ	—	ܗ	hē
w	ו	wāw	6	ܘ	—	ܘ	waw
z	ז	zayin	7	ܙ	—	ܙ	zayn
ḥ	ח	ḥêth	8	ܚ	ܚ	ܚ	ḥēth
ṭ	ט	ṭêth	9	ܛ	ܛ	ܛ	ṭēth
y	י	yōdh	10	ܝ	ܝ	ܝ	yūd
k	כ, ך*	kaph	20	ܟ	ܟ	ܟ	kōph
l	ל	lāmadh	30	ܠ	ܠ	ܠ	lōmadh
m	מ, ם	mêm	40	ܡ	ܡ	ܡ	mīm
n	נ, ן	nūn	50	ܢ	ܢ	ܢ	nūn
s	ס	sāmekh	60	ܣ	ܣ	ܣ	semkath
'	ע	'ayin	70	ܥ	ܥ	ܥ	'ē
p	פ, ף	pê	80	ܦ	ܦ	ܦ	pē
ṣ	צ, ץ	ṣādê	90	ܨ	—	—	ṣōddē
q	ק	qōph	100	ܩ	ܩ	ܩ	qōph
r	ר	rêš	200	ܪ	—	ܪ	rēš
ś	שׂ	śîn	300	ܫ	ܫ	ܫ	šīn
š	שׁ	šîn					
t	ת	tāw	400	ܬ	—	ܬ	tāw

*The second symbol after the comma is used only as a final in a word.

syllables with vowels, especially "long vowels" and "diphthongs":
' for *a, ā*; *h* for *-ah*; *w* for *aw, ō, ū*; *y* for *ay, ē, ī*. When the language
went out of ordinary use, the pronunciation was retained by oral
tradition among the practitioners of the Jewish religion. In the sixth
century A.D., a system of showing vowels in detail was devised;
since then, the diacritical marks of this *masoretic* (from *masōrah*
'tradition'?) vocalization (of the Old Testament text) have been
used in teaching Hebrew, and are usually referred to as vowel points

(a text with vowels shown is "pointed"). In transliteration it is sometimes customary to use the circumflex to mark "long" vowels for which the lengthening letters ', *w*, *y* are written, and the macron to show other "longs"; such writings as *ê* for *y* preceded by the *ē* vowel symbol, and *ē* for the *ē* symbol without *y* are in a sense transcriptions rather than exact transliterations.

The complete system of vowel signs is:

◻̤ *ā*, *â*; also *o* (short)	◌֟◻ *î* or *ī*	◻֔ *u*
◻̠ *a*	◻֒ *i* (short)	◻֘ *ă*
◌֟◻̤ *ê*	◌֝ *ô*	◻֚ *ĕ*
◻̤ *ē*	◌֝ *ō*	◻ֻ *ŏ*
◻֒ *e*	◌֝ *û* or *ū*	◻֒ *ə* (shwa), or no vowel

If we were to provide Hebrew with an exact system of transliteration which transliterated each symbol, we would have to use something like the following:

' *b b· g g· d d· h w z ḥ ṭ y k k· l m n s ' p p· ṣ q r ś š t t·*

Here *b*, *g*, *d*, *k*, *p*, *t* are read as /β, γ, ð, x, f, θ/ and *b·*, *g·*, *d·*, *k·*, *p·*, *t·* are read as /b-, -bb-; g-, -gg-; d-, -dd-; k-, -kk-; p-, -pp-; t-, -tt-/. The final forms of *k*, *m*, *n*, *p*, *ṣ* could be transliterated as *k,,, m,,, n,, p,,, ṣ,*. The stretched letters ', *h*, *l*, *m*, *t* could be transliterated ·', *h-*, *l-*, *m-*, *t-*. The vowels would be: *ā*, *a*, *ēy*, *ē*, *e*, *iy*, *i*, *ōw*, *ō*, *ūw*, *u*, *əa*, *əe*, *əo*, *ə*.

For indicating the way to accent phrases in chanting prayers and the like, a large number of additional diacritics were invented. It cannot be said with certainty that these were only indicators of musical or chanting additions to the linguistic material; they may have been, in part, accent and intonation indicators.

In writing Syriac, various styles of the alphabet developed. The one given here is the Jacobite form; Nestorian is slightly different in appearance (see References and Notes). Since Syriac was also a religious language not in ordinary use, it was necessary to add diacritical marks for spirantal alternants of stops and for vowels, to preserve the traditional pronunciation. As in Hebrew, the stop-spirant alternation involved *b-bh*, *g-gh*, *d-dh*, *k-kh*, *p-ph*, *t-th*. The spirant forms were shown by a dot under the letters, the stops by a dot over the letters.

Vowels were sometimes shown, as in Hebrew, by ', w, y. Eventually systems developed for systematically indicating all vowels, at least in sacred texts. Western Syriac (Maronite) used the Greek vowel letters, thus: $^{∠}a$, $^{⌐}e$, $^{⊤}i$, $^{○}o$, $^{∠}u$, written above the preceding consonant. In Eastern Syriac a system more like the Hebrew is used: $\dot{ℸ}\ a$, $\ddot{ℸ}\ ā$, $ℸ\ e$, $ℸ̣\ ē$, $ℸ$ (with y) i, $\dot{ℸ}$ (with w) o, $ℸ̣$ (with w) u.

8.32. The Arabic alphabet originally consisted of the 22 usual Semitic letters, in the usual order, with six additional letters for sounds preserved in Arabic but lost in the other languages. Using the modern letter forms (as written when isolated) the alphabet in that order was (with the old numerical values, before the introduction of the numerals from India):

ت	ش	ر	ق	ص	ف	ع	س	ن	م	ل	ك	ى	ط	ح	ز	و	ه	د	ج	ب	ا
t	š	r	q	ṣ	f	'	s	n	m	l	k	y	ṭ	ḥ	z	w	h	d	j	b	'
400	300	200	100	90	80	70	60	50	40	30	20	10	9	8	7	6	5	4	3	2	1

The added letters were:

ث	خ	ذ	ض	ظ	غ
θ	ḫ (x)	ð	ḍ	ẓ	γ
500	600	700	800	900	1000

When the writing of Classical Arabic was standardized for the preservation of the Koran (Qur'ān), in the seventh century, the letters that had come to look alike in shape and were distinguished only by dots, were put next to each other in the alphabet, and the traditional order was largely lost. The letters *h, y, w*, which (along with ') often indicated "long" vowels, were put at the end of the alphabet. Some attention seems to have been paid to phonetic similarity in ordering some of the letters. By the seventh century, Arabic had developed extremely cursive forms, with different shapes for most of the letters in initial, medial, and final positions (with spaces between words). The standard Arabic alphabet, as used in modern printing, is given in the table below.

The Arabic Alphabet

Letter in isolation	Name of letter	Trans-literation*	Letter at beginning of a word	Letter internal in a word	Letter at end of a word
ا	ʾ·alif	· (zero)	ا	ا	ل
ب	ba·ʾ	b	ب	ؠ	ب
ت	ta·ʾ	t	ت	ت	ت
ث	θa·ʾ	θ (th)	ث	ث	ث
ج	jiym	j	ج	ج	ج
ح	ḥa·ʾ	ḥ (ḥ', ḥ)	ح	ح	ح
خ	xa·ʾ	x (ḫ; kh)	خ	خ	خ
د	da·l	d	د	د	د
ذ	ða·l	ð (dh)	ذ	ذ	ذ
ر	ra·ʾ	r	ر	ر	ر
ز	za·y	z	ز	ز	ز
س	siyn	s	س	س	س
ش	šiyn	š (sh)	ش	ش	ش
ص	ṣa·d	ṣ (s', ṣ)	ص	ص	ص
ض	ḍa·d	ḍ (d', ḍ)	ض	ض	ض
ط	ṭa·ʾ	ṭ (t', ṭ)	ط	ط	ط
ظ	ẓa·ʾ	ẓ (z', ẓ)	ظ	ظ	ظ
ع	ʿayn	ʿ	ع	ه	ع
غ	γayn	γ (gh)	غ	‍غ	غ
ف	fa·ʾ	f	ف	ف	ف
ق	qa·f	q	ق	ق	ق
ك	ka·f	k	ک	ک	ك
ل	la·m	l	ل	ل	ل
م	miym	m	م	م	م
ن	nuwn	n	ن	ن	ن
ه	ha·ʾ	h	ه	ه	ه
و	wa·w	w	و	و	و
ى	ya·ʾ	y	ؠ	ؠ	ى

*The transliterations in parentheses are "popular" ones.

A large number of ligatures exists; a few examples are:
ﻚ *l·*, ﺑ *b·*, ﻬﻤ *hm·*, ﺤﺑ *bḥ*, ﻚ *k·*.

The vowels are represented thus:

$$\acute{\ } \, a \qquad آ \; a· \, (\bar{a})$$
$$\underset{\cdot}{\ } \, i \qquad ﻰ \; iy \, (\bar{\imath})$$
$$\acute{\ } \, u \qquad و \; uw \, (\bar{u})$$

Final /a·/ is written ‿ *ay* in a few words. There are also a few instances of ' denoting /a·/; we transliterate these as *ā*. The signs *,* ́ *,* ᵒ were used in Classical Arabic to represent the final "indefinite" case endings of nouns, which are said to have been pronounced /an, in, un/; they are usually omitted in modern printing of Arabic. These signs are simply doubling of the vowel signs, and therefore could be transliterated as *aa, ii, uu*; to avoid confusion with some modern transcriptions in which double vowels mean long vowels, we use the transliterations *ã, ĩ, ũ*. Absence of a vowel is shown by ᵒ, which we leave untransliterated.

The phoneme /'/ [ʔ] is indicated by the sign ʾ, called *hamzah* (the symbol is perhaps derived from the letter ع ?), placed over (and, with *i*, under) '·*alif*, and sometimes over *wa·w* or *ya·*'; after a "long vowel" or a consonant, *hamzah* stands alone on the line, or with a support under it, ئ. We transliterate *hamzah* by ', the initial combination آ being transliterated '·. When an initial *hamzah* with its following vowel is elided, the sign ٱ, called *waṣlah*, is written—ا. This is also transliterated by '; so that ' followed or preceded by a vowel means *hamzah*, while when it is followed by a consonant it means *waṣlah*. If two '·*alifs* come together, to represent the sequence /'a·/, they are written as آ '·*alif-maddah*, and we transliterate by ·*a*·.

Doubling of a consonant is shown by ّ, called *tašdiyd*; we transliterate by : after the letter. When *l* of the article ·*al* is assimilated to certain initial consonants, the *l* is written, but *tašdiyd* is placed over the consonant; thus we transliterate *ld* in such a case by *ld*:.

The letter *h* in final position with two dots over it denotes the morphophonic t of the feminine ending -atu(n); this writing is transliterated -*aħũ* (and -*aħu*); in modern Classical Arabic the ending is read simply as /a/, and transliterated -*aħ* (-*ah*).

The transliteration given first in the above lists represents every sign of the writing system, and is exact. The transliterations in parentheses are usual or conventional ones: *ā, ī, ū* for *a·, iy, uw*; *an, in, un* for *ã, ĩ, ũ*. The alternative transliterations *th, kh*, etc. are not reversible, unless printed with an underline—th, kh, etc. Symbols with ˗ are those of the United States Board on Geographic Names. (See References and Notes for more details on Arabic writing, and for material on the phonemes of Classical Arabic and their relation to the writing system.)

The numerals in Arabic, which are the source of our "Arabic numerals", and which originally came from India, are now written and printed thus:

١ ٢ ٣ ٤ ٥ ٦ ٧ ٨ ٩ ٠
1 2 3 4 5 6 7 8 9 0

In saying numbers, the units come before the decades, but otherwise the largest number comes first; nonetheless, the numerals are written in the same order as in our writing system, so that ١٩٦٥ = 1965 is said "one thousand nine hundred five and sixty".

The Arabic alphabet is used for writing the languages of many areas where the religion is Islam. All the letters are retained to maintain unchanged the spelling of Arabic loanwords, but in the native language some of these letters fall together with others in sound, and some new letters have to be invented. The basic principles of writing consonants and of omitting vowels are retained.

An example is Persian (an Iranian language). The following symbols are added:

$$ پ \quad چ \quad ژ \quad گ $$
$$ p \quad č \quad ž \quad g $$

The letters θ, h, δ, s, d, t, z, ‘ are pronounced like s, h, z, s, z, t, z, ’ respectively; γ and q are used interchangeably for the phoneme /q/ (which has an allophone [γ]); w is /v/. The vowels /æ, o, e/ are not regularly written at all, but when they are, the Arabic symbols for a, u, i are employed; final /e/ is written with h; /i/ is written y, /u/ is w, /a/ is ·.

Another Iranian language, Pashto (Afghanistan), is also written in Arabic letters. Extra letters for retroflex sounds are:

ټ ډ ړ ڼ ښ ږ also: څ ځ
t d r n s z $č$ j

The example of Urdu is mentioned in 8.01.

8.33. The Ethiopic writing system has departed most from the original Semitic. It was first used in the same way as all Semitic writing, and differed in no important way from South Arabian writing. Then, when Coptic Christianity came to Ethiopia, the native alphabet was systematically reworked and expanded, under the influence of the Greek-derived Coptic alphabet. We may conjecture an original system of 22 letters, with vowels omitted, and written from right to left. The modern shapes of the original letters are:

አ በ ገ ደ ሀ ወ ዘ ሐ ጠ የ ከ ለ መ ነ ሰ ዐ ፈ ጸ ቀ ረ ሠ ተ
’ b g d h w z h t y k l m n s ‘ f s q r $š$ t

That these are developments from the older Semitic alphabet letter shapes is evident in nearly every instance. South Arabian inscriptions exist with almost identical letter forms.

When the alphabet was adapted to the writing of Gez, the old religious language, the direction of writing was changed, going from left to right. Some new letters were added, and the writing of vowels was introduced: the vowel symbols were written small and as diacritics, and were physically attached to the consonant symbol. The result is that it looks as if there were about 250 letters or symbols, and that the system is a syllabary. In principle and in form, however, it is not a syllabary, but an alphabet with a relatively small number of basic symbols.

In present-day Amharic there are some additional letters for palatalized consonants, and each of these occurs with the six vowel signs, and alone. There are also some combined symbols for clusters with /w/.

The Amharic Writing System

Consonant	Vowels						
	Ca	Cu	Ci	Cā	Cē	Ce or C	Co
hV	ሀ	ሁ	ሂ	ሃ	ሄ	ህ	ሆ
lV	ለ	ሉ	ሊ	ላ	ሌ	ል	ሎ
ḥV	ሐ	ሑ	ሒ	ሓ	ሔ	ሕ	ሖ
mV	መ	ሙ	ሚ	ማ	ሜ	ም	ሞ
šV	ሠ	ሡ	ሢ	ሣ	ሤ	ሥ	ሦ
rV	ረ	ሩ	ሪ	ራ	ሬ	ር	ሮ
sV	ሰ	ሱ	ሲ	ሳ	ሴ	ስ	ሶ
syV (shV)*	ሸ	ሹ	ሺ	ሻ	ሼ	ሽ	ሾ
qV	ቀ	ቁ	ቂ	ቃ	ቄ	ቅ	ቆ
bV	በ	ቡ	ቢ	ባ	ቤ	ብ	ቦ
tV	ተ	ቱ	ቲ	ታ	ቴ	ት	ቶ
tyV (chV)	ቸ	ቹ	ቺ	ቻ	ቼ	ች	ቾ
ḫV	ኀ	ኁ	ኂ	ኃ	ኄ	ኅ	ኆ
nV	ነ	ኑ	ኒ	ና	ኔ	ን	ኖ
nyV	ኘ	ኙ	ኚ	ኛ	ኜ	ኝ	ኞ
'V	አ	ኡ	ኢ	ኣ	ኤ	እ	ኦ
kV	ከ	ኩ	ኪ	ካ	ኬ	ክ	ኮ

*Alternate transliterations are shown in parentheses.

The Amharic Writing System   (continued)

Consonant	Vowels						
	Ca	Cu	Ci	Cā	Cē	Ce or C	Co
kyV (khV)	ħ	ħ·	ħ.	ħ	ħ	ħ	ħ
wV	ⲱ	ⲱ.	Ⴓ	Ⴓ	Ⴓ	ⲱ·	Ⴓ
'V	0	0·	ዒ	ዓ	ዔ	ዕ	ዖ
zV	ዘ	ዙ	ዚ	ዛ	ዜ	ዝ	ዞ
zyV (zhV)	ዠ	ዡ	ዢ	ዣ	ዤ	ዥ	ዦ
yV	የ	ዩ	ዪ	ያ	ዬ	ይ	ዮ
dV	ደ	ዱ	ዲ	ዳ	ዶ	ድ	ዶ
dyV (jV)	ጀ	ጁ	ጂ	ጃ	ጄ	ጅ	ጆ
gV	ገ	ጉ	ጊ	ጋ	ጌ	ግ	ጎ
t'V	ጠ	ጡ	ጢ	ጣ	ጤ	ጥ	ጦ
ty'V (ch'V)	ጨ	ጩ	ጪ	ጫ	ጬ	ጭ	ጮ
p'V	ጰ	ጱ	ጲ	ጳ	ጴ	ጵ	ጶ
s'V	ጸ	ጹ	ጺ	ጻ	ጼ	ጽ	ጾ
z'V	ፀ	ፁ	ፂ	ፃ	ፄ	ፅ	ፆ
fV	ፈ	ፉ	ፊ	ፋ	ፌ	ፍ	ፎ
pV	ፐ	ፑ	ፒ	ፓ	ፔ	ፕ	ፖ
qwV	ቈ	—	ቊ	ቋ	ቌ	ቍ	—
ḫwV	ኈ	—	ኊ	ኋ	ኌ	ኍ	—
kwV	ኰ	—	ኲ	ኳ	ኴ	ኵ	—
gwV	ጐ	—	ጒ	ጓ	ጔ	ጕ	—

In the table "The Amharic Writing System", the rows headed
syV, tyV, nyV, kyV, zyV, dyV, t'yV were added for Amharic; all
these letters involve the addition of a palatalizing marker (ʾ or some
substitute for it): the pronunciations involved seem to be, respectively, [š], [č], [ń], [x], [ž], [ʒ'], [č']. In Amharic, the old ḥ is [h], š is
[s], and ' is [ʔ], thus being equivalent, respectively, to h, s, and ';
ḫ is [x], and it is not stated whether it represents a different phoneme
from ky. The letters transliterated t', ty', p', s', z (also d') represent
glottalized sounds (lenis) [t̪'] or [t̪ˢ'], [č'], [p̣'], [ṣ'], [ʒ'].
Amharic also uses the following additional ligatures:

ሏ   ሟ   ሯ   ሷ   ሧ   ቧ   ቷ   ጧ   ኗ   ኟ   ኳ   ዟ

lwā mwā rwā swā sywā bwā twā tywā nwā nywā kywā zwā

$$\text{ᚗ}\quad\text{ᚙ}\quad\text{ᚚ}\quad\text{᚛}\quad\text{᚜}\quad\text{᚝}\quad\text{᚞}\quad\text{᚟}\quad\text{ᚠ}\quad\text{ᚡ}$$

zywā   ywā   dwā   t'wā   t'ywā   s'wa   fwā   myā   ryā   fyā

For numerals Gez used Greek letters adapted in style to the Ethiopic system, and marked off by special signs above and below each number:

፩	፪	፫	፬	፭	፮	፯	፰	፱	፲	፳	፴	፵	፶	፷	፸	፹	፺	፻
1	2	3	4	5	6	7	8	9	10	20	30	40	50	60	70	80	90	100
α	β	γ	δ	ε	ϝ	ζ	η	θ	ι	κ	λ	μ	ν	ξ	ο	π	ϟ	ρ

8.4. INDIC ALPHABETS

8.40. The systems of writing that are used in India and that have developed elsewhere from the Indic writing have been discussed in terms of their history and structure in 7.3 and its subdivisions (7.30, General historical; 7.31, Sanskrit writing; 7.32, other Indic alphabets; 7.33, Tibetan, Burmese, Cambodian, Siamese, Malayan alphabets). Here we shall examine the historical development of letter shapes in India, and present full details of the devanagari writing; the other systems developed from it are set forth in the subsections following.

The Devanagari Alphabet

अ आ इ ई उ ऊ ऋ ॠ ऌ ए ऐ ओ औ
'a   'ā   'i   'ī   'u   'ū   'ṛ   'ṝ   'ḷ   'e   'ai   'o   'au

क ख ग घ ङ   च छ ज झ ञ   ट ठ ड ढ ण
ka kha ga gha ña   ca cha ja jha ña   ṭa ṭha ḍa ḍha ṇa

त थ द ध न   प फ ब भ म   य र ल व
ta tha da dha na   pa pha ba bha ma   ya ra la va

श ष स ह
śa ṣa sa ha

The first 13 letters (a 14th, $\bar{ḷ}$, is sometimes listed—made like $ḷ$, but with an extra hook at the bottom, in the same way as $\bar{ṛ}$ compared with $ṛ$) are indicators of a vowel (short or "long"), with the preceding initial onset, marked '. The next 33 letters are consonant symbols, and in the form here given also represent the vowel *a* following the consonant. The arrangement of all the letters is a product of phonological insight; the consonants, especially the five groups of stops, are grouped by place of articulation and then by manner of release and voicing. Four semivowels and four spirants follow. The phonetic order is from back to front—velar, palatal, retroflex, dental, labial—from voiceless to voiced to nasal, from unaspirated to aspirated.

Examination of the symbols shows that in many instances they are derived from some nearby symbol: '*ā* from '*a*, '*ī* from '*i*, '*ū* from '*u*; '*ṛ*, '*ṝ* from '*a*; '*ai* from '*e*; '*o*, '*au* from '*a*; *ṭa*, *ṭha*, *ḍha* from *da*; *pha* from *pa*, '*l* from *la*, *ba* from *va*. The ultimate origins of the symbols can in most cases be traced to some Semitic form; a few such possible connections are presented below.

If we tried to transliterate in terms of an exact system for each symbol as such, the result might be the following for the vowel letters:

'ᵃ 'A i ī u ū '_ṛ '_ṝ l_ṛ l_ṝ e e· 'A· 'A··

Then the separate unmodified consonant letters would have to be transliterated perhaps thus: kᵃ ᴋᵃ gᵃ ɢᵃ ñᵃ cᵃ ¢ᵃ jᵃ ᴊᵃ ñᵃ ṭᵃ Ṭᵃ ḍᵃ ᴅᵃ nᵃ tᵃ ᴛᵃ dᵃ ᴅᵃ nᵃ pᵃ ᴘᵃ bᵃ ʙᵃ mᵃ yᵃ rᵃ lᵃ vᵃ śᵃ ṣᵃ sᵃ hᵃ; the small capitals and ¢ indicate a different letter as a transliteration, and are to be understood as representing the aspirates.

The original pronunciations of the letters in Sanskrit, with the phonemic analyses that we believe held at the time, are:

vowels—*a* /a/ [v], *i* /i/ [iᵛ], *u* /u/ [uᵛ]; *ā* /a·/ [aᴿ], *ī* /iy/ [iⁱᐯ], *ū* /uw/ [uᵘᐯ]; ṛ, ṝ, ḷ /·r, ·r·, ·l/ [ɪ, ɪᴵᴵ, ɪ̣]; *e* /ay/ [æe̞], *ai* /a·y/ [aᵉⁱ], *o* /aw/ [ᴐǫ], *au* /a·w/ [aᵉᵃ]; modern pronunciation is [ᴇ·] for *e*, [aⁱ] for *ai*, [ɑ·] for *o*, [ɑᵘ] for *au*;

consonants—/k/ [k], /kh/ [k'], /g/ [g], /gh/ [gᴴ], /ŋ/; /c/ [¢], /ch/ [¢'], /j/ [ᴊ], /jh/ [ᴊᴴ], /ñ/; /ṭ/ [ṭ], /ṭh/, /ḍ/, /ḍh/, /ṇ/; /t/ [ṭ], /th/ [t'], /d/, /dh/, /n/; /p/, /ph/ [p'], /b/, /bh/, /m/; /y/ [i̢ᐱ], /r/ [ɪ], /l/ [ḷ], /w/ [ɥᐱ(+)]; /ś/, /ṣ/ [ṣ], /s/ [ṣ], /h/ [ᴴ]; modern pronunciation of *c*, *ch*, *j*, *jh* is as affricates [č, č', ǰ, ǰᴴ]; *r* as [rᵃ] or other "*r* sounds"; *v* as [v] or [β] or [w]; *ś* as [š] or [ś], *ṣ* as [š] or [ṣ] or [s]; *h* as [h] or [ᴴ].

Additional signs used are: *visarga* **:** *ḥ*, phonemically /h/, phonetically [h]; *anunāsika* or *anusvāra* **˙** *ṅ*, phonemically /n/, phonetically possibly vowel nasalization. In exact transliteration these would be ʰ and ⁿ. A letter **ॐ** *ḻ* (retroflex) sometimes occurs.

Vowels other than "initial" vowels (see list below) are written as diacritics with the letters (in parentheses are the possible exact transliterations, taking into account the actual similarities of the forms).

a included in a letter	(-ᵃ, but omitted	*ā* ा after a letter	(-ᴬ)
when one of the others below is present)			
i ि preceding a letter	(ⁱ-)	*ī* ी after a letter	(-ᴬⁱ)
u ु under a letter	(-ᵤ)	*ū* ू under a letter	(-ū)
ṛ ृ under a letter	(-ᵣ)	*ṝ* ॄ under a letter	(-r̄)
ḷ ॢ under a letter	(-ₗᵣ)		
e े over a letter	(-·)	*ai* ै over a letter	(-··)
o ो after a letter, or		au ौ after a letter, or	
े over and ा after	(-ᴬ·)	ै over and	
		ा after	(-ᴬ··)

Examples of the vowels with क *ka* are:

का कि की कु कू कृ कॄ कॢ के कै को कौ
kā   ki   kī   ku   kū   kṛ   kṝ   kḷ   ke   kai   ko   kau

A sample line is given, as normally printed (the first double line of the famous tale of Nala and Damayanti):

आसीद्राजानलोनाम   वीरसेनसूतोबली
āsīdrājānalonāma   vīrasenasūtobalī
āsīd rājā nalo nāma,   vīra·sena-sūto balī
'was [a]king Nala [by]name'   'Hero·army-son [the]mighty'

If printed with the words separated, this line would be as follows:

आसीद् राजा नलो नाम वीरसेनसूतो बनी

As is seen, when consonant clusters are written, the consonant letters are combined in ligatures (transliterated by the sequence of consonant letters). A sampling of devanagari ligatures:

कृ क्क क्त क्त्य क्व क्न क्र क्र्य क्ष ग्ध ग्न ङ्क च्च
kṛ   kka   kta   ktya   ktva   kna   kra   krya   kṣa   gdha   gna   ṅka   cca

छ छु ज्ज ज्ञ ञ ध्य त्स राट ष्ण त्त त्म्य त्स्य

ccha chra jja jña ñja ṭṭya tsa ṇṭa ṇṇa tta tmya tsya

टु म्ब य्य रु रू ष्क छ्य स्त्र ह्य

dru mbra yya ru rū ṣka ṣṭrya stra hya

The principle involved in the ligatures is to use the essential parts of the letters and to combine them. For *r*, however, the practice is as follows: a preceding *r* is written as ꞈ over the next letter (exact transliteration ʳ-)—र्क *rka* (ʳkᵃ); a following *r* is written ⸜ (-ᴿ)—प्र *gra* (gᴿᵃ); with *ṛ* it is the vowel that is written in full—ऋ *ṛ* (ʳ'ᵣ). Final consonants without vowels have *virāma*   : क् -*k*, स् -*s* (*k*ₒ, *s*ₒ). In manuscripts and older printed Sanskrit works, words are not divided from each other, and a line is simply written solid to the end; but in works printed outside of India, and in some modern printing in India, words are separated by spaces, especially if this does not involve breaking up a ligature.

It has been implied that it would be difficult to trace all the letter forms of devanagari back to their origins. One of our sources (Diringer, see References and Notes) has an extended table showing various forms of letters found in different parts of India at different times. A few selections will be sufficient illustration:

Trans-literation	Devanagari	Brahmi	Early North Indian	Early South Indian
a	अ	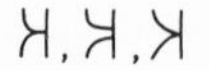 ㅐ,ㅕ,ㅕ	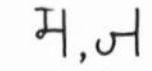 ㅏ,ㅓ	 ४,५
ka	क	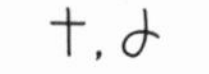 +,ʤ	 ↑,ᴀ	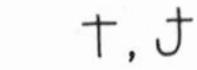 +,ᵴ
ga	ग	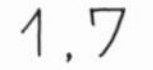 𝟏,ᒥ	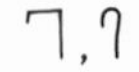 ᒧ,ᒧ	⌒
ta	त	 λ,⅄	C,ϲ̄	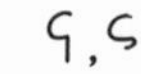 ५,५
ba	ब	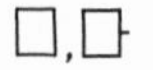 □,□⁺	�	ଥ
sa	स	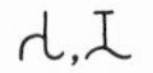 ⅆ,ᒣ	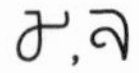 ♂, କ	⚊

There is no doubt that writing in India started with Aramaic writing in the seventh or eighth century B.C. But there would, in fact, be little profit in trying to trace the letters; once a writing system starts, its variants can be extreme, and almost any letter form can end up looking like something else.

8.41. To exemplify the differences that can develop in letter forms deriving from one original source, we present the Bengali, Gujerati, Orissa, Kanarese, Telugu, and Tamil alphabets compared with devanagari.

Alphabets of India

Trans-literation	Devanagari	Bengali	Gujerati	Orissa	Kanarese	Telugu	Tamil
'a	अ	অ	અ	ଅ	ಅ	అ	அ
'ā	आ	আ	આ	ଆ	ఆ	ఆ	ஆ
'i	इ	ই	ઇ	ଇ	ಇ	ఇ	இ
'ī	ई	ঈ	ઈ	ଈ	ಈ	ఈ	ஈ
'u	उ	উ	ઉ	ଉ	ಉ	ఉ	உ
'ū	ऊ	ঊ	ઊ	ଊ	ಊ	ఊ	ஊ
'ṛ	ऋ	ঋ	ઋ	—	ಋ	ఋ	—
'ṝ	ॠ	ৠ	—	—	ಌ	ౠ	—
'ḷ	ऌ	ৡ	—	—	ಌ	—	—
'ḹ	ॡ	ৡ	—	—	ೡ	—	—
'e	ए	এ	એ	ଏ	ಎ	ఎ	எ
'ē	—	—	—	—	ಏ	ఏ	ஏ
'ai	ऐ	ঐ	ઐ	ଐ	ಐ	ఐ	ஐ
'o	ओ	ও	ઓ	ଓ	ಒ	ఒ	ஒ
'ō	—	—	—	—	ಓ	ఓ	ஓ
'au	औ	ঔ	ઔ	ଔ	ಔ	ఔ	ஒள
ka	क	ক	ક	କ	ಕ	క	க
kha	ख	খ	ખ	ଖ	ಖ	ఖ	—
ga	ग	গ	ગ	ଗ	ಗ	గ	—
gha	घ	ঘ	ઘ	ଘ	ಘ	ఘ	—
ña	ङ	ঙ	—	ଙ	ಙ	ఙ	ங
ca	च	চ	ચ	ଚ	ಚ	చ	ச

Alphabets of India (continued)

Trans-literation	Devanagari	Bengali	Gujerati	Orissa	Kanarese	Telugu	Tamil
cha	छ	ছ	છ	ଛ	ಛ	ఛ	—
ja	ज	জ	જ	ଜ	ಜ	జ	ஜ
jha	झ	ঝ	ઝ	ଝ	ಝ	ఝ	—
ña	ञ	ঞ	—	ଞ	ಞ	ఞ	ஞ
ṭa	ट	ট	ટ	ଟ	ಟ	ట	ட
ṭha	ठ	ঠ	ઠ	ଠ	ಠ	ఠ	—
ḍa	ड	ড	ડ	ଡ	ಡ	డ	—
ḍha	ढ	ঢ	ઢ	ଢ	ಢ	ఢ	—
ṇa	ण	ণ	ણ	ଣ	ಣ	ణ	ண
ta	त	ত	ત	ତ	ತ	త	த
tha	थ	থ	થ	ଥ	ಥ	థ	—
da	द	দ	દ	ଦ	ದ	ద	—
dha	ध	ধ	ધ	ଧ	ಧ	ధ	—
na	न	ন	ન	ନ	ನ	న	ந
pa	प	প	પ	ପ	ಪ	ప	ப
pha	फ	ফ	ફ	ଫ	ಫ	ఫ	—
ba	ब	ব	બ	ବ	ಬ	బ	—
bha	भ	ভ	ભ	ଭ	ಭ	భ	—
ma	म	ম	મ	ମ	ಮ	మ	ம
ya	य	য	ય	ଯ	ಯ	య	ய
ra	र	র	ર	ର	ರ	ర	ர
la	ल	ল	ળ	ଳ	ಲ	ల	ல
va	व	ব	વ	ଵ	ವ	వ	வ
śa	श	শ	શ	ଶ	ಶ	శ	—
ṣa	ष	য	ષ	ଷ	ಷ	ష	ஷ
sa	स	স	સ	ସ	ಸ	స	ஸ

Alphabets of India (continued)

Trans-literation	Devanagari	Bengali	Gujerati	Orissa	Kanarese	Telugu	Tamil
ha	ह	হ	હ	ଛ	ಹ	హ	ஹ
ḷa	ळ	—	ળ	—	ಳ	ఴ	—
ḻa	—	—	—	—	ೞ	—	—
-ṁ	ं	ং	◌	—	೦	ం	—
-ḥ	ः	ঃ	—	—	ಃ	ః	—
h	—	—	—	—	ೱ	—	—
no V	◌਼	◌	—	—	—	—	—
Cā	ा	া	િ	ା	ೆ	ా	ா
Ci	ि	ি	િ	◌	ಿ	ి	ி
Cī	ी	ী	ી	◌	ೀ	ీ	ீ
Cu	ु	ু	ુ	◌	ು	ు	ு
Cū	ू	ূ	ૂ	◌	ೂ	ూ	ூ
Cṛ	ृ	ৃ	ૃ	—	ೃ	—	—
Cṝ	ॄ	◌	—	—	ೄ	—	—
Cḷ	ॢ	—	—	—	◌	—	—
Cḹ	ॣ	—	—	—	◌	—	—
Ce	े	ে	◌	—	ೆ	ె	ெ
Cē	—	—	◌	—	ೇ	ే	ே
Cai	ै	ৈ	◌	—	ೈ	ై	ை
Co	ो	ো	◌	ୋ	ೊ	ొ	ொ
Cō	—	—	—	—	ೋ	ో	ோ
Cau	ौ	ৌ	◌	ୌ	ೌ	ౌ	ௌ
1	१	—	૧	୧	೧	౧	௧
2	२	—	૨	୨	೨	౨	௨
3	३	—	૩	୩	೩	౩	௩
4	४	—	૪	୪	೪	౪	௪

Alphabets of India (continued)

Trans-literation	Devanagari	Bengali	Gujerati	Orissa	Kanarese	Telegu	Tamil
5	५	—	५	৵	೫	౫	௫
6	६	—	૬	৬	೬	౬	௬
7	७	—	૭	৭	೭	౭	௭
8	८	—	૮	୮	೮	౮	௮
9	९	—	૯	୯	೯	౯	௯
0	०	—	૦	୦	೦	౦	௦

The only one of these alphabets that departs in any serious way from devanagari is the Tamil one, where unneeded letters are omitted. The others retain nearly everything, even though some letters are used only in Sanskrit loanwords.

8.42. The writing system that has been applied to the Tibetan language since the ninth century A.D. developed from a North Indic alphabet after the seventh century. The letters are easily seen to be derived from forms close to those of devanagari, and the writing style used in public documents and in printing still exhibits the horizontal upper lines (sometimes broken) from which the letters seem to hang, as in devanagari. There are 30 letters, with five additional ones for transcribing Sanskrit; and, as in all Indic writing, there are many ligatures. The letters in unmodified form are understood as including the vowel *a*, and there are vowel diacritics for other vowels; there are two "vowel-initial" letters—'*a* and "*a*. Each syllable is set off by a final point or dot, since Tibetan is basically a language with monosyllabic morphemes, like Chinese.

In modern Tibetan dialects, syllables begin with plain (voiceless), aspirated, or voiced stops or affricates (some of which may be phonemically clusters such as /tr, ty, th/), or with one of the sibilants, a semivowel, a liquid or nasal, or /ʔ/ or /h/; and there is no evidence that in the older language there were complex consonant clusters at the beginnings of syllables. The traditional spelling of Tibetan includes, however, many syllables with consonant-cluster ligatures as initials: *dka, bska, mkha, mkhya, "pra,* etc.; the ones transliterated here are pronounced in modern Central Tibetan as /ka, ka, kha, thya, thra/ respectively. It has been conjectured by some that the first one or two letters of such combinations represented in Old Tibetan prefixes that were either vowelless or had a weak vowel of the [ə]-type, and which had grammatical significance. This conjecture seems entirely out of line, however, with the evidence of related languages or of the modern dialects. Others have thought the prefixed letters indicated various kinds of tones; in modern Tibetan there is a relation between the tones that syllables have and the simple or complex written initials; and this idea may be part of the correct explanation, even though the tone system that was intended does not seem to be deducible from the written evidence. Another possible explanation is that the prefixed letters were mnemonic devices to indicate the different meanings of homonymous morphemes. The present author is inclined to this last theory, and believes it to be at least partly true; if this theory can be proved, then the Old Tibetan writing system was alphabetic and phonemographic, and, at the same time, sememographic. Also, Tibetan syllables are often written with one or more final consonants, which sometimes represent a single consonant phoneme, but at other times are "silent", with occasional effect on the preceding vowel. The original function of these final clusters is also unknown; they, too, may have been sememographic devices, in part.

The Tibetan alphabet is given below in its usual order, with the usual transliteration, which is of the type used for Indic in general, with notations of the modern values of the letters.

The Tibetan Alphabet

	Trans-literation	Modern values of the letters
ཀ	ka	/k/ with high tone on the following vowel, /ʹ/
ཁ	kha	/kh/—always with /ʹ/
ག	ga	/k/ with low tone, /ʽ/; with preceding silent letters—/g/ with /ʽ/
ང	ña	/ŋ/ with /ʽ/
ཙ	ca	/č/ with /ʹ/
ཚ	cha	/čh/ with /ʹ/
ཇ	ja	/č/ with /ʽ/; -/ǰ/ with /ʽ/
ཉ	ña	/ñ/ with /ʹ/; -/ñ/ with /ʽ/
ཏ	ta	/t/ with /ʹ/
ཐ	tha	/th/ with /ʹ/

The Tibetan Alphabet   (continued)

	Trans-literation	Modern values of the letters
ད	da	/t/ with /'/; -/d/ with /`/
ན	na	/n/ with /'/; -/n/ with /`/
པ	pa	/p/ with /'/
ཕ	pha	/ph/ with /'/
བ	ba	/p/ with /'/; -/b/ with /`/
མ	ma	/m/ with /'/; -/m/ with /`/
ཙ	ča	/c/ [tˢ] with /'/
ཚ	čha	/ch/ [tˢ'] with /'/
ཛ	ja	/c/ with /'/; -/ʒ/ [dᶻ] with /`/
ཝ	va	/w/ with /`/
ཞ	ža	/š/ with /`/
ཟ	za	/s/ with /`/
འ	"a	/w/ and /y/ with /`/
ཡ	ya	/y/ with /`/
ར	ra	/r/ with /'/; -/r/ with /`/
ལ	la	/l/ with /'/; -/l/ with /`/
ཤ	ša	/š/ with /'/
ས	sa	/s/ with /'/
ཧ	ha	/h/ with /'/; -/h/ with /`/
ཨ	'a	/'/ with /'/; -/'/ with /`/
ཊ	ṭa	
ཋ	ṭha	
ཌ	ḍa	Sanskrit transliterations
ཎ	ṇa	
ཥ	ṣa	
ི	i	/i/
ེ	e	/e/
ོ	o	/o/, and /ø/ before certain silent finals
ུ	u	/u/, and /ʉ/ before certain silent finals

Numerals: ༡ ༢ ༣ ༤ ༥ ༦ ༧ ༨ ༩ ༠

Punctuation: initial ༄, internal ।, final ॥, syllable end ·

The ligatures (often written out as separate letters in modern times) are sequences of the stops *k, kh, g, t, th, d, p, ph, b* followed by *y, r, l, v* (not all the combinations occur); *r, l, s* followed by the stops and stop combinations, and a few others.

The combinations with subscript *r*, ྲ, and subscript *y*, ྱ, are used to denote, in modern pronunciation, retroflex and palatal consonants respectively (phonemically perhaps /Cr/ and /Cy/). With superscripts and prescripts (that is, letters written over or before others), each phoneme is represented by a large number of spellings, although most combinations consistently represent the same phonemes.

The details of the spelling of silent letters in Tibetan, both initial and final, the various irregular spellings, the morphophonic alternations that are shown in the spelling, and those that are not—all these raise a number of interesting questions about the writing system and also about the history of the language. The answers remain to be found, in most cases. It is suggested that if some of the writing is really sememographic, the adapters of Sanskrit writing to Tibetan may have known Chinese, with its different characters for homophones, and carried over into their alphabet the sememographic characteristics of a logographic writing system; it would be enlightening to know what principles they followed, if any.

8.43. This section concludes the discussion of alphabets derived from India by listing the Burmese, Cambodian, and Thai alphabets, with their transliterations. Explanatory notes on special writing practices follow the lists.

The Burmese alphabet is based on a South Indic form of writing, introduced by Buddhist missionaries who wrote in Pali, a Prakrit (Middle Indic) language. Most of the letters of the original alphabet are retained, even the initial vowel signs, but in many cases the distinctions of sound between different symbols are not made; there is also evidence of change in Burmese pronunciation.

The table below gives the letters of the alphabet in their usual Indic order, with an Indic transliteration (as for devanagari), a suggested conventional transcription, and a suggested phonemicization (which is discussed following the table).

As in all Indic alphabets, the consonant letters without a vowel symbol indicate the initial consonant or cluster followed by the vowel /a/; in Burmese the vowel has the "constricted tone", *à*, phonemicized here as vowel followed by terminal glottal constriction, /a'/. With the lengthening symbol ါ (used with *kh, p, w, d, g, ng*) or ာ (elsewhere) following, the vowel has the "low tone", *á*, phonemicized

The Burmese Alphabet

Character	Indic transliteration	Conventional transcription	Phonemicization
အ	('a)	'a	/'a'/
အာ	('ā)	'á	/'a/
ဣ	('i)	'i	/'i'/
ဤ	('ī)	'i	/'i/
ဥ, ဥ	('u)	'u	/'u'/
ဦ	('ū)	'ú	/'u/
ဧ	('e)	'ei	/'ey/
အဲ	('ai)	'i	/'i'/
ဩ	('o)	'o	/'oh/
ဪ	('au)	'ó	/'o/
က	(ka)	ka	/ka'/
ခ	(kha)	kha	/kha'/
ဂ	(ga)	ga	/k'a'/ [g]
ဃ	(gha)		
င	(ṅa)	nga	/ŋa'/
စ	(ca)	sa	/sa'/
ဆ	(cha)	hsa	/sha'/
ဇ	(ja)	za	/s'a'/ [z]
ဈ	(jha)		
ည	(ña)	nya	/nya'/
ဋ	(ṭa)	ta	/ta'/
ဌ	(ṭha)	hta	/tha'/
ဍ	(ḍa)	da	/t'a'/ [d]
ဎ	(ḍha)		
ဏ	(ṇa)	na	/na'/
တ	(ta)	ta	/ta'/
ထ	(tha)	hta	/tha'/
ဒ	(da)	da	/t'a'/ [d]
ဓ	(dha)		
န	(na)	na	/na'/
ပ	(pa)	pa	/pa'/
ဖ	(pha)	hpa	/pha'/
ဗ	(ba)	ba	/p'a'/ [b]
ဘ	(bha)		
မ	(ma)	ma	/ma'/
ယ	(ya)	ya	/ya'/
ရ	(ra)	ra	/ya'/ and /ra'/
လ	(la)	la	/la'/
ဝ	(va)	wa	/wa'/
သ	(sa)	tha	/θa'/ (and /θ'/ [ð])
ဟ	(ha)	ha	/ha'/

here as simply the vowel itself, /a/. With the symbol း following, we have the "high tone", *â*, which we analyze as /ah/. When a syllable is written with certain final consonant letters, it has the "glottal tone", which we believe is a final /t/. Unstressed nonfinal syllables, usually called "atonic", are written the same as constricted ones; I hold that they have a phoneme of absence of stress, and write /ă/.

The Burmese sounds [g, z, d ,b, ð] are described as having a gradual onset of voicing. We phonemicize them as clusters of /k, s, t, p, θ/ with the phoneme /'/, here allophonically the onset of voice. The conventional *g, z, d, b* are then /k', s', t', p'/; there is no separate spelling for /θ'/ [ð], but *th* is used.

The symbols for /y, w, h/ as second members of clusters have special combining forms: ယ *ya* > ျ, ရ *ra* > ြ, ဝ *wa* > ွ; ဟ *ha* > ှ. Letters in final position indicating final consonants without a following vowel have a special sign added to them— ် : က *ka*, but က် *-k*. The final letters for all the stop consonants, and for the sibilants, are pronounced as final /t/. The symbols for nasals, and for *l* and sometimes *y*, in final position indicate the vowel nasalization we treat as /n/ (conventionally often written *ng*).

The representation of vowels other than /a/ is complex, involving special vowel signs, "silent" final letters (consonants), and other devices. It is further complicated by the writing of the "tones". However, the general principles of "tone" writing are simple, as has been indicated for /a/. "Low tone" is shown by the "lengthener"; also, it is inherent in syllables ending in final /n/ and is written with various nasal symbols. "High tone" is always marked by the symbol : *-ḥ* = /h/, following any other vowel or "tone" sign, "Constricted tone" is unmarked, or is indicated by a subdot ့, which countermands, as it were, any other "tone" indicator. The final /t/ is indicated by various final consonant letters.

Vowel and "tone" signs are:

ာ or ါ *á* = /a/; –ာ: or ါ: *â* = /ah/; –ာ. or ါ. *à* = /a'/
ို with final nasal (*N*) or stop consonant (*C*) symbols; *ai-* = /ay/-
ော *au* = /aw/
ဲ or no vowel sign and a final *-y*; *e* = /e/
ေ *éi* = /ey/; ေ : *êi* = /eyh/; ေ . *èi* = /ey'/
ိ with final stop or sibilant symbols (*C*); *eiC* = /eyt/
ိ· or ိ with final nasal symbols (*N*); *eiN* = /eyn/
ိ·: or ိN: = /eynh/; ိ : or ိN. = /eyn'/
ော် *ó* = /o/; ော: *ô* = /oh/; ော. *ò* = /o'/

Q̓ *óu* = /ow/; Q̣: *óu* = /owh/; Q̣. *ôu* = /ow'/; ⊆C *ouC* = /owt/
⊆ or ⊆N *óun* = /own/; ⊆·: or ⊆N: *óun* = /ownh/; ⊆·. or ⊆N. *ôun*
    = /own'/
Q̣ *i* = /i/; Q̣: *î* = /ih/; Q̣ ì = /i'/; -C ìC = /it/
-Ɛ *ing* = /in/; Ɛ: *îng* = /inh/; -Ɛ. *ìng* = /in'/
⊆ or ⊆*u* or *ú* = /u'/ or /u/; ⊆: or -⸜: *û* = /uh/
ȫ with final *t* or *w*; *uC* = /ut/
O *w(a)* with final *t* or *w* (or some others) = /ut/
ȫ or ȫN (and also the *w* symbols); *ún* = /un/ etc. for /unh, un'/

The above listing does not include all the rare and irregular spellings, but shows all the usual ways of writing vowels and "tones".

It is interesting to examine how Indic writing was used to show the "tones" in Burmese. The "high tone" ^ = /h/ is inherent in the symbols for the /e/ vowel if not modified. The "constricted tone" ` = /'/ is inherent in the symbols for /ey/ and /u/ if not modified, and also in all unmodified consonant symbols (the vowel being /a/); that is, graphs for short vowels were taken as properly symbolizing /V'/. The "glottal" or "stop tone" -C = /t/ is inherent whenever a final stop or sibilant or affricate is written, the different consonants having different inherent vowels. The "low tone" ' = /V/ is inherent in all other vowel symbols, including those followed by nasal symbols. A special symbol, the subdot, indicates ` = /'/ where necessary to countermand an inherent symbolization. The "high tone" ^ = /h/ is regularly symbolized by ⁝, which is the Indic *visarga* = *ḥ*, and seems to justify our analysis as /h/.

Burmese writing exhibits the adaptation of an alphabet first devised for an Indic language to a Tibeto-Burman language of quite different structure. It solved the problem of "tone" representation in terms of a recognition of the phonemic structure of the language, and without recourse to sememographic devices or "silent" letters of the kind that seem to have developed in Tibet.

___

Writing was brought to Cambodia at about the same time as to Burma—fifth or sixth century A.D. The structure of the Cambodian language (Khmer, of the Mon-Khmer family) seems to be much more like that of an Indic language than is the structure of Burmese, and adapting the Indic writing system presented fewer problems. Modern Cambodian has 12 vowel phonemes, but since the Indic alphabets have always been rather cavalier about writing vowels, writing the Cambodian vowels seems to have been no great problem.

The letters of the Cambodian alphabet, with the conventional Indic type of transliteration, are given below.

The Cambodian Alphabet

ಜ	*a*	ῆ	*ka*	౮	*ṭa*	႘	*pa*	ಕ	*śa*
ಜා	*ā*	೨	*kha*	೪	*ṭha*	౪	*pha*	೪	*ṣa*
೮	*i*	೬	*ga*	೩	*ḍa*	౧	*ba*	೪	*sa*
೩	*ī*	೪೮	*gha*	೪ಟ	*ḍha*	೫	*bha*	೫೧	*ha*
೪	*u*	೦	*ña*	೪ೲ	*ṇa*	೪	*ma*	೫	*ḷa*
೪	*ū*	೮	*ca*	೫	*ta*	೪೪	*ya*		
೪	*e*	೪	*cha*	೪	*tha*	೪	*ra*		
೪ೲ	*ai*	೫	*ja*	೪	*da*	೪೪	*la*		
೪೪	*o*	೪೪೪	*jha*	೪೪	*dha*	೪	*va*		
೫೪	*au*	೧೪೪	*ña*	೪	*na*				

...ʃ	...	....	...	...	๒ʒ...	...ʃ	...
ā	*i*	*ī*	*u*	*ū*	*e*	*o*	*ṁ*

೨	๒	๓	๔	๕	๖	๗	๘	๙	๐
1	2	3	4	5	6	7	8	9	0

The letters for retroflex sounds—*ṭ, ṭh, ḍ, ḍh, ṇ, ṣ*—seem to be used only in writing Indic loanwords, and do not represent separate phonemes in either the older or the modern Cambodian language. The vowel symbols have been adapted to the non-Indic vowel system by writing sequences of vowels and by using *y* and *v* (/w/) in sequence with vowel symbols.

The Indic alphabet came to Siam (Thailand) by way of Cambodia. The Siamese alphabet has forms that resemble those used in Cambodian, but are somewhat more cursive. They are supposed to have been devised by King Ramkhamhaeng, and the first record of them is an inscription of this king assigned to 1283 A.D. The modern Siamese forms are directly descended from those of the thirteenth century, with minor changes; the system used in Laos is merely a slight stylistic variant of the Siamese one.

The alphabet given below is first transliterated by a simplified version of a system devised in Siam in 1940; this simplified version is now being used by the Siamese government. It omits diacritical marks and writes æ and œ as *ae* and *oe*. Siamese spelling of names and other words of Indic origin is conventional and traditional, and does not correspond to the modern pronunciation. The Latin-letter forms of these names often vary between transliteration and transcription, and sometimes show a mixture of the two. The origin of the Siamese letters is shown (or suggested, in doubtful cases) by trans-literation symbols of the Indic type in parentheses.

In the Siamese alphabet the order of the letters is, beginning with *ka*, that of the devanagari, with new letters inserted in places that usually show their provenience. Siamese being a language with tones, it was necessary to find a way of representing them. Since there were a larger number of consonant letters than was needed for the consonant phonemes, the extra letters (including some that seem to have been invented for this very purpose) were used to show tones. The letters are divided into three classes —high, middle, low. All middle and low consonants inherently denote middle tone, and high consonants denote rising tone. Because the basic names of the letters are all /Cɔh/, and because many letters represent the same

The Siamese Alphabet

THE CONSONANT SYMBOLS

Siamese letter	Indic trans-literation	Other transliterations (see text)	Tone class	Phonemic value (see table of Siamese tones)
ก	*ka*	*k-, -k* [*k*]	middle	/k-, -k/
ข	*kha*	*kh-, -k* [*kh*]	high	/kh-, -k/
ฃ	modified *kha*	*kh-, -k* [*kh'*]	high	obsolete; replaced by [*kh*]
ค	*ga*	*kh-, -k* [*k'*]	low	/kh-, -k/
ฅ	modified *ga*	*kh-, -k* [*k''*]	low	obsolete; replaced by [*kh*]
ฆ	*gha*	*kh-, -k* [*k'h*]	low	/kh-, -k/
ง	*ña*	*ng* [*ng*]	low	/n/
จ	*ca*	*ch-, -t* [*c*]	middle	/ty-, -t/
ฉ	*cha*	*ch-, -t* [*ch*]	high	/thy-, -t/
ช	*ja*	*ch-, -t* [*c'*]	low	/thy-, -t/
ซ	modified *ja*	*s-, -t* [*s'*]	low	/s-, -t/
ฌ	*jha*	*ch-, -t* [*c'h*]	low	/thy-, -t/
ญ	*ña*	*y-, -n* [ny]	low	/y-, -n/
ฎ	*ṭa*	*d-, -t* [*ḍ*]	middle	in Sanskrit and Pali words /t', t/
ฏ	modified *ṭa*	*t-, -t* [*ṭ*]	middle	in Sanskrit and Pali words /t/

The Siamese Alphabet (continued)

THE CONSONANT SYMBOLS

Siamese letter	Indic transliteration	Other transliterations (see text)	Tone class	Phonemic value (see table of Siamese tones)
ฐ	ṭha	th-, -t [ṭh]	high	in Sanskrit and Pali words /th, t/
ฑ	ḍa	th-, -t [ṭ']	low	in Sanskrit and Pali words /th, t/
ฒ	ḍha	th-, -t [ṭ'h]	low	in Sanskrit and Pali words /th, t/
ณ	ṇa	n [ṇ)	low	in Sanskrit and Pali words /n/
ด	ta	d-, -t [d]	middle	/t'-, -t/
ต	modified ta	t-, -t [t]	middle	/t-, -t/
ถ	tha	th-, -t [th]	high	/th-, -t/
ท	da	th-, -t [t']	low	/th-, -t/
ธ	dha	th-, -t [t'h]	low	/th-, -t/
น	na	n [n]	low	/n/
บ	pa	b-, -p [b]	middle	/p'-, -p/
ป	modified pa	p-, -p [p]	middle	/p-, -p/
ผ	pha	ph-, -p [ph]	high	/ph-, -p/
ฝ	modified pha	f-, -p [f]	high	/f-, -p/
พ	ba	ph-, -p [p']	low	/ph-, -p/
ฟ	modified ba	f-, -p [f']	low	/f-, -p/
ภ	bha	ph-, -p [p'']	low	/ph-, -p/
ม	ma	m [m]	low	/m/
ย	ya	y-, -(omitted) [y]	low	/y/
ร	ra	r-, -n [r]	low	/r-, -n/
ล	la	l-, -n [l]	low	/l-, -n/
ว	va	w-, -(omitted) [w]	low	/w/
ศ	ṣa	s-, -t [ṣ]	high	/s-, -t/
ษ	śa	s-, -t [ś]	high	/s-, -t/
ส	sa	s-, -t [s]	high	/s-, -t/
ห	?	h-, -(omitted) [h]	high	/h/
ฬ	?	l-, -n [ḷ]	low	/l-, -n/
อ	'a	'- [']	middle	/'/
ฮ	ha	h-, -(omitted) [h]	low	/h/

The Siamese Alphabet

THE VOWEL SYMBOLS*

Siamese letter	*Indic trans-literation*	*Other transliterations (see text)*	*Phonemic value (see table of Siamese tones)*
··ะ, ·ั··	..*ḥ*, ?	*a* [*a*:, *a*]	/a', a/
··า	..$^{-}$	*a* [*a*$^{-}$]	/ah/
·ิ·	..*e*	*i* [*i*]	/i'/
·ี·	..*ai*	*i* [*ī*]	/iy/
·ึ·	modified *e*	*u* [*i*]	/ɨ'/
·ือ·ื·	modified *e*..'*a*; modified *e*	*u* [*ï*', *ï*]	/ɨy/
·ุ·	..u	*u* [*u*]	/u'/
·ู·	..ū	*u* [*ū*]	/uw/
เ··ะ, เ·็·	^{i}*ḥ*, ^{i}..?	*e* [*e*:, *ĕ*]	/e', e/
เ··	^{i}	*e* [*e*]	/ey/
แ··ะ, แ·็	^{ii}..*ḥ*, ^{ii}..?	*ae* (*æ*:, *æ̆*]	/æ', æ/
แ··	^{ii}..	*ae* [*æ*]	/æh/
โ··ะ, —	?..*ḥ*, nothing	*o* [o:, °]	/o', o/
โ··	?..	*o* [*o*]	
เ··าะ	^{i}..$^{-}$*ḥ*	*o* [*e*$^{-}$:]	/ɔ', ɔ/
เ··อ	^{i}..'*a*	*o* [e']	/ɔh/
เ·ั·วะ, ··ว	^{i}..?*wḥ*,..*w*	*ua* [eaw:, °w]	/uh/
·ั·ว	..?*w*	*ua* [aw]	/uwh/
เ··ียะ	^{i}*eyḥ*	*ia* [eīy:]	/ih/
เ··ีย	^{i}*ey*	*ia* [*eīy*]	/iyh/
เ··ือะ	^{i}*e'aḥ*	*ua* [*eï*':]	/ɨh/
เ··ือ	^{i}*e'a*	*ua* [*eï*']	/ɨyh/
เ··อะ	^{i}..'*aḥ*	*oe* [*e*':]	/ə', ə/
เ··อ, เ··ิ	^{i}..'*a*, ^{i}..*e*	*oe* [*e*', *ei*]	/əh/
—ำ	..ṁ$^{-}$	*am* [*a*$^{m-}$]	/an/
ใ··	?	*ai* [*ay*]	/ay/
ไ··	?	*ai* [*aý*]	/ay/
เ··า	^{i}..$^{-}$	*au* [*e*$^{-}$]	/aw/

* Where two vowel symbols are given in the first column, the second symbol is before a final consonant.

sound as one or more other letters, the letters have been given additional names which are words spelled with the letter: *khŏh khày* 'kh egg', *khɔh khwahy* 'kh water buffalo', *khɔh rákhan* 'kh bell' (as if *c* were called "k cat", *k* "k kill", and *q* "k quick").

In the table "The Siamese Alphabet" the Siamese letter is followed by the Indic transliteration (historical); then by the official simplified form of transliteration, and the exact transliteration in brackets; then by its designation in one of the three tone classes, and then by indications of its phonemic value. The names of the letters are not given here (see References and Notes—Haas).

The detail of the complicated system of vowel writing suggests that the "long vowels" and "diphthongs" were formerly different in phonemic makeup from what they are now (or at least partially different). It should be noted that certain other sequences of a vowel with one or two semivowels also occur phonemically: these are written with the vowel symbols—short or long—followed by *y* or *w*; those that occur are: /iw, ew, æw, iyw, eyw, uy, oy, ɔy, əy, uwy, owy, uhy, ihw, ïhy, æhw, ahw, əhy, ahy, ɔhy/.

The tones of Siamese are low /ˋ/, falling /ˆ/, high /ˊ/, rising /ˇ/, middle /=/ (they also occur as single tones—low /ˋ/, high /ˊ/, middle /⁻/—on certain short vowels). The tones are indicated by writing the tone symbols ı ๒ ๓ ๔ (which are forms of the numerals 1, 2, 3, 4—see table of Siamese tones), and omitting a symbol, and the value of the symbols depends on the type of initial consonant and the kind of syllable. The two kinds of syllables are "live"—those ending in a "long vowel" or a "vowel cluster" (/ih, ïh, ûh/), or in /y, w, m, n, ŋ/; and "dead"—those with final short vowels, i.e., /Vˀ/, or with short vowels and /p, t, k/.

Siamese Tones

Symbol	Middle consonant		High consonant		Low consonant		
	Live	Dead	Live	Dead	Live	Dead, short	Dead, long
ı	low /ˋ/	does not occur	low /ˋ/	—	falling /ˆ/	falling /ˆ/	—
๒	falling /ˆ/	falling /ˆ/	falling /ˆ/	falling /ˆ/	high /ˊ/	—	high /ˊ/
๓	high /ˊ/	high /ˊ/	—	—	—	—	—
๔	rising /ˇ/	rising /ˇ/	—	—	—	—	—
none	middle /=/	low /ˋ/	rising /ˇ/	low /ˋ/	middle /=/	high /ˊ/	falling /ˆ/

In addition to the complexity of representation of the consonants, vowels, and tones, Siamese also has many traditional spellings of Sanskrit and Pali loanwords; these constitute irregularities in the spelling system. Siamese is an example of a writing system which is carefully contrived to represent most of the phonemic structures of the language, but which does it in rather complicated and inefficient ways.

The forms of the numerals in Siamese are:

๑	๒	๓	๔	๕	๖	๗	๘	๙	๐
1	2	3	4	5	6	7	8	9	0

The Western forms of the numerals are now sometimes used in books and especially in school mathematics.

It is customary in writing and printing Siamese to run words together (as in Sanskrit), and to leave spaces only at the ends of clauses and sentences. Spaces also have some other uses, and some punctuation marks other than spaces are used.

8.5. SPECIAL ALPHABETS

8.50. All alphabets are intended to represent the phonological systems of languages in some way, but, because of their history and the presence of other kinds of written symbols, there is no ordinary alphabet in existence that represents only the phonology and does so with exactness in terms of the phonemic system. Sometimes allophones are written, some phonemes are omitted because of inadequate analyses, some morphophonic relations are shown and others are ignored, and here and there sememographic and logographic symbols are used.

Whenever a writing system, especially an alphabet, is adapted to a new language, there is phonological examination of that language, and if new symbols are devised, the new system becomes what is often called a "phonetic alphabet". Even before modern linguistics developed, special "phonetic" symbols were provided for the description of new sounds. Instances of such symbols have been mentioned in Chapter 7 and previously in this chapter.

In the nineteenth century "universal phonetic alphabets" began to be invented. Many have been devised since, and all are very much alike in general principles: new symbols are added by modifying old ones by means of added hooks or lines or crossbars, or by elongation or distortion of some part of the symbol; letters are taken from other alphabets; diacritics are used for further differentiation.

To aid the reader in interpreting phonetic transcriptions in systems other than the one used in this book (see Chapter 2, especially 2.23), we present some descriptions or statements of various systems, and indicate how the symbols may be compared with ours. The comparison is thorough for the alphabet of the International Phonetic Association (IPA) and for the Americanist system first compiled by Sapir in 1916.

One of the earliest phonetic alphabets of modern times was devised by Richard Lepsius (1810–84), who was a German Egyptologist and Africanist. Lepsius used diacritical marks widely. His vowel symbols were *a, e, i, o, u* modified as follows:

ā long, *ă* short, *ẹ* (that is, a letter with a line under it) "open" vowel, *e̦* "close" vowel, *ã* nasalized, *o̦, u̦* front rounded; *i̦, e̦* central or back unrounded; *g̦* indefinite vowel. Our equivalents would be, respectively, a:, a or ă or a˘, ɛ or ɛ (and other special symbols), e, ą, ø, ʉ, ɨ or ï, ë, ə.

Special consonant and other symbols were, with our equivalents (where different) in brackets:

ʒ [ɋ], *k̃* [ȼ], *č, ṭ, kh* [k'], ' [ʔ], *g̃* [ɟ], *j, ḍ, ḏ* [dₓ], *ṅ* [ŋ], *ń* [ñ], *ṇ, h̃* [ħ], χ [x], *š* [s̩], *ś* [ś], *s̩* [sₓ], *ϑ* [θ], γ, *ž, δ* [ð], *y, w, w̰* [β], *ř* [ʀ], *ɣ* [ɹ], *l'* [ḷ].

Clicks were shown as / [ȼᴬ], / [ṭᴬ], / [ṭᴬ], // [lᴬ], used alone and with following *g* or *ṅ* for voiced or nasalized varieties.

Tones were to be shown thus: high level *a₁*; low level *a_L*; high rising *a¹*; low rising *aᴸ*; high falling *a˅*; low falling *aᴧ*; high "circumflex" *a̬*; low "circumflex" *aᴧ*.

As is evident, the Lepsius system was limited in applicability, and needed much expansion to be widely usable. Carl Meinhof, who worked on the comparative linguistics of Bantu, from the end of the nineteenth century until the 1930s, used Lepsius's alphabet as a base, and expanded it for wider applicability in African studies. Symbols were added, as for voiceless vowels—*a̯*, nonsyllabic vowels—*i̯*, diphthongs—*a͡i, a͡u*; the tone marking was improved—high *a'*, low *a̗*, and others in this iconic fashion; *á* and *à* were used for primary and secondary stress; consonant releases were explicitly marked—glottalized *p'*, voiceless lenis *b̥*, unreleased *t̰*; clicks were shown by a triangle attached to the top of such letters as *t, l*.

In 1907 the journal *Anthropos* published an alphabet designed for wide anthropological use; this was devised largely by Father Wilhelm Schmidt, and has been added to over the years. This alphabet was essentially the Lepsius-Meinhof usage somewhat more systematically applied. All these alphabets, which differ little among themselves and have been used in various European linguistic specialty areas, with modifications and additions as necessary, go in strongly for complex arrays of diacritics. They are hard to write, harder to type, impossible to print until special pieces of type are prepared. In the course of time, many European printing houses, and some in the United States, have acquired many of the special types, but the inherently unsystematic nature of the alphabets, and of the devising and adding of new symbols, has not made these systems popular except in the highly specialized fields they started in.

On the other hand, the IPA system was explicitly aimed at the widest possible use, its symbols were carefully designed, type for printing and typewriting has been provided as new symbols were invented, and the alphabet has become well known in language-teaching work and in European (including British) linguistic work. We compare its symbols with ours (many of ours being simply the IPA symbols) in terms of vowels, consonants, and diacritics.

Vowel (and Semivowel) Symbols

TRAGER						IPA					
i	ʉ	ɨ	ʉ	ɯ	u	i	y	ɨ	ʉ	ɯ	u
I	ʊ	ɪ	ʊ	ʮ	U	I, ʟ	Y	ɪ	ʊ	—	U, ɷ
e	ø	ə	ɵ	ɤ	o	e	ø	—	ɵ	ɤ	o
E	Œ	ə	ʚ	∆	Ω	—	—	ə	—	—	—
ɛ	œ	ɜ	ɞ	ʌ	ɔ	ɛ	œ	ɜ	—	ʌ	ɔ
æ	ɶ	ⱱ	ɷ	Λ	ɯ	æ	—	ɐ	—	—	—
Æ	ɒ	a	ɐ	ɑ	ɒ	a	—	—	—	ɑ	ɒ
y	ɥ	ɣ	ʍ	ɥ	w	j	ɥ	—	—	—	w

The basic vertical division of the IPA vowels is into six areas, though the presence of ə implies a seventh. Diacritics are available for the blank spaces.

Consonant Symbols

TRAGER

IPA

The IPA consonants are not classified exactly the same as ours, but the two systems fit together rather well in most particulars. Additional symbols in IPA are: palatalized ţ ḑ ŋ = our t_y d_y n_y; ʤ = our ś ź or š̌ ž̌ ; g for our g when ɡ is used for our q; velarized ł ᵗ đ ȿ ᵹ = our l_x t_x d_x s_x z_x; p' t' etc. for glottalized as in our system; ɓ ɗ = our b" d"; ơợ = our s_w z_w; ʔʒ = our š_w ž_w; "flapped l" ɹ = l¹; clicks ʇ = tᴬ, ʖ = lᴬ, ʗ = tᴬ, ʞ = kᴬ; e̩ ɛ̩ etc. = our e_ɪ, ɛ_ɪ, etc.; ʍ = w.

The IPA diacritical marks, with ours following the equal-sign, are: ~ = ̫; ◦ = ∧; v = v; ̈ = ̈; . = ̩; ̜ = ̫; + = <; – = >; ∩ = ̫; ω = w; ɔ more rounded = _w; ͻ less rounded = ̫; :, ·, �‿ degrees of length; n̩ = ņ; ̩ medium stress; ā, a̲ high and low level tone; á, a̗ high and low rising tone; à, a̗ high and low falling tone; â rising-falling tone; ǎ falling-rising tone.

In general keeping with the usages of the IPA, a conference held in Copenhagen in 1925 reached agreement on the use especially of certain diacritical marks, and certain symbols about which there had been disagreement between systems. The outstanding conclusions of the conference may be listed thus:

long vowels [a·], half-long [a.], overlong [a··];
strong stress ['a], medial stress [ˌa], extra-strong stress ["a];
tones—level [̄], rising ['], falling [ˋ], over vowel symbols, or at
     different heights before them, as ['a, ˈa, ˌa], etc.;
syllabic consonant [n̩], nonsyllabic vowel [i̯];
voicelessness of voiced consonant [n̥], voicing of voiceless consonant
     [h̬] or [ḥ];
nasalization [a̰];
overrounding [a̫]; underrounding [a̫];
dental [t̪]; retroflex [ţ] or [t̪]; etc.;
palatal [ɟ, ḑ, ȷ, ŋ, ş, ᶾ, ķ, ḡ] = respectively our [ȼ, ɟ, l, ñ, ś, ź, ḵ, ĝ];
shibilants: [š, ž, ş, ᶾ, ȿ, ᶻ] = respectively our [š, ž, ś, ź, ȿ, ż];
spirants: [φ, β, θ, δ, χ, γ]; [ȷ] for our [y] or [ŷ]; [x] for our [x];
velars and postvelars: [ᴋ, ɢ, ɴ, ʀ, ʀ] = respectively our [q, ɢ, ŋ̣, ʀ, ẏ];
glottal sounds: ['] = our [ʔ]; [h] and ['];
r-sounds: [r, r̩, r̂, ř, ɹ, ʀ] = respectively our [r, r̩, r_y, ř, ʀ, ʀ];
affricates: [ts], etc. = our [tˢ], etc.
clicks: [tᴬ];
front rounded vowels [̈], central rounded vowels [˙].

As is seen, many of these modifications of IPA are of the kind that are used in the system preferred in this book.

In various countries, intensive dialect studies have been made and special alphabets have been devised for them. These are usually provided with a wealth of diacritics to show all kinds of details and minor differences of sound.

A German dialect alphabet was published in 1877. Its basic symbols are like those of the IPA, with diacritics like those of the Meinhof and Anthropos systems. Various modifications were published at later dates by groups and individuals (14 such systems are given in our source), but essentially all these systems were alike.

Various systems for recording Romanic dialects have also been in use since the late nineteenth century. French and Swiss dialects, Italian dialects, and Spanish dialects have been the most frequently recorded. The differences between them are slight, and they all use about the same symbols and the same diacritics as the German dialect alphabets.

The recording of modern Slavic dialects has also been done in various phonetic alphabets based on the same principles as the dialect alphabets mentioned just previously. More attention has been paid to symbols for palatalized consonants than was done in Romanic, for instance; and the established Slavic orthographic symbols, such as c [tš], č, š, ž have been used as starting points. Since the 1930s dialect work has been done in the Soviet Union on the varieties of Russian, White Russian, and Ukrainian; the phonetic alphabets were based on Latin letters originally, but there are indications that more recently there have been phonetic alphabets based on Cyrillic. These apparently start with the kinds of modified letters that have been devised for the Cyrillic orthographies of various languages of the Soviet Union, and then add other symbols by means of diacritics of the same type as are used in other phonetic alphabets.

Finno-Ugric languages and dialects have been studied both in Central Europe and in Russia. The usual types of phonetic alphabets have been devised, with the symbols c, ʒ [dᶻ], č, ǯ, š, ž used in the same way as for Slavic. Cyrillic-based alphabets for the study of these languages are now used in the Soviet Union. The various Turkic languages have usually been recorded in very much the same symbols as have been used for Finno-Ugric. An early use of Cyrillic was by Böhtlingk for Yakut (a Turkic language) in 1851.

The various transcriptions used for Chinese and other languages of eastern Asia are often partly phonemic (see 8.52). (For material discussing these languages, see References and Notes).

The Americanist system presented by Sapir in 1916 was based on older American systems of transcription, and on the various European systems in existence at the time. An attempt was made to establish a system with the widest possible coverage. On the whole, it was a highly successful attempt, and Americanists used the system (and still use it) very consistently. It must be pointed out, however, that many of the refinements of detail were never applied in practice. In 1934 Sapir and some of his colleagues suggested certain changes to bring the system more in line, in a few details, with other systems. The changes were adopted by most workers in the field. The system used in this book stems in certain ways from the Americanist system, at the same time that it tries to reconcile itself with the IPA.

In the original Sapir system, the vowel table is based on Sweet, *A primer of phonetics* (Oxford, 1902). The classification involves these dimensions: high, mid, low tongue height; front, central, back tongue position; narrow and wide tension (i.e., tense and lax); and lip rounding or its absence. The system provides 36 basic vowels, and there are 27 symbols and nine blanks. Arranged in terms of our vowel table, in so far as possible, the symbols are given in the table below (Sapir's examples in parentheses).

The consonant system is of the general kind found in other systems, but is expanded and adapted to take care of sounds found in American Indian languages. The basic manners of articulation are: stops, spirants, affricates, nasals, laterals, lateral affricates, trills; stops are subdivided into voiceless, voiced, "intermediate" (= voiceless lenis),

Phonetic Vowel Symbols (Sapir System)*

i (Fr. *fini*)	*ü* (Fr. *lune*)	˙ɩ	*u̇* (Swed. *hus*)	*ï*	*u* (Ger. *gut*)
ɩ (Eng. *bit*)	ü̇ (Ger. *Mütze*)	˙ι	u̇̇	ï̇	ʋ (Eng. *put*)
e (Fr. *été*)	*ö* (Fr. *peu*)	—	*ȯ*	α (Eng. *but*)	*o* (Ger. *so*)
ε (Eng. *men*)	ö̈ (Ger. *Götter*)	—	ɔ̇	*a* (Ger. *Mann*)	ɔ (Ger. *Volk*)
—	ω̈ (Fr. *peur*)	—	ω̇	—	ω (Eng. *law*)
ä (Eng. *man*)	—	*ȧ* (Fr. *patte*)	—	—	—

*The symbol ə is used for an "indeterminate" vowel.

aspirated, glottalized; spirants, affricates, laterals, lateral affricates; trills are voiceless, voiced, and glottalized; nasals are voiceless and voiced. The places of articulation are: bilabial rounded, bilabial unrounded, dentilabial (= labiodental), interdental, linguodental, linguoalveolar, cerebral (= cacuminal), dorsodental, dorsal, dorsopalatal [these last three are hard to identify as real sounds]; c-sounds [c = š, hence shibilants] divided into advanced, central, retracted; advanced palatal (= prevelar), central palatal (= mediovelar), back palatal (= postvelar), glottal, laryngal. Symbols are provided for most of the possible positions formed by the manners and places of articulation as coordinates. Stops are shown by the usual basic symbols p, b, t, d, k, g with diacritics and additions; spirants are shown by f, v, s, z, and other symbols (see below); affricates are shown by stop plus spirant symbols; nasals are basically m, n; laterals are l-symbols; and trills are shown by r-symbols; Greek letters are freely used.

The table of consonants begins thus:

$p_\text{w} \quad b_\text{w} \quad B_\text{w} \quad p'_\text{w} \quad p'_\text{w} \sim p_\text{w}! \quad h \; w \quad h \sim h! \quad ph \; bw \; ph \sim ph! \quad M_\text{w} \; m_\text{w}$

$p \quad b \quad B \quad p' \quad p' \sim p! \quad \varphi \; \beta \quad \dot\varphi \sim \varphi! \quad p\varphi \; b\beta \; \dot{p}\varphi \sim p\varphi! \quad M \quad m$

Dentilabials are: $f, v, f' \sim f!, pf, bv, \dot{p}f \sim pf!$; interdentals θ, ϑ [= ð], $\theta' \sim \theta!, t\theta, d\vartheta, t\theta' \sim t\theta!$

The lingual and cerebral basic symbols are $t, d, D, s, z, N, n, l \sim L, l, R, r$. Linguodentals are $\underset{\cdot}{t}, \underset{\cdot}{d}$, etc.; linguoalveolars are the unmodified symbols; cerebrals are $\underset{\cdot}{t}, \underset{\cdot}{d}$, etc.

The "dorsal" sounds are shown by $\tau, \delta, \Delta, \sigma, \mathfrak{z}, \nu, \nu, \Lambda, \lambda$, modified as are t, d, etc.

The shibilants are shown by c, j (also with $_\land$ and .) for our š, ž; $tc = \check{c}, dj = \check{\jmath}$; there are also stop symbols in this position—$\tau y, ty, \underset{\cdot}{t}y$, etc., but these were given in parentheses in the table, and have had little actual use. Nasals and laterals in this place of articulation are shown by devices analogous to those for stops: Ny, ny, ly, ly, and $\nu y, \nu y, \Lambda y, \lambda y$.

Back consonants are k, g, G, χ or x, γ, P, ρ, with $_\land$ and ., etc.

In the 1934 revision, $\check{s}, \check{z}, c, \mathfrak{z}, \check{c}, \check{\mathfrak{z}}$ (or $\check{\jmath}$), λ, λ were substituted for $c, j, ts, dz, tc, dj, tl, dl$ respectively.

As is evident, the system used in this book can be considered a further systematization (and simplification) of the Sapir system.

8.51. To supply the reader of this book with a readily accessible list of symbols, including diacritics, available for use in phonemic alphabets, a compilation of all symbols printed in the book and

others found to exist in various type fonts is given below. The
symbols given are roman, but italic equivalents exist for most.

Symbols Available for Phonetic Alphabets

a ɑ ᴀ ɐ ᴅ ɤ æ Æ ɷ ᴀᴏ a á â à ă ä ã ą ȧ å ӥ ᴩ ӕ ӓ
b ɓ ʙ β ƀ б ь ḅ
c ç ȼ ȼ ɕ ɔ ɘ ċ č ḍ ç ç ɔ̇ ɔ̈ ч ц
d ɖ ᴅ ð ɖ ɖ ɖ ɖ ḍ ɔ̣ ᴀ
e ᴇ ɛ ɘ ɘ з é ế ë ẽ é ê ě ë ẽ ȩ ė ḗ ɛ̌ э ɛ
f ɸ ɟ Φ
g ɡ ɢ ĝ ǧ ɣ ŷ ẏ ʏ ʏ г ғ
h ʜ ḥ ḥ ḥ ʰ н ħ ʰ ʜ ꜧ
i ɪ ɩ ь ị ï ï ɨ ɨ и й ы
j ǰ ᴊ ɟ ɟ̂ ĵ ʮ
k ᴋ ʞ ḳ ḳ
l ɫ ʟ ḷ ʟ ʟ ᴊ ᴊ ʎ ᴋ λ ʎ̣ ɭ л љ
m ɱ ᴍ ṃ
n ᴨ ɳ ŋ ń ñ ἡ ɲ̂ ɲ ɴ њ ν
o Ω ɔ ø Œ œ ω ɯ ö ɔ̈ Ω̈ ɔ̇ ῶ ⊖ Ω̇ ó ô ò ŏ ǫ ♂
p ᴩ ṗ п π
q ǫ ♀ ϙ
ɾ ғ ɹ ʅ ρ ʀ ʁ я я
s ᵴ ʂ ᵴ ʂ ś š ṡ ṣ ṣ ʃ ш щ
t ᴛ θ ϑ ʈ ṭ ɟ ⱦ ϑ
u ᴜ ʉ ʉ ü ü ú ů ɯ ᴙ ъ ю
v ʋ ᴠ ʌ
w ᴡ w ᴡ ẅ ẇ ẘ ц
x ẋ x̧ x̣ x̣ ẋ x̌ x̌ χ ξ ψ
y ÿ ʏ ʮ y̧ ʏ
z ᵶ ᴢ ȝ ź ž ᴢ ż ż ζ ж

8.52. The adaptation of existing alphabets and the invention of
new alphabets have always had as their purpose the rendering of

the language in such a form that the reader is able to reproduce the words and phrases in their proper phonological form. Syllabaries and logographic writing systems were also based on phonological considerations. Only the modern "universal" phonetic alphabets were intended for the representation of other than the phonemic structures of languages.

As has been seen in the discussions (in the various chapters of this book) of the ways in which languages are written in their regular orthographies, and in the discussion (in Chapter 7 and in the present chapter) of writing systems and specifically of alphabets, the phonemic systems of languages are rarely represented with anything approaching completeness, or with consistent and complete regularity. Consonants are most often adequately shown, vowels are well indicated in many systems, though not necessarily with full accuracy, length and accents of various kinds are most often poorly indicated or not shown at all, and transitions and intonation patterns (or their analogs) are rarely indicated in any consistent way. All writing systems, including alphabetic ones, also show other than phonological structure: words or other morpheme units or sequences are usually indicated, homophonous items are often differentiated in spelling, styles of discourse and the nature of material as actually spoken or not are often shown, special devices like capital letters are used for special meanings, logograms—numerals and the like—are common, and even paralanguage is sometimes written.

In the light of all this, the use of an alphabet to represent the phonemic system of a language is not the only problem involved in devising or applying a writing system. Considerations of all kinds of other cultural factors must be held in mind. For languages that are sociologically or politically or otherwise subordinate to other languages, the transition from literacy in the subordinate language to literacy in the superordinate language must be considered. The writing of loanwords, the use of traditional punctuation, the retention of common logograms (numerals and others), the "logic" of paragraphing and italicizing and other special devices—all must be held in mind in devising a writing system.

In a country like Mexico, the writing of an Indian language must conform to Spanish writing habits. This necessity has been proved many times: a phonemic orthography using *k* and omitting *c* and *qu* has been rejected, or a spelling with many accent marks (for tones) has proved "difficult". An Aztec orthography using *qu* before *e* and *i*, and *c* elsewhere for /k/, writing *ts*, *ch*, *tl*, *cu* for /c, č, λ, kw/ respectively, and denoting /w/ by *hu* or *u*, is much preferable to one in which the phonemic symbols are used. In writing Maya, the traditional use of *c* for /k/ (with the use of *qu* before *e, i* if desired) and of *k* for /q/, is preferable to the use of *k* and *q*. In writing a tone language, devices that restrict the number of diacritics on a page are desirable; examples of such restrictions could be found in our sources, but the analyses on which they are based are incomplete (for one thing, transitions are not analyzed), and there is not enough experience to show whether the systems work with native-speaking learners.

In the Soviet Union it was found that new Latin-letter orthographies were not successful; Cyrillic was substituted in the late 1930s. These replacing systems were so devised as to retain Russian loanwords with a minimum of change. The use of new letters and of diacritics was also restricted, especially in the more recent systems. Latin-letter orthographies have been retained where they have been long established, as in the Baltic republics.

The only widespread attempt to foster a native spelling system in the United States in recent times has been made for Navaho. During the Second World War, and after, Navahos were taught to read their own language and were then taught English. A few concessions to English spelling habits were made (*sh* for /š/, *ch* for /č/), but otherwise the writing was phonemic. The Indian schools taught basic literacy in this system also. There have been no studies of its effectiveness, however, and very little effort is made to continue use of the system. The reasons for apparent failure here are probably almost entirely outside of the system or the Navaho language; they stem from improperly trained teachers, the lack of any reading material in Navaho, and the overwhelming pressure of the dominant English-speaking culture.

As an example of what would have to be done to provide a phonemically accurate yet sociologically acceptable writing system, we shall imagine that the English-speaking peoples reach the high level of general education necessary to make them receptive to some kind of changes in English spelling. Such a situation is not foreseeable, so the following can be read as a kind of science fiction.

For the consonant phonemes the following system could be used: *p, t, k, b, d, g, c* (or *ch*) /č/, *j, f, th* /θ/, *s, sh* /š/, *v, dh* /ð/, *z, zh* /ž/, *m, n, ng* /ŋ/, *l, r, w, y, h*. The only problem here would be whether to write *ng* before *k*—*thingk* or *think*—and how to write words with /ŋg/— *fingg'r* for present *finger*?

The vowel phonemes are harder to decide on: *i, e, u* in *pit, pet, put* are simple, but how to write present *cat, cut, cot*? If we decide on *a* for /æ/, then we need *u* for /ə/, and have to change the spelling of *put*; if we use *ae* for /æ/, and *a* for /ə/, items like *cat* and *cut* become *kaet* and *kat*, and present-day habits are seriously disturbed. And then what about *cot*? Writing *kot* will do, because we shall have to use a cross-dialectal spelling in any case. What about the vowels /ɨ/ and /o/, and /a/ in recent loans where it might not be American /a/ varying with British /ɔ/? The solutions could be: write *i'* for /ɨ/ initially or after another vowel, otherwise simply '; write *o'* for /o/ in weak syllables (*o* in *obey*, which would become *o'bey*), otherwise write cross-dialectically with *ow*; write *aa* in foreign words for /a/. Already for the basic vowels, questions of dialect difference have presented themselves.

For the complex nuclei, a number must be selected as standard, and the others excluded or provided for only in dialect writing or other special cases. Suppose we take as our base the Eastern American and Southern British standard pronunciations of the words *bee, bay, buy, boy, who, how, hoe, law, spa, beer, bare, bar, bore, boor, burr* (the items with *r* will have to be written in terms of dialects that "pronounce r", i.e., have terminal retroflexion). These words could then be respelled thus: *biy, bey, bay, boy, huw, haw, how, loh, spah, bihr, behr, bahr, bohr, buhr b'r* respectively; except for *bey, boy, spah*, and possibly *bahr* and *bohr*, these do grave violence to existing habits.

The writing of compounds would present the gravest of problems. If a hyphen is suggested for /+/, and we write *buk-keys* for *bookcase*, should we write *ays-kriym* or *ays kriym* for *ice cream*? And how about *high school*—should it become *hay skuwl* or *hay-skuwl* or *hayskuwl*?

Short of using stress marks in a completely phonemic manner, no easily learned system of marking stresses could be devised. And what about the changes of stress in sentences?

As for terminals and pitches, no feasible improvement of present punctuation would be good enough to bother about.

All the uses of capitals, indentations, spacing, italics, boldface, small capitals, would have to be retained, as well as differences in size and style of type.

The considerations set forth above indicate that there is considerable room for real inventions in the realm of writing systems, and that any reform of spelling is not simply a matter of systematizing the graphic representation of segmental phonemes. It has been suggested—perhaps not seriously—that if the teaching of spelling were stopped, orthography would reform itself.

The author of this book has experimented for years—as a leisure-time activity—with possible spelling-reform systems for English. The more he has learned about literate cultures in general, and about the culture of English-speakers in particular, the more he has become convinced that no such reform would be acceptable. Only a collective act of will, intellectually prepared for and emotionally acquiesced in, an act comparable to a mass "conversion"—and thus a basic change in the culture—could bring about such a change. Of course, the English-speaking community numbers over 250 million; but a community of 50,000 would apparently have just as much trouble.

For the reader who is skeptical of the conclusion, the preceding paragraph is transcribed into the full form of the system suggested in the preceding paragraphs. The author's own idiolect is used as a base, and all kinds of special devices for cross-dialectal spellings and individual variations are included.

Dhi ohth'r av dhis buk haez i'ks-periment'd f'r yihrz—aez a liyzh'r-taym aektivitiy—widh posib'l speling-ri-fohrm sist'mz for Ingglish. Dha mohr hiy haez l'rnd a-bawt lit'r't kalc'rz in jen'ral, aend a-bawt dha kalc'r av Ingglish-spiyk'rz in partikyul'r, dha mohr hiy haez bi-kam kan-vinst dhat now sac ri-fohrm wud biy ak-septib'l. Ownliy a kalektiv aekt av wil, in-t'lekcuwaliy priy-pehrd-fohr aend iymowshanaliy aekwiyest-in, an aekt komparab'l tuw a maehs "kan-v'rzhan"—aend dhas a beysik ceynj in dha kalc'r—kud bring a-bawt sac a ceynj. Av kohrs, dhi Ingglish-spiyking kamiwnitiy namb'rz owv'r tuw-handr'd aend fiftiy milyan; bat a kamiwnitiy av fiftiy-thawzand wud a-paer'nt-liy haev j'st aez mac trab'l.

The crusading spelling reformer is probably only angered by such a demonstration. But the teacher of reading, the ordinary literate person, the believer in the uses of applied science, the nondoctrinaire social scientist—and anyone else for that matter—should give it much thought.

A language, a spelling system, an alphabet, even a specific homophonous pair like *meet* and *meat*, all are items in a vast cultural complex. No change in any part can avoid bringing about change elsewhere. Any change in any part of a culture CAN be willed and CAN be brought about, but the cultural price must be known and must be willingly paid. The ANTHROPOLOGY of spelling reform is as yet an almost completely unexplored field.

CONCLUSION

Chapter 9

LANGUAGE
AND SOCIETY

9.0. LITERARY, RELIGIOUS, AND OFFICIAL LANGUAGES

9.00. In the ancient world in which Western culture originated there were several languages which were literary languages, in the sense that some dialect in which one or more important works of literature were composed came to be used for literary purposes by speakers of other dialects. The literary language came to include material from the other dialects, and thus became a language that, in its totality, was not the native spoken dialect of anyone. Such a literary language tended to preserve its forms against change: and when it was written down this tendency increased, so that with time the language might become rather different from any real spoken language.

Examples of ancient literary languages are several of the Greek dialects, and finally Classical Greek in the form called *koinế*, 'the common [= uniform, used in common] one'. Classical Latin (8.12) is another ancient literary language.

In the Near East in ancient times there were a number of languages in which literature was composed, but these were originally religious languages, and will be mentioned in the next section (9.01). The same is true of India and south Asia as a whole.

In China a literary language developed and was written down over 2,000 years ago, and has persisted in its written form to this day.

Classical Greek, Classical Latin, and written Chinese developed in societies in which no single text or set of texts of a religious nature was of sufficient importance to impose its language as the model. It was rather a succession of literary works that set the standard. Literary Greek started with the Homeric poems, included some literary efforts in other dialects, and finally settled on a compromise between prominent local dialects as the literary standard. Literary

313

Latin started with literary works at a time when Rome was expanding its political power, and grew with the growing empire. Literary Chinese probably began as the written form of some dialects that were close to each other and came to be written in a more or less uniform manner thereafter.

There were undoubtedly some other literary languages in the ancient world. But most of the languages used for literary purposes started as religious languages, which will now be considered.

9.01. In many societies religious rituals and other materials are recited and memorized in such a way that their language persists relatively unchanged over long periods. When writing is introduced, the form of the language used for religious purposes becomes fixed. If the literary works that are produced ·stem from the religious material, the religious language becomes a literary language. In such cases, its development and change are usually controlled (*hampered* might be a better word) by the conservativeness of the religious tradition. Literary languages that started as religious languages often exhibit a considerable difference from any spoken language used by the society.

In ancient Egypt the language that was recorded when writing was invented was a religious language. It remained such for a long time, and when literary and technical and practical matters were written, at a later date, they were to a large extent still couched in the style of the religious language.

In Sumer the first written documents were religious texts. The language continued to be used for some 2,000 years with comparatively little change, and then, when there finally were no more native speakers left, it was still used as a religious language by people who spoke languages that were completely unrelated to it. This phenomenon—the use of a religious language that is not closely or at all related to the spoken language of a group—has also taken place elsewhere.

In India, Vedic Sanskrit became an unwritten religious language, and continued in use in this way for centuries. Then writing was introduced, and the religious language thenceforth remained fixed and immutable. As literary and other uses of Sanskrit developed, there arose some modifications in the language, but Sanskrit remained essentially the same, and remains so to the present. Later Pali, a Prakrit (a language less controlled than Sanskrit, and less archaic), was set up as the religious language of Buddhism, and as such spread far outside of India, to peoples of other languages, such as Burmese, Thai, Cambodian, and others. A very special religious language that developed in India has been called by Western scholars Buddhist Hybrid Sanskrit; the writers of this language, speakers of Middle Indic dialects, probably felt that they were writing Sanskrit, but adapted it to various popular usages; this language was really quite artificial, and yet in essence not much more so than other special styles that have become religious languages.

Hebrew became the religious language of the ancient Jews, and gradually ceased to be an ordinary spoken language. The spoken language was Aramaic, and Hebrew continued in use as a fixed and unchangeable religious language, with few if any other uses. As the Jews spread out of Palestine, they took Hebrew with them as their religious language, though in all cases they spoke the language of the country they lived in. Though fixed in its written form, Hebrew nevertheless changed its pronunciation in keeping with the phonological changes of whatever language was being spoken; these changes were most marked in the Hebrew used by speakers of Yiddish in central and eastern Europe in the period since the Middle Ages. When Hebrew was revived as a modern secular language, it was given a new phonology partly based on the traditional pronunciation before the changes set in. It is now an artificially restored language, with a partly artificial structure (modeled after the languages of western Europe), and is an official language (see 9.03). In religious usage, however, the traditional forms persist, and even the older phonology is retained in part.

When the Koran was written, the Arabic dialect of Mecca became a religious language. This Classical Arabic persists as a religious language, and is also, in various modified forms, a literary and official language.

The Christian religion began among Greek-speaking Jews, and the literary Greek of the time became the first Christian religious language; in the course of translation from Hebrew of various sacred texts, and as a result of its use, often by non-Greeks, to write about new ideas, this Christian Greek became a kind of specialized dialect, for which the term Hellenistic Greek is often used. It early began to show some of the changes from the *koinē* that eventuated in Modern Greek.

As Christianity spread, the Bible was translated into many languages, and these became, in the Biblical version, religious languages. There was the Latin of the Vulgate, showing already some of the traits that appeared in Romanic. Then there were the Armenian and Georgian versions in the fifth and sixth centuries, and the Old Church Slavic one in the ninth. The first two did not spread beyond the speakers of the two languages, and thus became literary as well as religious languages. Old Church Slavic, however, became and remains the religious language of the eastern and most of the southern Slavs, as well as of the Rumanians; it never became a literary language, but it influenced the modern Slavic languages.

In western Europe, Latin remained as the religious language, and from this usage there developed various modified forms referred to as Medieval Latin, and which in some instances became literary and even official languages.

After the Protestant Reformation, many European languages were used to translate the Bible. In some cases this was the first written use of the language, and it was thus a religious language. In other cases, a literary language was used for the Bible translation. The King James version of the Bible is in seventeenth-century literary English; its language exhibits some specialization, and has influenced subsequent literary English, but it is essentially a literary, not a religious language. In Germany and Scandinavia the Bible translations were important in fixing and developing the literary languages.

In modern times, since the nineteenth century, missionaries have been translating parts or all of the Bible into hundreds of languages. In every case, whether the translation is well or badly done, the result is a newly created religious language. Most of these religious languages do not even become adopted by the recent converts for whom they are intended; but in some cases they become literary languages, at least for small numbers of people.

9.02. Modern literary languages have in some cases developed directly from various religious languages, as has been indicated above. In other instances, they have come into being alongside of religious languages and under the influence of them to a greater or lesser extent, but have had an independent existence. In still other cases, they are direct (or less direct) descendents of ancient literary languages. Some of the more important ones in the Western World or in the world as a whole will be mentioned here.

After Latin, the first literary languages on the continent in western Europe were the Romanic languages. French literature, in various dialects, dates from the tenth century, and the dialect of Paris began to be the predominant one in the twelfth century. Spanish and Portuguese literatures also began in the tenth century, and eastablished themselves in several dialects; by the fourteenth century central Portuguese and Castilian Spanish were the literary languages. Italian emerges as a literary language from about 1200 on. None of these Romanic languages, with the possible exception of Parisian French, were official languages until much later (see 9.03).

In the British Isles, Irish had become a literary language as early as the fourth century, and it continued as such until English rule was firmly established some eight centuries later. Then Irish ceased to be more than a native language oppressed and suppressed by a colonial overlord. In the 1920s, with the establishment of self-rule in Ireland, the language was revived as an official language, but as a literary language it is little used. In England various dialects of Old English had been used as literary languages from the eighth century, following a literary tradition brought from the continent in the poem *Beowulf*. Then in the tenth century King Alfred established West Saxon as the model for literary usage. English fell into disuse as a literary and official language at the Norman Conquest (1066), and Norman French was the official language (with some considerable literary use) for about 300 years. After this the English of London became the literary as well as official language.

In Germany, east to the present Baltic countries, various Low German, Middle German, and High German dialects were used as literary languages, and also in official documents. With the Reformation the mixed Middle German-High German dialect officially in use in several German states began to be the standard religious, literary, and official language throughout Germany. Over the years, it has become also a spoken language, with social and geographical varieties. In the Low German, Bavarian, and Swiss areas, standard German is still only an official, literary, and religious language for many people.

In the Netherlands various Flemish and Hollandish dialects were used as literary languages in the Middle Ages. Then, after the Reformation, a kind of common Hollandish-Flemish literary language established itself, and became the official and standard Dutch of today. Afrikaans has become a literary language in the last half-century, but Dutch is still a preferred religious language for many Afrikaans speakers.

In Iceland there was literary use of the language from the tenth century, and various forms of Old Norse were written on the continent. Swedish and Danish grew up as literary and official languages with the development of Sweden and Denmark as nations. Swedish was also the language of most literate Finns until the nineteenth century. In Norway, Danish was the official language for some centuries, and became the spoken and literary language of the literate until the creation of a Norwegian literary language in the nineteenth century.

The several Slavic languages now in use all began their existence as literary languages, at various times from the twelfth century (Russian) to the twentieth century (Macedonian). Old Church Slavic was a religious language, but also had some use as a literary language in Bulgaria, and elsewhere in various national recensions as the separate languages of the Eastern and Southern Slavs began to develop.

In Asia the various modern literary languages began their development at various times. Chinese and Japanese go back many centuries; Korean is more recent. The modern languages of India go back in some cases as much as 500 to 700 years, and the same is true of modern Persian.

Modern Arabic as a literary language is a special development of a religious language. Modern Hebrew is a revival of a religious language.

In the Pacific areas, in Africa, and in the Americas, none of the indigenous languages can be said to have developed into literary languages as yet.

9.03.   Any language that has ever been used to write a state document of any kind can be said to have been or to be an official language. All the languages mentioned in the previous three sections as religious or literary languages have also been official languages. In some cases they have been established as such by specific action of a sovereign or a ruling body, but more often the usage has come about more or less spontaneously, and any official action taken later has been merely confirmatory.

The rise of modern nations has brought with it an increase in the technical statement of rules and regulations, and accordingly more explicit indications of what languages are used for what purposes. Official languages are now usually legally established, and the limits of their use in respect to other possible languages are often clearly stated.

Everywhere in the United States it is taken for granted that English is the official language. In New Mexico, Spanish is a second official language, in the courts and in the legislature, but not as the language of instruction in the schools. In Puerto Rico, Spanish is the first language, and English has special status. Wherever there are Indians, it is considered that their languages can always be used by them in their dealings with various government agencies, and interpreters are provided for. However, except for Navaho, the use of these languages is little different, legally and practically, from that of the languages of immigrants who have not learned English. In the deliberations of the Navaho council, Navaho is officially used and is even written. In Louisiana, French has some standing as a second language, but only quasi-officially.

In Canada, English and French have equal legal standing. In Quebec, English is a minority language but its standing is maintained. Elsewhere in Canada, French speakers find themselves at a disadvantage practically though not legally.

Further discussion of countries with more than one official language can be found in 9.11.

In the world as it was politically organized in the nineteenth century, and until after the First World War, a map of official languages was relatively easy to draw. In North America, English began at the United States-Mexican border, and covered everything north of there, except for the province of Quebec and the islands of St. Pierre and Miquelon. In the latter three areas, French was shown as the official language. Beginning in Mexico, everything south of there to the tip of South America was officially Spanish—except British Honduras with English, Brazil with Portuguese, and the Guianas, which showed English, French, and Dutch. The West Indies showed Spanish in Cuba and Puerto Rico and in the Dominican half of the island of Haiti; French in the Haitian half of Haiti, in Guadeloupe, and in Martinique; Dutch in Curaçao and Aruba; Danish in the Virgin Islands (English after 1917); and English elsewhere. Greenland was Danish, as were Iceland and the Faroes.

In Europe, German was the ruling language in Germany and in the Austro-Hungarian Empire (with Hungarian sometimes specifically shown separately for Hungary and Slovakia). In the Balkans, the picture shifted as the Slavic countries emerged in the Balkan wars (just before the First World War) and Turkish was replaced. In Switzerland, French, German, and Italian were equally official. In the rest of Europe, there were the national languages, following national boundaries. All of the Russian Empire was shown as Russian speaking. Polish, Ukrainian, and the Baltic languages did not officially exist.

In Africa, only the colonial languages were shown officially— English, French, German, Portuguese, Spanish. In Asia outside of Russia, there were Turkish, Arabic, Persian, English in India and Burma, Chinese in China, French in Indo-China, English in Malaya and in the Philippines.

The official picture was simple. Details on many of the unofficial languages were not available, and were often even suppressed by governments.

After the First World War, a host of new countries appeared in Europe, and new official languages were set up. After the Second

World War, the number of new countries increased rapidly. There are at the time of publication well over 100 members of the United Nations, and for many of them the language situation is very muddled. There are countries where the situation has been stable for years, such as the United States; there are others—as the new countries in Africa—in which language use is hopelessly confused, with former colonial languages persisting at the same time that one or more native languages are clamoring for recognition.

To determine the official languages of all the nations of the world, and to determine the extent of their use, and what other languages are permitted or are in use, would be a task of considerable proportions. One could start with official statistics and old maps, but these would be very far from providing the needed data.

The United Nations has five official languages: English, French, Spanish, Russian, and Chinese. The selection was governed by a number of factors, which may be guessed at as follows:

ENGLISH—250,000,000 native speakers, and an equal number already more or less acquainted with the language; extensive land areas— 10,000,000 square miles (more than 25,000,000 square kilometers) of territory for native speakers; the eminence of the British Empire in the nineteenth century, and the succession of the United States to the position of world economic and other leadership.

FRENCH—50,000,000 native speakers, and perhaps an equal number under French influence (former colonies and the like); old tradition of French as the language of diplomacy; traditional acceptance by many of French as a second language, learned for the purpose of wider communication.

SPANISH—145,000,000 native speakers, and a few million elsewhere; large territory—Mesoamerica, South America; importance of Spanish-speaking countries in the betterment of the world's economic situation.

RUSSIAN—a total of some 225,000,000 people, in the Soviet Union and adjacent to it, who speak Russian, or are under its official influence (125,000,000 native speakers, and 50,000,000 or so with Russian as a second language); vast territory, 8,000,000 square miles (about 21,000,000 square kilometers); extensive role in westernization of Asian peoples; political, scientific, technological importance.

CHINESE—600,000,000 people, of whom at least half speak some form of Northern Chinese; large territory; important influence in Asia. The inclusion of Chinese as one of the languages had political overtones: it was a sop to the non-Communist government in Taiwan, whose representatives needed it only slightly, being largely Western-educated; the UN also had in mind mainland China, which had not yet become Communist. Chinese gets little use in UN deliberations, but may get much more when China is admitted.

9.1. LANGUAGE AND REALITY

9.10. The ideal relation of a language to the society of the people speaking it would be that of one to one: each society having its own language, and only one language; each language spoken by one society, and only one society. In strict terms, such a situation may only have existed, theoretically, at the time when language had been invented, had been learned by all the members of the inventing group, but had not yet been passed on to other groups—if there ever was such a time.

In practical terms, however, we can speak of a unilingual society as one in which all the members become native speakers from infancy, regardless of any social stratifications or other subgroupings that may exist. In such a society, any nonnative speakers are outsiders who have come in later—as visitors, by marrying in, as slaves, and so on. In small societies, whatever they may be called—bands, tribes, or the like—unilingualism is the rule, and it appears always to have been.

As societies expand in numbers of members, and in territory covered, there are likely to arise geographical and social dialect differences. So long as these differences are minimized and pushed back by constant interaction between the subgroups, the society remains, in theory and practice, unilingual.

In a unilingual society, any differences in language usage among members are in terms either of personal differences in experience, education, intelligence, and personality; or are structured in terms of social and/or geographical dialects. A chief speaks differently from his weapon bearer, a professor from his student, a father from his child; the city people and the country folk talk differently; the mountaineers have a strange dialect in the opinion of the lowlanders; and so on.

In some societies, social dialects are very different from each other, yet such societies are still unilingual if all the members think their language is unified. In India, for instance, there are villages where three or four dialects are spoken, by members of different castes; but this differs only in degree from the situation in an American city where the university professor speaks a different class dialect from the maintenance man who comes in to clean his office.

As the modern nations developed, they often decreed an official language in attemps to create a unilingual society, or to maintain one. There have been many such actions since the growth of modern nationalism, and especially in the twentieth century.

A unilingual society has, in theory, a relatively easy time of it expressing its ideas of reality. When the political leaders talk about the goals of the nation, when government and law are discussed, when the moral virtues are extolled, when teachers propound the knowledge that students should acquire, when religious leaders reiterate the eternal verities—when any one of these things takes place, the speakers and the hearers are supposed to understand each other and to act accordingly. Unfortunately, the ideal is often far from the truth. In unilingual societies there are many instances of lack of mutual comprehension despite the use of the same language. Someone will say, "He and I don't speak the same language." And, in effect, this is true: even small differences in the nonlinguistic culture can bring about differences in meaning. And such differences can cause serious frictions and disputes.

Societies that are in themselves unilingual but which share their language with one or more others experience possibilities of lack of comprehension that are like those within a single unilingual society, but of greater significance. In the English-speaking world, the divergence between the United States and Canada on the one hand— where what may be called North American English is spoken —and, on the other, the countries where "Commonwealth" or "Empire" English is spoken is the most important. The realities of the universe that are talked about in the one group are different from those in the other. Within North American English, Canadian and American necessarily differ in terms of the differences in political and social structure; but from some points of view, the English language is more varied in use between, say, Mississippi and Maine, than it is between the United States as a whole and Canada. Within Commonwealth English, one starts with greater differences of history and social structure and political organization, but at some levels— those above the very essence of everyday individual living—there is an attitude that makes for similar orientations and mutual comprehension; yet a Scotsman from Edinburgh and a Londoner, even if both are educated speakers of what is superficially "Received Pronunciation", may be worlds apart in all kinds of understanding of specific linguistic usages, while the Edinburgh man and an American, if both are, say, university professors, may actually speak a language in common, in terms of philosophy and world outlook.

Other instances of multisocietal languages are French in Quebec and in France; German in Germany, Switzerland, and Austria; Spanish in Spain and the various countries of Latin America; Portuguese in Portugal and Brazil. In all of these instances, the problems of mutual comprehension, and the cross-cutting of different levels and statuses in the societies, are comparable, analogous, and even parallel to those in the English-speaking world.

9.11. Whether by the accidents of history—as in the case of Switzerland—or by specific intention—as in present-day India, there are societies or nations in the world which present large measures of cultural unity but which employ more than one language, that is, are multilingual. In multilingual societies, the same reality, or similar aspects of several realities, are presented and are talked about in several languages. The amounts of sameness or of difference depend on many historical factors.

It has been said over and over that a language, a culture, an ethnic group, do not necessarily coincide or fail to coincide in any specific way. A language may be spoken in several societies, a culture may be common to speakers of several languages; an ethnic group may be unicultural and/or unilingual, or it may include speakers of many languages or members of many cultures, or any combination of the possibilities.

In a long-established, cohesive multilingual society like that of Switzerland, the several languages used are somewhat in the position of the social or geographical dialects of a unilingual society. But there are important differences. The French of Switzerland is fairly uniform—it is a kind of colonial French—but it is culturally differently oriented from the French of France. The Genevan speaker of French is not a Frenchman, he is a Swiss; yet his being French-speaking also makes him part of a larger, less well-defined culture, that of all those who speak French. The German of Switzerland is fragmented into numerous local dialects, but is also unified by the fact that its speakers all get educated in standard German; and this makes them also part of the multisocietal world of speakers of German. The Swiss who speak Italian are theoretically in the same position as the Swiss who are French or German speakers; but because they are fewer in numbers, and because their Italian dialects have been subjected to standardization for a relatively short period, they do not belong to as large an outside world linguistically. The Swiss who speak the several Rhetic languages—Romansch, Ladin, Friulan—have no outside linguistic world, and may be supposed to be the most "Swiss" of all, and thus the most multilingually unicultural. Impressionistically, however, it is the German Swiss who are most "Swiss" and yet perhaps the least multilingual; the Italian Swiss are the least "Swiss"; and the French Swiss are the least unicultural.

In the society that may be called North American (English), a society that at first seems to be unilingual, and part of an even larger unilingual entity, there are seen to be included some groups that are not English-speaking. This North-American society is multi-lingual first because of the French in Quebec, then because of the Spanish spoken in the southwestern United States, and finally be-cause of the small enclaves of Indians scattered all over, and the presence of as yet unassimilated immigrant groups. The French-Canadians are culturally part of North America in this sense, and not of the French-speaking world. They are linguistically French, but fight a constant and losing battle to keep their French from becoming a mere calque and replica of English.

In the case of Switzerland, official equivalents of the things that need to be said in more than one language were worked out long ago, and the spoken languages have adapted to each other also. In Canada, official versions in French of something originally put into English sound like translations, even if they are good translations. But a French-Canadian newspaper, especially in its sport columns, let us say, is not a translation of English but an actual transposition of the English into a live kind of French, even if the French appears on examination to be a calque of the English and very different from anything that would be written in France.

The Spanish of the Southwest of the United States has much less status as a language of literary and official use than the Frecnh of Canada, and is accordingly much more like a version of the dominant English. The official Spanish equivalents of English usage, as in New Mexico, show little concern with what might be said in Mexico south of the border. The unofficial renderings, as in the "Spanish columns" of newspapers, are often amusingly "incorrect" Spanish, when they are not stilted translations.

Turning now to a newly established multilingual nation, India, we have to realize first of all that at many levels of the culture the multilingualism is not new at all. For several thousand years the cultures of the Indian subcontinent have been in contact, and the use of many languages has been practiced. Now a new situation exists: a modern nation and political entity is actively engaged in carrying on its nationwide affairs in Hindi, under the influence of English and with a widespread continued use of English; and it must translate and transform the Hindi and/or English, or sometimes a kind of amalgam of the two, into some two dozen other languages— some Indic and some Dravidian—which have to a large degree never been used for the kinds of expression now required.

As Western culture more and more overlays the other cultures of the world, its practitioners come more and more to constitute a multilingual society. The various subcultures thus created are themselves in most cases necessarily multilingual. The unilingual groups of various size become increasingly multicultural. Japan, unilingual and unicultural in the middle of the nineteenth century, becomes multicultural (Japanese and Western cultures in various mixtures at various levels of the society) and multilingual (English and other Western languages used in science and for international communication). In Mexico, the dominant Spanish speakers become more "Americanized", and also more Mexican by expressly including Indians as first-class citizens, making the society more multilingual; the Indians, entering into the larger society, become multicultural. The tale is often told of the Mexican Indian who walks from his village to a city; he has a pair of shoes, but keeps them in his suitcase or in a bag or tied together over his shoulders, and he walks barefoot; on reaching the city, he puts on his shoes, and by this act transforms himself into a member of Mexican society at large—changing cultures by an outward material symbol. If he works three months, decides he has amassed a sufficient competence, and goes back to the village, he takes off his shoes on leaving, and becomes an Indian again. Linguistically too he changes: in the city he speaks Spanish— learning to do so if he hasn't learned before—and in the village he speaks his native Indian language. In the United States too there are many instances of Indians who "go back to the blanket", or go back and forth between cultures, and are multilingual.

The various instances of multilingual societies and multisocietal languages and the overlappings and subdivisions that have been mentioned are just the merest sampling, and can at best only suggest the numerous kinds of problems, in all realms of the structures of languages as well as of other cultural systems, that remain to be investigated. The anthropological linguist and the linguistic anthropologist, if they are not one and the same, can look forward to a tremendous expansion of their field of study in the next century. The hope may be expressed that they will be able to meet the challenge.

9.12. In all the instances of the spread of a language to a new society, discussed in the preceding section and elsewhere in this book, there are implied the influences of an indigenous language on the new language that overlays or supersedes it, and conversely the influence of the superordinate language on the indigenous one.

In nineteenth-century historical linguistics these notions were discussed in terms of substratum and superstratum. In Roman Gaul, for instance, Gaulish was the substratum to Latin, and its influence was called in to explain things in French that did not happen to Latin elsewhere. In postmedieval France, Francian was the superstratum, and its phenomena were traced into the dialects it pushed back or replaced.

The influence of the superstrate language can often be documented directly. The influence of a substrate language can usually only be speculated about, for lack of definitive data.

With modern linguistic observation, and the recording of cultural changes and developments as they are in process, it will become possible to chart the substrate and superstrate influences in detail, to systematize them, and perhaps to draw generalizations from them as to what happens, and how, and when. Then, by extrapolation, it may become possible to clarify and explain past instances of similar phenomena.

9.13. In the discussion of meaning in Chapter 4, and specifically in 4.2 and its subsections, allusion was made to the relation of language to the rest of culture in terms of the so-called Whorf hypothesis. For fuller comprehension of the connection of language and reality, we would have to have analyses of cultural systems other than language that are analogous to the analyses of languages that can be made by such procedures as have been discussed in this book.

In the subsection just preceding, the problem of layers of linguistic systems, in time, was touched upon. Reconstructions of the history of languages as structures, even as vocabularies, can be made. And as they are made, historical connections become clarified. But the attaining of such clarity can only bring new problems in the matter of the relation of language and reality. For the historical reconstruction of other cultural systems has not reached anywhere near the level of adequacy found in linguistic history.

The most valuable contribution to general anthropological theory that linguistics can make is to demonstrate that human behavior can be analyzed descriptively and the analyses compared historically. The rest of culture must be analyzed system by system (and there are many systems) by means of procedures appropriate to the subject matter. When such analyses begin to exist, as a few already do for kinship or some aspects of technology, and here and there in other parts of culture, that is, when there are "grammars" of time systems or of kinship systems or of government or of religion, then such grammars can be compared with the grammars of their languages, and insights into the interrelations of the systems can be gained, "Reality", or rather the many realities that are culture, can then be reconstructed. And when enough reconstruction has been done, we may some day have an anthropological history of mankind.

9.2. LANGUAGE AND A UNITED WORLD

9.20. Human beings communicate chiefly by talking. Where languages differ, some kind of auxiliary communication system must be found. In most cases, it is an auxiliary language.

Auxiliary languages are of many kinds. A language that acquires superior prestige for any reason may serve as an auxiliary means of communication for speakers of other languages of less prestige. An imposed language, as by conquest, may become an auxiliary language for the conquered. Where languages in contact have approximately equal prestige, a compromise pidgin language may emerge. The language of a conquered people may become an auxiliary language for the conquerors. A pidgin may emerge in a situation of little actual interaction between superior and subordinate peoples, and become auxiliary for both groups. A religious language may become an auxiliary language under some circumstances. Official languages may be specified as auxiliary languages. The situations and the possibilities are many and varied.

We can mention some instances of auxiliary languages that have been used or have developed in the world of Western culture. Latin in pre-Anglo-Saxon Britain was an auxiliary language, and as the language of the church it continued to be used in this way in England and Ireland, as also on the continent of Europe all through the Middle Ages. After the Norman Conquest, English became an auxiliary language for the conquerors, and eventually supplanted French. In the colonial countries after 1500, the languages of the colonizers served as auxiliary languages in many instances until they simply supplanted native languages. In Mexico the Spanish used Aztec as an auxiliary, and in Peru and Ecuador it was Kechuan. In Brazil the Portuguese used Tupi ("Língua Geral"). Various forms of Pidgin English became auxiliaries—on the China coast, in the Pacific, in North America; one of these, as Neomelanesian, has become a creole, and is still an auxiliary language. A French pidgin was auxiliary in Haiti, and became a creole. Papiamento is a Spanish pidgin, now a creole. Russian pidgins as auxiliaries arose in the northern regions of Finland and in Central Asia and Mongolia. The Indians of the Northwest United States had an auxiliary pidgin, Chinook Jargon. In medieval Europe, a pidgin Romanic, Lingua Franca, was a generalized auxiliary in the Mediterranean area. In the East Indies, a pidgin Malay, now transformed into Bahasa Indonesia, became an auxiliary; Bahasa Indonesia remains an auxiliary language, has become a creole, and is on the way to becoming a primary language. The languages of the United Nations are auxiliary languages for the members who speak other than those five official languages. From the eighteenth century on into the present, French has been used as an auxiliary language in international diplomacy. English is now frequently used as an auxiliary language in international scientific and other gatherings.

9.21. In the Western world the use of Latin as an auxiliary language declined after the Renascence, and the use of French in its place never quite attained the same universality. By the eighteenth century the idea of doing something about the problem of international communication began to be looked upon as a challenge to human ingenuity. The creation of an artificial language for the purpose began to be suggested. It appears that several hundred projects of constructed international auxiliary languages have been put forth. Most of them have never attracted any popular attention, being for the most part wholly at variance with any of the realities of linguistic structure. Such unrealistic codelike systems, often so made as to be only visual, continue to be devised.

A few devisers of constructed languages have been wise enough to make them as much like ordinary languages as possible. This takes away the stigma of the term "artificial", for in point of fact every natural language has many aspects that are just as artificial as those of any constructed language. Every technical jargon, every scientific nomenclature, every vocabulary of a new technology—all these are artificial in the sense of being made up for the specific purpose. And every pidgin language is also artificial, for somebody deliberately set about to create it by "simplifying" and modifying some natural language. Moreover, it should be remembered that we hold language as such to be an invention, the first cultural invention (see 1.11). Any attempt to provide a language for a special purpose, such as international communication, is therefore necessarily an elaboration of the basic invention that is language. Language is an artifact, and any constructed international auxiliary language is an artifact—is "artificial".

In 1879 a German named Martin Schleyer published a constructed language he called VOLAPÜK 'world speech'. It was based on European languages, especially the Germanic ones, and for a few years had considerable vogue. But it had some marked defects: the phoneme /ü/ was rejected by speakers of English, of the Romanic languages other than French, of Slavic, and of many other languages; the formation of words from the existing vocabularies of Europe was whimsical—as *vola* from *world* or *Welt*, *pük* from *speech* or *speak*; and the grammatical system was complex.

In 1887, a much better-constructed language, ESPERANTO, was presented by Dr. L. L. Zamenhof, a Russian subject living in Lithuania. Esperanto had an extensive but not too strange phonemic system, and an extremely simple inflectional system; derivation was along seemingly conventional lines. Esperanto caught the fancy of those who had become disillusioned with Volapük, and at one time was said to have 100,000 active partisans; there are still many. Esperanto was so successful in its way, that the name has become a common noun for an auxiliary language or other medium of common communication. Structurally Esperanto is a regularized, slightly overinflected Romanic language, with a considerable number of non-Romanic vocabulary items (*birdo* 'bird' < English, but pronounced /bírdo/, suggesting *beard* [!]; *vosto* 'tail' < Russian *xvost*), and a grammatical tendency to treat affixes as stems, so that in effect the inflected forms and derivatives are phrases: from the base *bel-*, meaning 'beauty', are derived *belo* 'a beautiful thing', *bela* 'beautiful' (adjective), *belulo* 'a beautiful person', *beleco* (*c* = /ts/) 'beauty'; from the general demonstrative base *l-* are derived *lo* 'essence, entity', *la* 'the' (adjective); the affixes *-ul-* and *-ec-* are made into bases and, with the nominalizer *-o*, result in *ulo* 'person' (possessing some characteristic), *eco* 'state or quality'. Similarly, *Esperanto* 'the hopeful one' < *esper-*, base, 'hope'; *-a-*, present time; *-nt-*, active participle; *-o*, nominal; literally 'hope-now-doing-entity'.

Dissatisfaction with some of the special characteristics of Esperanto led to the creation in 1901 of IDO (literally, 'offspring'), a "more natural" version of Esperanto. Ido had some success, but never became anywhere nearly as popular as Esperanto.

In 1922, Edgar deWahl presented OCCIDENTAL, a still more "natural" language, much more like ordinary Western Romanic than is Esperanto. It met with practically no success as such, but some of its principles were subsequently adopted as guidelines for developing Esperanto.

In 1928, Otto Jespersen proposed NOVIAL ("new International Auxiliary Language"). This was much less synthetic or agglutinating than Esperanto, and was constructed more along the lines of English. It is a sort of "analytic", Germanicized Romanic.

In 1903, Giuseppe Peano, an Italian mathematician, had proposed LATINO SINE FLEXIONE 'Latin without inflection', using the standard Latin vocabulary, in stem form, and incorporating the international scientific and technical vocabulary. After the Second World War, Latino sine flexione came to be called INTERLINGUA, and has been fostered by a number of persons and groups interested in the adoption of an international auxiliary language. Interlingua has been somewhat freed from its original dependence on Latin, and is now a kind of generalized and internationalized Latin in ultra-Romanic form.

All the constructed international auxiliary languages (i.a.l.'s)—including the five last mentioned, which are all carefully thought out and have excellent characteristics—have had objections raised to specific items of their structure. Esperanto is said to have some difficult phonemes—/c, č, ζ, ǰ, x/ (spelled *c, ĉ, dz, ĵ, ĥ*)—to have superfluous inflection (accusative, plural of adjectives), and to be too rigid in its derivational procedures, and too agglutinative. Ido is characterized as too logical in its difference from Esperanto. Occidental is called too natural, Novial is said to be too analytic, Interlingua is too Latin. These objections all have merit, but are insignificant compared to the following: all the Western-based, Romanic-type, i.a.l.'s are just as difficult for a non-Westerner to learn as is any natural Western language, and are much less useful and usable; any constructed language is going to have sounds and forms that are strange or difficult for most—or at least many—speakers of natural languages the world over. The conclusion from these last two objections is that it would be best to adopt some natural language as the preferred i.a.l., despite the advantage this would give its native speakers.

In all the criticisms leveled at constructed i.a.l.'s, including those just mentioned, no attention is paid to a factor of supreme anthropological importance, namely, the semological structure and metalinguistic use of an i.a.l. Every natural language has a semology based on its historically developed structure. Any i.a.l. based on Romanic or Germanic or Latin, or on any other natural language, is bound to have a semology that starts from and is limited by its history. Every natural language develops a metalinguistic in terms of the culture or cultures of its speakers. Any i.a.l. based on a natural language or a group of natural languages cannot avoid having a biased metalinguistic. Given the acceptance of these judgments, no i.a.l. has any advantage over a natural language, and serves no real purpose.

The considerations just mentioned also militate against the use of a "simplified" form of a natural language, such as Basic English. The native speakers of English cannot—and will not—learn to truncate and mutilate their language; and the learners of Basic English would only find the learning of real English more difficult.

The anthropologist of language must be aware of the arguments against constructed i.a.l.'s alluded to above, and must recognize their validity. In his role as human being and humanist, however, he can point to the historical possibilities discussed in 9.13, and can then suggest some possible future remedies for the difficultues. That is the subject of the next, and last, subsection.

9.22. A world riven by strife, in the form of "hot" wars and "cold" wars, "police actions" and "preventive activities", "maintenance of peace" and "unyielding resistance to agression", firm resolve to combat any "ism" one dislikes while talking about accommodation and coexistence—such a world would welcome a means of communication that would make sense to everybody. What are the chances of such a world language?

The first, and frankest, answer must be that the chances are, as of now, almost nonexistent. There are several dozen dominant cultures in the world of today, each more or less directly identified with a specific language. The United States, the Soviet Union, the British Commonwealth or what is left of it, western Europe, central Europe, the Mediterranean countries, the Near East, India and Pakistan, southeast Asia, China-Korea-Japan, the Pacific—and all their subareas—are all pointing to futures that contradict or interfere with each of the others in some way. Analogously, English (American and British), Russian, French, German, Italian, Arabic, Hindi-Urdu, Vietnamese, Indonesian, Chinese, Japanese—all these languages, and others, are fighting for supremacy.

As of the 1970s, there is no possibility of a single world language. But what of the future?

To the last question, the answer is necessarily optimistic, but also necessarily vague as to specific times and places. Yes, there will be, some day, a world language. But it cannot come into existence until there is a world culture. What are the basic necessities for such a world culture?

After historical reconstructions (of the kind suggested in 9.13) of the relationships of cultural systems to each other have been made, there can then be effort along the following lines. The analyses of time and space must be unified. Chronology, weights and measures, astronomical descriptions of the universe, these are, in various degrees, already achieving unity. Everybody now counts hours and minutes and seconds, and the days they form, in the same way. But weeks and months and years still vary, though the Western form is widespread. The biological and neurological studies of man are still far from consensus, and until they come to agreement, no unified way of talking about people can exist. All peoples talk, but most languages are still undescribed and unanalyzed; hundreds, perhaps thousands, of linguistic and ethnolinguistic studies remain to be done. Technologically, much of the world is superficially unified; but in vast areas, modern technology is still unknown, and until it becomes known, no linguistic meeting of minds can take place. The economic systems of the world are many, and as long as the myths about them persist, there can be no one way of talking about them. Agreement on values is extensive, but disagreement on details is of such magnitude as to wipe out, in large part, the agreement; intercultural discourse about values is still blocked by almost insuperable differences. In economics, the world is still a milling, striving, conflicting mass of opposed interests; no consensus is in sight, but it will probably come, and then communication will be possible. The world's governments range far and wide—there are "authoritarian" ones, and there are "democratic" ones; the terms will continue to lack concrete significance until extensive studies of their semologies and metalinguistic contexts have been made. There is no world religion, so agreement on what is the best "way of life" is impossible.

The preceding paragraph may sound hopeless to some. But it is not really that. Mankind began as a small group of individuals, one of whom invented language, and taught his fellows to behave culturally. Mankind has become thousands of groups, with an equally large number of languages, behaving culturally at crosspurposes. By talking, and continuing to talk, to each other, mankind may once again become one: a grouping of many groups of individuals, with one language, one ethic, one goal. It may take centuries, but it can't help happening. A million or more years ago, man began talking. He talked himself into diversity, and has talked himself into worldwide conflict. He will talk on, and will talk himself into unity and agreement.

In the beginning of humanity was the word, and, with humanity, the word goes on.

REFERENCES
AND NOTES

The references given here are in part general, for background or additional reading, and in part specific, for given topics. They do not constitute a complete bibliography, but many of them contain extensive bibliographical material which would lead the interested reader to further details on the subjects treated.

Included with the references are notes of various kinds, usually giving supplementary explanations of details, or indicating other treatments of the subject. Often, there are also indications of the development of the study of a particular topic or of a particular specialty.

More extensive discussions of specific languages, supplementing the material in the present book, are provided in two books projected for future publication and tentatively entitled *English and its relatives* and *The Non-Western languages*. Reference to these publications is made by the initials *E&R* and *NWL* respectively: chapter and section numbers in these volumes are necessarily tentative.

References and notes are arranged by the numbered sections and subsections of chapters. The omission of a section or subsection number indicates that no references are given for that part of the text, and that there are no notes on it.

PART I. CHAPTERS 1, 2, 3, 4

1. Summaries of the subject matter of Chapter 1 and of the general content of this book may be found in:

TRAGER, GEORGE L. Language. *Encyclopaedia Britannica* v. 13, pp. 696–703, 1955. [Continued in print through 1964.]

———. Linguistics. *Encyclopaedia Britannica* v. 14, pp. 162A–162H, 163; 1956. [Continued in print through 1964.]

―――. The languages of the world. *Collier's Encyclopedia* v. 14, pp. 299–310. New York: The Collier Publishing Co., 1962.

1.00. The Biblical story of the Tower of Babel is a well-known explicit account of the origin of language differences.

1.10. The modern biological classifications were established by Linnaeus in the following work:

LINNÉ, CARL VON. *Caroli Linnaei, sveci, ... Systema naturae sive Regna tria naturae, systematice proposita per classes, ordines, genera, & species.* Lugduni Batavorum, 1735. Facsimile, Uppsala: Bokgillet, 1960. ['Carolus Linnaeus, the Swede's ... System of nature or the three Kingdoms of nature, systematically set forth by classes, orders, genera, and species. Louvain.'] [The three "kingdoms" are animal, vegetable, and mineral.]

Some useful readings on the evolution of man are:

CARRINGTON, RICHARD. *A million years of man: the story of human development as a part of nature.* New York: New American Library, 1964. "A Mentor Book." 304 pp. (Originally published by World Publishing Co., New York, and Weldenfeld and Nicolson, London, 1963.) [Ch. 7, The australopithecines, pp. 76–83. New findings are taking place constantly, and new conclusions may require updating of such a chapter at any time.]

CLARK, W. E. LeGros. *History of the primates.* Chicago: Univ. of Chicago Press, Phoenix Books, 1959. vi+186 pp. ["The fossil 'Australopithecinae' of South Africa", pp. 101–119. See comment on preceding item.]

KRAUS, BERTRAM S. *The basis of human evolution.* New York; Evanston, Ill.; and London: Harper, 1964. 6 p. l., 384 pp.

LASKER, GABRIEL WARD. *The evolution of man.* New York: Holt, 1961. xvi+239 pp.

MONTAGU, ASHLEY. *Man: his first million years.* New York: New American Library, 1958. "A Mentor Book." 192 pp.

OAKLEY, KENNETH P. *Man the toolmaker.* Chicago: The Univ. of Chicago Press, Phoenix Books, 1957. vi+159 pp.

1.11. For a speculative consideration of the origin of language, see:

HOCKETT, CHARLES F., and ROBERT ASCHER. The human revolution. *Current Anthropology* 5:135–168, 1964. [Comment by the present author, pp. 163–164.]

1.13. On culture see the following:

WHITE, LESLIE A. *The science of culture.* New York: Grove, c1949. (Evergreen Books: E–105.) [Especially Part I, and Ch. I, II, III.]

————. Man, culture, and human beings. *Michigan Alumnus Quarterly Review* v. 66, no. 10, p. 1–10, Dec. 5, 1959.

Any general introduction to anthropology will give the reader details about the various aspects of cultural behavior, and examples from specific cultures among the societies of the world. Though old, the following is still to be recommended, in any of its editions or reprintings, as among the best:

KROEBER, ALFRED L. *Anthropology*. New York: Harcourt, c1923. x+523 pp.

1.21. The definition of language given here is a fuller version of that found on p. 5 of the following:

BLOCH, BERNARD, and GEORGE L. TRAGER. *Outline of linguistic analysis*. Baltimore: Linguistic Society of America, 1942. 82 pp.

A similar definition is given on p. 7 of:

SAPIR, EDWARD. *Language*. New York: Harcourt, c1921. vii+258 pp. [The definition is on p. 8 of the paperback reprint as a "Harvest Book", HB7, 1956 (copyright renewed 1949).]

On the "dances" of bees, see:

VON FRISCH, K. *Bees: their vision, chemical senses, and language*. Ithaca, N.Y.: Cornell Univ. Press, c1950.

KROEBER, A. L. Sign and symbol in bee communication. *Proceedings of the National Academy of Sciences* 38:753–757, 1952.

1.22. The original presentation on paralanguage is:

TRAGER, G. L. Paralanguage: a first approximation. *Studies in Linguistics* 13:1–12, 1958.

Kinesics was first expounded in:

BIRDWHISTELL, R. L. *Introduction to kinesics*. Louisville, Kentucky: Univ. of Louisville, [1954]. 2 p.l., 75+[2] pp. [Originally printed by Foreign Service Institute, U.S. Department of State, 1952.]

1.3. A good introduction to the study of language change is:

STURTEVANT, E. H. *Linguistic change: an introduction to the historical study of language*. With a new introduction by Eric P. Hamp. Chicago: Univ. of Chicago Press, [1961]. xviii+165 pp. [Phoenix Books, P60. Originally published in 1917.]

1.34. A good discussion of the varieties of American English is the chapter "The dialects of American English", by Raven I. McDavid, Jr., pp. 480–543 of the following:

FRANCIS, W. NELSON. *The structure of American English.* New York: Ronald, c1958. vii+614 pp. [Except for the chapter mentioned, the book should be used with caution, as it contains many inaccuracies, especially in phonemic transcriptions.]

The grouping of American English dialects in our text is that of Henry Lee Smith, Jr. (see the Preface); see References for 2.44.

1.4.   For works on writing see References for Ch. 7 and 8.

2.   Works on general phonetics, on phonemics and its theory, and specific analyses of phonological systems may serve as general background for or as further reading on the material in this chapter. Specific references are given for some of the sections and subsections. It may be noted that this chapter constitutes a full summary presentation of the author's views of the theory and methodology of phonology, and in that sense is independent of other general discussions.

2.0.   This section summarizes (with some restatement) views expounded in the articles "Language" and "Linguistics" by the author, cited for Ch. 1, and in the following:

TRAGER, G. L. *The field of linguistics.* Norman, Okla.: 1949. 8 pp. *Studies in Linguistics, Occasional Papers,* 1 [=SIL:OP 1]. [2nd printing, 1950; reprinted by Foreign Service Institute, U.S. Department of State, 1952; by Johnson Reprint Corporation, N.Y., 1963.]
———. *Linguistics is linguistics.* Buffalo: 1963. 28 pp. (SIL:OP 10.)

2.1.   The diagram in subsection 2.11 is taken from p. 12 of:

TRAGER, G. L. *Phonetics: glossary and tables.* 2nd ed., rev. Buffalo: 1964. 26 pp. *Studies in Linguistics, Occasional Papers,* 6_2 [Originally published in 1958.]

2.2.   This section (subsections 2.20–2.23) is based in its analyses and tables on the work cited for 2.1. That publication should be consulted for technical details. The treatment here is more descriptive and discursive.

There are many other books on phonetics, but the systems of analysis in them differ in one way or another from that presented here. The reader should beware of confusion if he consults them before fully assimilating the present system. However, with this system as a point of departure, comparison with or transition to others is not difficult.

2.20.   For data on the acoustics of sounds see:

JOOS, MARTIN. *Acoustic phonetics.* Baltimore: Linguistic Society of

America, 1948. 136 pp. (Language Monograph 23.)

2.23. The International Phonetic Association (IPA) publishes a journal, *Le Maître Phonétique*. This was started in May 1886 as *Dhi Fonètik Tîtcer*, was printed from May 1887 as *dhə fonetik tîtcər*, from September 1887 to December 1888 as *ðə fonetik tîtcər*. In January 1889 the present French title was adopted, and has been printed both in ordinary French orthography and as *lə mɛ:trə fɔnetik*. The text of the journal is entirely in phonetic transcription—or rather in partially or fully phonemicized transcription—except for book titles and proper names. Supplemental publications, describing the phonetic system of the IPA, have appeared at intervals, with the text in ordinary orthography, in various European languages. An English version is:

The principles of the International Phonetic Association. London, 1949. 53 pp.

The Americanist alphabet was published in:

American Anthropological Association. *Phonetic transcription of Indian languages.* Washington, D.C.: United States Government Printing Office, 1916. 15 pp., 2 tables. (Smithsonian Miscellaneous Collection, v. 66, no. 6.)

The tables in Trager, *Phonetics* [References, 2.1] are to be found as follows: Table of vowel classification, p. 16; Table of consonant classification, p. 22; list of diacritical symbols, pp. 25–26.

The sketches of languages referred to will be found in the projected volumes, *English and its relatives* (*E & R*) and *The Non-Western languages* (*NWL*).

2.30. The techniques of phonemic analysis are discussed in the various general introductory textbooks of linguistics. The following may be mentioned:

GLEASON, H. A. *An introduction to descriptive linguistics.* Rev. ed. New York: Holt, c1961. viii+503 pp. [Ch. 16–21.]

HILL, A. A. *Introduction to linguistic structures.* New York: Harcourt, c1958. xi+496 pp. [Ch. 2–5.]

HOCKETT, C. F. *A course in modern linguistics.* New York: Macmillan, c1958. xi+621 pp. [Ch. 2–6, 10–13.]

In Bloch and Trager, *Outline of linguistic analysis* [References, 1.21], the general sections of Ch. 3, "Phonemics", namely 3.1 to 3.6, are still an excellent though concise statement of principles and techniques.

See also the first Reference for 2.4.

2.31. For transition-phoneme theory see:

TRAGER, G. L. Some thoughts on "juncture". *Studies in Linguistics* 16:11–22, 1962.

2.4. The treatment of English phonology is based on the following work:

TRAGER, G. L., and HENRY LEE SMITH, JR. *An outline of English structure.* Norman, Okla.: 1951. 92 pp. *Studies in Linguistics: Occasional Papers,* 3. Reprinted by American Council of Learned Societies, 1956, 1957, 1959, 1961, 1962, 1965, 1966.

Other, older analyses of English exist, some differing seriously from the Trager-Smith one in theory and method. None, however, is as complete, or as widely accepted at the present time. The text indicates some of the differences between those systems and the one used here.

2.42. For the variety of allophones the phoneme /t/ sometimes exhibits, see:

TRAGER, G. L. The phoneme "t", a study in theory and method. *American Speech* 17:144–148, 1942.

See Hill, *Introduction to linguistic structures* [References, 2.30], Ch. 6, "Phonotactics", for discussion of consonant clusters.

2.44. The list of key words for determining dialect areas was originally devised by Henry Lee Smith, Jr. for use in a radio program entitled "Where are you from?" which he conducted from 1939 to 1941; the list has subsequently been revised and reduced. On the basis of these words and of the observations made by him during the program and elsewhere at that time and since, Dr. Smith was able to delimit the eight areas set forth in 1.34. The presentation here differs in some few details from Dr. Smith's own, but is given with his permission and approval.

3. The general theory on which this chapter is based is to be found in the appropriate parts of the articles "Language" (Trager) and "Linguistics" (Trager) cited for Ch. 1; see also References, 2.0.

3.1. The procedure for analyzing morphemes is illustrated in Trager and Smith, *Outline of English structure* [References, 2.4], Part II, "Morphemics", pp. 53 ff. Other discussions and treatments are to be found in the general works cited for 2.30.

Much of the detail of sections 3.10, 3.11, 3.12 is based upon a large number of specialized technical studies abstracted and summarized for purposes of class presentation, and has not been previously published in the discursive form that is presented here.

The English examples are from, or follow the analysis of, *An outline of English structure*; for French see *E&R*, 5.2 and subsections and References to that section; for Taos see *NWL*, 9.22. The treatment of English initial *fl-*, *gl-* as "psychomorphs" is in:

MARKEL, NORMAN N., and ERIC P. HAMP. Connotative meanings of certain phoneme sequences. *Studies in Linguistics* 15:47–61, 1961.

3.2. The general statement made above for 3.1 applies to this section also. Some of the discussion is based on material that has not yet been published.

3.20. For French nonphonemic stress in words and phrases, see: HADEN, ERNEST. Accent expiratoire. *Studies in Linguistics* 16:23–39, 1962.

For the treatment of English words in *-ation*, etc., see: TRAGER, FELICIA HARBEN. English *-sion*, *-tion* nouns. *Canadian Journal of Linguistics* 7:86–94, 1962.

For Japanese see References for *NWL*, Chapter 6; for Thai see References for *NWL*, Chapter 5; for Nootka see *NWL*, 9.12.

3.3. The principles of syntactic analysis presented here are those used by the author in his own work, and are in large part those elaborated by Henry Lee Smith, Jr. since 1955, partly in collaboration with the present author. The material is as yet largely unpublished.

The analytical procedures usually referred to by the terms "transformational" and "generative" are considered here to be in the realms of philosophy and philosophical mathematics, and not within the realm of linguistic science; they eschew data and proceed from speculatively arrived at theoretical positions to results having no applicational utility. No further reference to them will be made.

Kenneth L. Pike and his associates have been working for some years with techniques for syntactic analysis which they designate as "tagmemic". Many of their procedures and results resemble those discussed here, but the theoretical base is different: they seem to neglect phonological entities as syntactic boundary markers, and their syntax stems from meaning, rather than leading to it.

3.4. See *OES* [References, 2.4] for the morphemics of English. A number of modifications have been made here, in terms of work done since that publication, but largely still unpublished.

See also the general works previously cited—Hill, Gleason, Hockett [References, 2.30]; Francis [References, 1.34].

3.40. The theory of morphophonic analysis and its application to English are developed in the following articles by H. L. Smith. The treatment in the present work does not necessarily agree in all details with Smith's presentation, but there is no basic difference of approach.

SMITH, HENRY LEE, JR. The concept of the morphophone. *Language* 43:306–341, 1967.

————. *English morphophonics: implications for the teaching of literacy.* n.p.: New York State English Council, c1968. 1 p.l., iv+119 pp.

3.43. For the treatment of English personal pronouns see:

TRAGER, G. L. A componential morphemic analysis of English personal pronouns. *Language* 43:372–378, 1967.

3.44. On English *-tion,* cf. Felicia Harben Trager, cited for 3.20. Ablaut is treated here along the lines followed by Henry Lee Smith, Jr. in his recent work (unpublished). His and the present author's formulations do not necessarily coincide in detail, though the theoretical approach is the same.

4.00. For a preliminary treatment of semology, see:

JOOS, M. Semology: a linguistic theory of meaning. *Studies in Linguistics* 13:53–70, 1958.

4.02. The quotations from Lewis Carroll may be found in the following (or any other edition):

The complete works of Lewis Carroll. Illustrated by John Tenniel, introduction by Alexander Woolcott. New York: Modern Library, n.d. xi+1293 pp. ["Jabberwocky" occurs on pp. 153–155. Alice's comment is on p. 155. In the Preface to the 1896 edition of *Looking-glass,* Carroll says "Pronounce *slithy* as . . . 'sly, thee'; make the 'g' *hard* in 'gyre' and 'gimble' . . ." (p. 138 of the edition cited here). The Preface of *The hunting of the snark* has the remarks alluded to, on p. 754. In *Looking-glass,* Humpty-Dumpty explains "Jabberwocky" to Alice on pp. 215–217; compare that explanation, a whimsical one, with our serious one.]

4.1. Semology as defined in this book has not been very much studied. Henry Lee Smith, Jr. has done much work on it in connection with his studies of the structure of English, but the material is largely unpublished.

A special study of the relation of semology to other parts of an analysis is:

TRAGER, G. L. Taos IV: morphemics, syntax, semology in nouns and in pronominal reference. *International Journal of American Linguistics* 27:211–222, 1961.

A specific consideration of a small semological area may be found in:

TRAGER, G. L. Semology, metalinguistics, and translation. *Papers in linguistics in honor of Léon Dostert*, pp. 149–154. The Hague, Paris: Mouton, 1967. [An analysis of the meanings of a Taos verb base in several of its occurrences.]

4.2. For discussion of what has been called the "language-and-culture" or "Sapir-Whorf" hypothesis, see:

Language, thought, and reality: selected writings of Benjamin Lee Whorf. Edited and with an introduction by John B. Carroll, foreword by Stuart Chase. New York: Wiley; and Technology Press of Mass. Inst. of Technology, c1956. vi+278 pp.

HOIJER, HARRY, ed. *Language in culture: proceedings of a conference on the interrelations of language and other aspects of culture.* Chicago: Univ. of Chicago Press, 1954. xi+286 pp. [Also as Memoir no. 79, American Anthropological Assoc.]

TRAGER, G. L. The systematization of the Whorf hypothesis. *Anthropological Linguistics* 1:1:31–35, 1959.

The articles by Whorf which aroused interest in the ideas on the relation of language to the rest of culture are reprinted in *Language, thought, and reality* [above]. The conference recorded in *Language in culture* was devoted to a discussion of many aspects of Whorf's ideas, with several different points of view being taken. The paper by the present author listed just above attempts to lay down guidelines for productive and systematic study of the "language-and[∼ in]-culture" idea; it was part of a symposium devoted to the subject.

A discussion of the relation of language to the rest of culture in terms of historical reconstruction is:

TRAGER, G. L. Linguistics and the reconstruction of culture history. *New interpretations of aboriginal American culture history.* 75th anniversary volume of The Anthropological Society of Washington. Washington, D.C., 1955. pp. 110–115.

4.21. See *NWL*, 9.3, for the phonology of Taos.

4.22. See *E&R*, Ch. 8, for Russian, and Ch. 11 for its relation to English.

4.3. Many studies of loanwords in many languages have been made. Most of them are accurate enough and make interesting reading, though very few are structurally based, and practically none that the author knows of really trace the phonological and other changes in detail, as we have tried to do.

Three studies by the author are:

TRAGER, G. L., and GENEVIEVE VALDEZ. English loans in Colorado Spanish. *American Speech* 12:34–44, 1937. [Nonstructural; prephonemic.]

TRAGER, G. L. The days of the week in the language of Taos Pueblo, New Mexico. *Language* 15:51–55, 1939. [The material was updated in the next item.]

———. Spanish and English loanwords in Taos. *International Journal of American Linguistics* 10:144–58, 1944. [The stress and tone markings were changed in Taos I: ..., *IJAL* 14:155–156, 1948; see References, *NWL*, 9.22.]

On bilingualism see:

HAUGEN, EINAR. *Bilingualism in the Americas: a bibliography and research guide*. University, Ala.: Univ. of Alabama Press for the American Dialect Society, 1956. 159 pp. (Publ. Amer. Dial. Soc., 26).

———. *The Norwegian language in America: a study in bilingual behavior*. Philadelphia: Univ. of Penna. Press, 1953. 2 vols.

4.34. The development of pronominal *one* in English is discussed in:

TRAGER, G. L. French *on* = English *one*. *Romanic Review* 22:311–317, 1931.

4.4. No specific references on lexicography are given. All large dictionaries contain at least some discussion of the problems involved in compiling them. For translation as such see References, 4.5.

4.41. For Arabic roots (= bases), see *NWL*, 2.2.

4.5. Problems of translation have been discussed by dictionary makers, philosophers, and literary people, but rarely by linguists. In recent years much attention has been given to these problems by Christian missionaries working for the American Bible Society, the Wycliffe Bible Translators, or other groups (mostly evangelical Protestants). Many missionaries are now well trained as linguists, and can contribute much to the understanding of the problems of translation.

The following work is aimed at translators of the Bible, but is a linguistically sound discussion of translation as a whole:

NIDA, EUGENE A. *Bible translating, an analysis of principles and procedures, with special reference to aboriginal languages.* New York: American Bible Society, 1947. vii+362 pp.

See also:

————. *Message and mission: the communication of the Christian faith.* New York: Harper, c1960. xvii+253 pp. [An anthropologically sound discussion of communication across cultural boundaries. See especially Ch. 9, "Scripture translation and revision as techniques of communication", pp. 189–205.]

A popular account of the work of the Wycliffe Bible Translators is:

WALLIS, ETHEL EMILY, and MARY ANGELA BENNETT. *Two thousand tongues to go: the story of the Wycliffe Bible translators.* New York: Harper, c1959. ix+308 pp.; maps, illus.

PART II. CHAPTERS 5 and 6

5. For discussions of the historical approach to languages see Sturtevant [References, 1.3].

PEDERSEN, HOLGER. *Linguistic science in the 19th century, methods and results.* Authorized translation by J. W. Spargo. Cambridge, Mass.: Harvard Univ. Press, 1931. x+360 pp. [Paperback reprint, *The discovery of language* . . ., Bloomington, Ind.: Indiana Univ. Press, 1962.]

5.02. The history of various languages is discussed in the volumes *E&R* and *NWL*.

5.1. The material in this section is based on standard sources. See:

BAUGH, ALBERT C. *A history of the English language.* New York: Appleton-Century-Crofts, 1935. xiii+509 pp.

See also any history of England; and, especially for the early traditional lore:

BEDE'S *History of the English church and people* (published in a modern translation by Penguin Books, 1955).

5.10. For Celtic see *E&R*, Ch. 6.

5.11. For Germanic see *E&R*, Ch. 3.

5.13. For details of changes in English spelling see *E&R*, Ch. 1.

5.2. See References for Ch. 6, as well as the volumes *E&R* and *NWL*.

5.20. See *E&R*, Ch. 1.

5.21. For Germanic loanwords in Finnish, see *NWL*, Ch. 7.

6. Discussions of theory and method in comparative linguistics are found in most of the standard textbooks and works of reference. See the following:

BLOOMFIELD, LEONARD. *Language.* New York: Holt, 1933. [Ch. 18, The comparative method. Also Ch. 17 and 20–25.]

SAPIR, EDWARD. *Language.* New York: Harcourt, 1921; Harvest Books (paperback), 1956. [Ch. 7, Language as a historical product: drift; Ch. 8, Language as a historical product: phonetic law.]

HOCKETT, C. F. *A course in modern linguistics* [References, 2.30]. [Linguistic ontogeny, Ch. 41; phylogeny, Ch. 42–54.]

Most of the theoretical work in comparative linguistics has been done in connection with specific articles in the various fields since early in the nineteenth century. There have been few general synthesizing efforts. The following may be mentioned:

HOENIGSWALD, HENRY M. *Language change and linguistic reconstruction.* Chicago: Univ. of Chicago Press, c1960. viii+168 pp. [Bibliography, pp. 160–165.]

HOCKETT, C. F. The terminology of historical linguistics. *Studies in Linguistics* 12:57–63, 1957.

HYMES, DELL H. Genetic classification: retrospect and prospect. *Anthropological Linguistics* 1:2:50–66, 1959. [Bibliographical footnotes.]

6.00. For historical data on English see *E&R*, Ch. 1.

6.01. Sir William Jones is quoted and referred to by L. Bloomfield, *Language* [References, 6], p. 12; and at greater length by:

JESPERSEN, OTTO. *Language, its nature, development, and origin.* London, 1922. pp. 33–34.

See *E&R*, Ch. 9, for Indic languages; and *NWL*, Ch. 4, for Dravidian languages. For Semitic languages see *NWL*, Ch. 2.

6.10. The statements about Greek *máti* and Malay *mata* are synthesized from available dictionaries and other standard sources.

For the phonemic and phonetic reconstruction of Old Church Slavic see the text of *E&R*, 8.33; for Indo-European (or Indo-Hittite) see *E&R*, 11. For Azteco-Tanoan see Whorf and Trager, cited in References, 6.23.

6.11. The standard work on the development of the Romanic languages, which are used here and in the following subsections to exemplify comparison and reconstruction, is:

MEYER-LÜBKE, WILHELM. *Grammaire des langues romanes* ... traduction française par Eugène Rabiet. Paris: H. Welter, 1890. Reprinted by G. E. Stechert and Co., New York, 1923. 4 vols.

The lists of words compared in our text were compiled by the present author. The phonemicizations of the several languages and the discussion of developments are his own, based on his experience in the Romanic field, and in linguistics generally. The details, and some of the generalizations, depart from tradition only to the extent necessitated by the author's present linguistic theories.

For Latin see *E&R*, Ch. 4; for French see *E&R*, Ch. 5.

6.22. The treatment of reconstructions as formulas of correspondence, suggesting the general nature of the original phonemic system, is well presented by Bloomfield (*Language* [References, 6], Ch. 18): "A reconstructed form, then, is a formula that tells us which identities or correspondences of phonemes appear in a set of related languages" (pp. 302–303); "The comparative method tells us, in principle, nothing about the acoustic shape of reconstructed forms; it identifies the phonemes in reconstructed forms merely as recurrent units" (p. 309). See also:

LANE, GEORGE S. Changes of emphasis in linguistics with particular reference to Paul and Bloomfield. *Studies in Philology* 42:465–483, 1945: "It [the historical method] is incapable of describing them [the sounds of a reconstructed language]" (p. 466).

The view discussed in the present book, that reconstruction of PHONETIC detail is often possible and is implicit in phonemic reconstruction, was voiced by the present author in a comment on Lane's article:

TRAGER, GEORGE L. Changes of emphasis in linguistics: a comment. *Studies in Philology* 43:461–464, 1946: "We all know that when we reconstruct the *t* of *ten* and the *d* of *decem* ... into something we call 'Indo-European *d*' and symbolize by *d, we are dealing with an entity that was ... some kind of coronal voiced stop" (p. 463). [An oversight in proofreading resulted in the printed text of the article having "'Indo-European *t*' and symbolize by *t" and "coronal voiceless stop", and also "*t" four lines beyond the cited material; these errors have not heretofore been corrected in print.

See *E&R*, Ch. 11, for details on the phonetic reconstruction of Indo-European.]

See *E&R*, Ch. 3, for Germanic. See *E&R*, Ch. 11, for Indo-Hittite as a whole.

6.23.   The original hierarchy of terms was proposed in:

WHORF, B. L., and G. L. TRAGER. The relationship of Uto-Aztecan and Tanoan. *American Anthropologist* 39:609–624, 1937. [Footnote 5, p. 610.]

Suggestions for expanding such hierarchies are found in:

LAMB, SYDNEY M. Some proposals for linguistic taxonomy. *Anthropological Linguistics* 1:2:33–49, 1959.

The set of hierarchical terms developed in the text of 6.23 and expanded as needed elsewhere (*E&R*, *NWL*) by intercalation of additional terms is more finely subdivided than the original hierarchy (Whorf and Trager), and differs in detail from Lamb's proposals.

The emphasis on binary comparison is the present author's own elaboration of what seems to be the basic theoretical point of departure.

For the Romanic languages see *E&R*, Ch. 4.

The Portuguese "future phrase" may be seen in the form *fallaré* 'I'll speak' or *fallar . . . he*; see *E&R*, Ch. 5.

Glottochronology and lexicostatistics are discussed in the following works (there are many others):

LEES, ROBERT E. The basis of glottochronology. *Language* 29:113–127, 1953.

GUDSCHINSKY, SARAH J. The abc's of lexicostatistics (glottochronology). *Word* 12:175–210, 1956.

SWADESH, MORRIS. Diffusional cumulation and archaic residue in historical explanations. *Southwestern Journal of Anthropology* 7:1–21, 1951.

HYMES, DELL H. Lexicostatistics so far. *Current Anthropology* 1:3–44, 1960.

———, and others. More on lexicostatistics. *CurrAnthro* 1:338–345, 1960.

BERGSLAND, KNUT, and HANS VOGT. On the validity of glottochronology. *CurrAnthro* 3:115–153, 1962. [Comment by G. L. Trager, p. 146.]

The comparison of Macro-Mixtecan and English was made in an article written with tongue-in-cheek and deadpan mock seriousness;

it is one of a small number of excellent hoax articles in various fields of science designed to dispel error by ridicule rather than anger:

CALLAGHAN, CATHERINE A., and WICK R. MILLER. Swadesh's Macro-Mixtecan hypothesis and English. *Southwestern Journal of Anthropology* 18:278–285, 1962.

PART III. CHAPTERS 7 and 8

7. This chapter is a summary of a very extensive field. It is included in this book on language and languages because languages must be presented in some written form, and native writing systems are informative about language history as well as about pronunciation and morphemic structure.

No attempt is made to cite extensively the literature dealing with the writing systems that are discussed. Pertinent summarizing or basic works are mentioned below, when they exist.

Much of the presentation is a statement of the present author's appraisal of current views (where they are referred to), of his own analyses of problem areas, and of his guesses about possible answers to as yet unsolved questions.

For writing in general see:

GELB, I. J. *A study of writing.* Rev. ed. Chicago: Univ. of Chicago Press, c1963. xix+319 pp. [First ed., 1952, of which the German translation, with some additions and revisions, was supervised by Gelb: *Von der Keilschrift zum Alphabet; Grundlagen einer Schriftwissenschaft.* [Stuttgart]: Kohlhammer, [1958]. 291 pp. [The prejudices of Gelb in discussing any writing systems except those he believes to have originated in Mesopotamia, are such as to cast doubt on the validity of all his conclusions. The factual data are usable, however.]

DIRINGER, DAVID. *The alphabet: a key to the history of mankind.* London and New York: 1948. 2nd ed., 1949. [Also as *L'alfabeto nella storia della civiltà,* Florence, 1937.]

———. *Writing.* New York: Praeger, c1962. 261 pp. 78 photographs, 49 line drawings, and 3 maps. [*Ancient peoples and places,* v. 25.) [Updates and replaces, in a somewhat more popular form, the preceding item.]

FRIEDRICH, J. *Extinct languages.* New York: Philosophical Library, 1957. x+182 pp.

PEDERSEN, HOLGER. *Linguistic science in the 19th century* ... [References, 5]. [Especially Ch. 6, pp. 141–239.]

NEWBERRY, JOHN STRONG. The prehistory of the alphabet. *Harvard Studies in Classical Philology* 45:105–156.

See also References for Chapter 8 and its subdivisions.

7.01. The drawing of the Australian shield is from:
LINTON, RALPH. *The tree of culture*. New York: Knopf, 1955, p. 163.
The kinship chart is taken from the full chart in:
TRAGER, G. L. The kinship and status terms of the Tiwa languages. *American Anthropologist* 45:557–571, 1943. [Discusses the kinship terms of Taos, Picuris, Sandia, and Isleta; see *NWL*, 9.22.]

7.03. The figures on literacy are based on the maps on pp. 142–143 of the *Encyclopaedia Britannica World Atlas*, Chicago, 1964.

7.1. On Sumerian and other cuneiform, and Egyptian and Semitic writing, see:
BARTON, G. A. *The origin and development of Babylonian writing*. Leipzig, 1913. 2 vols.
GARDINER, A. H. The nature and development of the Egyptian hieroglyphic writing. *Journal of Egyptian Archaeology* 2:61–75, 1915.
————. The Egyptian origin of the Semitic alphabet. *Journal of Egyptian Archeology* 3:1–16, 1916.
SPRENGLING, MARTIN. *The alphabet: its rise and development from the Sinai inscriptions*. Chicago, 1931.

7.10. For the Semitic languages see *NWL*, Ch. 2.

7.11. The two Egyptian symbols in their three stages are from Gelb [References, 7], p. 76, and may also be found in:
STEINDORFF and SEELE. *When Egypt ruled the East*. Chicago, 1942. p. 123.

The signs are V22 and W9 in Gardiner's Sign List, pp. 524 and 528, respectively, of:

GARDINER, A. H. *Egyptian grammar*. 3rd ed. Oxford, 1957, reprinted 1966.

V22 represents a whip, but does not spell the word for 'whip'; it is usually used as *mḥ* 'fill'; W9 represents a stone jug with a handle, and there is a word *nḥnm* meaning this vase with its oil; also used to spell *ḥnm* 'join', and also for the name of the god *Khnum*. (These details are from Carleton T. Hodge of Indiana University—personal communication.)

7.2.   On Greek and Latin writing see:

ROBERTS, E. S., and E. A. GARDNER. *An introduction to Greek epigraphy*. Cambridge, 1887–1905. 2 vols.

CARPENTER, RHYS. The alphabet in Italy. *American Journal of Archaeology* 49:452–464, 1945.

For Gothic, Slavic, other Greek-derived alphabets, and modern orthographies, see the general references in *E&R* for the several chapters dealing with the languages.

7.21.   For the Greek *koiné* see *E&R*, Ch. 7. For Oscan and Umbrian see *E&R*, Ch. 4.

7.22.   For the extension of Latin to new areas see *E&R*, 4.11. For the Roman transcription of Greek see *E&R*, 4.22.

7.23.   For French spelling see *E&R*, 5.1.

7.24.   For the ancient languages of Anatolia see *E&R*, Ch. 10.

7.3.   For writing in India see *E&R*, Ch. 9.

7.32.   The Dravidian languages are treated in *NWL*, 4.1.

7.33.   Tibetan and Burmese are treated in *NWL*, Ch. 6. Siamese and Cambodian are treated in *NWL*, Ch. 5, which see also for Indonesian.

7.40.   For the Chinese writing system see:

KARLGREN, BERNHARD. *Sound and symbol in Chinese*. London, 1923. 112 pp.

For the Chinese language see *NWL*, Ch. 6.

7.41.   A treatment of Japanese writing is:

YAMAGIWA, J. K. *Introduction to Japanese writing*. Ann Arbor, Mich., 1943.

The Japanese text displaying all the writing systems now in use in Japan is from the translator's introduction to the translation of Trager and Smith's *An Outline of English structure* (Tokyo: Taishukan, 1958; translated and annotated by Akira Ota), p. 1, last sentence of first paragraph. The analysis and interpretation of the symbols were supplied by my colleague John J. Chew (now of the University of Toronto).

The Japanese language is treated in *NWL*, Ch. 6.

The Korean examples are taken from:

LUKOFF, F. *English for Koreans*. Washington, D.C.: American Council of Learned Societies, 1954. xv+480 pp.

For the Chinese-based Vietnamese writing see:

NGUYỄN, DÌNH HOÀ. Chữ Nôm, the demotic system of writing in Vietnam. *Journal of the American Oriental Society* 79:270–274, 1959. [The actual Chinese equivalents of the *chữ nôm* characters cited were supplied and commented on by Dr. Fred C. C. Peng, whose work on Chinese is cited in *NWL*, Ch. 6; the phonemic analysis of Chinese is discussed in that chapter also.

7.50. For discussion of precursors of writing in native America, see the following:

MALLERY, G. Pictographs of the North American Indians—a preliminary paper. Bureau of American Ethnology, *Fourth Annual Report* (1882–1883). Washington, D.C.: United States Government Printing Office, 1886. pp. 3–256, 83 plates, 209 figures.

————. Picture writing of the American Indians. Bureau of American Ethnology, *Tenth Annual Report* (1888–1889). Washington, D.C.: USGPO, 1893. pp. 1–807, 54 plates, 1290 figures.

STEWARD, JULIAN H. Petroglyphs of California and adjoining states. *Univ. of Calif. Publications in American Archaeology and Ethnology* 24:47–239, 1929.

7.51. For Mayan and Aztec writing see the following:

KNOROZOV, ÜRIĬ V. *Pisʹmennostĭ drevnix Maĭä; la escritura de los Maya antiguos*. Moscow, 1955.

————. New data on the Maya written language. *Journal de la Société des Américanistes* 45:209–216, 1956.

————. The problem of the study of the Maya hieroglyphic writing. *American Antiquity* 23:284–291, 1958.

MORLEY, SYLVANUS GRISWOLD. *An introduction to the study of the Maya hieroglyphs*. Bureau of American Ethnology, *Bulletin 57*. Washington, D.C.: United States Government Printing Office, 1913. 284 pp.

THOMPSON, J. ERIC S. *Maya hieroglyphic writing* . . . 2nd ed. Norman, Okla.: Univ. of Okla. Press, 1960.

————. *A catalogue of Maya hieroglyphs*. Norman, Okla.: Univ. of Okla. Press, 1962.

WHORF, BENJAMIN LEE. Decipherment of the linguistic portion of the Maya hieroglyphs. *Annual Report of the Smithsonian Institution*. 1941:479–502.

DIBBLE, CHARLES E. The Aztec writing system. In Hoebel, Jennings, and Smith, *Readings in anthropology*. New York: McGraw-Hill, 1955. pp. 296–302.

KIMMEL, DONALD. Special types of speech scrolls in native manuscripts. *Mesoamerican Notes* 2:104 and plates IVA and IVB, 1950 (Mexico City College, Dept. of Anthropology).

7.53. On the Cherokee syllabary see:

MOONEY, JAMES. The sacred formulas of the Cherokees. Bureau of American Ethnology, *Seventh Annual Report* (1885–1886). Washington, D.C.: United States Government Printing Office, 1891. pp. 301–397.

———. Myths of the Cherokee. Bureau of American Ethnology, *Nineteenth Annual Report* (1897–1898). Washington, D.C.: USGPO, 1900. pp. 3–548, 20 plates, 3 figures.

PILLING, JAMES C. *Bibliography of the Iroquoian languages.* Bureau of American Ethnology, *Bulletin 6.* Washington, D.C.: USGPO, 1888. vi+208 pp.

The Cherokee example was supplied by the late Professor J. F. Kilpatrick of Southern Methodist University. It is a conjuration, discussed in the following paper by him and his wife (a great-great-granddaughter of Sequoya):

KILPATRICK, JACK FREDERICK, and ANNA GRITTS KILPATRICK. Cherokee burn conjurations. *Journal of the Graduate Research Center* 33:17–21, 1964 (Dallas: Southern Methodist Univ.).

See also:

CHAFE, WALLACE L., and J. F. KILPATRICK. Inconsistencies in Cherokee spelling. *Symposium on language and culture: Proceedings of the 1962 annual spring meeting of the American Ethnological Society* 60–3.

The educational experiment referred to in the text has produced the following publications:

WALKER, WILLARD. *ᎪᎯᏫᎵ ᎪᏟᎳᎩ ᎪᎯᎵᏘᎫ ᎪᏍᎬᏘꮄᏫᎫ* [di-go-we-li di-tsa-la-gi di-go-li-tse-di di-de-lo-kwa-s-do-di] *Cherokee primer.* Tahlequah, Okla., 1965. Copyright 1965 by the Carnegie Corporation Cross-Cultural Education Project of the University of Chicago. 2 p. l., 68 p. [Rev. ed., December, 1965.]

[———]. *An experiment in programmed cross-cultural education: the import of the Cherokee primer for the Cherokee community and for the behavioral sciences.* Tahlequah, Okla., 1955. Dittoed, [10]l.

ᏣᎳᎩ ᎠᏰᎵ ᎪᏪᎵ ᎦᎴᏓᏅᎢ [tsa-la-gi a-ye-li go-we-li ga-le-da-nv-i] *Cherokee Newsletter.* Tahlequah, Okla., 1965. [The syllabary as given in the text is taken from this publication.]

The material on the Cree syllabary as used for Eskimo is taken from:

Canada, Ministry of Northern Affairs and National Resources, Welfare Division. *Tentative standard orthography for Canadian Eskimo.* Ottawa, Canada, 1962. 2nd ed. Spiral bound; parts separately paged. [The material was compiled or edited by R. C. Gagné, and is very good in its anthropological linguistic discussion; there are sample texts and comparisons with older orthographies. The syllabary was supplied on a mimeographed sheet included with the above publication in the covering correspondence.]

Eskimo in print. *Time*, June 29, 1959, p. 37. [An article on the journal *Inuktitut*, with a sample of a few lines in the syllabary.]

△ ₋ₒ ∩ ⊃ᶜ[*Inuktitut*], January 1965. 58 pp., illus.

8.   The alphabets presented in the tables of this chapter are, in part, common forms of writing widely available, and these are reproduced in the most accessible typefaces. Others, less common, are reproduced from existing compilations by photographic or other copying. Sources are given below.

Transliterations and phonemic interpretations are for the most part the present author's. He is also responsible for the notes to the tables, and for guesses about the origins of the more obscure characters.

The best sources of alphabets are the following:

Alphabete und Schriftzeichen des Morgen- und des Abendlandes. Berlin: Reichsdruckerei, 1924. 86 pp. [This list of 'alphabets and writing symbols of the Orient and Occident' contains excellent examples of many alphabets, etc., with useful notes.]

United States Government Printing Office. *Style manual* ... Rev. ed., January 1953. Washington, D.C.: USGPO, 1953. v+492 pp. [Ch. 25, Foreign languages, pp. 329–430, was revised for this edition by a committee headed by the author of the present book and including John G. Mutziger and Henry Lee Smith, Jr. It contains spelling rules, rules for syllabication, and the like for many languages, presenting tables of the alphabets, with any diacritical marks that are used—including Latin-letter orthographies, with indications of pronunciation. Sample texts, word lists, abbreviations, and other useful data are also included.]

United States Government Printing Office. *Specimens of type faces* ... Washington, D.C., 1951. 262 pp. [This book, compiled for office use at the GPO, is useful in illustrating Latin letters with numerous diacritical marks, in various typefaces, as well as Cyrillic and Greek type.]

The following Russian publication is especially useful for the Soviet Union:

GILÄREVSKIĮ, R. S., and V. S. GRIVNIN. *Opredeliteli äzykov mira po pisĭmennostäm* ['List of the languages of the world by writing systems']. 2nd ed., rev. Moscow: Izdatelĭstvo VostočnoĮ Literatury, 1961. 303 pp. [This book gives a short specimen text and an alphabet, with some historical notes, for the languages of the Soviet Union and also the world as a whole. There are no indications, even by way of transliterations, of the phonemic uses of the alphabets; this is especially regrettable for the new letters added to Cyrillic for various Soviet languages.]

8.01. The Serbocroatian language is treated in *E&R*, 8.33. The Urdu equivalents of Hindi devanagari are given in *Alphabete und Schriftzeichen* . . . [References, 8], p. 37.

8.02. The Board on Geographic Names, of the Division of Geography of the U.S. Department of the Interior, has issued many publications on transliteration and employing the transliterations the Board has adopted. Some of these transliteration systems are given or referred to in the *Style manual* cited above. See also the following:

Romanization guide for Arabic, Bulgarian, Chinese, Faroese, Greek, Hebrew, Icelandic, Japanese, Korean, Mongolian, Nepali, Persian, Russian, Serbo-Croatian, Thai. Based on the systems as used by the United States Board on Geographic Names [cover title]. [Title p.:] "Romanization Guide." [Replaces *Transliteration Guide*, issued August 1961 by the Department of State.] The Geographer, Office of Research in Economics and Science, Bureau of Intelligence and Research, U.S. Department of State, and Office of Geography, Department of the Interior. July 1964. iv+51 pp.

8.10. The material on Greek is compiled from standard sources.

8.11. The Etruscan alphabets are taken from Diringer, *Writing* [References, 7], p. 176, and:

HUS, ALAIN. *The Etruscans.* New York: Grove Press; London: Evergreen, 1961. Table on p. 81.

The Etruscan language is discussed in *NWL*, 1.11.

8.12. For the Oscan and Umbrian alphabets see:

BUCK, C. D. *A grammar of Oscan and Umbrian* . . . Boston: Ginn, 1928. pp. 22 ff.

The two languages are treated in *E&R*, Ch. 4.
The West Greek forms are compiled from Diringer and Gelb [References, 7].

8.13. Some of the historical discussion of Latin-letter forms is based on Diringer [References, 7], pp. 165–177.
The spelling of Latin is discussed in *E&R*, 4.20.

8.21. The Coptic alphabet is from *Alphabete und Schriftzeichen* . . . [References, 8], p. 7. The Gothic alphabet is from:

STREITBERG, WILHELM. *Gothisches Elementarbuch*. 4th ed. Heidelberg, Winter, 1940.

The Gothic writing system is also discussed in *E&R*, 3.30.

8.22. The Armenian and Georgian alphabets are from *Alphabete und Schriftzeichen* . . . .
The Armenian language is treated in *E&R*, Ch. 10. Georgian is treated in *NWL*, 1.3.

8.23. The Glagolitic and Old Church Slavic Cyrillic are from standard works on Old Church Slavic. The modern alphabets are from standard sources. See also Gilärevskiĭ [References, 8].
For the transliterations see:

TRAGER, G. L. The transliteration of Russian and other Slavic alphabets. *Studies in Linguistics* 1, no. 20, 1943. 4 pp. [Needed corrections have been made in the present text.]

The Slavic languages are treated in *E&R*, Ch. 8.
The phonemics of Old Church Slavic is treated in:

TRAGER, G. L. Old Church Slavic writing and phonemes. *Prace Filologiczne* 18:145–151, 1964. [As printed, this article has a number of serious misprints. See *E&R*, 8.24, for discussion and corrections.]

8.24. For the Old Irish language, see *E&R*, Ch. 6.
The discussion of the Germanic futhark is based on:

PEDERSEN. *Linguistic science in the 19th century* . . . [References, 5]. pp. 229–230, 233–239.

See also Diringer, *Writing* [References, 7].
Discussion of the application of runic writing to Old English is found in:

WOOLFSON, A. P. *A graphemic, diaphonemic, and morphophonic interpretation of the early and late Old English dialects*. Buffalo dissertation, 1967. Unpublished.

8.3.   For Semitic writing see:

PEDERSEN. *Linguistic science in the 19th century* ... [References, 5]. pp. 176–188.

GELB. *A study of writing* [References, 7]. pp. 122–152.

DIRINGER. *Writing* [References, 7]. pp. 112–148.

8.30.   For the orthographies of the Semitic languages see *NWL*, Ch. 2.

The Egyptian, Ugaritic, and Canaanite symbols are compiled from Pedersen [References, 5], p. 179; Gelb [References, 7], pp. 77, 130, 137; Diringer, *Writing* [References, 7], pp. 115, 130.

In discussing "The Old Persian /l/ phoneme", *Journal of the American Oriental Society* 76:24–26, 1956, Herbert H. Paper has made the suggestion which we have alluded to that the Old Persian writing system was in some way modeled on Semitic writing with influences from Babylonian cuneiform and the Royal Achaemenid Elamite cuneiform. It is not likely, however, that the Ras Shamra alphabet could have survived to serve as a specific model (personal communication from H. H. Paper, Nov. 1964).

8.31.   The Hebrew and Syriac letters and the remarks about them are taken from *Alphabete und Schriftzeichen* ... [References, 8]. See also any textbook, and:

MORAG, SHELOMO. *The vocalization systems of Arabic, Hebrew, and Aramaic; their phonetic and phonemic principles.* The Hague: Mouton, 1962. 85 pp.

8.32.   For Arabic see the works mentioned in 8.31, and any Arabic grammar. Also see *Romanization guide* [References, 8.02]. See the treatment of the Arabic language in *NWL*, 2.20. For Persian see:

PAPER, HERBERT H., and MOHAMMED ALI JAZAYERY. *The writing system of Modern Persian.* Washington, D.C.: American Council of Learned Societies, 1955. 30 pp.

8.33.   The Amharic transliteration given here was originally developed by the present author for use with geographic names in Ethiopia. See:

U.S. Board on Geographic Names. *Transliteration system for Amharic geographic names.* Washington, D.C.: Department of the Interior, 1951. 3 pp.

8.4.   The alphabets presented in the subsections 8.40 to 8.43 are taken from standard sources. Some of the interpretations and transliterations are the present author's.

8.40. For Sanskrit writing in detail see:

WHITNEY, WILLIAM DWIGHT. *Sanskrit grammar.* Cambridge, Mass.: Harvard Univ. Press, 11th issue, 1967, of 2nd ed., 1889.

The sample illustrating the development of Indic letter shapes is from Diringer, *Writing* [References, 7]. p. 146–147.

8.41. The several Indic alphabets are reproduced from *Alphabete und Schriftzeichen* ... [References, 8]. pp. 45–49, 51–54.

8.42. For Tibetan writing see:

MILLER, ROY ANDREW. *The Tibetan system of writing.* Washington, D.C.: American Council of Learned Societies, 1956, 30 pp.

8.43. Burmese writing is described in:

JONES, ROBERT B., JR., and U KHIN. *The Burmese writing system.* Washington, D.C.: American Council of Learned Societies, 1953. 37 pp.

The Burmese letter forms are compiled from the above and from *Alphabete und Schriftzeichen* ... [References, 8], p. 55.

The Cambodian alphabet is from *Alphabete und Schriftzeichen* ... [References, 8], p. 55.

For Siamese (Thai) writing see:

HAAS, MARY R. *The Thai system of writing.* Washington, D.C.: ACLS, 1956. 115 pp.

The Siamese alphabet in printed form is found in *Alphabete und Schriftzeichen* ... [References, 8], p. 56.

For a statement of the phonemic structure of Siamese see:

TRAGER, G. L. Siamese phonemes: a restatement. *Bulletin of the Institute of History and Philology,* Academia Sinica, v. 29, pp. 21–29 (Studies presented to Yuen Ren Chao on his sixty-fifth birthday). Taipei, Taiwan, 1957.

8.5. Examples of phonetic symbols in this section are taken from the following works:

Lautzeichen und ihre Anwendung in verschiedenen Sprachgebieten. Berlin: Reichsdruckerei, 1928. 116 pp. [A companion volume to *Alphabete und Schriftzeichen* ... (References, 8).]

BLOCH, BERNARD, and GEORGE L. TRAGER. *Tables for a system of phonetic description.* New Haven, Conn.: 1940. 8 pp. [Out of print.]

TRAGER, G. L. *Phonetics: glossary and tables.* Buffalo, N.Y., 1958. 27 pp. *Studies in Linguistics, Occasional Paper,* 6; 2nd ed. rev. 1964. 26 pp.

The principles of the International Phonetic Association. London, 1949. 53 pp. [And subsequent versions of the material in *Le Maître Phonétique, passim.*]

See also the References for 2.23, and the text of Chapter 2, especially 2.2 and 2.3 and their subsections.

8.50. Material on the writing of Chinese and other eastern Asian languages in transcription will be found in *NWL*, Ch. 6 and 7.

8.52. On some problems of application of phonemic and other principles of writing to orthographies for previously unwritten languages, see:

SMALLEY, WILLIAM A., and others. *Orthography studies: articles on new writing systems.* London: United Bible Societies; Amsterdam: North Holland Publishing, 1964. vii+173 pp.

CONCLUSION. CHAPTER 9

9. This chapter is a summarizing and concluding one. The statements made are in large part opinions of the author based on his experience with and reading in the fields involved. Direct and precise citation and documentation are in most cases unnecessary.

References for specific details and for the specific languages mentioned are to be found in the volumes *E&R* and *NWL*, for the appropriate chapters and sections. It does not seem necessary to list them here; the reader interested in the bibliography can seek it in the books noted.

9.0. Studies of the growth or establishment of literary, religious, and official languages as anthropological phenomena, or of their vocabularies from the semological point of view, do not exist apart from the histories of the nations or religions involved, or elsewhere than in literary or linguistic studies in general or of the specific languages. The References alluded to just above can only guide the reader to the beginning of the search for such material of this nature as exists.

9.1. Some general and specific references on the relation of language to reality have been given for Ch. 4, especially 4.2.

Recent political, historical, and sociological studies often mention diversity of language within various nations, but few linguistically sound studies of the phenomena involved have ever been made. Such as exist are highly technical.

9.12. Discussions of substrate and superstrate languages are often found in philological works dealing with the European languages especially. Very few theoretically sound linguistic data emerge from such studies, beyond what is said in the text of this section. There are no useful references in this connection.

9.13. For this subsection reference should be made to the materials cited for 4.2, and especially to Trager, "Linguistics and the reconstruction of culture history", cited there. See also:

TRAGER, G. L. A schematic outline for the *processual* analysis of culture. [Formulated in 1962; issued, with revisions, by xerox reproduction at the Center for Advanced Study in the Behavioral Sciences, Stanford, Calif., May 1963; reissued, in dittoed form, at Buffalo, January 1965.] 3 l. Now in print in:

———. Language and psychotherapy. Ch. 9, pp. 70-82 of *Methods of research in psychotherapy*, edited by L. A. Gottschalk and Arthur H. Auerbach. New York: Appleton-Century-Crofts, c1966. [See pp. 75–78.]

9.21. There is a wide literature on artificial auxiliary languages, and most of it is of such a popular or speculative nature as to merit no attention here. The following may be listed:

JACOB, H. *A planned auxiliary language* ... London, 1947. [Reviewed by N. A. McQuown, *Language* 26:175–185, 1950. The review is a thorough commentary on the problems of constructed languages, and is the source of some of the specific data in our text.]

SHENTON, H. N., E. SAPIR, O. JESPERSEN. *International communication, a symposium on the language problem*. London, 1931. 120 pp. [Now outdated, but useful for the situation before the Second World War and the events that followed it.]

GODE, ALEXANDER. The signal system in Interlingua—a factor in mechanical translation. *Mechanical Translation* 2:55–60, 1955.

On Basic English, see:

OGDEN, C. K. *Basic English: a general introduction with rules and grammar*. London: Kegan Paul, Trench, Trubner, 1930. 100 pp.

INDEX

This index includes names of persons mentioned in the text and names of authors listed in the References and Notes. Titles of some works referred to frequently or for which no author is named are also listed. Reference is by page numbers.